To Bill Keeth —

Best wishes,

Bith Simmons

Who Adjusts?

_____

PRINCETON STUDIES IN

INTERNATIONAL HISTORY AND POLITICS

Series Editors
John Lewis Gaddis
Jack L. Snyder
Richard H. Ullman

———————————————

Who Adjusts?

DOMESTIC SOURCES OF FOREIGN ECONOMIC POLICY DURING THE INTERWAR YEARS

Beth A. Simmons

PRINCETON UNIVERSITY PRESS

PRINCETON, NEW JERSEY

Library of Congress Cataloging-in-Publication Data

Simmons, Beth A., 1958–
   Who adjusts? : domestic sources of foreign economic policy during
the interwar years / Beth A. Simmons.
      p.   cm. — (Princeton studies in international history and
politics)
   Includes bibliographical references and index.
   ISBN 0-691-08641-9
   1. International economic relations—History—20th century.
   2. Gold standard—History—20th century.   I. Title.   II. Series.
HF1411.S454   1994   337'.09'04—dc20   93-2272

ISBN: 0-691-08641-9

This book has been composed in Times Roman

Princeton University Press books are printed on acid-free paper
and meet the guidelines for permanence and durability of the
Committee on Production Guidelines for Book Longevity of the
Council on Library Resources

Printed in the United States of America
1   3   5   7   9   10   8   6   4   2

For my father, Charles N. Simmons
and the memory of my mother, Barbara A. Simmons

———————————

CONTENTS

FIGURES

TABLES

ACKNOWLEDGMENTS

THIS BOOK developed out of a dissertation that was completed at Harvard University in 1991. My greatest intellectual debt is to my three thesis advisers, Professor Robert Keohane (Committee Chair), Professor James Alt, and Professor Stephan Haggard. Their comments and suggestions were useful during every phase of this project, and without their help and encouragement this study could not have been completed. I also benefited from extensive comments on a penultimate draft by Barry Eichengreen, Brad Delong, and Kenneth Oye and discussions with Alberto Alesina and Gary King. The basic argument of this book and some preliminary findings were presented at the University of Michigan's Center for Political Studies and the University of Chicago's Program on International Politics, Economics, and Security (PIPES). These seminars provided useful discussion and criticism that helped to improve the final product.

It is difficult to imagine a more collegial setting in which to work than in the Political Science Department at Duke. Thanks to my colleagues here for all the encouragement and support they have provided toward the completion of this book, and for the opportunity to present my findings at our Friday seminar series. John Aldrich, John Brehm, and Paul Gronke provided insights on particular modeling questions that came up in Chapters 3, 4, and 6. Two Duke graduate students—Dean Lacy and Brian Loynd—gave me useful advice on how best to present my statistical findings. Bill Bernhard assisted in research on Belgian economic policies during the thirties. Lyle Scruggs assisted me in rating the independence of the various interwar centrals banks. Of course, I retain full responsibility for all errors of fact, judgment, and interpretation. Adam Krob compiled the index.

The Duke University Research Council provided funds to assist in the transformation of the dissertation into this book. I am also grateful to the following institutions, which have provided generous financial support for my research and writing over the course of my graduate career: Harvard MacArthur Fellowship in International Security, Center for International Affairs, Harvard University, 1990–1991; Ford Dissertation Fellowship in European Society and Western Security, Center for International Affairs, Harvard University, 1989–1990; Krupp Scholarship for Dissertation Research (for research in France), 1987–1988; Morris Abrams Award, The Jewish Vocational Society, 1987; Jens Aubrey Westengard Scholarship, Harvard University, 1986.

Finally, I would like to acknowledge the support of my husband, Lt. Col. Bruce Jackan, whose presence was an inspiration, and whose stints in service to his country in Saudi Arabia, Iraq, Angola, and Panama provided me with long lonely stretches of time to get something accomplished.

Who Adjusts?

Chapter 1

INTRODUCTION

WHY WAS international economic conflict so prevalent in the years between the First and Second World Wars? The twenties and thirties have come to be known as a period of rampant economic nationalism, monetary instability, commercial collapse, and "beggar-thy-neighbor" foreign economic policies that shook the fragile international economy. Protectionist policies improverished trading partners, reduced the global welfare, and arguably made the Great Depression even worse than it otherwise might have been. Unilateral devaluation disrupted trade and injected uncertainty into international economic relations. The living standards of millions were at stake in the choice of foreign economic policies; indeed, economic conflict was a prelude to military conflict on a scale unprecedented in modern history. What we need to understand, then, is why individual states chose either to break or to abide by the prevailing norms of internationally accepted economic policy: why some states maintained gold standard requirements of currency stability and relatively liberal trade, while others chose to adjust to balance of payments deficits by devaluing and erecting barriers to trade—in effect, pushing the costs of adjustment onto their trade partners.

Many scholars of international relations have argued that the nature of the international system contributed to economic conflict. The war had been an inconclusive test for hegemonic power in Europe, and brought only a tense transitional period in which states openly prepared to settle accounts. No single economic power had both the willingness and the ability to support a liberal international economic system. The system of alliances was weak and multipolar, arguably lessening states' incentives to "invest" in cooperation. International organizations were thought to be mere fig leaves for the pursuit of raw state interests. Realism, with its mercantilist economic corollary, is nowhere more widely accepted than it is in interpreting the "twenty years' crisis" that reigned between the two world wars of this century.

The interwar years pose something of an anomoly for some of the most powerful explanations of state behavior that have been advanced in the international political economy literature. The spectacle of the most powerful state in the international system refusing to exercise leadership to ensure economic openness poses a puzzle for theories of hegemonic stability. The *variations* in policies over the two decades and from country to country cannot be easily attributed to the uncertainty engendered by systemic multipolarity. Episodic economic cooperation despite the presence of obvious suboptimalities arising in markets for capital, currency, and goods presents problems for functional theories that focus on the gains to be derived from international cooperation. What these explanations lack is a systematic consideration of the domestic incentives and constraints that states faced in framing their external economic policies during the interwar years.

This study argues that an important part of the explanation for international economic outcomes during the interwar years arose from the internal politics and institutions prevalent within many countries after the Great War. In the face of balance of payments deficits, governments could choose to adjust *internally* by reducing prices and demand, or adjust *externally* with "beggar-thy-neighbor" policies that pushed the problem of adjustment onto a country's trade partners. Is there a political explanation for the choice of adjustment strategy? To answer this question I draw on theoretical work that has developed the logic of strategic behavior—the temptation to dump currencies that are likely to be devalued, the logic of competitive devaluation, the individual rationality of tariff retaliation—but go beyond these by testing for the political conditions associated with the decision to defect from the gold standard and liberal trade. A profile emerges of the domestic political characteristics associated with benign, norm-abiding adjustment during the interwar years: stable governments and quiescent labor movements contributed to international economic cooperation, while domestic political and social instability undermined it. Conservative polities with independent monetary institutions tended to maintain currency stability, but threw up protective barriers to trade, while left-wing governments and governments that could influence their central banks tended to reduce trade protection but sacrificed the gold value of their currency. In short, there is a clear relationship between states' willingness to play by the international economic "rules of the game" and patterns of domestic politics. While this study does not supplant systemic theorizing, it does have crucial implications for the international outcomes with which international relations scholars have been concerned: international economic cooperation and conflict, and the role and durability of international rules or norms.

THE PROBLEM: EXPLAINING INTERNATIONAL ECONOMIC RELATIONS DURING THE INTERWAR YEARS

Key to understanding economic conflict and cooperation during the interwar years is to understand states' willingness and ability to play by the international economic "rules of the game" on which the gold standard was based. As will become clear in the following chapter, the gold standard had three basic requirements. First, states had to make their balance of payments a higher priority than the condition of their domestic economy. Second, states had to maintain reasonably open trade relations in order that gold standard adjustment could take place. And third, exceptional finance had to be provided by either the central banks or private banking consortia from surplus countries in some cases if fixed rates were to be maintained.

Systemic theorizing alone has been insufficient for interpreting the patterns of national gold standard compliance during the interwar years, and the reason has to do with the indeterminacy of systemic constraints on governments' economic policy choices. Based on systemic conditions (relative size, relative economic productivity, relative degree of trade dependence, for example), scholars have deduced (or sometimes imputed) a set of state preferences that are hypothesized to shape their international economic policy choices and hence systemic economic stability. The classic statement is Charles Kindleberger's interpretation of the collapse of the international economic system during the 1930s as a breakdown in international leadership.[1] He viewed systemic stability and open, liberal economic relations as "public goods" that are best provided by the dominant economic power in the system. He argued that international economic stability could best be provided by one power willing to provide countercyclical international lending and to keep its markets open despite recession, to maintain a stable value for its currency and encourage other states to do the same, to ensure the coordination of macroeconomic policies, which in the context of the gold standard meant to refrain from the sterilization of gold inflows, and finally to act as lender of last resort when other countries were experiencing balance of payments deficits or currency crises.

International relations theorists have tried to test Kindleberger's suggestive insights by exploring the extent to which economic stability and openness are actually associated with a hegemonic system.[2] In some versions, the theory is used to predict more cooperative policies from the hegemon itself.[3] In the last several years, however, several basic flaws have been exposed in the logic that would predict an association of hegemonic structure or position and more cooperative foreign economic policies or stable international outcomes.[4] Fur-

[1] Charles P. Kindleberger, *The World in Depression*, 1929–1939 (Berkeley: University of California Press), 1986.

[2] With respect to international trade, see Stephen Krasner, "State Power and the Structure of International Trade," *World Politics*, Vol. 28, 1976, 317–347; and David Lake, *Power, Protectionism, and Free Trade: International Sources of U.S. Commercial Strategy, 1887–1939*, (Ithaca: Cornell University Press), 1988. The importance of hegemonic dominance has been especially central in the discussion of shifts in international monetary regimes. Robert O. Keohane and Joseph S. Nye, *Power and Interdependence: World Politics in Transition* (Boston: Little, Brown), 1977; Keohane, *After Hegemony: Cooperation and Discord in the World Political Economy* (Princeton: Princeton University Press), 1984.

[3] It is also considered but discounted by two of the most important international political economy studies of the collapse of the Bretton Woods system. See Joanne Gowa, *Closing the Gold Window* (Ithaca: Cornell University Press), 1983; and John Odell, *U.S. International Monetary Policy: Markets, Power, and Ideas as Sources of Change* (Princeton: Princeton University Press), 1982.

[4] Duncan Snidal, for instance, has pointed out that cooperation among a small group of powers is possible; see "The Limits of Hegemonic Stability Theory," *International Organization*, Vol. 39, No. 4, Autumn 1985, pp. 579–614. Conybeare has pointed out that hegemonic powers are more likely to abuse their market size to implement optimal tariffs than to maintain openness; see, John A. C. Conybeare, *Trade Wars: The Theory and Practice of International Commercial Rivalry*; and

thermore, the entire approach is based on the *supposition* that the strongest incentives facing states in the system are indeed external and can be deduced from systemic variables. But it is important to recall that Kindleberger himself was not *puzzled* by the United States' unwillingness to open its markets, maintain a stable currency, and maintain countercyclical capital flows during the Depression. He understood the domestic political incentives facing American policymakers (and deplored these actions nonetheless).[5] The point is quite general: without some information about the preferences of the dominant economic power and the other states in the system, the logic of systemic hegemonic theory is less than compelling.[6]

The same point can be made in the application of game theory to external economic policy choice and international economic outcomes. Game theory provides a framework for understanding states' choices under given assumptions regarding the number of actors, their preference structures, and how much value they place on future interactions. These factors define the strategic setting, and game matrices are usually devised to depict a dichotomous policy choice often generically labeled "cooperate" or "defect." Some very powerful findings have emerged from applications of game theory to international political economy, though the bulk of the work has employed various forms of the Prisoner's Dilemma. The key parameters influencing states' behavior in this context are the probability of future interactions, the length of actors' time horizons, and the number of players involved. Iteration, long time horizons, and small numbers make cooperative outcomes more likely.[7]

The logic is unassailable, as long we make the correct assumptions about the nature of the game, which in turn rests on correctly identifying states' preferences. A Prisoner's Dilemma in international trade means that the participants are conditional free traders: in repeated play they will cooperate only if they believe their trade partners will as well. Once again, this is an empirical issue. Does each state have the same incentives to engage in free trade? What influ-

---

James Alt et al. have shown that when the costs of enforcement and reputation are considered, the outcome of a hegemonic system need not be stable; see "Reputation and Hegemonic Stability: A Game-Theoretic Analysis," *American Political Science Review*, Vol. 82, June 1988, pp. 445–466.

[5] For example, see Charles P. Kindleberger, *The World in Depression*, pp. 192–196.

[6] A similar point can be made regarding other systemic arguments for states' foreign economic policy choices. Recently, for example, Joanne Gowa has argued that a bipolar international political system is better than a multipolar one in providing for free trade. However, the relationship between bipolar systems and free trade appears to be subject to the domestic political and economic organization of the major alliance partners (contrast the interwar German-led authoritaritan alliance and the Cold War Soviet bloc with the liberal postwar trade principles of Western Europe and the United States). This is not to deny that system characteristics do have an independent effect on the propensity to select free trade policies, but the propensity is likely to be much greater for alliances composed of polities for whom free trade is consistent with their domestic political and economic organization.

[7] Kenneth Oye, Robert Keohane, and Robert Axelrod, *Cooperation Under Anarchy*, special issue of *World Politics*, Vol. 38, No. 1, October 1985.

ences the relative value they put on free trade versus protection? The key variable may be systemic or structural (the degree of dependence of a state's economy on international trade), or it may be domestic or institutional (the nature and organization of domestic interest groups). But game theory itself does not assign logical priority to any specific level of analysis in determining state preferences. For the analysis to have any sort of an empirical basis (as opposed to a purely theoretical consideration of the properties of a given game), the researcher must develop a model of state preferences, the determinants of which may be domestic or external.

In contrast to trade policy, international monetary cooperation raises the further problem of what it means to "cooperate," and who the relevant "players" are. This is because currency values are determined not only by governments (their macroeconomic policies, central bank intervention), but by markets as well (their decision to hold the currency or sell it). Few political scientists have offered formal game-theoretical analyses of international macro-economic policy coordination,[8] but it is inconceivable that macroeconomic preferences—an essential determinant of exchange rates—could be under-stood without reference to domestic political conditions. On the other hand, the strategic problems underlying the relations between governments and holders of their currency is somewhat better understood.[9] Fixed exchange rate regimes approximate an N-person Prisoner's Dilemma among an issuer and holders of a currency. The "dilemma" only grows acute, however, when the *credibility* of the issuer of the currency is in question. What remains unanalyzed in this model are the factors that influence each player's perception of a high risk of defection by the opposing player(s). In other words, what conditions cause markets to suspect that issuers will be tempted to inflate their currency and to devalue?

To answer this question, it is necessary to draw from the scholarship in both international political economy and comparative political economy[10]—two literatures that until recently have remained somewhat distinct despite their common concern of explaining governments' economic policy choices.[11] While the international political economy literature concentrates on external

[8] Economists have done so. See Koichi Hamada, *The Political Economy of International Mone-tary Interdependence* (Cambridge: MIT Press), 1985. Political scientists representations have often been informal. See Robert D. Putnam and Nicholas Bayne, *Hanging Together: The Seven Power Summits* (Cambridge: Harvard University Press), 1984, which discusses the events leading up to the Bonn macroeconomic agreement in terms that easily suggest a game of chicken between the United States and Germany.

[9] See Kenneth Oye, "The Sterling-Dollar-Franc Triangle: Monetary Diplomacy, 1929–1937," *World Politics*, Vol. 38, No. 1, October 1985, pp. 173–199.

[10] I use this term broadly to include work done by political scientists who have tried to explain economic policy choice/outcomes, as well as economists (fewer in number) who have incorporated political variables—for example, political and social stability, political polarization, electoral and party systems, and domestic monetary institutions—into their analysis.

[11] The reasons for the relative independence of the development of the comparative and the international political economy literature are related to the issue—much debated in international

constraints and opportunities (including retaliation/punishment, greatly expanded joint welfare gains, and the role of international institutions), the comparative political economy subfield provides domestic political and institutional arguments as to why governments might have different preferences over such economic outcomes as rates of economic growth, inflation, and unemployment, and the policy levers they pull to attempt to influence these. Both literatures provide plausible hypotheses regarding a government's ability to make credible commitments to exchange rate stability. A nontendentious approach would examine whatever set of variables from any level of analysis that would speak most clearly to the problem of a credible, noninflationary macroeconomic policy commitment.

Political economists working from a comparative perspective in the 1960s began to address this problem by looking at the influence of class-based political organizations on economic policy preferences. E. S. Kirschen and others discovered systematic differences between parties of the Left and the Right in their macroeconomic objectives: socialist political groupings' dominant policy objective was full employment and improvements in income distribution, center groupings placed price stability above full employment (though both were ranked as significant), and conservatives unambiguously placed price stability at the top of their list of economic objectives.[12] This pioneering study of attitudes spawned a research program, which attempted to quantify the effects

---

relations theory—of the appropriate level of analysis. Among international relations scholars there is a presumption that the unique contribution of the subfield should be to shed light on how the *systemic* setting in which states operate influences their behavior. Accordingly, systemic theorizing is often viewed as the raison d'être of international relations theory. Kenneth Waltz's exhortation to international relations theorists to avoid reductionism (subunit analysis) reflects such a position. Kenneth Waltz, *Theory of International Politics* (New York: Random House), 1979. International relations scholars also emphasize parsimony: the ability to make significant inferences about state behavior on the basis of limited information. Explanations emanating from a higher level of aggregation, such as the system level, are viewed as an appropriate first cut, and for some theorists are the only acceptable resolution to the trade-off between elegance and accurate prediction. Systemic explanations are viewed as more parsimonious than those from other levels of analysis, hence "We should seek parsimony first, then add complexity while monitoring the adverse effects that this has on the predictive power of our theory," and "initial explanations should seek to account for the main features of behavior at a high level of aggregation—such as the international system as a whole—while subsequent hypotheses are designed to apply only to certain issue areas [or countries]." Robert O. Keohane, "Theory of World Politics: Structural Realism and Beyond," chap. 7 in Keohane (ed.), *Neorealism and Its Critics* (New York: Columbia University Press), 1986, p. 188 and passim. Finally, international relations theorists point to the potential for domestic theories of international political economy to encounter the fallacy of composition. Economic conflict may arise from barriers to communication, information, intractible numbers of players, or the difficulty states have making a credible advance commitment to cooperate, rather than specific attributes of the states themselves. Rational-choice explanations of policy choice and international regime development exemply this approach.

[12] E. S. Kirschen et al., *Economic Policy in Our Time, Vol. 1: General Theory* (Amsterdam: North Holland), 1964. See Kirschen's informative preference chart on p. 227.

of party in power on actual macroeconomic outcomes. Douglas Hibbs's analysis of macroeconomic outcomes confirmed Kirschen's preference mapping: both time-series and cross-sectional data seem to suggest that in periods and nations governed by the Left, generally higher levels of employment and inflation prevailed than was the case under center or right-wing governments.[13] The theory that left-wing and right-wing parties prefer and pursue distinct macroeconomic policies has recently been amended to take into consideration the organization of the labor market and the emergence of neocorporatist structures.[14] But it has also been attacked as irrelevant when international economic interdependence is high and integrated goods and financial markets force a convergence in the macroeconomic policies of competing trade partners.[15]

This last observation has led some scholars to downplay social class explanations in favor of theories that look at the degree of social conflict and political instability themselves. Early sociological interpretations of inflation suggested that it might be a short-term way of containing political conflict among groups and sectors.[16] More recently, theories on the relationship between political

[13] Douglas A. Hibbs, "Political Parties and Macroeconomic Policy," *American Political Science Review*, Vol. 71, No. 4, December 1977, pp. 1467–1487. For a critical review of Hibbs's findings, arguing that they exaggerate the differences between the parties, see Nathaniel Beck, "Parties, Administrations, and American Macroeconomic Outcomes," *American Political Science Review*, Vol. 76, No. 1, March 1982, pp. 83–93. For other empirical tests of the impact of parties on economic policy outcomes, see Paul F. Whiteley, "The Political Economy of Economic Growth," *European Journal of Political Research*, Vol. 11, No. 2, June 1983, pp. 197–213; and Peter Lange and Geoffrey Garrett, "The Politics of Growth: Strategic Interaction and Economic Performance in the Advanced Industrialized Countries," *Journal of Politics*, Vol. 47, No. 3, August 1985, pp. 792–827. For further discussion, see Walter F. Abbott and J. W. Leasure, "Income Level and Inflation in the United States," in Nathan Schmukler and Edward Markus (eds.), *Inflation Through the Ages: Economic, Social, Psychological and Historical Aspects* (New York: Brooklyn College Press), 1983, pp. 804–819. For a sophisticated account that includes union structure and party preferences, see Fritz W. Scharpf, "A Game-theoretical Interpretation of Inflation and Unemployment in Western Europe," *Journal of Public Policy*, Vol. 7, No. 3, pp. 227–257. Other important works on representation of class interests include Andrew Martin, "The Politics of Economic Policy in the United States: A Tentative View from a Comparative Historical Perspective," *Sage Professional Papers in Comparative Politics*, No. 01-040 (Beverly Hills, Calif.: Sage), 1973; Edward Tufte, *Political Control of the Economy* (Princeton: Princeton University Press), 1978.

[14] Philippe C. Schmitter, "Interest Mediation and Regime Governability in Contemporary Western Europe and North America," in Suzanne Berger (ed.), *Organizing Interests in Western Europe and North America* (Cambridge: Cambridge University Press), 1981, pp. 285–327; Colin Crouch, "Conditions for Trade Union Wage Restraint," in Leon N. Lindberg and Charles S. Maier (eds.), *The Politics of Inflation and Economic Stagnation* (Washington, D.C.: Brookings Institution), 1985; Gary Marks, "Neocorporatism and Incomes Policy in Western Europe and North America," *Comparative Politics*, Vol. 18, No. 3, 1986, pp. 253–277.

[15] For a review and partial refutation of these arguments, see Geoffrey Garrett and Peter Lange, "Political Responses to Interdependence: What's 'Left' for the Left?" *International Organization*, Vol. 45, No. 4, Autumn 1991, pp. 539–564.

[16] See Colin Crouch, "Inflation and the Political Organization of Economic Interests," chap. 9 in Fred Hirsch and John H. Goldthorpe, *The Political Economy of Inflation* (Cambridge: Harvard University Press), 1978, pp. 217–239.

instability and inflation have developed two strands: one that emphasizes that weaker governments are *unable* to implement politically costly inflation controls, and another that postulates that weaker governments actually have a shorter time horizon than politically secure ones, and so *rationally choose* to postpone adjustments that would curb inflation.[17] Both hypotheses should have profound consequences for international economic cooperation. In either case, unstable governments can be expected to "defect" from international macroeconomic agreements that require a stable exchange rate, maintenance of balance of payments equilibrium, and debt repayment. One can expect the cooperative outcome of the iterated Prisoner's Dilemma to unravel when a player is domestically unstable, since markets know that unstable governments heavily discount the prospects of future cooperation.

Finally, recent work in the political economy of domestic institutions suggests that the credibility of a state's monetary commitments may depend on the independence of its monetary institutions.[18] Politically independent central banks can carry out a policy of monetary stability, even if to do so would be temporarily politically painful. Lower inflation rates have been found to be associated with more independent banks, although the "optimal" degree of credibility is still debated in the literature.[19] If these models are correct, then central bank independence should not only be interesting from a comparative political economy perspective, but it should also have a direct bearing on the stability of a fixed exchange rate regime—an outcome of central interest to scholars of international political economy.

Scholars concerned with foreign economic policy choice or international economic relations can readily incorporate these testable hypotheses in a way that would be logically consistent with well-developed systemic and strategic paradigms. If it is true that left-wing governments have preference orderings that differ in predictable ways from governments of the Right (or if markets act on the assumption that they do), then these preferences should be reflected in the structure of the game and affect the stability of cooperative outcomes. If a government is politically unstable, this is relevant to the value it will put on present costs versus future benefits of any given policy choice, as well as the value it places on future international interactions (i.e., relatively little). If an international monetary commitment is made by a government whose monetary policies are conducted by an independent central bank, then there would be less reason to expect defection through inflation, severe balance of payments crisis, or devaluation. To artificially segregate international and domestic influences

[17] For a discussion and empirical test, see Sule Ozler and Guido Tabellini, "External Debt and Political Instability," NBER Working Paper No. 3772, July 1991.

[18] Kenneth Rogoff, "The Optimal Degree of Commitment to an Intermediate Monetary Target," *Quarterly Journal of Economics*, Vol. 100, 1985, pp. 1169–1189.

[19] Susanne Lohmann, "Optimal Commitment in Monetary Policy: Credibility versus Flexibility," *American Economic Review*, Vol. 82, No. 1, March 1992, p. 273.

could in fact lead to a misunderstanding of international economic relations. Domestic determinants of preference orderings, time horizons, and credibility should be integrated into an explanation as to why certain states found it difficult to abide by the rules of the gold standard as practiced during the interwar years.

THE ARGUMENT OF THIS BOOK

Under what conditions, then, did economic policymakers choose to abide by the rules of the gold standard, and under what conditions did they tend to break the rules? In answering these questions, it is important to keep in mind that governments may be motivated for political reasons to stimulate (or avoid deflating) their domestic economy, and, more importantly, they may be *perceived* by rational forward-looking markets (anyone holding their currency, or any factor of production operating within the economy) as variably subject to such temptation. These governments' problem is that there is no foolproof way to assure markets that they will resist the temptation to try and engineer stimulation or resist the temptation to go back on a commitment to deflate. Rational forward-looking markets search for evidence of a government's commitment. They react negatively to evidence that a government might renege on its commitment to deflate (or to avoid inflation): evidence of political instability, labor unrest, demands of left-wing constituencies. On the other hand, the commitment of a government constrained by an independent monetary authority is more believable to market agents than that of a government which can simply run the printing press. Both quantitative evidence and qualitative evidence for the interwar years suggest that, where governments could not make credible commitments to avoid inflation, the result was capital flight, inflation, and incipient deficit in the current account. The implications for an international monetary regime based on gold were clear: where commitments to avoid inflation and maintain external balance were unbelievable, pressure for devaluation and protection mounted.

Both external and domestic constraints and incentives shaped states' choice of adjustment strategy. Externally, a high degree of economic openness placed limits on the benefits of tariff protection and raised the risk of foreign retaliation, putting a premium on adjustment through the exchange rate. The dominant traders, on the other hand, could exploit their monopoly position to stem balance of payments deficits through protection. Even when these external conditions are controlled, however, the decision of how to cope with deficits is constrained by domestic political factors. Since devaluation cut into the value of investment and creditors' savings, it was avoided by center-right governments and strong independent central banking institutions. On the other hand, trade protection imposed serious costs on the abundant factor of production, labor. The preference of the conservatives was to protect and defend the currency; that of the Left was to devalue and liberalize trade. Some governments were so weak and unstable, however, that they took virtually no internal adjustment measures; they chose the path of least resistance and protected domestic producers while allowing the currency to depreciate. Ultimately, the gold standard depended on the ability and willingness of policymakers—who faced both external and domestic constraints—to adhere to a stringent set of austerity norms that could be costly in the short term.[20]

Before proceeding further, I should be explicit about what this study does *not* try to do. First, it is not a defense of the gold standard. The argument is *not* that the norms of the gold standard were "good" in any global welfare maximizing sense. Few economists would be likely to argue that widespread protection was anything but welfare reducing, but the case is far from clear for fixed exchange rates.[21] Recent research in economic history has thrown into question the assumption that was widely held by policymakers for most of these two decades: that economic stability depended on monetary stability, and that monetary stability could only be maintained by tying the national currency to gold.[22] However, following contemporary policymakers, I view the gold standard as a

[20] Note that my arguments about externalization are essentially for the short to medium run. No country can adjust to external economic imbalance indefinitely through pure externalization, since protection and devaluation do pose domestic economic costs over time.

[21] See Barry Eichengreen, "A Dynamic Model of Tariffs, Output, and Employment under Flexible Exchange Rates," *Journal of International Economics*, Vol. 11, 1981, pp. 341–359. The welfare-decreasing effects of protectionism are among the few points on which economists are virtually in unanimous agreement. Bruno Frey et al., "Consensus and Dissensus Among Economists: An Empirical Study," *American Economic Review*, Vol. 74, pp. 986–994. For the argument that tariffs worsened the spread of the Depression, see Allen Meltzer, "Monetary and Other Explanations for the Start of the Great Depression," *Journal of Monetary Economics*, Vol. 2, 1976, pp. 455–472; Christian Saint-Etienne, *The Great Depression, 1929–1938: Lessons for the 1980s* (Stanford: Stanford University Press), 1984. I am grateful to Barry Eichengreen for pointing out to me that while devaluation in the thirties may have stimulated the economy of the devaluing country, it tended to have negative transmission effects when taken unilaterally and without a concomitant expansion in the devaluing country's money supply. See also Ehsan U. Choudhri and Levis A. Kockin, "The Exchange Rate and the International Transmission of Business Cycle Disturbances: Some Evidence from the Great Depression," *Journal of Money, Credit, and Banking*, November 1980, pt. 1, pp. 565–574; Barry Eichengreen and Jeffrey Sachs, "Exchange Rates and Economic Recovery in the 1930s," *Journal of Economic History*, Vol. 95, No. 4, December 1985, pp. 925–946; Wallace E. Huffman and James R. Lothian, "The Gold Standard and the Transmission of Business Cycles, 1833–1932," in Michael D. Bordo and Anna J. Schwartz (eds.), *A Retrospective on the Classical Gold Standard* (Chicago: University of Chicago Press), 1984, pp. 455–511.

[22] Barry Eichengreen's recent study carefully and persuasively documents the extent to which adherence to fixed exchange rates actually encouraged the Depression to spread and to deepen. Eichengreen, *Golden Fetters: The Gold Standard and the Great Depression, 1919–1939* (New York and Oxford: Oxford University Press), 1992. Nonetheless, contemporary policymakers clearly viewed the gold standard as the norm for appropriate economic policy choice. Kenneth Mouré's recent history of the franc Poincaré illustrates the excruciating economic distress governments sometimes put their economies through in order to maintain their currency's gold parity. Mouré, *Managing the Franc Poincaré* (Cambridge: Cambridge University Press), 1991.

normative bench mark for appropriate foreign economic policy, and go on to explain the conditions associated with the decision to devalue and to protect. The global welfare implications of the gold standard are a crucial concern of economic history, but do not directly bear on the issue of abiding by the rules that is the focal point of this study.

Second, it is not possible to treat every conceivable policy option designed to address external economic imbalance. Quantitative import restrictions and currency and capital controls are mentioned only in passing, yet they were clearly used to externalize the costs of adjustment by a number of states.[23] Attention is drawn to these alternatives in interpreting the quantitative results and in discussing the cases. The focus here is on devaluation and tariff protection, the two most pervasive means of resisting internal adjustment during the interwar years.

Third, this study does not pretend to supplant systemic international relations theory, but rather to supplement it. Because the study deals with the twenties and thirties, it cannot test for the relative impact of such systemic variables as multipolarity, bipolarity, or hegemony. There is simply not enough variation in the system as a whole during our seventeen-year period to rule these variables in or out. Effectively, the essential nature of the system is held constant. Still, it is possible to test some structural arguments: we can assess the extent to which the policy choices of larger powers, highly trade dependent countries, and net external creditors, for instance, were different from their opposites. But this should not be construed as an effort to supplant broader systemic theorizing.

TOWARD AN EXPLANATION OF THE POLICY MIX: METHODOLOGY AND ORGANIZATION

Two methodologies are used here to make the case for domestic sources of foreign economic policy choice: comparative cases and quantitative analysis. A dualist methodological approach has tremendous advantages in unraveling a problem as complex as the political influences on the adjustment policy mix.[24]

---

[23] There is a sophisticated subset of the endogenous tariff literature that is concerned with modeling the choice between tariffs, quotas, and other tax-cum-subsidy options. See Ronald Findlay and Stanislaw Wellisz, "Endogenous Tariffs, the Political Economy of Trade Restrictions, and Welfare," in Jagdish Bhagwati (ed.), *Import Competition and Response* (Chicago: University of Chicago Press/NBER), 1982; Kent Jones, "The Political Economy of Voluntary Export Restraint Agreements," *Kyklos*, Vol. 37, 1984, pp. 82–101; Wolfgang Mayer and Raymond Riezman, "Endogenous Choice of Trade Policy Instruments," *Journal of International Economics*, Vol. 23, 1987, pp. 377–381.

[24] The prevalent "either-or" debate between methodological schools has been counterproductive, and does not need to be reviewed here. For a good recent review of the strengths of each, see Charles C. Ragin, *The Comparative Method: Moving Beyond Qualitative and Quantitative Strategies* (Berkeley: University of California Press), 1987. For an argument that cases cannot on their own either generate or test theory, see Christopher H. Achen and Duncan Snidal, "Rational

First, descriptive statistics provide some sense of where a particular case fits into a broader distribution of cases. If an argument is to be made that Belgium's trade dependence contributed to its liberal trade policy, it is useful to know just how trade dependent and how liberal Belgium was compared to other states. Secondly, the statistical analysis complements the case studies by parceling out the relative influences of several variables, which is impossible to do convincingly using a small number of cases. The cases, on the other hand, reveal far more about the political *processes* that link the explanatory variables with the dependent variables. Overall, combining methodologies provides a parallax on the problem that is difficult to achieve with a single approach. To choose one method to the exclusion of the other is like closing one eye and trying to make judgments about distance: it is easy to lose perspective. The most convincing conclusions will ultimately be those on which the regressions agree with the archives.

As a first cut, a macroscopic, quantitative, time-series cross-sectional analysis is used that covers from twelve to twenty-one countries for most of the interwar years.[25] The criteria for choosing the countries were that they were part of the European-American economic system during the interwar years, that they were independent countries (colonies and dominions were excluded), and that sufficient data could be found to justify their inclusion into a quantitative analysis. The unit of analysis is a "country-year," and the number of observations could reach a theoretical 357, were it not for the problem of missing data and the inclusion of lagged or moving-averaged variables. For most of the regressions presented, the number of observations ranges between 140 and 300, depending on the included explanatory variables.

The countries that were eventually included in this analysis could fairly be described as constituting the European-American core of the interwar economic system.[26] Thus, conclusions cannot be legitimately drawn about the politics of balance of payments adjustment and the correlates of the policy mix for countries in the non-European periphery.[27] While this is one limitation of

Deterrence Theory and Comparative Case Studies," *World Politics*, Vol. 41, No. 2, January 1989, pp. 143–169.

[25] I originally intended to include twenty-three countries, but as will be seen in the following chapters, Romania and Yugoslavia are almost always excluded from the multivariate analysis due to missing data. The number of countries varies because of case attrition, which in turn depends on which variables are included. Each presentation of the results indicates the identity of the included countries.

[26] With the exception of Japan, which is included because of its economic connections with this core group (the United States was its major trading partner for much of the period).

[27] I have intentionally omitted what many economists have called the (non-European) "periphery"—the semideveloped countries of Latin America, Africa, Asia, and Australasia. There are good methodological and practical reasons for doing so. Economic historians have documented quite well the particular vulnerability of the peripheral regions to the upheavals of the late 1920s and

the study, it may not be overly serious, since there is still a high degree of variation among the included countries with respect to degree of development, industrialization, wealth, and regime type, so that the results may have an acceptable degree of generality. The most stringent efforts were made to avoid selecting these cases on the basis of balance of payments pressures or the policy mix selected to address these pressures. Hence, the United States' balance of payments position was as favorable for the period as a whole as Austria's was dismal. The Dutch florin was as stable as the Greek drachma was mercurial. Belgium's customs averaged less than 6 percent of the total value of its imports for the period as a whole, while the comparable figure for Bulgaria was more than 22 percent. In short, despite the fact that the study is limited to the European-American core, the cases chosen do not artificially truncate the policy choices I am trying to explain. They are delimited only by geography and data availability.[28]

The core theoretical claim is fleshed out in Chapter 3, and a quantitative political/economic model for capital flight and current account deficit follows. This marriage of disciplines raises the question of precisely which variables should be included in a "political/economic" model of external economic imbalance. In the interest of parsimony, my rule has been to include only those economic variables that are reasonably widely accepted as influencing the outcome in question, and *only* those economic variables that the government or monetary authority does not directly control. This means that policy variables— the money supply, bank rate, and fiscal budget—are excluded from the equation. If policy variables were to be controlled, we really would not have an explanation for the relationship between the political variable and the observed outcome.[29] In practical terms, the difficulty is one of multicollinearity: the

---

1930s. See C. A. Diaz-Alejandro, "Stories of the 1930s for the 1980s," in P. Aspe Armella, R. Dornbusch, and M. Obstfeld (eds.), *Financial Policies and the World Capital Market: The Problem of Latin American Countries* (Chicago: University of Chicago Press), 1983; Barry Eichengreen and Richard Portes, "Debt and Default in the 1930s: Causes and Consequences," *European Economic Review*, Vol. 30, June 1986, pp. 599–640.; H. Fleisig, "The United States and Non-European Periphery During the Early Years of the Great Depression," in H. Van der Wee (ed.), *The Great Depression Revisited: Essays on the Economics of the Thirties*, 1972.

[28] It is possible that the problem of missing data introduces some bias into the analysis. It is frequently the less developed countries within the European core that also happen to be missing data. Thus, it was difficult to find statistics on Bulgaria, Greece, Poland, Romania, Spain, and Yugoslavia—countries whose lesser developed status may be correlated with distinctive patterns on the dependent variables. But data were also missing for Belgium, Canada, and Switzerland in a number of instances, so that it is not obvious that the loss of data introduces serious selection bias.

[29] As an illustration, if we are interested in testing for the impact of the central bank on the current account, it makes little theoretical sense to include the money supply and the bank rate in the equation. My hypothesis assumes distinctive policy patterns among politically independent central banks; the interpretation of the institutional coefficient is questionable if both of its major policy levers are controlled in the equation.

inclusion of both the political variable and the policy instrument washes out the effects of both. The solution has been to control for economic variables, including external shocks, that are largely beyond the control of governments or monetary authorities.

The development of a political/economic model for capital flows, current account deficit, currency depreciation, and tariff policies also raises the contentious issue of the direction of causation. At the risk of oversimplification of their position, economists are often skeptical of claims that political variables have an "independent" effect on economic outcomes. Often they prefer to conceptualize the political variables as endogenous to economic forces, or as epiphenomena of economics, that contribute relatively little to a causal understanding of economic outcomes. To bolster the causal argument, here the political variables are made to compete with lagged economic variables, and successive versions of the model are tested for stability and explanatory power. Where political variables can compete effectively with lagged economic variables in a multivariate regression and where political variables are only weakly correlated with prior economic conditions, a convincing case can be made that politics have an important independent causal effect on economic outcomes. It is an exceedingly demanding test for politics, but the data stand up to the skeptics rather courageously.

The second methodology employed is the comparative case method. Two chapters review selected cases in detail in order to confirm the plausibility of the quantitative analysis. The cases were chosen, first, because they represented deterioriating external economic imbalance, and second, because they contained variations on the explanatory variables that were found to be significant in the quantitative analysis.[30] Hence, the stabilization of the French franc (1923–1926) provides interesting variations over time in three of the variables that were significant to an explanation of capital flight and changes in the currency value. In those few years, France was ruled by a center-right government, a left-wing coalition, and finally by a broad-based (but conservative) coalition of National Union. France experienced a few years of relatively stable government, followed by constant cabinet collapse, and finally again relative stability under the regime of Raymond Poincaré. Finally, while formally independent, the central bank went from extremely weak leadership under Georges Robineau to a strong and assertive posture under Emile Moreau. France during

---

[30] All of the cases selected for intensive comparison involve countries with pluralist democratic regimes. This has some advantages and some shortcomings: On the one hand, "regime type" is held constant, so that inferences can better be made on the impact of other variables. On the other hand, any observations regarding the impact of other variables, such as instability, party in power, organization of the labor and capital market—must be understood as being contingent on the presence of pluralist democracy. No firm conclusions can be drawn about the way in which other variables may interact with regime type to produce different results. The results of the case comparisons are limited to pluralist democracies.

the 1920s is nearly the ideal case to study three variables that were subjected to systematic testing in Chapters 3 and 4.

Case studies are also employed to compare how states handled balance of payments deficits under the depressionary conditions of the thirties. In Chapter 7, Britain, Belgium, and France are compared.[31] The rationale for selecting these cases, again, is that they represent instances of deteriorating external position and that they provide variance on the explanatory factors revealed to be of importance to the policy mix in previous chapters. Britain was the largest trader in the sample, while Belgium accounted for a much smaller share of world trade. Belgium was the most highly trade dependent country in our sample, while France possessed a highly diversified economy and was potentially self-sufficient. Labor unrest varied over time for each of these countries, with France sustaining the most serious degree of social unrest among the three. Similarly, France was highly politically unstable, while Britain and Belgium enjoyed fairly stable governments during these years. Finally, there is variation within each country over time in the political orientation of party in power. Britain went from a Labour government to a conservative "National" government, while Belgium went from conservative Catholic domination to a coalition that admitted Socialists. France is the extreme case of a swing from center-right government to a far left coalition of Socialists and Communists who cooperated to form the Front Populaire. This trio of cases provides sufficient leverage into the question of the determinants of the policy mix to flesh out the story suggested in the broader statistical analysis.

This study is designed to answer the question "Who adjusts?" in a cumulative fashion. Its design is cumulative on two levels. Within the quantitative chapters (3, 4, and 6), the progression is from a set of simple descriptive statistics of the dependent variable, to a partial regression analysis based on economic variables, and finally to a multiple regression that includes economic and political explanations, as well as some structural control variables. One reason for presenting results in this way is to use the available data to the best advantage. The greater the number of included variables, the higher the case attrition. Simpler presentations take in a larger number of cases. The second reason is that we can assess the impact of adding a political component to the basic economic model. We can look for evidence that the political explanations either increase the proportion of explained variation, reduce the variance of the included variables, or produce fitted variables that are superior to those generated by other models. For these reasons, each chapter is organized *internally* to build

---

[31] The typical troika for studying systemic breakdown and retaliation during this period consists of Britain, France, and the United States. It would have been inappropriate to select the United States because, while it devalued and threw up tariffs, it was never in a negative or seriously declining balance of payments position. If it is the policy mix we are interested in explaining, then the case cannot be chosen on the basis of this mix. To do so would introduce selection bias into the choice of cases.

toward an estimate of the impact of politics on the balance of payments and the policy mix.

Furthermore, the chapters are organized serially to build a cumulative picture of the policy mix. Chapter 3 concentrates on explaining why countries get into current account difficulties and experience capital flight in the first place. Chapter 4 explores the extent to which the same factors are associated with the decision to devalue or to allow the currency to depreciate. Chapter 5 pauses to check our findings against a historical case in point. The case of the stabilization of the French franc concentrates on the influences on the current account, capital flows, and currency depreciation that have been discussed up to this point. Chapter 6 extends the quantitative analysis to cover the decision to raise tariffs, and Chapter 7 presents three more cases that concentrate on the trade-offs involved in choosing to deflate, to devalue, and/or to protect. This method of inquiry allows us to move easily from economic to political explanations, from quantitative findings to case studies, and from single to multiple policy choices. It provides a reasonably thorough examination of the pressures and opportunities confronting states when they faced the decision of whether or not to abide by the gold standard norms.

FINDINGS

The gold standard required national economic policymakers to place external balance above domestic economic balance, to stabilize and maintain the value of their currency, and to try and maintain a reasonably open market for international trade. Adherence to these norms was the ideal toward which most of the economic conferences and bilateral negotiations of the day were directed. Yet the ability and will to adhere to these norms were highly conditioned in some cases not only by structural features of a country's domestic economy and its relationship to the international economic system, but also by the domestic political constraints policymakers faced and the preferences they held based on their own political objectives.

Countries that were most likely to choose a cooperative policy mix were small, and had highly trade dependent economies. They were led by stable governments and were characterized by a quiescent labor force. When these characteristics prevailed, it was possible to sustain domestic economic policies that were consistent with external equilibrium. Large traders took advantage of their size to implement more restrictive trade policies. Countries that had the luxury of being insulated from the rest of the international economic system were the worst offenders of the gold standard norms: even in the absence of severe balance of payments pressures, they tended to protect and, to a lesser extent, to devalue, forcing the smaller and more trade dependent countries to adjust to these hostile moves.

Unstable governments were also disruptive to international economic relations. By every criteria, they were unwilling—or unable—to cooperate. They tended to overconsume,[32] ringing up larger and larger current account deficits. Political instability shook the confidence of capital, which fled in the face of political uncertainty. Largely as a result of both current account pressure and capital flight, governments with a brief life expectancy allowed their currencies to depreciate much more frequently than did those with a firm grip on political authority. There is even scant evidence, though it is not strong, that unstable governments were also associated with higher tariffs. Governments that were not likely to be in office for long were singularly unsuited to international economic cooperation. Any benefits such cooperation promised in the medium to long term were discounted in the face of the high present costs of internal adjustment.

Finally, there was a distinction in the policy mix favored by conservative polities and that favored by polities in which labor was better represented. The former tended to defend the currency, but raised tariffs. The latter tended to do the opposite. Hence, higher left-wing representation was associated with currency depreciation but also with the alleviation of tariff barriers (which were deemed a "tax on consumption"), while center-right parties defended the currency but protected. Moreover, where the central bank was most independent from government, the currency tended to be stronger, but there was also a slight tendency to restrict imports. The distinct interests of capital and labor are evident in the mix taken. It is difficult to imagine a *selective* implementation of international economic norms that could be more politically driven.

[32] Technically, the correct term here is "absorption," not consumption. In the Keynesian framework, consumption is only one component of total absorption, to which must be added government spending and investment.

Chapter 2

THE INTERWAR GOLD STANDARD

THE INTERWAR gold exchange standard never worked as smoothly as had the international monetary system before the First World War. A crucial reason was that the social and political landscape had changed so radically in so many countries from 1913 on that the commitment to the norms of international adjustment implicit in the gold standard simply were not credible under the conditions that tended to prevail in many countries at the close of the war. This chapter will first provide an introduction to the interwar gold standard, and point out how this system depended on a highly credible commitment on the part of its participants to deflate if necessary in order to defend their currency. It will also show that post–World War I conditions had changed from prewar conditions in ways that undermined the credibility of that commitment in many states. The second section outlines the norms of the interwar gold exchange regime. It first describes the adjustment mechanism, then outlines three implicit adjustment norms, and finally discusses the ways in which states might negotiate so that deficit adjustment might be facilitated by loans or credits from the major lending houses or central banks of surplus countries. The third section discusses theories that shed light on the selection of a policy mix and introduces the explanatory variables that are the empirical core of this study.

THE PREWAR AND INTERWAR GOLD STANDARDS

Expectations during the interwar years about how states experiencing balance of payments disequilibrium should adjust evolved from beliefs about how adjustment had taken place under the prewar "classical" gold standard. Compared to the international monetary chaos that followed, the nineteenth-century gold standard was a model of stability. Without doubt, exchange rates were far less stable in the interwar years than during the gold standard years of the late nineteenth century that preceded them.[1] The only substantial devaluations between 1880 and 1914 were those of Portugal, Argentina, Italy, Chile, Bulgaria, and Mexico. By contrast, almost every European country devalued its currency in the twenties and again, as did the United States, during the Depression.

Why the gold standard worked so well in the earlier period but was so fragile

---

[1] In his classic account of the prewar international gold standard, Arthur I. Bloomfield wrote, "Only a trifling number of countries were forced off the gold standard, once adopted, and devaluations of gold currencies were highly exceptional." *Monetary Policy Under the International Gold Standard: 1880–1914* (New York: Arno Press), 1978, p. 6

in the twenties and thirties was a puzzle to contemporaries and is still debated today. As a recent study by Barry Eichengreen notes,[2] its robustness did not depend on halcyon economic conditions: the prewar system had survived serious economic downturns in the mid 1890s and the early 1900s. Its stability did not depend on calm capital markets: before the war foreign lending had fluctuated significantly, and financial crises were commonplace. Its workability did not depend on the concentration of financial hegemony in one center: both Paris and Berlin were important financial centers in the nineteenth century, and it is not obvious that the distribution of financial power was any more concentrated than between London, Paris, and New York during the interwar period.[3] Nor could the stability of the prewar system be attributed to a greater willingness on the part of central banks to play by the "rules of the game": in neither period did they consistently contract their money supplies when losing gold reserves or expand it when gaining them.[4]

Where these systems differed greatly was their credibility. "There was no question," Eichengreen writes in reference to the prewar years, "that at the end of the day the authorities at the center of the system would take whatever steps were necessary to defend gold convertibility."[5] When such a commitment was beyond doubt, capital holders would act in anticipation of an unflagging defense of a weak currency, and would ultimately reinforce the authorities' efforts to correct incipient market pressures. But what made the prewar commitment more credible than that of the interwar period? The answer appears to be twofold: minimal domestic political opposition to the gold standard; and prompt and significant international central bank collaboration in times of crisis. In this chapter, I argue that the new political and social conditions unleashed by World War I undermined the certainty that states would be willing and able to maintain the gold standard. And in addition to the oft-cited postwar enmities among the major powers, international cooperation was also hampered by the *expectation of defection on the part of the deficit country*. Where domestic political conditions were not expected to be conducive to maintaining a stable currency, to cooperate was, for the surplus/strong-currency country, to be on the losing end of a one-way bet. While the stability of the system would have been enhanced by international cooperation, international cooperation

---

[2] Barry Eichengreen, *Golden Fetters: The Gold Standard and the Great Depression, 1919–1939* (New York and Oxford: Oxford University Press), 1992, chap. 2.

[3] Melchior Palyi, *The Twilight of Gold* (Chicago: Henry Regnery), 1972, *passim*.

[4] See Ragnar Nurkse, who found that central banks in fact tended to offset international reserve flows rather than accommodate them. *International Currency Experience* (Geneva: League of Nations), 1944; and Arthur Bloomfield, *Monetary Policy Under the Gold Standard, 1880–1939* (New York: Federal Reserve Bank of New York), 1959, who found that countries' discounts rates tended to rise and fall together, contrary to theoretical expectations. Surplus countries were in fact reluctant to adjust to the demands of external equilibrium, often for fear of inflation, as evidenced by the reluctance to lower discount rates when reserve ratios rose.

[5] Eichengreen, *Golden Fetters*, p. 65.

was ultimately conditioned by its expected payoff—the best predictor of which was the complexion of the deficit/weak-currency country's domestic politics. Hence, we return again to the question: what conditions contributed to a country's ability to maintain a credible commitment to gold?

Exclusionary Politics and Monetary Stability during the Nineteenth Century

One reason why the international monetary system was stable during the nineteenth century was because of the excellent fit it enjoyed with prevailing domestic political institutions and practices. With little resistance, the gold standard could be managed in most countries between 1870 and 1913 from the top down. Disturbances in the balance of payments, which placed downward pressure on the currency, could be countered by the central bank discount rate or interest rate increases that would constrict short-term finance, discourage investment, and damp down the level of domestic economic activity and depress prices, reducing the incipient deficit and reversing selling pressure on the currency. External balance could then be maintained, though at a cost to the level of domestic economic activity.[6]

Compared to the twentieth century, there was little political resistance during the nineteenth century to the primacy that the gold standard placed on external balance, even when this was achieved at the expense of the domestic economy. This lack of resistance may be largely attributable to exclusionary politics as well as to laissez-faire political philosophies that did not recognize state responsibility for the economic well-being of its citizens. Political systems that excluded, marginalized, or were otherwise able to ignore the widespread economic and social pain caused by the whipsawing of the domestic economy were unquestionably able to maintain a fixed monetary standard. Political philosophies that could justify an exclusive focus on external balance and shun responsibility for economic misery at home buttressed the credibility of the gold standard.

Between 1870 and 1914 there was an increasingly perceptible shift in the balance of power between classes that eventually challenged the institutional and philosophical supports of externally oriented monetary policies. These years of intensified industrialization and urbanization saw a growing demand for the recognition of the rights of workers—a shift that was increasingly recognized by the grudging acceptance of the right of the state to interfere with employers' exploitation of their workers, to regulate conditions of employment, and to develop basic standards of public health. By the 1880s a somewhat

---

[6] The prewar gold standard was not successful at ensuring either domestic price stability or economic growth. Barry Eichengreen (ed.), *The Gold Standard in Theory and History* (New York: Methuen), 1985, pp. 6–9. The inability of the gold standard to deal with the dual demands of internal and external equilibrium was a major reason for its breakdown under the new political circumstances of the interwar years. Palyi, *Twilight of Gold*, passim.

more positive view of the role of the state in the economic well-being of a nation was gaining currency. Bismarck's policies are often cited as a first step on the road to the "welfare state," but in England as well the need for a more active policy of social reform was making its way into progressive thought about the responsibilities of the state toward the welfare of its citizens. Increasingly, liberalism's earlier tenets were being challenged by new doctrines of state action and responsibility.

Only gradually, as the right to vote was extended to workers and the poor, were these ideas translated into tangible political demands. Universal male suffrage only began to take hold in many European countries after the turn of the century.[7] Among the earliest to extend universally the right to vote were France, Switzerland, and Germany,[8] each of which in 1848 extended suffrage to all male citizens in their twenties and older. Britain maintained various property, tax, and educational requirements and inequalities until 1918, though it is true that these were liberalized in 1868 and again in 1885. The Scandinavian countries were fairly early enfranchisers: by 1900 Norway had virtually universal male suffrage, and by 1907 in Finland all men and women over the age of twenty-four were entitled to vote by secret ballot. Sweden gave up its high economic qualifications in favor of universal male suffrage in 1909. In Austria, landowning and minimum tax contributions greatly restricted suffrage until the abolition of the curial system in the 1907 Reform Law; universal and equal adult suffrage was not extended to all citizens over twenty years of age until 1919. Belgium and the Netherlands also had tax minima that effectively excluded most laborers until 1894, and until the Great War, those who owned property or had a higher-education diploma were awarded additional votes. Denmark prevented workers who did not have their own household from voting until 1915. Italy used a combination of tax and wealth minima, as well as educational requirements, to limit the electorate; in fact, these requirements were tightened in 1894 to reduce the number of eligible voters, contrary to the liberalization trends in other countries. Like most other European countries, however, Italy did extend universal manhood suffrage in 1919, but free and fair elections did not survive the rise of fascism in 1924. In general, it is fair to say that until the turn of the twentieth century—and for some countries, not until after World War I—large portions of working-class persons could effectively be prevented from voicing their political and, potentially, their economic demands via the ballot box. By the beginning of the interwar period, most systems of

[7] For a concise review of suffrage requirements and voting procedures for many Western European countries, see Peter Flora, *State, Economy, and Society in Western Europe, 1815–1975* (Frankfurt am Main: Campus Verlag), 1983, pp. 95–148.

[8] One must be cautious in attributing too much to the extension of the franchise in Germany at this time. First, the electoral law was in fact highly favorable to the Junkers; moreover, the Reichstag was hardly a popularly controlled legislature during this time. See N. Stone, *Europe Transformed, 1878–1919* (Cambridge: Harvard University Press), 1984, p. 184.

exclusion and inequality had been dismantled in favor of universal male suffrage.

Workers were increasingly expressing their demands outside of parliamentary politics as well. Spurred by accelerating urbanization and the depression in agriculture of the 1870s, labor began to concentrate in the cities. During the 1880s, thanks largely to falling food prices, real wages grew (as did profits), muting potential labor disputes for the time being. By the early twentieth century, however, serious social unrest led to demands for universal suffrage in Austria; general strikes in Belgium, the Netherlands, Sweden, and Italy; revolutionary uprisings in Russia and Romania; and nearly to civil war in Hungary.

Italy during the 1890s was a harbinger of the potential for domestic political conflict to undermine international monetary policy commitments. Italy's toehold on parliamentary politics after unification was extremely tenuous, and was further undercut by the depression of the 1890s.[9] Bank failures led to accusations of political corruption, and a violent peasant uprising and tax revolt broke out in Sicily in 1893. Agricultural disasters in 1897 threatened famine in many areas, contributing to the growing strength of the Socialist party. Violent disturbances emanated from the south, and culminated in violent unrest in Milan in the spring of 1898, causing the fall of the government. The election that followed led to a majority for the parties of the Left and the leadership of Giovanni Giolitti, but not without serious monetary crisis. Italy was one of the most politically unstable of the European countries during the late nineteenth century, and one of only three European devaluations between 1880 and 1914. In Italy around the turn of the century, fissiparous domestic politics contributed to monetary chaos and foreshadowed the tensions between domestic politics and gold standard promises that would become all too apparent after the war.

The Great War itself hastened many of the changes that in many countries had begun in the opening years of the twentieth century. In the West, the mixing of classes and income levels in military service, the influx of women into industrial occupations, and the sudden upward surge of trade unionism and participation in industry were clearly altering the political and social landscape on which economic adjustment would fall. The experience of national mobilization for total war legitimized the demands for political equality that had been building since the late nineteenth century.[10]

Political representation of the working classes grew across Europe after the

[9] In Italy, parliamentary politics had come under attack for its "cynical bargains within a narrow clique without much regard for the country as a whole." James Joll, *Europe Since 1870: An International History* (New York: Harper and Row), 1973, p. 124.

[10] For example, for an account of the social effects of the war in Britain, see A. Marwick, *The Deluge* (London: Bodley Head), 1965, and *Britain in the Century of Total War: War, Peace, and Social Change, 1890–1967* (London: Penguin), 1968.

war. Social Democratic party membership made major advances in Austria, Sweden, Denmark, France, and Norway, and membership in the British Labour party climbed over the course of the two interwar decades.[11] And it was only after the war that Social Democratic and Labour parties participated in governments. The British Labour party first contested elections in 1900, but it had only a small representation in Parliament before the war. Labour seats peaked at 47 percent of Parliament in 1929, and Labour governments were formed for the first time in 1924 and again in 1929. In Germany, the Social Democrats had been a significant party since the 1890s, but led democratic governments for the first time in 1919–20 and again in 1928. France experienced its first moderate Left government in 1924 through 1926, and again in 1932 through 1933, and a more radical Socialist-Communist coalition between 1936 and 1938. In Belgium, working-class parties accounted for 14 percent of the seats in parliament in 1914, and the proportion jumped to 37 percent in the first postwar election. The Norwegian Labor party experienced a similar postwar jump: with 18 percent of the parliamentary seats held in 1912, its representation grew to 39 percent in 1927, and it formed its first government in 1935. Though patterns varied across countries, workers undeniably had an unprecedented voice in governance following World War I.

Increased political representation was accompanied by a revolution in labor organization and industrial action. In Britain, Germany, Sweden, Denmark, and Norway, a steady upward trend in unionization had taken off around the turn of the century, and took a gargantuan leap during World War I. The number of union members doubled in Britain and more than trebled in France after the war. Massive strikes erupted across Europe in the early twenties. In Italy, the number of working days lost jumped from 912,000 in 1918 to more than 22 million in 1919 and more than 30 million in 1920. France's pattern was similar. Germany's strikers took their greatest toll in 1924, when more than 36 million working days were lost. The most disruptive of all was the British general strike of 1926, which cost workers and the economy 162 million working days.[12] Organized labor's primary concerns—for political access, employment opportunities, a living wage, and growing demands for a social safety net—were increasingly incompatible with a fail-safe commitment to gold. The old patterns of domestic economic adjustment that were needed to maintain external economic balance and a stable currency would come under increasing stress as a result.

Governing coalitions were far more fragile as a result of the new social and political forces that emerged during the interwar years. For the overwhelming

---

[11] Stefano Bartolini, "The Membership of Mass Parties: The Social Democratic Experience, 1889–1978," chap. 7, in Hans Daalder and Peter Mair, *Western European Party Systems* (London: Sage), 1983, pp. 177–220.

[12] All statistics on strike activity are from B. R. Mitchell, *European Historical Statistics*, Series C2, (London: Macmillan), pp. 181–185.

TABLE 2.1
Average Cabinet Duration for 17 Countries,
1870–1913 and 1923–1939

	Average Cabinet Duration (years)	
	1870–1913	1923–1939
Austria/Hungary	2.3	0.93 (Aus.)
		1.5 (Hun.)
Belgium	3.3	1.3
Bulgaria[a,b]	1.09	1.2
Denmark[a]	2.15	4.25
France	1.34	0.63
Germany	1.86	1.42
Greece[a]	0.55	0.84
Italy	1.5	1.41
Japan	2.6	1.06
Netherlands	2.26	2.13
Norway	2.26	2.13
Romania	1.16	0.73
Spain	0.86	0.65
Sweden	2.69	1.7
United Kingdom	1.65	1.31
Yugoslavia[a,b]	0.97 (Serbia)	1.13

Source: Arthur S. Banks, Cross-Polity Time-Series Data, Segment
1, Field M.

[a]Countries for which prewar cabinets had longer duration than interwar ones.

[b]1878–1913

majority of European countries, significant cabinet changes were far more frequent during the interwar years than had been the case between 1870 and 1913 (though the United States and Canada do not fit this trend). Table 2.1 clearly indicates the shorter average cabinet duration during the interwar years compared to the decades of the "classic" gold standard.

Even the well-established democracies—Britain, France, the Netherlands, Belgium, Sweden, and Norway—experienced greater political instability during the interwar years than they had prior to the Great War. The war had had even more revolutionary consequences for the political systems of Central and Eastern Europe, of which the Bolshevik revolution is only the most dramatic example. Prewar regimes in Germany and Bulgaria fell. While the former country moved toward an unstable democracy, the latter engaged in economic policies so harsh toward the owners of wealth and capital that economic recovery was paralyzed for several years.[13] Hungary briefly experienced Communist dictatorship under Bela Kun; civil war broke out in Poland and later in Spain.

In short, the interwar period was unprecedented for most countries in the extent to which polities were struggling with the newly organized forces and demands of a broader, more inclusive democracy. Some lost the struggle and abandoned the democratic project. Others persisted and gradually formed a domestic consensus that could support the new demands of the Left. Still others experienced periods of prolonged instability, waivering between competing societal demands and changing governments with alarming frequency. In each case, the way in which competing demands were filtered through the political systems of these states could not help but have a drastic impact on a country's unquestioned commitment to gold.

These social and political changes directly influenced the stability of the gold standard. Whereas during the nineteenth century virtually every European government—and many others besides—had gold standard commitments that were beyond any reasonable doubt, those commitments did not ring true where political and social instability meant politically convenient solutions and where the Left refused to sacrifice labor for the sake of the currency. During the nineteenth century, markets *knew* that governments would defend their legal gold parity. Indeed, it often had been unnecessary actually to do so; market confidence itself had had an equilibratory effect on those rates. But this credibility rested on the widely held assumption that the role of monetary policy was to defend the currency, an assumption which in turn rested on domestic political systems that could ignore economic turmoil. The political reforms of the early twentieth century forewarned that all was not well with this set of priorities, just as they were prescient of the newly emerging demands for an increasingly elaborate welfare state. The nineteenth-century gold standard put a high premium on external equilibrium, often at the expense of internal economic conditions, and it could be justified among the narrow enfranchised classes as a necessary condition for the conduct of international trade and investment.[14] Political marginalization of the working classes ensured unanimity. But the politics of inclusion and the concomitant breakdown in nineteenth-century consensus meant that primacy could no longer unquestionably be given to external balance and currency stability. For the first time, most governments

[13] G. T. Danaillow, *Les Effets de la Guerre en Bulgarie* (Paris: Presses Universitaires de France), 1932.

[14] T. E. Gregory, *The Gold Standard and Its Future* (London: Methuen), 1932. The Macmillan Committee echoed this sentiment just before Britain departed from gold in 1931: "International trade, commerce, and finance are based on confidence. One of the foundation stones on which that confidence reposes is the general belief that all countries will seek to maintain so far as lies in their power the value of their national currency as it has been fixed by law." The Macmillan Report, reprinted in Eichengreen, *The Gold Standard in Theory and History*, p. 196.

faced seriously competing policy goals. In the Western democracies, struggles over income shares between capital and labor led to demands for resources greater than those that could easily be satisfied consonant with the external constraint of a fixed gold parity, creating inflationary pressures within some economies.[15] For the first time in history, workers were more nearly the political match of holders of capital, setting the stage for a "war of attrition"; that is, a period of prolonged conflict over economic policies that arguably contributed to inflation and currency depreciation.[16] The central divide was often not only over which sectors of society should shoulder the heavy fiscal burdens stemming from World War I, but also over the rate of economic growth itself. Deflation would have its most devastating impact on the unfortunate members of the working class who were thrown out of work, but it would benefit creditors and the rentier.[17] As Kindleberger has written, "What was critical was that the postwar position made it necessary for sectors in society to struggle over the income distribution. . . . [T]he issue [was] whether deflation and unemployment would saddle a major share of the load on the working class, as contrasted with the rentier. Keynes observed in 1922 that the choice between inflation or deflation comes down to an agonizing outcome of a struggle among interest groups."[18]

As John Ruggie has pointed out in his discussion of the evolution of the post–World War II economic order, these struggles were not easily digested by an international monetary system fixed to gold.[19] Open domestic conflict undermined the certainty that a government would honor its commitment to defend the currency in light of pressures to inflate. Those with liquid capital, whose decisions constituted the ebb and flow of currency markets, associated political

[15] Colin Crouch, "Inflation and the Political Organization of Economic Interests," chap. 9 in Fred Hirsch and John H. Goldthorpe, *The Political Economy of Inflation* (Cambridge: Harvard University Press), 1978, pp. 217–239.

[16] John Goldthorpe has hypothesized that inflation takes off when conflict between social groups becomes more intense and more evenly matched. John H. Goldthorpe, "The Current Inflation: Towards a Sociological Account," in Hirsch and Goldthorpe, *The Political Economy of Inflation*, pp. 186–216. The phrase "war of attrition" is used by Barry Eichengreen, *Golden Fetters*, and by Alberto Alesina and Allan Drazen, "Why Are Stabilizations Delayed?" Unpublished essay, Harvard and Tel-Aviv Universities, May 1990.

[17] Charles S. Maier believes that it is possible to predict an "inflation prone coalition" that includes (though is not limited to) workers concerned with high wages and full employment. Charles S. Maier, "The Politics of Inflation in the Twentieth Century," chap. 2, in Hirsch and Goldthorpe, *The Political Economy of Inflation*, pp. 37–72.

[18] Charles P. Kindleberger, *A Financial History of Western Europe* (London: Allen and Unwin), 1984, p. 323. See also Manfred G. Schmidt, "The Politics of Unemployment and Labor Market Policy," *West European Politics*, Vol. 7, No. 3, July 1984, pp. 5–24.

[19] John Gerard Ruggie, "International Regimes, Transactions, and Change: Embedded Liberalism in the Postwar Economic Order," in Stephen Krasner, *International Regimes* (Ithaca: Cornell University Press), 1983, pp. 195–231.

instability with inflation, or at the very least uncertainty.[20] More generally, markets tried to anticipate any set of political conditions or government policies that hinted at a weak commitment to gold. Whenever they detected a crack in credibility, they sold the currency in question to avoid exchange losses. These actions were often self-fulfilling prophecies. The turmoil of domestic politics gave holders of liquid capital ample incentive to destabilize the interwar gold standard.

The Role of International Monetary Cooperation

Unfortunately, the gold *exchange* system magnified some of these effects by similarly shaping the incentives of foreign central banks. With the 1922 monetary conference at Genoa, the British had secured agreement on the principle that the smaller countries should hold a portion of their reserves in the currency of the major gold centers (Britain, France, and the United States), and that these in turn would hold gold and make it available upon demand. While this would allow for the expansion of central bank reserves and relieve the deflationary pressures associated with maintaining a strict relationship between gold reserves and the money supply, the risk was that central banks would abandon any currency suspected of weakness. Since sterling, dollars, French or even Swiss francs were all reserve currencies, it was fairly costless to move one's reserves from one to another depending on the mood of the market. An extraordinary degree of confidence was necessary to trust the value of one's own central bank reserves to the monetary policy of a foreign country. Not only was there the temptation to cash in foreign exchange holdings as they grew in relation to a relatively inelastic supply of gold,[21] but there was also the option of purchasing a reserve currency based on its status as "most credible" among the top four. Even central banks were tempted to watch politics and play the market.

This leads to a second important distinction between the prewar gold system and the interwar gold exchange standard. During the earlier period, there was little question that the occasional foreign exchange crisis would be handled cooperatively among the three major money centers of Europe: London, Paris,

[20] For analyses that emphasize the need for political stability in order to achieve economic stabilization, see Thomas Sargent, "Stopping Four Big Inflations," in R. Hall (ed.), *Inflation: Causes and Effects* (Chicago: University of Chicago Press), 1982, and "Stopping Moderate Inflations: The Methods of Poincaré and Thatcher," in Rudiger Dornbusch and Mario H. Simonsen, *Inflation, Debt, and Indexation* (Cambridge: MIT Press), 1984; and Rudiger Dornbusch, "Lessons from the German Inflation Experience of the 1920s," in Rudiger Dornbusch, Stanley Fischer, and John Bossons (eds.), *Macroeconomics and Finance: Essays in Honor of Franco Modigliani* (Cambridge: MIT Press), 1987.

[21] Feliks Mynarski, *Gold and Central Banks* (New York: Macmillan), 1929. This problem applies to any international monetary system in which expanding foreign trade is financed by a "convertible" key currency. Robert Triffin, *Gold and the Dollar Crisis* (New Haven: Yale University Press), 1960.

and Berlin.[22] During the Baring Crisis of 1890, which was sparked by the news of the Argentine rebellion and potential bond default, the Bank of England used its slender reserves to act as lender of last resort, and quickly received short-term loans of £3 million and £1.5 million from the central banks of France and Russia, respectively. Confidence was restored so quickly that gold never crossed the channel.[23] Sterling faced another serious crisis in 1906, due to unusually heavy American borrowing in the London market. The Banque de France offered to support sterling with a loan, and ended up purchasing sterling bills to support the exchange.[24] The following year, a financial panic centered in the United States stimulated a gold drain from the Bank of England that caused the British central bank to raise its discount rate to the highest level in more than thirty years. Continental central banks accommodated the British by allowing their reserves to decline and gold to flow to Britain, where it could be used to finance the increased demand for gold in the United States.[25] These and other episodes of instantaneous international cooperation made the nineteenth-century gold standard stable—if only because publics *believed* the international community's support for the gold standard was virtually inviolable.

The contrast with the interwar period is a stark one. Some of the reasons are well known. The war and the nature of the peace had sown conflicts that were manifest in international monetary relations. Inter-Allied war debts and German reparations poisoned the relationship between France, Britain, and Germany and threw sand into plans to stabilize the mark in 1924.[26] Differing ideas over the merits of the gold standard versus the gold exchange standard retarded central bank cooperation between Britain and the United States from 1928 to 1931.[27] Competition between France and Britain for financial influence on the Continent complicated financial stabilization in Central Europe.[28] To say that international financial and monetary cooperation was not taken for granted is an understatement. It was an uphill battle for most of these two decades.

Publics may have cheered the nationalistic policies of their leaders, but markets were greatly disturbed. When the Federal Reserve Bank of New York, the Bank of England, and J. P. Morgan and Company all hesitated to support the franc in 1924 and 1925, the French franc sank as capital fled. When central bankers could not arrange long-term financing to support the Belgian franc in

[22] Eichengreen, *Golden Fetters*, chap. 2, passim.

[23] Arthur D. Elliot, *The Life of George Joachim Goschen* (London: Longmans, Green), 1911.

[24] Harry White, *The French International Accounts, 1880–1913* (Cambridge: Harvard University Press), 1933, p. 195.

[25] Ira Cross, *Domestic and Foreign Exchange* (London: Macmillan), 1923, p. 217.

[26] Stephen A. Schuker, *The End of French Predominance in Europe: The Financial Crisis of 1924 and the Adoption of the Dawes Plan* (Chapel Hill: University of North Carolina Press), 1976.

[27] S.V.O. Clarke, *Central Bank Cooperation, 1924–1931* (New York: Federal Reserve Bank of New York), 1967.

[28] Competition between London, Paris, and, to a lesser extent, New York is a major theme of Paul Einzig, *The Fight for Financial Supremacy* (London: Macmillan), 1931.

1925, they withdrew their support and the franc lost an eighth of its value in four hours. When negotiations over reparations nearly collapsed in the spring of 1929, markets fled the reichsmark. When the Banque de France hesitated to extend the Bank of England a loan to defend the pound in the waning summer of 1931, speculators and even other central banks delivered the coup de grace. The international climate was uncertain. An international gold standard could not survive without international cooperation, yet for high political and a myriad of petty reasons, such cooperation was notably in short supply.

Yet one of the central reasons for the shortage of international cooperation that hardly ever receives serious treatment is that central banks, treasuries, and private sources of emergency capital were themselves wary to go out on a limb to cooperate with their foreign counterparts who were likely to defect. There was a real hesitation to provide assistance to a deficit country that did not seem ready or able to take action to alter fundamentally its own deteriorating position. One of the primary reasons the French were denied financial assistance between 1925 and 1926 was that there was little confidence that the unstable Cartel des Gauches would implement a financial and fiscal policy that would prevent the hemorrhage of private capital from France. One of the most significant reasons for the breakdown in international cooperation as the British struggled to maintain sterling's parity in 1931 was that foreign central bankers were demanding bigger unemployment compensation cuts than the Labour party could supply. Yes, the interwar gold standard depended on international cooperation for its stability, and indeed, such cooperation was only intermittently forthcoming. But what incentive did the Federal Reserve Bank of New York or the Bank of England have to extend the French emergency credits when French leaders refused to balance the budget?

To summarize, any fixed system of exchange rates requires an extraordinary degree of credibility if parities are to be maintained. One of the starkest contrasts between the operation of the gold standard before and after World War I was the degree of certainty that governments would reliably pursue macroeconomic policies consonant with external balance and fixed rates of exchange, and that in those instances in which a country experienced a run on its reserves international cooperation would be forthcoming. The drastic sociopolitical changes of the First World War undermined confidence in the possibility of internal adjustment. These domestic changes in combination with the animosities that flowed from that conflict created fateful hesitancies with respect to international assistance. The uncertainty these combined conditions placed on financial and foreign exchange markets was overwhelming.

THE NORMS OF GOLD STANDARD ADJUSTMENT

In reconstructing the international economic system in the early 1920s, monetary authorities turned to the system that appeared to have served them so well before the war. The late-nineteenth and early-twentieth-century gold standard constituted a loosely held set of prescriptions about how a country should deal with an incipient deficit or a downward selling pressure on its currency. This system's premise was that individual nations' monetary systems were based on a gold standard regime, which included the convertibility of domestic money into gold at a fixed price, the freedom for private citizens to import and export gold, and a fixed relationship between the money supply (bills in circulation) and the gold reserve. When adopted by a number of countries, these conditions established a fixed exchange rate system between national currencies.

The Adjustment Mechanism

The classic model of gold standard balance of payments adjustment was that described by David Hume in the middle of the eighteenth century.[29] His rendition of the "price-specie-flow" mechanism was based on a stylized economy in which two categories of commodities—goods and gold—were traded. When prices of goods rose domestically, residents tended to substitute less expensive imports for home goods. In the absence of production increases, residents of the foreign country would have to cut their consumption to accommodate increased foreign demand for their goods. Gold would then flow from the country with the higher prices for goods to that with the relatively higher price for gold. In other words, the resulting balance of trade settlement was made by gold shipments from the deficit to the surplus countries.

When opportunities for arbitrage are taken into account (when a capital market is considered in addition to the market for goods and gold), international adjustment will not take place through relative price differences, but rather through interest rate differentials and capital flows.[30] In this case, when domestic prices for securities rise (which is to say, interest rates fall), capital flows from the country in which interest rates are low to the country in which they are high, until security prices and interest rates are once again equalized internationally. Thus, the balance of payments deficit (the sum of the trade balance deficit plus the capital outflow) would not have to be covered fully by an international transfer of gold. If compensating capital flows should fully cover the trade imbalance, there need not be any gold transfer at all.

The critical step in the adjustment process was the effect that incipient gold flows had on the level of economic activity within each country. Central banks maintained gold reserves that were used to back a given multiple of notes, and financial institutions practiced fractional reserve banking that allowed them to

[29] David Hume, *Essays: Moral, Political, and Literary*, Vol. I (London: Longmans, Green), 1898. First published in 1752; recently reprinted in abridged form in Barry Eichengreen, *The Gold Standard*, pp. 39–48.

[30] P. B. Whale, "The Working of the Prewar Gold Standard," *Economica*, Vol. 4, February 1937, pp. 18–32.

"create money" by extending loans on the basis of deposits. A central bank that was losing gold was supposed to raise its discount rate, increasing the cost of funds for financial institutions, which would induce the institutions to hold larger precautionary reserves and reduce the money available to the economy. The central bank might try directly to reduce the money supply by an open-market sale of securities. The point is that gold outflows should be accompanied by efforts to reduce the domestic money supply, which in turn should contract the economy's level of economic activity, lower domestic prices, and improve the balance of payments.

Two points should be stressed about the adjustment mechanism. First, central banks could take measures in anticipation of actual gold flows, which is one reason why the physical movement of gold was often unnecessary. A higher discount rate in the deficit country would attract the capital necessary to finance its deficit, while lower rates in the surplus country would have the opposite effect. Second, in theory, this adjustment mechanism was supposed to operate symmetrically in both surplus and deficit countries, although the norm (and the necessity) for adjustment by deficit countries was much stronger than that for countries in surplus. Thus, gold flows or the central bank's anticipation of incipient flows would set off an increase in the money supply (stimulation) in the surplus country and a decrease in the money supply (a dampening effect) in the deficit country. Rising domestic prices in the surplus country would then encourage foreign purchases (imports or purchases of foreign securities), and falling prices in the deficit country would encourage home purchases and a preference for domestic over foreign investments. Whether the system was stabilized "automatically" via gold flows or was "managed" by central bank policy, the monetary prescription for a deficit country was the same: an increase in interest rates and/or contraction of the money supply was necessary to relieve the external pressure. In theory, equal but opposite policies were to be implemented in surplus countries.[31]

The adjustment mechanism could be severely undermined unless markets were allowed to clear, as described above. In the goods market, price effects had to be able to influence consumption patterns. Trade restrictions or protection efforts were ways of disrupting or delaying the adjustment process. The corollary in the capital market is obvious: if capital is not permitted to move

---

[31] For a general review of the workings of a gold standard, see Richard N. Cooper, *The Gold Standard: Historical Facts and Future Prospects*, Brookings Papers on Economic Activity, Vol. 1 (Washington D.C.: Brookings Institution), 1982; Kenneth W. Dam, *The Rules of the Game: Reform and Evolution in the International Monetary System* (Chicago: University of Chicago Press), 1982, chap. 2, pp. 15–40. For the historical conditions of its operation, see Leland Yeager, "The Gold Standard Before World War I," chap. 15, in Yeager, *International Monetary Relations: Theory, History, and Policy* (New York: Harper and Row), 1966, pp. 295–309; R. G. Hawtrey, *The Gold Standard in Theory and Practice* (London: Longmans, Green), 1947. On the practical operation of the gold standard, see articles collected in Eichengreen, *The Gold Standard*, especially those by Robert Triffin, Donald N. McCloskey and J. Richard Zecher, and W. M. Scammel.

freely in response to interest rates, the adjustment mechanism will not operate as smoothly as it should.

Implied Norms of Gold Standard Adjustment

The gold standard provides the normative baseline against which this study analyzes the policy choices of deficit and surplus countries. There are two reasons for using gold standard "norms." The first is that present-day economic theory does not speak with sufficient unity or certainty in the area of international macroeconomic adjustment to justify substituting more modern understandings of deficit and surplus adjustment and burden sharing for those that prevailed in the interwar years.[32] The second is that even if economic theory were to converge on a consensus in this area, it would be senseless to impose those understandings on the decisionmakers of the twenties and thirties. Policy choice should be interpreted as far as possible in the context of beliefs and norms that prevailed among contemporaries.[33]

Prewar experiences with the gold standard generally informed monetary and political authorities' conception of external adjustment well into the interwar years. Some fifty nations participated in the interwar gold standard, and there was for most of the period a broad consensus over the economic policies that were needed to maintain the system. Several implied norms were widely shared among those that aspired to reestablish and maintain the gold standard. Not all were equally salient, nor were responsibilities for gold standard maintenance symmetrical for deficit and surplus countries. This is because a country with a surplus does not face an equally finite limit to the reserves it can accumulate, and hence it experiences little economic pressure to alter its policy.[34] The norms listed below reflect those that were broadly accepted by most countries, roughly in the order of importance.

Norm 1: External balance takes priority over the domestic economy. The basic premise of the gold standard was that countries were supposed to pursue macroeconomic policies that were compatible with the maintenance of fixed parities. Currency stability was the first goal of the gold standard. Devaluation was thought to risk the disruption of trade and investment, and was viewed as a

---

[32] Economists today differ not only on the magnitude of transmission effects from changes in domestic fiscal and monetary policies from one economy to another, but in some cases even differ on the sign of the transmitted effect.

[33] The effect of beliefs and perceptions on policy choice is underscored by Robert Jervis, *Perception and Misperception in International Relations* (Princeton: Princeton University Press), 1976; and Ernst B. Haas, "Words Can Hurt You," in Stephen Krasner (ed.), *International Regimes* (Ithaca: Cornell University Press), 1983, pp. 23–59, although I am not concerned here to develop an evolutionary epistemology that would identify ideas per se as an important independent explanatory variable.

[34] Leland B. Yeager, *International Monetary Relations*, p. 48.

government's default on its obligations. It also caused an immediate loss on the balance sheets of foreign central banks that were holding the depreciated currency as part of their foreign exchange reserves. During the Depression, devaluation was often associated with efforts to "obtain an unreasonable competitive exchange advantage," as it was put in the concurrent declarations of the Tripartite Agreement in 1936.[35] In contrast to post–World War II thinking on the subject, devaluation during the interwar years was not accepted as a legitimate form of economic adjustment.[36]

Because of the significance attached to fixed exchange rates, external balance had to have priority over the domestic economy when these were in conflict. Conflict would arise when a deficit country experienced an economic slowdown (external balance demanded further contraction but domestic conditions justified stimulation), and when a surplus country experienced potential inflationary pressures (external balance would justify further demand stimulation and internal balance the opposite).

The primacy of external balance was clearly stated by the Macmillan Committee during one of the deepest years of the British depression: "[C]ountries which are losing gold must be prepared to act on a policy which will have the effect of lowering prices, and countries which are receiving gold must be prepared to act on a policy which will have the effect of raising prices."[37] In the face of 2.63 million unemployed Britons (some 21.5 percent of the work force), and despite the fact that wholesale prices in 1931 had declined some 12.5 percent and consumer prices had dropped 6.2 percent, the report still called for price compression to improve the declining British balance of payments. The report also called for surplus country (American) price stimulation, as British monetary authorities had been doing for most of the decade. A clearer statement of the priority to be given to external balance over the needs of the domestic economy is difficult to imagine.

There was a notable hierarchy of prescribed actions underlying this general norm. The clearest and most widely understood prescription fell on the fiscal policy of deficit countries. *Deficit countries were entreated to get their houses in order and to practice financial orthodoxy.* The First Interim Report of the Cunliffe Committee (1918) provided the most explicit statement of these policies, but its assumptions were similar to those held in a number of countries in

[35] Tripartite Monetary Agreements of 25 September 1936, printed by the Bank for International Settlements, Monetary and Economic Department, Basel, Switzerland, January 1937.

[36] Devaluation in the postwar period has often been viewed as a necessary part of an expenditure switching policy mix that is designed to encourage the flow of investment and other resources into the traded-goods sector. The interwar norm against devaluation has been criticized as misguided. Kindleberger, for one, considers the 1933 dollar depreciation to have been "useful" in that it raised prices in the United States but did not depress them abroad. Charles P. Kindleberger, *The World in Depression, 1929–1939* (Berkeley: University of California Press), rev. ed., 1986, p. 227.

[37] *Report of the Macmillan Committee on Finance and Industry*, Cmd. 3897, London, HMSO, 1931, paragraph 42.

the twenties.[38] Published on the heels of wartime budgets and outlays for reconstruction, the report came out clearly for financial orthodoxy and balanced budgets within deficit countries in order to reduce domestic demand and stabilize the currency. The need for a return to "financial orthodoxy" in order to facilitate currency stabilization was also a major theme at the International Financial Conference held at Brussels in 1920 and the conference at Genoa in 1922.[39]

The proper conduct of fiscal policy was a norm that fell exclusively on deficit countries. There was absolutely no expectation that surplus countries would "artificially" stimulate their own domestic demand through public expenditures for purposes of influencing their external position. The opportunity to discuss coordinated public works—a form of coordinated reflation—presented itself during the preparations for the World Economic Conference in the spring of 1933, but the idea was made moot by unilateral American action to devalue the dollar, and was in any case vehemently opposed by the French. Had the idea flown, it still would not have amounted to a norm for *surplus* country behavior, since it would have applied to all of the major economies regardless of their external position. The idea of using fiscal policy to influence the balance of payments was an orthodox prescription that applied overwhelmingly to the deficit countries.[40]

The second prescription again fell on deficit countries. *Deficit countries were to pursue stringent monetary policies and to avoid "undue" credit expansion.* The Cunliffe Report linked government borrowing with slack credit policies, noting that "the growth of purchasing power has exceeded that of purchasable goods and services," resulting in balance of payments deficits. The solution was to raise interest rates, which the report reasoned would lessen loan demands, check expenditures and economic activity, and lower domestic prices, with the result that imports would be discouraged and exports promoted. "When the exchanges are adverse and gold is being drawn away, it is essential that the rate of discount in this country should be raised relatively to the rates ruling in other countries," the report concluded.[41]

Although the expectation was somewhat weaker and the norm often resisted,

[38] Eichengreen, *The Gold Standard*, p. 19. *First Interim Report of the Cunliffe Committee on Currency and Foreign Exchanges after the War*, Cmd. 9182, London, HMSO, 1918, paragraphs 6–7.

[39] S.V.O. Clarke, "The Reconstruction of the International Monetary System: The Attempts of 1922 and 1933," *Princeton Studies in International Finance*, No. 33 (Princeton: Princeton University Press), 1973.

[40] Although intentional surplus fiscal expansion for purposes of improving *external* balance was not accepted as an adjustment strategy in the interwar years, after World War II appropriate reflationary policies for the surplus country were expanded to include stimulatory fiscal policies. See chapter 6 in Robert D. Putnam and Nicholas Bayne, *Hanging Together: The Seven Power Summits* (Cambridge: Harvard University Press), 1984, pp. 67–99.

[41] Cunliffe Committee Report, reprinted in Eichengreen, *The Gold Standard*, p. 177.

there was a broad understanding that *surplus countries should accommodate gold inflows by lowering interest rates and expanding the money supply accordingly*. To do otherwise was referred to as "gold sterilization," and surplus countries usually denied that they were engaging in such policies.[42] Relaxing monetary policy in response to gold inflows was meant to be reflationary: to stimulate growth, demand, and prices relative to the surplus country's deficit trading partners. Increased demand was meant to stimulate imports from deficit countries, and lower interest rates were meant to discourage further capital inflows, in these ways correcting an incipient balance of payments surplus.

Overall, the gold standard required that external balance be a higher priority than domestic economic balance. The strongest prescription was that deficit countries should balance their budgets. Next was the demand that deficit countries raise interest rates and implement restrictive monetary policies. Weakest of all was the expectation that surplus countries should accommodate rather than counter gold inflows by relaxing their monetary policies. The primacy of external balance was central to gold standard adjustment, but its prescriptions were much more salient for deficit countries than for those in surplus.

Norm 2: Liberal policies are preferred over external controls. The interwar economic system was far from a liberal international order. Barriers to the free exchange of goods, capital, and currency existed on a wide scale, especially in the years immediately following World War I and during the Depression. Nonetheless, there was an understanding that *external barriers to normal economic intercourse were disruptive to the adjustment mechanism*. Tariffs, import quotas, and capital and currency controls were efforts to improve the balance of trade or to prevent capital flight and currency depreciation *without* fundamentally altering domestic patterns of resource allocation and consumption. It was widely recognized that such barriers often had a negative impact on one's trading partners. These policies were perceived in the interwar years, as they are today, as hostile policy choices.

The preference for liberal external policies was a much weaker norm than that giving priority to external balance. Resistance to liberal trade policies in France, Germany, and Italy often diminished international consensus on the issue. In Britain, Labour supported lower tariffs, but Conservative governments interested in developing and maintaining a system of empire preferences wanted the option of using restrictive measures for this political end. In the United States, the Republicans' high tariff tradition flew in the face of this norm.

While this norm was somewhat weaker than that which gave priority to

---

[42] The United States did not formally admit to a policy of gold sterilization until 1937, when collapse of the Gold Bloc caused large gold influxes into the United States. Board of Governors of the Federal Reserve System, *Federal Reserve Bulletin* (Washington, D.C.: GPO), 1937, p. 1.

external equilibrium, there is still some evidence of a commitment to the ideal of liberal external policies over external controls. Every major economic conference or international agreement during these years, as well as much bilateral negotiation, was aimed at reaching agreements on limiting these hostile adjustment strategies, though often with scant success. International economic conferences held in Brussels in the 1920s, Portorose (near Trieste) in 1921, and Genoa in 1922 strongly opposed stringent trade restrictions. The World Economic Conference held in Geneva in 1927 under League of Nations auspices met to negotiate a convention against import restrictions and to implement tariff reductions. The World Economic Conference held in London in 1933 was supposed to deal with the problem of trade barriers and exchange controls, and the Roosevelt administration proposed a "tariff truce" for its duration. The 1936 Tripartite Agreement indicated the desire of the signatories to dismantle their systems of import quotas and exchange controls.

The norm that liberal policies were to be preferred to external controls applied to both deficit and surplus countries. In contrast to the norms for internal adjustment measures, it was expected that surplus countries would refrain from implementing external restrictions that would disrupt the adjustment process. In fact, when surplus countries contravened this norm, the infraction was considered particularly egregious and elicited a negative reaction from the international community. Thus, the Smoot-Hawley tariff imposed by the United States Congress in June 1930 was a particular object of international invective. In the 1932 election campaign, Roosevelt himself attacked America's tariff policy as unworthy of a creditor nation and blamed it for having forced other countries off the gold standard.[43] Even if we discount the domestic electoral motivation for such an assessment, it indicates a recognition that surplus countries had a special responsibility to maintain reasonably liberal external policies.

Norm 3: Provision of supplementary financing.   The third and final norm that underlay the interwar gold standard was as weakly held as the second. This norm recognized that fixed exchange rates had to be supported with international liquidity, and often with exceptional finance, and that the responsibility for providing liquidity was primarily upon surplus countries or consortia organized by surplus countries. When it was available, exceptional finance was usually negotiated between the deficit government and either a surplus government, a multilateral organization, foreign central banks, or foreign bankers.[44]

---

[43] Kindleberger, *The World in Depression*, p. 124.

[44] Exceptional or compensatory finance is distinguished from market-based or independently motivated finance in that it is not made on the basis of profit-making calculations, but is meant to fill the gap in the demand for and supply of a currency after the market has cleared at a fixed rate of exchange. The distinction between independently motivated and compensatory transactions is made by Yeager, *International Monetary Relations*, pp. 48–51.

In the twenties, Austria, Belgium, Bulgaria, Danzig, Hungary, Greece, and Poland stabilized their currencies with specific stabilization loans or reconstruction loans from the League of Nations.[45] Denmark, Italy, Norway, Portugal, Switzerland, and the United Kingdom arranged temporary forms of credit (usually central bank credits) for stabilization purposes, though these were not always fully utilized. Bulgaria, Czechoslovakia, Estonia, Finland, Latvia, Romania, Yugoslavia, Lithuania, Sweden, and the Netherlands managed their preliminary stabilization without any loans or specific credit arrangements. Germany began its stabilization without credits specifically for that purpose, but within a year had access to capital inflows from the Dawes Loan, which greatly buoyed the mark. France was issued a stabilization credit, but it went unused, and the franc was eventually stabilized without outside assistance. Later in the decade, Poland received credits from a consortium of fourteen central banks to help stabilize its currency, and in 1929, Romania's monetary reform was underwritten by a similar form of external assistance.

Although the provision of external liquidity to support currencies under pressure and balance of payments adjustments was never formally institutionalized, it did receive important multilateral backing from the Bank for International Settlements, which was founded in 1930.[46] Within a year of its creation, the BIS extended credits to the central banks of Austria, Yugoslavia, Hungary, and Germany totaling some 750 million Swiss francs (US$145 million), although such sums were recognized as paltry compared to those in the financial disasters that avalanched throughout Central Europe in 1931.[47] In addition, the BIS organized informal consortia of central banks to extend emergency credits, and by the late 1930s, the BIS had developed facilities for reciprocal credits among central banks.[48]

The norm for the provision of liquidity was weak, especially if one is looking for a Bretton Woods–like commitment to large-scale public finance of balance of payments adjustments.[49] In particular, because it was often done on an ad hoc basis, the provision of liquidity was subject to many of the expectational problems that affected capital flight in general at this time. The problem was twofold. First, ad hoc exceptional financing was difficult to arrange because it was risky for the central banks or firms that made the bulk of the contribution. Furthermore, where the loan amount agreed upon was perceived as insufficient

[45] League of Nations, *Essential Facts About the League of Nations* (Geneva: League of Nations), various issues; Denys P. Myers, *Nine Years of the League of Nations, 1920–1928*, Ninth Yearbook (Boston: World Peace Foundation), Vol. 12, No. 1, 1929, pp. 58–67.

[46] On the origins of the BIS, see Beth A. Simmons, "Why Innovate? Founding the Bank for International Settlements," *World Politics* (Spring 1993), pp. 361–405.

[47] Leon Fraser, "The International Bank and Its Future," *Foreign Affairs*, Vol. 14, No. 3, April 1936, pp. 453–464.

[48] These were designed as much to make credits available for exporters as to support exchange rates. Bank for International Settlements, *8th Report*, Basel, Switzerland, 1938, p. 109.

[49] Dam, *The Rules of the Game*, pp. 69–70.

to salvage a currency under siege, market reactions would often render nig-
gardly assistance packages counterproductive.[50] In the absence of regularized
channels and sources, and facing risks that deficit countries would not be able to
stabilize even with external support, surplus countries often delayed or shirked
adherence to this norm.

Access to exceptional finance was often conditional, although the stringency
of conditionality varied considerably from client to client and was often implicit.[51] The most obvious cases of conditionality involved the League loans to
the smaller countries in the twenties, where domestic monetary institutions
were redesigned and finances administered by League officials. However, even
in bilateral cases among the major powers, loans often hinged on specific
political and financial undertakings regarding the timing and content of the
budget and the independence of the central bank. For example, France was
denied American credits after 1923 in part because of its government's failure
to ratify war debt agreements with the United States, and a loan to Britain was
delayed in September 1931 because the Labour party refused to cut unemployment insurance from the budget. There were no fixed rules, but potential
creditors often attached conditions (implied or explicit) to the provision of
liquidity.

Overall, there was an expectation that surplus countries would supply financial assistance to help stabilize the economies or defend the currencies of deficit
countries. This norm was weak. It was also subject to problems of collective
action and uncertainty that prevailed in the absence of institutionalized channels for financial assistance. But it was a customary practice established under
the prewar gold standard, and in many cases surplus assistance was critical to
the establishment and maintenance of fixed parities.

International Bargaining: Deficit Adjustment and Surplus Facilitation

Implementation of these norms was often negotiable. Whenever a country
faced balance of payments pressures that made it difficult to maintain a fixed
parity, these norms would provide salient points around which negotiations
would center for a resolution of the potential crisis. As a starting point, both
surplus and deficit countries would try and maximize the extent to which their
counterpart would fulfill the obligations implied by each of the three norms
given above. The central goal for surplus countries, in a stylized negotiation
over balance of payments adjustment, was for the deficit country to fulfill its
obligations implied in the first norm: to balance its budget and to restrict its

---

[50] Sir Henry Clay, *Lord Norman* (London: Macmillan), 1957, pp. 397–398.

[51] The practice of conditionality evolved much more fully after the Second World War. See
J. Keith Horsefield, *The International Monetary Fund, 1945–1960*, Vol. 2: *Analysis* (Washington,
D.C.: IMF), 1969, chaps. 18, 20, 21, 23; and Joseph Gold, *Conditionality*, IMF Pamphlet Series
No. 31 (Washington, D.C.: IMF), 1979.

monetary policy so that domestic demand would contract and capital would flow inward to help finance the balance of payments deficit. The central goal for deficit countries, on the other hand, was to secure as much assistance from surplus countries as possible and on the most generous terms. Since exceptional finance provided monetary authorities of deficit countries with the foreign exchange necessary to fill the gap between the greater supply and the weaker demand for their currency, it usually spared deficit countries from speculative attacks on their currencies, and gave them some "breathing space" in order to implement more fundamental reforms.

Breathing space was especially important to the process of deficit adjustment because the fiscal and monetary changes demanded by the first norm could entail some fairly severe economic costs in the short term. Balanced budgets usually meant sharp contractions in employment or wage cuts in the public sector, scaled-back public investment for reconstruction, and slashed public services and social benefits upon which many sectors of society depended for their standard of living. The most wrenching domestic debates took place over the importance of budget balancing when unemployment insurance for millions of citizens was at stake.

Balanced budgets also required new taxation, which threw salt into the wounds of social conflict that had opened up in many societies since the conclusion of the Great War. The need to present a balanced budget inevitably raised questions about the incidence of taxation. Socialist parties called for income taxes or, in the extreme, special levies on accumulated wealth. They strongly opposed taxes on the consumption of necessities. Business groups and industries preferred indirect taxes and other nonprogressive tax schemes. The rentier, from the upper social strata, also opposed progressive taxation.[52] The political costs to a government of imposing a revenue-raising solution upon these contending social forces was often so high that the decision did not get made until it was too late.

Restrictive monetary policies also posed problems for deficit countries. The most immediate difficulty was that raising interest rates would complicate the government's ability to finance its debt. To attract funds, governments would have to pay higher yields on bonds, further contributing to the fiscal dilemma. At the same time, credit restrictions would dampen business activity, encourage the drawing down of inventories, and cut into production with inevitable impact on unemployment. In the short run, restrictive monetary policies would usher in recession, the political fallout from which could be great.

Since placing external balance above internal balance could be extremely costly for a deficit country, it was tempting for the country to choose either to

---

[52] Alberto Alesina, "The End of Large Public Debts," chap. 2 in Giorgio Basevi (ed.), *High Public Debt: The Italian Experience* (Cambridge: Cambridge University Press), 1988, pp. 34–79, especially p. 39.

protect itself by contravening the liberalism norm or, in the extreme, to defect from the basic tenet of the gold standard by devaluing. Surplus countries had a strong preference to encourage deficit countries to continue to comply with norms one and two by offering stabilization financing, and negotiations over domestic orthodoxy in exchange for external financial support took place repeatedly under the gold exchange standard. Surplus countries could also try to encourage the compliance of deficit countries by offering to improve access to their own market by lowering tariff barriers or increasing import quotas. (This was one way France tried to consolidate the Gold Bloc and discourage its members from devaluing between 1933 and 1935.)

In summary, the central bargain between deficit and surplus countries included mutual policy adjustments consistent with the three norms cited above. Surplus countries tried to encourage a policy mix consistent with the first and second norms in exchange for living up to expectations regarding the third. At the margins, surplus countries may also have been willing to offer concessions in the form of increased economic openness. The most cooperative solutions to the problem of international adjustment were those that were most compatible with all three norms. A policy mix taken by the government of a deficit country that placed internal above external balance and bolstered this priority with protectionism and other external controls has been aptly labeled "beggar-thy-neighbor" by historians of the period.

Explaining Policy Choice during the Interwar Years

Despite the social and political changes wrought by the spread of industrialization and the First World War, the vast majority of countries attempted during the 1920s to return to a gold exchange standard, which rested on the adjustment norms sketched above.[53] Yet over the course of the next two decades, states displayed varying propensities to abide by these three norms. Why were some countries better able—or more willing—to live up to the demands of the gold exchange standard, while others more readily defected by allowing their balance of payments to deteriorate, and by devaluing or protecting? This section examines these outcomes and briefly outlines a set of expectations regarding the incentives states face to choose each. (Fuller theoretical reviews are found in the relevant substantive chapters.) In each case, the new political conditions of the interwar years influenced the policy choice taken. The stark contrast with the nineteenth century provides a plausible explanation as to why the interwar monetary system was more fragile than that of the prewar years. But it also explains the variation across countries over the course of the twenties and thirties, which is the primary focus of this study.

[53] The only exception in the twenty-three-country sample used in this study was Spain, which maintained flexible exchange rates throughout the interwar period.

Internal Adjustment

The gold standard entailed a commitment to deflate in the face of an incipient balance of payments deficit, hence reducing economic activity in the short run. If economic agents did not believe that the government would be able to act decisively to keep inflation under control and reverse the incipient imbalance, their behavior alone could frustrate the problem of adjustment, as will be discussed in greater detail in Chapter 3. What conditions signaled markets that governments were willing and able to engage in deflation if necessary? Conversely, what conditions undermined this confidence? I have argued above that the consensus born of nineteenth-century exclusionary politics was beginning to crumble around the turn of the century, and its demise was further hastened by World War I. Democratization, influence of the Left in governance, political instability, and labor unrest were plausible signals to economic agents that monetary policymaking could no longer remain insulated from brewing political demands. Market participants were assuaged wherever central banks could maintain their independence from these demands, but where monetary authority was manipulable by politicians, expedience was expected to prevail.

Regime Type. The shift from exclusionary elite-based politics to inclusive mass politics was one of the most important changes of the late nineteenth and early twentieth centuries. One could plausibly argue that the process of democratization undermined the narrow consensus that gave pride of place to external economic balance during the nineteenth century, yet during the interwar years several states gave up the democratic project in favor of varying degrees of repression. The power to repress demands for growth and to pass austere budgets by decree served to signal governments' potency in controlling popular inflationary pressures. Regimes resting on popular sovereignty on the other hand faced strong incentives to avoid policies that contribute to severe economic contraction in the short run.[54] Indeed, during the years between the wars, many countries found that deflation required some degree of suspension of popular government. Where democracy was not overthrown by authoritarian forms of governance, cabinets were at times empowered to rule by decree until fundamental fiscal reforms were implemented. In short, the new, more democratic politics of the twentieth century raised the possibility that domestic economic conditions would enjoy a far greater priority than they had in the past. Democracy and equality signaled markets that the gold standard was no longer inviolable.

---

[54] William Nordhaus, among others, has outlined a political and economic logic for expecting democratic systems to have higher than optimal inflation. William Nordhaus, "The Political Business Cycle," *Review of Economic Studies*, Vol. 42, 1975, pp. 169–190. Nordhaus's model is built around the assumption that policymakers can make trade-offs between levels of inflation and unemployment in the short run that will translate into the largest possible number of votes.

Political Orientation of Party in Power.   The hallmark of political change across Europe during the late nineteenth century was the gradual organization and representation of the working class into mainstream politics. But this was precisely the class whose interests were most immediately and vitally at stake whenever external balance dictated the need for domestic deflation. Higher interest rates dampened business expansion and reduced employment opportunities. Workers were among the first to experience the burden of adjustment through falling wages or increased unemployment. Furthermore, falling prices would shift the real burden of adjustment away from creditors (or those who saved a larger portion of their income) to debtors. In particular, cuts in government expenditures (fiscal retrenchment) would fall most heavily on low-level public employees and usually involved the withdrawal of support for public social expenditures not deemed "essential." For all these reasons, newly influential political parties that purported to represent the working class after World War I found the practical requirements of internal adjustment especially undesirable.[55] Their pronouncements in favor of balanced budgets and strong currency simply did not ring true given their constituency commitments. Left-wing parties—excluded from governing during the prewar period—were expected to balk at policies by which workers would bear the greatest domestic share of the burden of adjustment. When left-wing parties assumed the responsibility for governing in the twenties and thirties, markets anticipated inflationary pressures and responded accordingly, making it far more difficult to actually achieve the internal adjustment the gold standard required.

Labor Unrest.   One of the most painful aspects of internal adjustment is the compression of input prices necessary to improve the competitive position of a country's products on the world market. To make exports competitive, industries must be able to lower their costs, a large part of which is the cost of labor. Where workers resist wage compression, deflation will end in an intolerable level of unemployment rather than in a more competitive economy.[56] An important aspect of the ability to adjust internally is therefore likely to be the degree of labor quiescence in any given society. While labor and social unrest were significant in a number of European countries in the 1890s and after the turn of the

[55] For the post–World War II period, see Douglas Hibbs, "Political Parties and Macroeconomic Policy," *American Political Science Review*, Vol. 71, No. 4, 1977, pp. 1467–1487; Stanley W. Black, "The Use of Monetary Policy for Internal and External Balance in Ten Industrial Countries," in Jacob Frenkel (ed.), *Exchange Rates and International Economics* (Chicago: University of Chicago Press), 1983, pp. 189–225; Andrew Cowart, "The Economic Policies of European Governments, Part 1: Monetary Policy" *British Journal of Political Science*, Vol. 8, 1978, pp. 285–311.

[56] On the relationship between labor demands and inflation for the post–World War II period, see Stanley W. Black, *Politics Versus Markets: International Differences in Macroeconomic Policies* (Washington, D.C.: American Enterprise Institute for Public Policy), 1982; Robert J. Gordon, "The Demand for and Supply of Inflation," *Journal of Law and Economics*, Vol. 18, 1975, pp. 808–836.

century, these protests did not easily translate into improved wages as long as unionization remained low. Labor demands for wage and job security and reduced working hours posed new risks during the interwar years, due to labor's superior organization and political clout. No longer could such demands be ignored; on the contrary, they could be expected to reverberate throughout the economy in the form of inflationary pressure. The new politics of the interwar years shattered the certainty that governments would refuse to accommodate such inflationary pressures in the interest of maintaining low inflation, external balance, and currency stability. And in contrast to the post–World War II period, a well-developed corporatist framework simply did not exist during the interwar years in most countries to contain economic conflict and the threat of domestic inflation. If the politics of the interwar years were newly inclusive, they had yet to develop institutional forms to soften the rough edges of class conflict. In this context, strikes could encourage anticipatory market adjustments that frustrated a program of internal economic adjustment in the face of an incipient deterioration in the balance of payments.

Government Instability. While the price of adjustment may indeed be high in the short run, the longer term benefits may be great: a strong stable currency, competitive exports, the ability to disassemble artificial controls, a manageable rate of inflation, and an improved reputational standing at home and abroad are all benefits of reaching a sustainable equilibrium in the balance of payments. Governments that expect to enjoy these benefits may well choose to endure the bitter deflationary medicine required to enjoy economic health. But governments that rest on a politically precarious consensus are highly unlikely to take serious measures to deflate. The practical problem of assembling a consumption-cutting majority with uncertain coalitional support makes it difficult to pass deflationary budgets. Moreover, there is very little incentive for a potentially unstable government to implement unpopular restrictive measures, since their implementation will likely jeopardize the government's prospects of being around to enjoy the benefits of a well-adjusted economy. Unstable governments have notoriously short time horizons. Deflation requires the ability to withstand short-term pain for long-term gain. Unless a government is reasonably sure it will be in power when the price of adjustment begins to pay off, adjustment will be postponed. Growth, consumption, and inflation will continue; political opponents will be left to pay the bills. Unstable governments are only acting rationally when they avoid the restrictive policies needed to correct a balance of payments disequilibrium.

Central Bank Independence. The decision to deflate may not be made by the government alone. While politicians control fiscal policies, they may have much less control over the direction of monetary policy. This is especially true when monetary institutions are designed to be independent of government control. Central bankers that are not directly appointed or supervised by politicians are in a position to implement tight credit policies that damp down domestic demand and work to lower domestic prices, with relative freedom from governmental pressure. Politically controlled central banks, however, are much more likely to carry out the government's agenda. When the myriad pressures and concerns of governments outlined above are considered, it is highly unlikely that an independent central bank would advocate a monetary policy that is *more* permissive than that preferred by the government itself. More typically, independent central banks will implement monetary policies that are tighter on average than those under political control. Thus, the insulation of the monetary authority from politics may enhance the commitment to monetary stringency, and strengthen the commitment to gold standard adjustment.

Overall, the hypothesis that the policy mix will be pulled toward internal adjustment under specifiable domestic political and institutional conditions can be tested systematically. Internal adjustment should be associated with regimes that are able to keep democratic excesses under control; it may even be the case that authoritarian regimes are better able to compress their economies than are democratic regimes. Internal adjustment is also more likely under center-right governments that place a higher value on price stability than on growth, under polities with a quiescent labor force and a stable government, and in countries with a central bank that is relatively independent of politicians. *In short, the ability to comply with internationally accepted adjustment norms may be conditioned by the domestic political and institutional variables that influence a country's macroeconomic tastes more generally.* Repression, conservatism, and stability are likely to be consistent with gold standard adjustment; their opposites, with defection.

Externalization

MONETARY EXTERNALIZATION: DEVALUATION

The first mode of defection to consider is abandonment of the gold standard's first principle: to maintain fixed currency parity. Because of the central role of market expectations, it is not sufficient to think of international monetary politics in terms of pure reciprocity between *governments*. In an anticipatory model, *official* reciprocity can be undermined by market pressures flowing from expectations that governments will not be able to defend the prevailing parity. When markets act on their beliefs about each government's commitment to the priority of external balance (and exchange stability), their actions can virtually force norm defection, or at least make defection more likely. Under such circumstances, the ability of governments to influence one another's behavior through a calibrated tit-for-tat strategy is highly circumscribed.

For the reserve currency case, Kenneth Oye has analyzed this phenomenon in terms of two sets of N-person Prisoner's Dilemmas: one among the central bank of the reserve currency and holders of that currency, and the other among holders themselves.[57] If a currency is under pressure, he notes, dumping it to avoid exchange losses is individually rational. Holders act on their expectations about government policy and about the reactions of other market players. If they expect devaluation they should sell sooner rather than later. If a government foresees selling pressures, it may have an incentive to devalue pre-emptively, in order to prevent the massive conversion of its currency into gold. Oye concludes that the setting of fixed rates precluded the use of exchange rates for bargaining purposes, undermining the possibilities for reciprocity that might have kept the international economic system from disintegrating in the early thirties.[58]

But intergovernmental reciprocity is not the central issue: the government's *credibility* with any holder of its currency is. The willingness to hold a currency is linked to the degree of confidence that it will not be devalued. In the early thirties, confidence that governments could continue to pursue macroeconomic and monetary policies consistent with fixed gold parities was flagging, partly because it was incredible that governments representing labor would allow their constituents to suffer for the sake of the currency. As Kenneth Oye notes, "Monetary politics in the early thirties were conditioned by recognition of a short term tradeoff between domestic recovery and exchange rate stabilization, and *governments of the left, confronting high levels of unemployment preferred devaluation to deflation.*"[59] Whether or not governments of the Left actually preferred devaluation, markets expected that constituency pressures would encourage the Left to abrogate the first norm of the gold standard. Credibility crumbled, and with it, the international monetary system.

The key empirical question is, *What shattered credibility?* Anything that would lead markets to suspect that Norm 1 was at risk and to expect devaluation could discredit a government's policy. Conditions associated with an expansion in the money supply that were inconsistent with a fixed parity could lead the market agents to rearrange their assets and renegotiate their contracts. Thus, all the variables associated with expected macroeconomic expansion could spark capital flight to the extent that markets anticipate inflation and act on this expectation. The moment deflation appears politically unfeasible, selling pressure on the currency is expected to increase, making devaluation more likely.

Markets are expected to react to political conditions with which they associ-

[57] Kenneth Oye, "The Sterling-Dollar-Franc Triangle," pp. 173–199.
[58] Ibid., p. 180.
[59] Ibid., p. 178 (italics added).

ate a heightened risk of inflation or other forms of confiscation.[60] Governments with working-class constituencies may be perceived as being less willing to deflate and more likely to expand the money supply to protect employment than governments of the center-right. The result will be capital flight and currency depreciation. A similar effect should attend unstable domestic political conditions. Governments that are not expected to be in office for very long are not able to make credible policy commitments, and markets react by seeking more predictable conditions elsewhere. Severe labor unrest could also contribute to capital flight. As strikes spread, expectations of inflation are raised, even if negotiations do not result in higher real wages. Holders of capital, fearing inflation and possible depreciation, will shift their assets accordingly. Capital will flee, and the risk of depreciation will increase. On the other hand, credibility is likely to be enhanced if the central bank is seen as being above politics. Under a more independent central bank, the expansive preferences of the government are perceived as being less likely to influence monetary policy. Holders of liquid capital will prefer to move their assets to markets where the monetary authority is insulated from political pressures to inflate the money supply. Independent central banks are expected to be associated with internal adjustment and with fewer and more moderate devaluations.

To summarize, monetary defection is hypothesized to be conditioned by the strength of a government's reputation for defending the currency. Reputation is heavily conditioned by the economic agents' beliefs about a government's preferences, time horizons, and willingness to accommodate labor demands. The credibility of a monetary commitment will be heightened to the extent that actual control over monetary policy is centered in an independent—and preferably conservative—institution. To answer the question "Who devalues?" we would do well to consider the conditions that contribute to a loss of credibility in monetary affairs.

TRADE EXTERNALIZATION: TARIFFS

The decision to protect is governed by a somewhat different set of factors from those described above. Tariffs more centrally involve the real economy rather than capital markets. Tariffs are also much more directly under a government's control than is the external value of its currency, which in the final analysis is determined by supply and demand. Tariffs also may serve a number of different policy ends: they may be implemented to protect specific producers, to improve the overall balance of payments, or to raise domestic revenue (customs tax).

---

[60] When inflation is unanticipated, it is "confiscatory" in the sense that it involves an unambiguous transfer of wealth from the private sector to the public sector, resulting in what has been termed an "inflation tax." See, for example, Samuel Brittan, "Inflation and Democracy," chap. 7 in Fred Hirsch and John Goldthorpe (eds.), *The Political Economy of Inflation* (Cambridge: Harvard University Press), 1978, pp. 161–185. Economic agents that anticipate and adjust their portfolios are able to escape wealth losses associated with seigniorage.

Finally, tariffs are legislatively voted rather than determined in the relatively insulated confines of monetary institutions. Tariffs are much more a policy *choice* in the traditional sense than is currency depreciation or devaluation. When governments make monetary decisions, they are primarily involved in strategic interaction with *markets*; when tariffs are contemplated, the primary problem is the strategic reaction of other *governments*. Tariffs are much more usable as international bargaining tools. Considerations of interstate reciprocity and retaliation come to the fore.

Hence, in considering commercial policies it is critical to focus on those factors that shape international economic relations with other states. It would be a mistake to lump devaluation with tariff protection and refer to them generically as "defection," since the strategic actors in each game are distinct. The problem, then, is to explain the conditions that influence the preferred mix of externalization.

In the case of tariffs, the structure and size of the economy are likely to be two of the most important determinants of the decision to protect. The traditional economic literature suggests that the largest states, like monopolistically positioned firms, are able to influence prices and hence may alter the terms of trade in their favor by implementing an optimal tariff.[61] Additionally, states that are relatively self-sufficient can better afford to insulate themselves from the international economy. Highly trade dependent economies, on the other hand, must trade to survive. They will not be willing to engage in protection, both because it raises the price of their own imports and because of the risk of retaliation. There are excellent reasons to believe, as Peter Katzenstein has noted, that the optimal strategy for small, trade-dependent states is to maintain liberal trade policies.[62]

But there may be an ideological or distributional explanation for changes in tariff levels as well. Tariffs are taxes, and tariff protection affords particular domestic producers surplus rents above the value of their production. As with any tax, its attractiveness depends on how the burden falls on different sectors of the society. Tariff protection favors domestic producers and penalizes consumers. Particularly when customs were levied on imported necessities such as food, beverages, and tobacco [*sic*!], tariffs were viewed as consumption taxes that penalized the working class. Despite the fact that consumers were also producers (and hence an argument could be made, as it is often today, that protection has an employment justification), political parties that represented workers were programmatically and ideologically opposed to consumption

---

[61] Charles P. Kindleberger, *International Economics* (Homewood, Ill: Richard D. Irwin), 1968, chap. 7; Tibor Scitovsky, "A Reconsideration of the Theory of Tariffs," *Review of Economic Studies*, reprinted in American Economic Association, *Readings in the Theory of International Trade* (New York: McGraw-Hill), 1949, chap. 16.

[62] Peter J. Katzenstein, *Small States in World Markets: Industrial Policy in Europe* (Ithaca: Cornell University Press), 1985.

taxes that raised the cost of living for the working class. More generally, the application of the Stolper-Samuelson theorem—which holds that protection generally benefits the scarce factor of production and imposes a net cost on the abundant factor—might predict that demands for freer trade would emanate from labor and left-wing parties rather than from capital and parties of the right.[63] Furthermore, as the Left gains representation in governance, we might expect a reduction in tariff barriers, both across countries, and over time.

Finally, tariff protection is a mode of externalizing the costs of adjustment, unemployment, and the burden of taxation onto foreign producers, whereas dismantling tariffs or keeping them low forces the domestic economy to absorb the impact of changing economic conditions and to raise taxes internally.[64] One final hypothesis is that unstable governments—those that have low time horizons and that rest on precarious political coalitions—are less likely than more stable ones to take the risks and absorb the costs of maintaining lower tariffs. Less stable governments, on the other hand, find externalization an easy alternative. Unable to resist domestic pressures, they are more likely to take the path of least resistance and protect domestic producers rather than to allow price adjustments to ripple through the economy.

CONCLUSIONS

This chapter has laid the groundwork for understanding the sources of instability in the gold exchange standard that prevailed between the two World Wars. The classic gold standard depended not on financial hegemony of one preponderant power, or conducive economic conditions, but rather on the belief that governments were commited to macroeconomic policies with which a fixed relationship to gold would be compatible. The Great War fundamentally changed the political landscape that had been compatible with a credible commitment to gold: political systems in which demands of contending social forces could be marginalized; governments that were stable, if narrowly constituted; and the prevalence of political philosophies that justified a relative lack of governmental responsibility for domestic economic conditions and the welfare of citizens. Although these conditions no longer prevailed after 1920, in reconstructing the international economic order monetary authorities turned to the model of monetary order that had, in their estimation, served so well up to 1913. Some states, for given periods of time, were willing and able to maintain internal macroeconomic policies that were consistent with the demands of the

---

[63] Ronald Rogowski, *Commerce and Coalitions* (Princeton: Princeton University Press), 1988.

[64] As John Hansen has argued in his discussion of the determinants of American tariff policy, "tariffs were instruments of revenue, and the battles over tariff policy were battles over taxes, over how they should be raised and over who should pay them." John Mark Hansen, "Taxation and the Political Economy of the Tariff," *International Organization*, Vol. 44, No. 4, Autumn 1990, pp. 527–549, especially p. 528.

gold standard; but others, undermined by markets that doubted the sincerity of official commitments to deflationary policies and external balance, found the social and political costs far too high a price to pay for remaining on gold. As the following chapter will show, the political and social factors that distinguished the prewar from the interwar years are also useful in explaining *variations* in the commitment to gold among countries over the course of the interwar years themselves. Thus the stability of the international monetary system had as much to do with internal as with international politics during the two decades between the wars. The distinguishing factors in a country's ability to maintain external economic balance have largely to do with the credibility of its commitment to pursue "moderate" macroeconomic policies, a commitment that came under question in more and more cases with the close of World War I.

Chapter 3

THE DETERMINANTS OF EXTERNAL IMBALANCE

THE INTERWAR monetary system depended heavily on the assumption that each country declaring itself to be on the gold standard adhere to the most important of the three norms outlined in the previous chapter: that it place external balance above domestic economic conditions. Only by doing so would it be possible to maintain a fixed relationship with gold. This chapter develops a model and provides evidence to show that economic explanations alone do not fully explain why certain states had difficulties maintaining a reasonable balance of payments. When the determinants of capital flows and current account deficits (net exports and net interest payments) are closely examined, clear political patterns emerge. According to rules of national income accounting, these two variables ought to be identical but opposite, since capital inflows are necessary to finance a current account deficit. In practice, however, short-term capital movements were frequently speculative and did not correspond with the financing needs of the current account. In such a case, capital outflows contributed to domestic inflationary pressures, which in turn undermined a country's international trade competitiveness and tended to reinforce current account deficits.

This chapter begins by presenting a framework for analyzing the political variables that influence a country's external economic balance. Next, I test the effect of these variables on both capital flight and current account deficits. The strongest and most consistent finding is that unstable governments facing a high degree of labor unrest, with the power to manipulate the policies of the central bank, are associated with both capital flight and a deteriorating current account. Furthermore, representation of the Left in government aggravated the current account deficit. Overall, when controlling for economic conditions and foreign shocks, four domestic political variables had a significant impact on a country's ability to abide by the first norm of the gold standard. Why this is so becomes clear when we explore the critical role of credibility in influencing expectations, prices, and ultimately a polity's ability to keep its economy in rough economic balance with the rest of the world.

POLITICS, CREDIBILITY, AND EXTERNAL IMBALANCE

If politics affects the balance of payments, it would most likely be through the risk of increased domestic price levels, which would in turn raise the real exchange rate. An overvalued currency can stimulate capital outflows (by increasing the risk that the currency will be devalued) and can contribute to current account deficit (since the country's exports are likely to be overpriced compared to goods on the world market). A theory about the relationship between domestic politics and the balance of payments must therefore address how particular political conditions raise the risk of domestic inflation. It would have to be a theory about why governments try to achieve economic stimulation by manipulating the money supply, and how economic agents anticipate and react to these efforts.

The literature on time inconsistency in monetary policymaking is a useful point of departure. Monetary policymaking can be thought of as a strategic interaction between monetary authorities and economic agents. The announcement and implementation of monetary policy occur in stages, and the core problem is that the government's optimal policy choice is time inconsistent: assuming that governments would prefer to preside over a growing rather than a stagnant economy, it is rational for the government to *announce* stringent monetary policies, but to *implement* a stimulatory surprise. However, the government's effort to optimize economic growth is undercut if rational forward-looking economic agents anticipate expansionary monetary policies and rearrange their assets and renegotiate their contracts accordingly. When they do this, the outcome is not growth, but inflation. In deciding whether or not to take these preemptory actions, markets assess governments' anti-inflationary credibility: they look for indications in the motivations, values, and capabilities of the monetary authorities that give clues to policymakers' ability to resist the temptation to stimulate. While all governments may claim that they will implement responsible macroeconomic policies, markets will react against those whose credibility is weak. In that case, increases in the money supply will not be taken up by increased demand. Prices will rise, the real exchange rate will increase, and the risk of devaluation will grow. As the risk of devaluation increases, investors become increasingly unwilling to hold assets denominated in the suspect currency. Thus, the conditions that undercut government credibility are those associated with the withdrawal of foreign capital, and ultimately with the deterioration of the current account as well.[1]

Credibility and Monetary Policy

Economies managed by governments lacking credibility are more likely to experience capital outflows than economies led by credible governments. Credibility is in doubt whenever markets believe that the government will attempt to engineer an unexpected expansion of the money supply. The problem of credibility can be analyzed in game theoretic terms. Suppose that governments and markets are conceived as distinct sets of actors engaged in an effort to maximize

---

[1] For a good review of time inconsistency and monetary policy, see Keith Blackburn and Michael Christensen, "Monetary Policy and Policy Credibility: Theory and Evidence," *Journal of Economic Literature*, Vol. 27, March 1989, p. 2.

their own utility (however defined) in a setting in which each actor's welfare depends not only upon his own decisions, but also upon those of the opposing "player." These players are not by any means equals; the government is relatively centralized and can be assumed to initiate policy, while the market is quite decentralized (even internationalized) and reacts to the moves of the economic authorities.[2] Market agents do not pick strategies as a collective unit, but as atomistic individuals who seek to maximize their utility based on their best guess not only about how the government will act, but about how the rest of the market will respond as well.[3]

Whenever governments retain discretion over future policy choice, they are unable to commit *unequivocally* to a preannounced monetary policy. Hence, market actors make judgments about the government's future action by using all available information about its past patterns of behavior under analogous conditions. But this information will only be partial and imperfect; moreover, the government might wish to conceal or misrepresent its true preferences or other private information so as to convince the markets of its commitment to monetary stringency. Under certain conditions, there is a strong incentive for the government to pursue monetary policies that are more expansive ex post facto than those announced ante facto. Markets anticipate this possibility, and the result is monetary expansion in the second period that is much higher than if government policy had been credible in the first place.

Finn Kydland and Edward C. Prescott[4] have presented a simple model of monetary policy that explains why the problem of time inconsistency crops up in the types of games outlined above. Their model illustrates why governments with discretion can find it to their advantage to renege on their earlier monetary commitments. In this model, policymakers' utility depends on inflation levels and production levels. Policymakers want to achieve an "ideal" inflation rate but avoid the costs of inflation that exceed this level. These costs may include those related to the administrative difficulties of keeping up with price increases, as well as the redistributive consequences for fixed-income earners, nonindexed workers, and persons who hold their wealth in currency-denominated assets. The more monetary inflation exceeds the ideal level, the greater the disutility for the government.

[2] This is of course a simplification, because governments arguably respond to aggregate economic behavior. But the main point is that decentralized actors do not respond in concert as though they can affect government policy choice. In this sense, government is the leader and decentralized market actors are followers.

[3] For the moment this ignores the problem of important disparities in the political power within the private sector, which may lead to "collusion." It also ignores for now the possibility that government decisionmaking may actually be very decentralized and contradictory.

[4] Finn Kydland and Edward C. Prescott, "Rules Rather than Discretion: The Inconsistency of Optimal Plans," *Journal of Political Economy*, Vol. 85, No. 3, June 1977, pp. 473–491. This model has also been explored and extended by Robert J. Barro and David B. Gordon, "A Positive Theory of Monetary Policy in a Natural Rate Model," *Journal of Political Economy*, Vol. 91, August 1983, pp. 589–610.

Policymakers' utility also depends on achieving some ideal level of output and employment. An important assumption of the model, however, is that from the perspective of policymakers, *actual production and employment are always less than the ideal*. "Natural" output is assumed to be too low because of market distortions resulting from labor unions, whose wage demands drive up unemployment levels; taxes, which discourage production and growth; and unemployment compensation, which encourages workers to remain unemployed. The model takes these distortions as given and assumes that policymakers are dissatisfied with the "natural" level of production and employment.

Policymakers are therefore motivated to find a way to improve their economy's level of production. They can do this by attempting to engineer short-term trade-offs along the Phillips Curve. Aggregate output is conceived as a function of the "natural" rate of production plus some fraction of the difference between the expected and the actual rate of inflation. Assuming policymakers control either interest rates or the money supply, higher levels of inflation can purchase higher levels of output in the short run. Viewing total output as a function of the natural level plus a short-term wallop from unexpected monetary expansion means that policymakers have the "scope to influence output by engineering inflationary surprises."[5]

Key to this model are the expectations of the private sector regarding inflation. Using all available information, independent rational market actors behave according to their best guess about monetary policy and inflation rates in the near future. As in game theoretic frameworks, the market's expected rate of inflation and the government's chosen actual rate of inflation are mutually contingent. The government tries to minimize the deviation of inflation from desired levels and tries to improve growth by capitalizing on the short-term trade-off of inflation against growth and employment.[6] The only way it can improve growth, however, is by engineering stimulative monetary policies that are *not* anticipated by the market. If the market expects inflation, and renegotiates contracts that take the expected inflation into account, the result will be higher inflation without the growth for which the government had hoped. If market actors are rational and forward-looking, they understand governments' temptation to gain from unexpectedly stimulatory monetary policies that boost growth and employment. To the extent that they believe the government has a motivation for engineering stimulation, they revise their expectations upward, pushing up actual rates of inflation.

The central question is whether the government's commitment to price stability is credible to market participants, both domestic and foreign. In a one-

---

[5] Blackburn and Christensen, "Monetary Policy and Policy Credibility," p. 11.

[6] Governments are rational in this model, but tend to be somewhat myopic. Theoretical justifications for accepting a certain degree of governmental myopia are not difficult to find: election pressures, imperfectly informed constituents, and an unstable political system could contribute to official myopia. Even a "sophisticated" government might rationally defect (inflate) in repeated play if it believes the cost to its reputation will not be too great.

shot game, a lack of credibility leads to monetary expansion and a level of inflation that is higher than desired and higher than would be the case were the government able credibly to commit itself to a conservative monetary policy. In repeated games—the more realistic model for monetary policymaking— markets remember past patterns of government behavior, and the political conditions associated with that behavior, and they threaten to punish overly expansive monetary policies by adjusting to them. Market participants may hold down their inflationary expectations if inflation has been held down in previous periods, but raise them if inflation has increased recently. Governments then have to take into account the risk that their stimulatory policies will redound negatively to their reputation and contribute to an intractable inflationary spiral and perhaps, ultimately, to a painful contraction.[7]

The problem of time inconsistency and government credibility has important implications for capital flows, since the decision to hold assets in a particular currency rests on confidence that it will not be devalued. It also has implications for the current account, since domestic inflation makes exports increasingly uncompetitive under fixed exchange rates. What determines whether or not markets believe governments will actually implement announced policies? What conditions undermine government credibility? The model outlined above suggests five factors that may undercut the ability of the government to implement conservative monetary policies:

The market's judgments about the credibility of the regime.   The political and institutional setting within which strategic interactions between market and government take place may be greatly influenced by the nature of the political regime in question. Are regimes that have recourse to repression more likely to be able to achieve their announced monetary goals than others? There are good reasons to suppose that nondemocratic regimes might be more successful than democratic ones in imposing conventional fiscal and monetary restraint, while group conflict in a democratic society may imbue it with an inflationary bias. The sheer centralization of power may enable dictators to impose conventional fiscal and monetary restraint more successfully. They may be better positioned to ignore short-term domestic demands, which may enhance the monetary credibility of authoritarian regimes.[8] If democracies are viewed as less credible

---

[7] On the importance of reputation, see Robert J. Barro and David B. Gordon, "Rules, Discretion, and Reputation in a Model of Monetary Policy," *Journal of Monetary Economics*, Vol. 12, July 1983, pp. 101–121; and David Backus and John Drifill, "Inflation and Reputation," *American Economic Review*, Vol. 75, No. 3, June 1985, pp. 530–538.

[8] These propositions have been debated in the recent comparative literature on economic stabilization in developing regions. See Karen L. Remmer, "Democracy and Economic Crisis: The Latin American Experience," *World Politics*, Vol. 42, No. 3, April 1990, pp. 315–335; C. A. Diaz-Alejandro, "Southern Cone Stabilization Plans," in William Cline and Sidney Weintraub (eds.), *Economic Stabilization in Developing Countries* (Washington, D.C.: Brookings Institution), 1981; Robert R. Kaufman, "Industrial Change and Authoritarian Rule in Latin America: A Concrete Review of the Bureaucratic-Authoritarian Model," in David Collier (ed.), *The New Authoritarian-*

with respect to their monetary policies, they should experience higher inflation, greater capital flight, and a worse current account position.

Obversely, democracies may be under pressure to satisfy demands for consumption in ways that raise domestic prices. This plaint was often voiced in fiscally conservative circles in the twenties and early thirties.[9] More recently, Samuel Brittan has argued that liberal democracy, with its pressures for full employment, tolerates excessive injections of money into the economic system.[10] He argues that democracies are under strong political pressures to provide benefits for special-interest groups, but the inflationary pressures these demands engender are borne by a wide spectrum of the population whose votes are not likely to be influenced by the costs of inflation. The cumulative effect is an inflationary bias in democratic societies.[11]

Historical anecdotes seem to confirm the weakness of some democracies in controlling inflation. Several episodes of stabilization in the 1920s were accompanied by the transfer of extraordinary powers from parliaments to the finance minister, as was the case with France and Belgium in the mid-twenties. The perception seems to have been that a credible fiscal program was not possible under divisive democratic conditions. On the whole, the ability of democracies to make credible commitments to monetary goals may be weaker than the credibility of more repressive regimes.[12]

The market's judgments about policymakers' preferences.   Despite a past record of conservative monetary policy, market expectations can shift radically if

ism in Latin America (Princeton: Princeton University Press), 1979; Henry S. Bienen and Mark Gersovitz, "Economic Stabilization, Conditionality, and Political Stability," *International Organization*, Vol. 39, No. 4, Autumn 1985, pp. 729–754.

[9] Sir William Dampier-Whetham wondered, in considering the necessity of wage cuts, whether democracy "will not always prefer immediate benefits for the wage-earners to the ultimate welfare of the nations." *Lloyd's Bank Review*, July 1931, p. 269. Similarly, in his criticism of Keynes's case for not returning to gold, T. E. Gregory thought that Keynes had given far too much emphasis to popular "working class" sentiments. T. E. Gregory, *The First Year of the Gold Standard* (London: Ernest Benn), 1926, p. 18.

[10] Samuel Brittan, "Inflation and Democracy," chap. 7 in Fred Hirsch and John H. Goldthorpe, *The Political Economy of Inflation* (Cambridge: Harvard University Press), 1978, pp. 161–185.

[11] Weighing *against* the credibility of authoritarian regimes, however, is their scope for arbitary behavior toward investors. Specifically, authoritarian governments have a comparative disadvantage in attracting capital if markets fear that they will arbitrarily alter or interfere with property rights. Such interference during the interwar years sometimes took the form of forced conversion of government bonds to lower rates of interest, or restrictions on the export of foreign exchange, or the unhindered repatriation of profits.

[12] In principle, it would be desirable to distinguish corporatist democracies from pluralistic democracies, since the former may be more successful at reaching agreements on economic policy. Peter J. Katzenstein, *Small States in World Markets: Industrial Policy in Europe* (Ithaca: Cornell University Press), 1985; John H. Goldthorpe, *Order and Conflict in Contemporary Capitalism* (Oxford: Clarendon Press), 1984. But since these structures were not well developed during the interwar years, it is most important simply to compare democratic with nondemocratic regimes.

there are reasons to believe that policymakers' preferences have changed, or if new policymakers with different preferences come to power. Markets can be skeptical that governments resting on very different political coalitions or constituencies will continue the monetary policies of previous governments. In short, rational forward-looking economic agents understand the electoral impulse to please a core constituency, and they assess policy promises of the government accordingly.[13]

Markets are therefore likely to react differently to the promises of governments of the Right versus those of the Left. Since upswings in the business cycle are particularly beneficial for the working class,[14] governments of the Left may face a greater temptation to stimulate the economy to please their core constituency. Even if some inflation does result, the costs fall most heavily on fixed-income and creditor groups, who are more likely to be allied with center-right parties.[15] These distributional consequences are likely to be reflected in the macroeconomic preferences of political parties.[16] Markets anticipate these

[13] For a recent model that makes use of the assumption that electoral uncertainty leads market actors to have expectations based on the "average" of the policies that the two parties are expected to follow if elected, see Alberto Alesina and Jeffrey Sachs, "Political Parties and the Business Cycle in the United States, 1948–1984," *Journal of Money, Credit, and Banking*, Vol. 20, No. 1, February 1988, pp. 63–82. They provide evidence that such expectations can lead to expansion under the left-wing party and recession under the right-wing party for the first two years of its term in office.

[14] Several studies have found that the second half of the upswing in particular is associated with a dramatic rise in income share toward labor in most economies. See Jeffrey Sachs, *Wages, Profits, and Macroeconomic Adjustment: A Comparative Study*, Brookings Paper on Economic Activity, Vol. 2 (Washington, D.C.: Brookings Institution), 1979, pp. 269–332; G. L. Bach and James Stevenson, "Inflation and the Redistribution of Wealth," *Review of Economics and Statistics*, Vol. 61, February 1974, pp. 1–13; Albert Burger, "Relative Movements in Wages and Profits, " *Federal Reserve Bank of St. Louis Review*, Vol. 55, February 1973; Edwin Kuh, "Income Distribution and Employment Over the Business Cycle," in J. Dusenberry et al., *Brookings Quarterly Econometric Model of the United States* (Chicago: Rand McNally), 1975, pp. 227–278. Marxists have interpreted the second half of the business cycle as the triumph of the working class, and its reversal and attendant unemployment as an outcome engineered by the capitalist classes abetted by the state. Rafor Boddy and James Crotty, "Class Conflict and Macro-Policy: The Political Business Cycle," *Review of Radical Political Economics*, Vol. 7, Spring 1975, pp. 1–19.

[15] The literature on the distributional effects of various macroeconomic policy outcomes is vast. See Robinson G. Hollister and John L. Palmer, "The Impact of Inflation on the Poor," in K. E. Boulding and M. Pfaff (eds.), *Redistribution to the Rich and the Poor* (Belmont, Calif.: Wadsworth), 1972, pp. 240–270; Charles M. Metcalf, *An Econometric Model of Income Distribution* (Chicago: Markham), 1972; G. L. Bach and G. Ando, "The Redistributional Effects of Inflation," *Review of Economics and Statistics*, Vol. 39, 1957, pp. 1–13.

[16] E. S. Kirschen et al., *Economic Policy in Our Time, Vol. 1: General Theory* (Amsterdam: North Holland), 1964. See Kirschen's informative preference chart on p. 227; Douglas A. Hibbs, "Political Parties and Macroeconomic Policy," *American Political Science Review*, Vol. 71, No. 4, December 1977, pp. 1467–1487. For a critical review of Hibbs's findings, arguing that they exaggerate the differences between the parties, see Nathaniel Beck, "Parties, Administrations, and American Macroeconomic Outcomes," *American Political Science Review*, Vol. 76, No. 1, March 1982, pp. 83–93. For other empirical tests of the impact of parties on economic policy outcomes see

preferences, and whether justified or not, the Left is more likely to experience inflation, capital flight, and current account deficit.

Note that all this argument depends upon is a crack in government credibility. In some cases, left-wing parties gave plenty of signals that they might not be able to achieve their proclaimed monetary goals. Division within the ranks of the British Labour party in 1929–1931 over unemployment insurance gave the impression that the budget might be a source of inflationary pressure, just as the forty-hour workweek and other social policies damaged the monetary credibility of the French Front Populaire in 1936. In these cases, economic agents voted no confidence and took measures to protect themselves against government "defection."[17] Markets expect left-wing governments to take policies in the interest of their constituencies, and in the short term, deflation can convert a worker into an unemployment statistic.[18] If economic agents begin to renegotiate contracts based on an expectation of monetary inflation, and if holders of liquid capital flee in anticipation of it, the result would be a spurt in capital outflow and pressure on the current account. Left-wing governments are far more likely to be the victims of hostile market assessments, making them more susceptible to external economic imbalance.

Paul F. Whiteley, "The Political Economy of Economic Growth," *European Journal of Political Research*, Vol. 11, No. 2, June 1983, pp. 197–213; and Peter Lange and Geoffrey Garrett, "The Politics of Growth: Strategic Interaction and Economic Performance in the Advanced Industrialized Countries," *Journal of Politics*, Vol. 47, No. 3, August 1985, pp. 792–827. For further discussion see Walter F. Abbott and J. W. Leasure, "Income Level and Inflation in the United States," in Nathan Schmukler and Edward Markus (eds.), *Inflation Through the Ages* (New York: Brooklyn College Press), 1983, pp. 804–819; and Edward Tufte, *Political Control of the Economy* (Princeton: Princeton University Press), 1978. For a sophisticated account that includes union structure and party preferences, see Fritz W. Scharpf, "A Game-theoretical Interpretation of Inflation and Unemployment in Western Europe," *Journal of Public Policy*, Vol. 7, No. 3, 1987, pp. 227–257.

[17] Writers from Montesquieu to Marx and their followers have emphasized the role of "capital strike" as a bottom-line constraint on any capitalist economy. Liberals have celebrated this constraint, while Marxists have lamented it. Montesquieu saw the rise of foreign exchange as a constraint on sudden arbitrary actions of the sovereign, and Adam Smith saw movable property as a constraint on extortionist tax policies. See Albert O. Hirschman, *The Passions and the Interests* (Princeton: Princeton University Press), 1977. Fred Hirsch notes the "veto power" of capital in "The Ideological Underlay of Inflation," Conclusion, in Fred Hirsch and John H. Goldthorpe, *The Political Economy of Inflation*, pp. 263–284. For structural Marxists' arguments about the capitalist constraint on state actions, see Samuel Bowles and Herbert Gintiss, *Democracy and Capitalism* (New York: Basic Books), 1986; Michael Shalev, "The Social Democratic Model and Beyond: Two Generations of Comparative Research on the Welfare State," in Richard Tomasson (ed.), *Comparative Social Research*, Vol. 6 (Greenwich, Conn.: JAI Press), 1983; and José M. Maravall, "The Limits of Reformism: Parliamentary Socialism and the Marxist Theory of the State," *British Journal of Sociology*, Vol. 30, 1979, pp. 262–287.

[18] For an account of the political business cycle that makes use of government reactions to anticipated voter behavior, see Bruno S. Frey and Friedrich Schneider, "An Empirical Study of Politico-Economic Interaction in the United States," *Review of Economics and Statistics*, Vol. 60, No. 2, May 1978, pp. 174–183.

The market's judgments about policymakers' time horizon.   The third factor that can undercut a government's credibility is the prospect that it will not be in office much longer. Markets expect governments with short time horizons to put a much higher premium on current utility, and to highly discount the future. Thus, they act on the assumption that unstable governments are among the most likely to have time-inconsistent preferences with respect to the trade-off of inflation and production.[19] The impact on the balance of payments will be profound.

Why should markets expect instability to be associated with an inflationary surge? Primarily because unstable governments are assumed to have short time horizons. The put a much higher value on present than on future consumption, since they are not likely to be in office to enjoy the rewards of monetary stringency. It is the distribution of costs and benefits of monetary stringency over time that makes it unlikely that unstable governments will live up to their commitments: the costs are concentrated in the present, but the benefits will only be realized in the future. For a government with short time horizons, deferred gratification does not make sense.

Furthermore, unstable governments simply do not have the ability or the authority to make credible monetary commitments. Political instability can be expected to make it much more difficult to pass a balanced budget, which will be inflationary in combination with monetary accommodation. The political price tag on negotiating a consumption-cutting fiscal policy will be especially high for unstable governments, who may not possess reliable information on which social and parliamentary groups may be needed as allies in pushing through an unpopular budget. What raises the costs of domestic bargaining for unstable governments are political, economic, or social upheavals that produce an "altered cast of characters about whom reliable information is yet to be acquired."[20] Once a coalition is assembled, it can remain vulnerable to defection threats by one dissatisfied, strategically positioned partner. Moreover,

---

[19] While cabinet instability is used as an explanatory variable, there is already a well-developed literature on exactly what influences cabinet duration itself. Some researchers have emphasized attributes of the political or electoral system (Michael Taylor and Valentine Herman, "Party Systems and Governmental Stability," *American Political Science Review*, Vol. 65, March 1971, pp. 28–37), while others have emphasized the random nature of events that destabilize governments (Eric C. Browne, John P. Frendeis, and Dennis W. Gleiber, "An Events Approach to the Problem of Cabinet Stability," *Comparative Political Studies*, Vol. 17, pp. 167–197). For a unified model of cabinet duration, see Gary King, James E. Alt, Nancy E. Burns, and Michael Laver, "A Unified Model of Cabinet Dissolution in Parliamentary Democracies," *American Journal of Political Science*, Vol. 34, pp. 846–871. For a critique of this approach, see Paul Warwick and Stephen T. Easton, "The Cabinet Stability Controversy: New Perspectives on a Classic Problem," *American Journal of Political Science*, Vol. 36, No. 1, pp. 122–146. Here, I am not concerned with the causes of cabinet instability, with the exception of the role of economic disturbances on cabinet turnover, since this complicates the question of the direction of causation in the models that follow.

[20] Margaret Levi, *Of Rule and Revenue* (Berkeley: University of California Press), 1988, p. 28.

unstable governments can be expected to face extraordinarily high costs associated with assuring compliance, since their authority is likely to be low. Negotiation, reliable information, and consistent compliance have a higher price under conditions of political and social bouleversement. For a government that is not likely to be around to enjoy the benefits, the gain simply does not exceed the expected pain.

Where the life expectancy of the government is short, and hence its discount rate high, the strategic relationship with the market takes on characteristics of a one-shot game, where both players know the rational move is to defect.[21] Reciprocity—in this case, mutually cooperative actions on the part of the government and the private sector—is likely to break down when the government's time horizon is short.[22] Once economic agents expect government defection, they sell assets denominated in domestic currency and seek refuge in other markets. There are strong reasons, then, to expect political instability to be associated with inflation, capital outflows, and current account deterioration.

The market's judgments about institutional monetary constraints.   In most time-inconsistency models, government commitments are suspect because of the known desire to increase employment and output. Credibility may be weakened further if the central bank is perceived as the government's ally. If the government can lean on the central bank to inflate credit, or to facilitate the government's management of its short-term debt, this will have a profound effect on the behavior of the market. Inflation in the next period will be higher than optimal; indeed, higher than either the central bank or society would have desired it to be.[23]

That which buttresses the credibility of the central bank, then, will dampen the inflationary monetary bias, lower the real exchange rate, and encourage

[21] When actors' preferences are as in Prisoner's Dilemma, a strategy of defection dominates one of cooperation in one-shot play because there are no expected long-term benefits from future cooperation. Where the players put a high value on future benefits, reciprocity and cooperation are the most rational—and collectively stable—strategies. Michael Taylor, *Anarchy and Cooperation* (New York: Wiley), 1976; Robert Axelrod, *The Evolution of Cooperation* (New York: Basic Books), 1984, chap. 3. Another excellent discussion on the notion of discount rate and its implication for rational choice is found in Jon Elster, *Ulysses and the Sirens* (Cambridge: Cambridge University Press), 1979.

[22] Axelrod concludes that "one specific implication is that if the other player is unlikely to be around much longer because of apparent weakness, then the perceived value of w [the discount rate] falls and the reciprocity of TIT-FOR-TAT is no longer stable." Axelrod, *The Evolution of Cooperation*, p. 59.

[23] As Kenneth Rogoff has pointed out, extrapolating from the model of Kydland and Prescott, an economy may ultimately be better off with respect to its inflation rate if it appoints monetary authorities who are even more conservative with respect to the trade-off between inflation and unemployment than is the rest of society. Rogoff, "The Optimal Degree of Commitment to an Intermediate Monetary Target," *Quarterly Journal of Economics*, Vol. 100, 1985, pp. 1169–1189.

capital inflows.[24] There are several ways monetary credibility can be achieved institutionally,[25] but the most common way of bolstering the credibility of the central bank in the 1920s was to create institutional arrangements that would insulate monetary authorities from inflationary pressures. The orthodoxy of the 1920s was that "if the control of the operations of the central bank lies directly with the Government, it becomes fatally easy for Government to finance itself for a time by means of book entries and short loans from the Bank, a course which is the first step towards currency depreciation and inconvertibility."[26] Independent central banks were believed to be better able to resist inflationary finance, and hence were expected to be associated with capital inflows and a stronger current account.[27]

[24] Rogoff notes that the first best solution would be to eliminate the source of the market distortions which give rise to the time inconsistency problem in the first place, but the social costs of busting unions, cutting unemployment insurance, and eliminating distorting taxation may be too high. Ibid., p. 1176.

[25] These include choosing central bankers with extremely conservative reputations (see John T. Woolley, *Monetary Politics: The Federal Reserve and the Politics of Monetary Policy*, Cambridge: Cambridge University Press, 1984, chap. 3); devising rules that remove discretion completely from day-to-day monetary policymaking (see Milton Friedman, "Should There Be an Independent Monetary Authority?" in Leland Yeager, ed., *In Search of a Monetary Constitution*, Cambridge: Harvard University Press, 1962, p. 227); devising remunerative rewards and punishments for deviations from prespecified monetary goals, as suggested by Rogoff, "The Optimal Degree of Commitment," p. 1180. Many central banks in the 1920s in fact had such penalties written into their statutes. Several banks were to be "taxed" on excess increases in the money supply beyond the legal limit. For a sophisticated treatment of the issue of credibility versus monetary flexibility, see Susanne Lohmann, "Optimal Commitment in Monetary Policy: Credibility versus Flexibility," *American Economic Review*, Vol. 82, No. 1, March 1992, pp. 273–286.

[26] C. H. Kisch and W. A. Elkin, *Central Banks: A Study of the Constitutions of Banks of Issue, with an Analysis of Representative Charters* (London: Macmillan), 1928, p. 22.

[27] Recent studies have generally found that politically independent central banks are indeed associated with lower inflation. Examining twelve Western democracies for the sixties and seventies, King Banaian, Leroy O. Laney, and Thomas D. Willett present evidence that "monetary policy was less accommodative overall in the countries characterized as more independent." The more independent central banks were Germany, Canada, Switzerland, and the United States. "Central Bank Independence: An International Comparison," *Economic Review* (Federal Reserve Bank of Dallas), March 1983, pp. 1–13. Marc Levy found that there were no significant differences in the rate of monetary growth or the inflation rate between "dependent" and "partially dependent" central banks, but but that these groups combined differ significantly from the most independent central banks. "Effects and Causes of Central Bank Independence: Do Institutions Matter, and Why?" unpublished essay, Harvard University, 1988. Gerald Epstein and Juliet B. Schor present evidence to suggest that countries with more independent central banks pursued more restrictive policies in the fifties and sixties, at the expense of the working class. "Macropolicy in the Rise and Fall of the Golden Age," unpublished essay, Harvard University, June 1987. Alberto Alesina and Lawrence H. Summers, looking at an expanded group of countries, agree that more independent central banks tend to have lower inflation, but found no evidence that this was at the expense of the real economy. They conclude that "inflation benefits of central bank independence are likely to outweigh any output costs." "Central Bank Independence and Macroeconomic Performance: Some Comparative Evidence," unpublished essay, Harvard University and NBER, 1990.

The government's and market's judgments about market distortions (labor unrest). In the strategic model considered above, economic agents not only anticipate government policy, but they also try to anticipate the actions of other economic agents and assess government policy in light of those actions. Whenever economic groups (such as labor unions) try to protect their interests by negotiating improved wage contracts in the strategic atmosphere outlined above, two things happen. One result is a preemptive response on the part of monetary authorities. Since higher wages achieved through collective action contribute to market distortions in this model, from the perspective of the policymaker an even *higher* level of monetary inflation will be necessary to raise the economy's output and employment to the policymaker's "ideal level" in the following period. Second, there will be a preemptive response from the rest of the private sector. They anticipate the government's move, and bet on inflation. The result will be higher prices, and a deteriorating external position.

Therefore, we would expect capital outflows when there are signs that market distortions may undermine the government's production or employment objectives. One measure of impending distortion is increased strike activity.[28] When widespread industrial disputes rack the economy, the government anticipates greater labor market distortions in the future and is increasingly tempted to compensate for them by raising the money supply. Other market actors expect the government to do so, contributing to inflation. Notice it is not the outcome of the strike here that drives the model's conclusion (whether or not labor wins wage concessions is not of primary importance), but the fact that labor unrest per se damages the market's confidence that the government will achieve its monetary goals. Our expectation is that increased labor unrest is negatively associated with changes in capital flows, as economic agents shift to markets with less potential for inflation, and with current account deterioration as inflationary pressures erode the price advantage of a country's exports.

Summary of the Model and Expectations

The model presented here stresses economic agents' expectations regarding inflation under various political conditions. Inflation raises a country's real exchange rate, and heightens the probability of eventual devaluation. In anticipation of the exchange risk, economic agents shift out of assets denominated in the domestic currency. Preemptory adjustment to inflationary expectations is a self-fulfilling prophecy, with negative consequences for both capital flows and the current account. A political theory of the balance of payments must there-

---

[28] Among the countries in this sample, the three with the highest percentage of days lost due to strikes relative to their populations were Norway (47%), Sweden (30.5%), and the United Kingdom (29.8%). The three countries with the lowest percentages were Italy and Japan (.8% each) and Romania (1.3%). The years with the greatest number of working days lost due to strikes were 1926 (30.5%) and 1924 (27.2%). The years with the least were 1935 (2.9%) and 1938 (4.5%).

fore link investor confidence with specifiable political conditions that serve to undermine the willingness to hold domestically denominated assets. Models of time inconsistency for monetary policymaking are extremely useful in this regard: they point to the political and institutional conditions that undermine a government's credibility in meeting its monetary objectives. I have suggested five political conditions that impinge on credibility and hypothesize that each has the following effect on the balance of payments:

	Expected Direction	
Variable	Capital Flows	Current Account
Democratic regime	−	−
Left-wing government	−	−
Cabinet turnover	−	−
Central bank independence	+	+
Labor unrest	−	−

These hypotheses are tested below. Strong evidence emerges that a country's balance of payments, and hence its ability to abide by Norm 1 of the gold standard, was complicated by the vagaries of these domestic political conditions.

CAPITAL MOVEMENTS

International capital movements financed postwar reconstruction, international trade, and German reparations. They were also an important part of the gold standard adjustment mechanism. Countries experiencing losses of gold reserves or selling pressure on their currency were supposed to raise interest rates to attract the capital necessary to support fixed parities. But capital movements were very sensitive to domestic politics and social unrest. For example, capital outflows from Britain in response to the general strike in 1926 nearly toppled the pound in 1927, as short-term funds sought a more stable local environment. When capital shifted suddenly from one country to another, the impact on exchange rates could be devastating.

This section argues that domestic political conditions had an important impact on investor confidence, capital flows, and ultimately the ability to remain on the gold standard. Here, I model the conditions that caused capital to question a government's commitment to the first norm of the gold standard. I begin by presenting a simple economic model in which capital flows are influenced by three factors: interest rate differentials, changes in real exchange rates, and output growth. I then demonstrate that domestic political conditions have an impact *independent* of the effects specified in the economic model. The

results support an argument that markets fled uncertain and potentially inflationary domestic political conditions. On the other hand, independent central
banks tended to counter the influence of mercurial politics and to encourage
capital inflows, at least before 1931.

The results of this section are critical for an understanding of the conditions
that contributed to the breakdown of international monetary cooperation in the
interwar years. Domestic political turmoil drove investors to seek safer havens,
which in turn complicated economic stability and adjustment. One of the key
levers of control was out of monetary authorities' hands as long as uncertainty
reigned at home. The *international* dilemma among holders and issuers of
particular currencies was set off by *domestically* based doubts that the issuer
could keep its promise to maintain par. The prospects for international cooperation were substantially weakened when deficit countries lost the confidence of
capital.

Descriptive Statistics of Capital Movements, 1923–1938

Statistics on capital flows are available for eighteen countries in my sample for
most of the interwar years, though data are missing for many of the smaller
countries in the twenties and for the fascist countries in the thirties.[29] Overall, it
was possible to collect data on capital flows for 280 country-years. Figure 3.1
shows the yearly capital flows experienced by each country. In general, we
should expect the net creditor countries (first graph) to be capital exporters, with
flows in the negative region. Obversely, we should expect debtor countries
(second through fourth graphs) to be capital importers. The general shape of
these graphs shows the expected trends for the twenties, but a reversal in the
thirties. From about 1930 on, debtor countries imported very little capital;
indeed, Germany, Canada, and to a lesser extent Poland and Hungary began
exporting capital.

Among creditor countries, the United States was the largest exporter of
capital during the twenties, but it became a significant capital importer in the
thirties. The United States' inflows are mirrored by French outflows between
1934 and 1936, likely due to the overvaluation of the franc and speculation on
its devaluation. The United Kingdom was a significant net exporter of capital in
the twenties, but in the thirties its flows were approximately balanced. Among
the semideveloped democratic debtors, Canada had capital flows that showed
the sharpest peak and plunge from the summit of 1930. The steepest decline in
flows was that of Germany from 1928 to 1931. Between those years, Germany
went from inflows of over a billion dollars to an outflow of almost 600 million.

[29] Countries in our sample for which these data were missing include Austria, Belgium, Czechoslovakia (1923–1924), Greece (1923–1929), Italy (1933–1938), Japan (1937–1938), Romania
(1929–1938), Spain, Yugoslavia (1923–1925 and 1937–1938). See Appendix I for source and
measurement of capital flows.

Creditor Countries

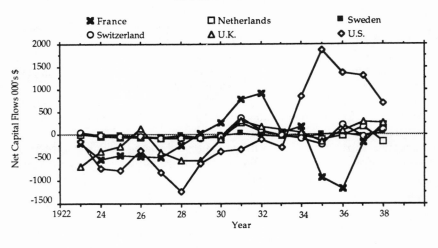

Semideveloped Democratic Regimes

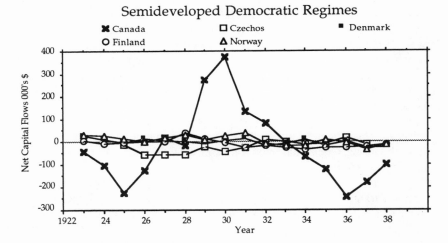

Figure 3.1: Net Capital Flows, by Country

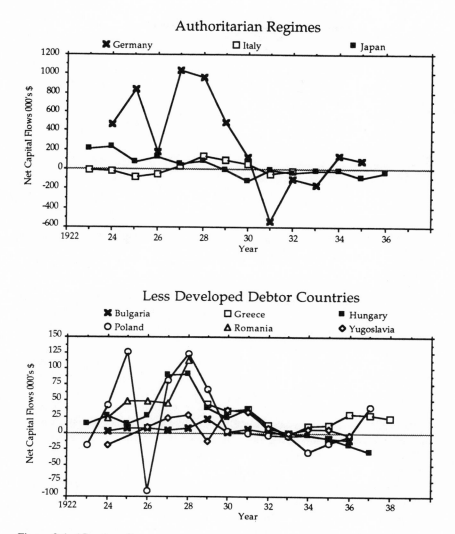

Figure 3.1: (*Continued*)

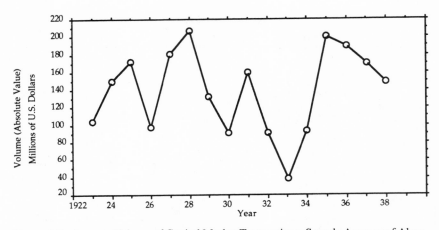

Figure 3.2: Average Volume of Capital Market Transactions: Sample Average of Absolute Values, by Year, 1923–1938

This steep decline has generally been attributed to the pull of the American Stock Exchange during the run up to October 1929, the high American interest rates that were meant to break the speculation, and the increasingly unstable political conditions in Germany.[30]

Capital flows were highly volatile in the interwar years. Figure 3.2 shows the total volumes of capital movements within the sample by year. The years with the largest overall volumes of movements were 1925, 1928, and 1935–1937. The two peaks in the twenties were mostly accounted for by lending to Germany (1925 was the first year of operation of the Dawes Plan). The peak in the thirties was largely due to the flows to the United States, as investors grew suspicious of the French franc and as political tension mounted in Europe before the war.

A different perspective on the significance of capital flows is provided in figure 3.3, which shows average capital flows as a proportion of a country's net national product. Canada exported the most capital in relation to its size, followed by the Netherlands and Poland. Poland, Greece, and Hungary—three countries in deep debt—were also net capital exporters for the period as a whole, while the United States, Sweden, Switzerland, and the United King-

[30] For a good account of German political instability at this time, see Henry Ashby Turner, *Stresemann and the Politics of the Weimar Republic* (Princeton: Princeton University Press), 1963, pp. 220–262. Industrial and unemployment conditions were also deteriorating rapidly. See Harold James, *The German Slump: Politics and Economics 1924–1936* (Oxford: Clarendon Press), 1986, p. 218. See also Erich Eyck, *A History of the Weimar Republic*, Vol. 2: *From the Locarno Conference to Hitler's Seizure of Power* (Cambridge: Harvard University Press), 1963, pp. 192–195.

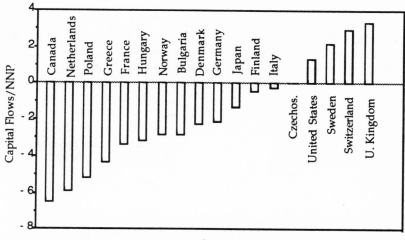

a. Average Capital Flows/Net National Product, 1923–1938; by Country

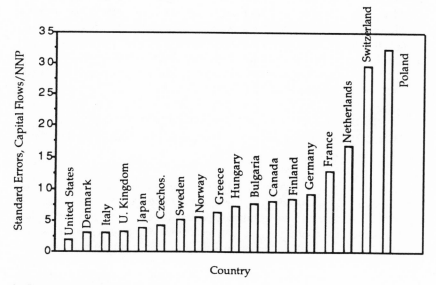

b. Standard Errors, by Country

Figure 3.3: Descriptive Statistics: Capital Flows

dom, all net creditors, imported more capital than they exported on average. Four Gold Bloc countries, Poland, Switzerland, the Netherlands, and France, had the greatest variation in capital flows as a share of net national product, while the United States and Denmark had the smallest.

What determined capital flows during the twenties and thirties? I test a simple economic model and then establish a framework for linking this model via market expectations and government credibility to domestic political conditions. Five political hypotheses are tested, controlling for economic conditions. Finally, I present the evidence and compare the model's fit with the actual capital movements for each country. The evidence is reasonably strong that governments whose credibility was weak were most frequently the victims of capital flight during the interwar years.

Economic Explanations for Capital Flows

Economic accounts emphasize that capital shifts among markets according to two price signals: the price of money in a given country relative to that prevailing elsewhere, and the inflation-adjusted exchange rate. Capital is expected to flow to markets in which interest rates are highest, and into currencies which are least likely to be devalued, that is, currencies with low real exchange rates. We would also expect capital inflows to be greatest to those regions that are growing the fastest. In short, capital flows to markets with the greatest demand, which offer the highest rate of return with the least exchange risk. Hence, changes in real interest rate differentials, real exchange rates, and output[31] are expected to be the primary economic determinants of capital flows (see Appendix I for sources and measurement of these variables).

$$\text{Capital Flows} = a + \beta_1(\Delta\text{Real Interest Rate Differential}) +$$
$$\beta_2(\%\Delta\text{Real Exchange Rate}) + \beta_3(\%\Delta\text{Index of Industrial Production}$$
$$[t - 1]) + e$$

Ordinary least squares estimation of the model explains very little of the variation in observed capital flows, but two of the three variables are statistically significant, and two of these confirm expected directions (table 3.1). Of these three variables, the clearest impact can be attributed to changes in the index of industrial production. With higher growth, more international borrowing was

---

[31] Changes in the real exchange rate have a mild correlation with interest rate differentials (.141). Changes in interest rate differentials are mildly associated with increases in the real exchange rate, which may contribute to an underestimation of these variables' effects in this model. This measure of output (the index of industrial production) is virtually uncorrelated with changes in the real exchange rate in the following year, but is weakly negatively correlated with real interest rate differentials ($-.075$), probably because of price increases that reduce real domestic interest rates in the following year.

TABLE 3.1
Five Models of Changes in Capital Flows for 12 Countries[a], 1924–1939
(Nonstandardized Coefficients; Standard Errors)

Variable	Econ. Model	Domestic Political(1)	Domestic Political(2)	Political Economic	Pol./Econ. w/Inflation Control
Intercept	−.048	.192	.027	.019	.021
Δ Real Interest Rate Differential	−.002 (.003)	—	—	−.007 (.004)	−.007 (.005)
%ΔReal Exchange Rate	−.480*** (.185)	—	—	−.495*** (.206)	−.505*** (.193)
%ΔIndustrial Production $(t - 1)$	.67*** (.231)	—	—	.403 (.246)	.335 (.293)
Democracy	—	−.113 (.139)	—	—	—
Left-wing Government (Democracies)	—	−.051 (.051)	−.016 (.026)	−.005 (.029)	−.003 (.03)
Cabinet Δ	—	−.106*** (.03)	−.109*** (.029)	−.135*** (.033)	−.135*** (.034)
Cent. Bank Indep. (1923–1931)	—	.022*** (.008)	.022*** (.008)	.024*** (.009)	.023*** (.009)
Labor Unrest $(t - 1)$	—	−.098* (.055)	−.102* (.055)	−.111* (.06)	−.113* (.06)
%ΔCost of Living Index $(t - 1)$	—	—	—	—	.254 (.592)
N	166	162	162	139	139
SER	.29	.281	.28	.282	.283
adj. R^2	.073	.096	.097	.187	.182
D.W.	2.231	2.314	2.308	2.419	2.427

Note: * = Significant at .10 level.   ** = Significant at .05 level.   *** = Significant at .025 level.
[a]Included countries: Canada, Czechoslovakia, Denmark, France, Finland, Germany, Hungary, Japan, Netherlands, Norway, Sweden, United Kingdom, United States. Excludes Austria, Belgium, Bulgaria, Greece, Italy, Poland, Spain, Switzerland, Romania, and Yugoslavia, due to missing data.

necessary to finance increased investment and consumption ($p < .0038$). There
is also a convincing relationship between changes in the real exchange rate and
and capital movements. The real interest rate is the only variable that does not
work well.[32] Of course, this test assumes that capital is internationally mobile,
which was not the case for many countries in this sample for the 1930s. Overall,
capital flowed to countries with better growth rates and to countries whose
exchange rates were becoming increasingly competitive given domestic price
levels. Conversely, capital flowed out of countries whose growth was faltering
and which appeared to be defending overvalued currencies.

Domestic Politics and Capital Flows: The Evidence

Capital flows were not just a function of economic variables during the interwar
years. There are good theoretical reasons to believe that markets reacted to the
political writing on the wall, as well as to prevailing economic conditions. The
theory outlined above suggested five political variables that undermined credibility and stimulated capital flight (see Appendix I for sources and measurement):

Regime Type.   One can hypothesize that democratic regimes are perceived as
less likely to be able to make credible monetary commitments. Since democratic regimes were coded *1* and nondemocratic regimes were coded *0*, we
would expect a negative relationship.

Left-Wing Government.   Commitments of monetary stringency are less likely
to be credible when they come from left-wing governments. This is four-point
scale measuring of the degree of left-wing participation in the government.
Observations are restricted to the democratic countries, since the Left was
repressed in the nondemocratic regimes in this sample. The higher the rating,
the greater the left-wing participation in government. Hence, we expect a
negative relationship between this variable and capital flows.

Political Instability.   The more unstable the government, the greater the expected capital flight. There are several possible ways to assess governments'
likely longevity. One way would be to establish a set of underlying political
conditions that are associated with cabinet duration, and then to use these
conditions as part of an explanation for deterioration in the balance of pay-

---

[32] This may be due to the strong assumption—forced on us by data limitations—that bank rates
are a satisfactory substitute for market rates of interest. It did not matter much to the analysis
whether the first or second difference of these interest rate differentials was used, or whether real
world interest rates (U.S. three-month Treasury bills) alone were used. Nor did it matter much to the
overall explanatory power of the model whether the effects of interest rates on creditors were
separated from those of debtors, although higher world interest rates were significantly associated
with capital inflows to the creditor countries.

ments.[33] Due to data limitations, I measure political instability by the number of times each year in which at least 50 percent of the cabinet changed, or else the prime minister was replaced. The minimum value for any given observation is 0, and the maximum is 7.[34]

Central Bank Independence.   The more independent the central bank from political interference, the greater the ability of the economy to attract foreign capital. Independence is measured by a scale that combines data on the method of making appointments, and the degree of governmental supervision of the central bank.[35] Higher scores indicate a greater degree of independence; hence, we should expect a positive relationship with capital flows (see Appendix II).

Labor Unrest.   Strikes engender inflationary expectations among market actors. Labor unrest is measured here as total working days lost due to strikes per population. Labor unrest is expected to be associated with capital outflows, yielding a negative relationship.

Control Variable: Changes in the Consumer Price Index.   Finally, to control for the possibility that capital outflows are simply stimulated by some exogenous inflationary shock, I control for inflation in the previous period. If the

[33] Possible indicators of underlying conditions might include indicators of social conflict; the number of parties in the government (a larger, more unwieldy coalition would be expected to be correlated with shorter cabinet duration); the percentage of the government's parliamentary majority (a larger majority would be expected to be associated with greater cabinet duration); or the degree of fractionalization of the parliament or of the government itself (a higher degree of fractionalization should be associated with cabinets of shorter duration). These hypotheses are found in David Sanders and Valentine Herman, "The Stability and Survival of Governments in Western Democracies," *Acta Politica*, Vol. 12, 1977, pp. 346–377; Michael Taylor and Valentine Herman, "Party Systems and Government Stability," p. 32; and Ekkart Zimmermann, "The Puzzle of Government Duration: Evidence from Six European Countries during the Interwar Years," *Comparative Politics*, Vol. 20, No. 3, April 1988, pp. 341–357. For measures of fractionalization see Giovanni Sartori, *Parties and Party Systems: A Framework for Analysis* (Cambridge: Cambridge University Press), 1976; Douglas W. Rae, "A Note on the Fractionalization of Some European Party Systems," *Comparative Political Studies*, Vol. 1, October 1968, pp. 413–418; Rae, *The Political Consequences of Electoral Laws* (New Haven: Yale University Press), 1971.

[34] The countries that were most stable on average by this definition for the period as a whole were Denmark and the United States, while the least stable were Austria and France. Switzerland was also among the three most stable in the sample; and Greece, Romania, and Spain were among the three least stable, but balance of payments information is missing for these countries. The year of greatest instability was 1933, followed closely by 1935 and 1926. The two most stable years were 1937 and 1927.

[35] Originally, I included measures of ownership and formal limits to the provision of liquidity in this measure, but both theoretical considerations (supervisory authority is clearly more important than ownership itself, which may be pro forma and need not imply policy input) and empirical problems (liquidity limits were difficult to determine with any degree of consistency across countries) led me to settle on this two-dimensional measure of independence.

political variables continue to have a significant correlation with capital outflows, then this would support an interpretation that the results found here are not simply an epiphenomenon of an inflationary shock that itself both destabilized the government and contributed to capital outflows. In other words, if the results of this political model hold even when the previous period's inflation is taken into account, then we can be relatively certain that political conditions have a significant impact on capital flows independent of the effects of a prior exogenous inflation.

To test this credibility-based interpretation of changes in capital movements the following equation was estimated using ordinary least squares (OLS):

Capital Flows = a + β_1(ΔReal Interest Rate Differential) + β_2(%ΔReal Exchange Rate) + β_3(%ΔIndex of Industrial Production [$t - 1$]) + β_4(Democracy) + β_5(Left-wing Government*Democracy) + β_6(Cabinet Turnover) + β_7(Central Bank Independence,23–31) + β_8(Labor Unrest[$t - 1$]) + β_9(%ΔCost of living Index[$t - 1$])) + e

The results of this equation, as well as two strictly political models of capital flows, are presented in table 3.1. In all versions of the model, three out of five of the domestic political variables are statistically significant in the expected directions. The variable that has the strongest correlation with capital flows in this model is cabinet instability.[36] The negative correlation signifies that higher turnover is associated with capital outflows, as our discussion of short time horizon and credibility would predict. This relationship will be explored more fully in Chapter 5, which examines the stabilization of the franc in the twenties. As that case illustrates, markets rejected the franc as long as extreme government instability made it unlikely that monetary policy would be anything but

[36] While the use of standardized coefficients to find the "relative weight" of each variable in determining the outcome is controversial due to sensitivity to the underlying distribution, the following seems to indicate just how important both cabinet instability and central bank independence are in explaining the flow of capital. (Since the coefficients are fairly constant across models, approximate average coefficients are reported.)

Variable	Standardized Coefficient
Real interest rate differentials	−.13
%ΔReal exchange rate	−.19
%ΔIndustrial production (IIP)	.11
Left-wing government (democracies)	−.01
Cabinet Δ	−.32
Central bank independence (1923–1939)	.20
Labor unrest ($t - 1$)	−.15
%ΔCost of living ($t - 1$)	.04

inflationary. With ten major cabinet changes between 1924 and 1926, it is plausible that the ensuing capital flight can be attributed at least in part to markets' assessment that French governments would not be able to achieve their proclaimed goals of balancing the budget and defending the franc as long as instability persisted.

Central bank independence also had a significant impact on capital flows, at least for the years between 1923 and 1931. This confirms my hypothesis and the conventional wisdom of the twenties, that independent central banks were important in establishing confidence, because they could refuse to monetize government budget deficits. This would explain why capital seems to have flowed more readily toward countries with such independent institutions, and away from those that were perceived as being under government control. The fact that the central bank variable is quite stable and highly significant across all versions of the basic model provides strong evidence that independence improves the monetary authorities' ability to make credible claims with respect to monetary policy.

This finding accords with what we know about the negotiating strategies of central bankers and financiers during this period. In the 1920s, the Bank of England and the Federal Reserve Bank of New York, along with prominent members of the American and British financial sectors, often conditioned their stabilization assistance on improvements in the institutional independence of national central banks. Where League of Nations assistance was involved, the British rewrote central bank statutes to try and insulate national monetary authorities from political pressures to finance government budget deficits. Even the Banque de France was pressured by the Americans and British between 1924 and 1926 to stand up to the Trésor. These patterns of behavior make perfect sense in light of the finding that negative changes in capital flows are associated with politically dependent central banks. External political pressures were brought to bear to improve the credibility of domestic monetary authorities.

The final domestic political variable that was statistically significant and in the expected direction was labor unrest. Since the time inconsistency model assumes that governments are tempted to inflate to overcome market distortions, then the greater the potential for these distortions, the greater the size of the needed stimulation, the more likely inflation and hence capital flight. These results underscore the plausibility of this interpretation, though only at about the 94 percent confidence level. The larger the number of working days lost to strikes, the more negative were changes in capital flows. The best example of this relationship is the case of the general strike in Britain (1926), involving more than 2.7 million workers and resulting in 167 million working days lost. The following year, capital outflows accelerated. In fact, capital left Britain more precipitously in 1927 (relative to the size of the British economy and the world volume of capital movements) than it did in either 1931 or 1932. Norway, too, experienced widespread strikes in both 1924 and 1931, and big negative changes showed up in the capital accounts in the following years.[37]

Two of the political variables apparently had little to do with capital flows. Whether or not a country was democratic did have the expected negative relationship with capital flows, but was not statistically significant ($p = .416$). The other domestic political expectation that we failed to confirm is the influence of the Left on capital flows ($p = .87$). The sign on left-wing participation is in the expected direction, but the standard error is so large that it is difficult to assign much impact to increased participation of the Left in the government.[38]

Finally, the economic controls included in the final version of the model provide good evidence that the political explanation advanced here is not simply an epiphenomenon of economic conditions. One might question whether cabinet instability leads to capital flight, as argued here, or whether an exogenous inflation both destabilizes governments and simultaneously encourages capital to flee. The inclusion of the change in the cost of living index in the previous period removes prior inflation as a plausible explanation of capital flight, and shows that the causal story outlined here is more likely. If the whole explanation was due to exogenous inflation (with endogenous instability), then cabinet turnover should have dropped out of the final model and change in the cost of living should have proved significant. This did not occur. Moreover, the cost of living index is barely associated with instability the next period (correlation $= -.027$). The instability variable also survives the inclusion of the index of industrial production in the previous period, which makes exogenous recession (with endogenous cabinet instability) an implausible explanation for the bulk of capital outflows. (The correlation between the index of industrial production and instability in the following period is $-.113$.) These data suggest that markets' distrust of unstable governments, rather than exogenous economic conditions, is the most convincing causal interpretation of the data.[39]

Fit between the Model and Actual Changes in Capital Flows

The combined political/economic model proposed here explained just under a fifth of the variance in capital flow changes for the period under consideration.

[37] Note that labor unrest is the only political variable that required a one-year lag. The relationship does not hold when contemporaneous observations are used. This is probably because strikes are the most volatile of the five political variables from year to year, and the timing of data collection may explain the need for the lag.

[38] The result is the same whether we consider the Left as a percentage of parliament or whether we use a dichotomous variable for governments with major left-wing participation versus governments with little or no left-wing participation; whether all regime types or democracies alone were considered; or whether the variable was lagged or considered contemporaneously with the dependent variable. There was no evidence that the Left had any impact on capital flows.

[39] Recall that the data have been standardized for the volume of capital movements in any one year, so that I am not modeling the collapse of capital markets in 1930, but rather the shifting of available capital to and from the countries in this sample.

Nonetheless, it explained this fifth with a high degree of certainty ($p = .0001$). Explaining a high proportion of variance is usually much more difficult when the dependent variable is a flow rather than a stock, as are capital movements. Figure 3.4 shows how well the combined model performed by comparing the fitted values with the actual observations of the dependent variable.

The countries for which the model is especially strong are France, Hungary, Japan (in the twenties), and to a lesser extent Norway and the United Kingdom. It is also reasonably accurate for the United States in the thirties. The pattern in the Netherlands is that of a small country that was subject to sharp swings as capital fled first the pound (the large positive change in 1931) and then the currencies of the Gold Bloc (the large negative change in 1932 and 1933). Outside of these exaggerations, the model works well for the Netherlands. Overall, for the more liberal market-oriented economies—where real exchange rates, interest rate differentials, and domestic political conditions can be expected to be especially relevant—this model generates fairly good fits.

The model is especially weak for Czechoslovakia, Germany, and Japan in the thirties. This should not be surprising since these countries had extensive capital and currency controls during that time, which would make the model much less applicable. All three of these countries had smaller capital outflows than the model would suggest because of the strict regulations prohibiting capital and currency transactions. Germany imposed exchange controls in the third quarter of 1931. Almost immediately, the model predicts negative changes where observed values jump to the positive region. The pattern observed in Japan clearly shows the effect of capital controls on changes in flows: Japan implemented stringent controls in the third quarter of 1932, a year of a negative change in flows when the model would have predicted a positive change. Immediately, capital flows improved, but the model continued to predict outflows on the basis of the underlying economic and political conditions. The same pattern applies to Czechoslovakia. Exchange controls were implemented in the third quarter of 1931. Unlike Germany and Japan, however, Czechoslovakia gradually liberalized controls over the course of the thirties. Accordingly, in 1932 and 1933 the model fits values much more negative than those actually observed. But the plots gradually come back together in 1934 and 1935, until they finally cross in 1937. As the Czechs liberalized their restrictions, the model provided a better fit with reality. It is likely that strict external controls play havoc with the model in several instances in the 1930s.[40]

Figures 3.5a and b show how the residuals are distributed on average by year and by country. If an important variable has been left out of the model, we should be able to discern a pattern in the clustering of the residuals in time or by economy type. I have already discussed the error that was introduced by applying free market assumptions to countries with severe currency controls. Yet the

[40] For an excellent review of Germany's, Japan's, Czechoslovakia's, and other countries' policies on exchange controls, see the League of Nations, *Report on Exchange Controls* (Geneva: Committee on Exchange Controls), 9 July 1938.

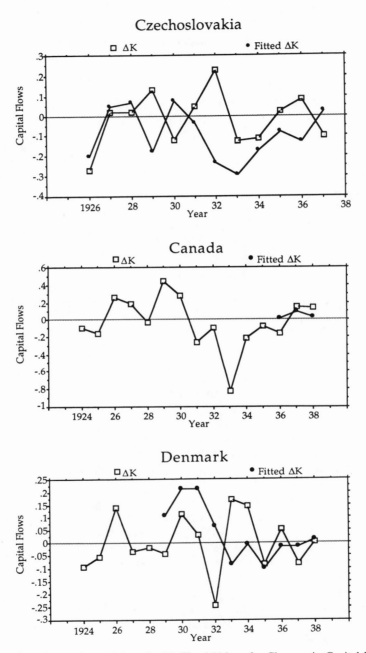

Figure 3.4: Comparison of Actual with Fitted Values for Changes in Capital Flows (Political/Economic Model)

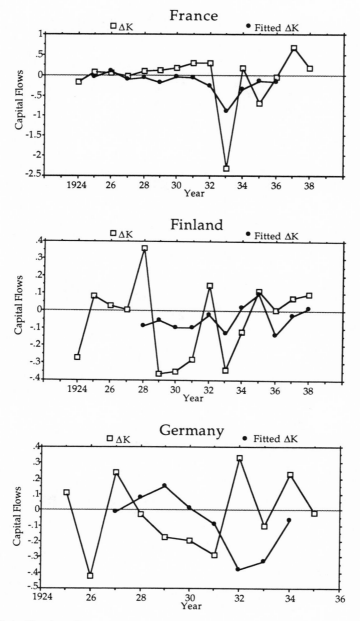

Figure 3.4: (*Continued*)

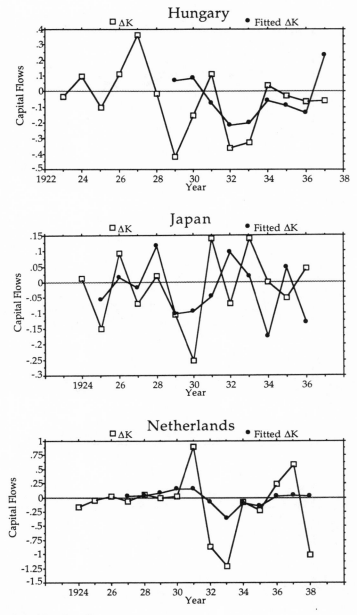

Figure 3.4: (*Continued*)

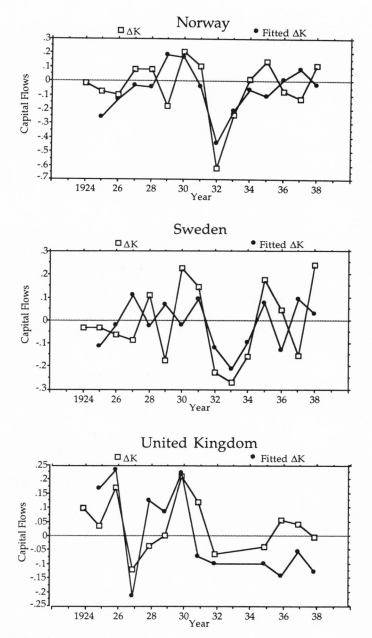

Figure 3.4: (*Continued*)

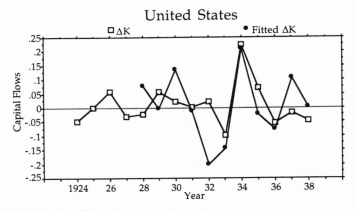

Figure 3.4: (*Continued*)

country residuals do not seem to fall into an easy liberal/democratic versus controlled/authoritarian pattern. France never implemented either currency or capital controls, and yet falls above the line with Germany and Czechoslovakia. Hungary had relatively stringent controls, and yet falls below the line with the liberal Netherlands. There does not appear to be any obvious pattern to the residuals by country.

A pattern in the residuals is somewhat more worrisome by year, although there appears to be no obvious problem of autocorrelation (the Durbin Watson statistic is in the acceptable range of about 2.4). But all three of the extreme outliers are years in which devaluations of one of the major currencies took place: 1931 and 1936 are well above the line, while the year of dollar deprecia- tion (1933) is well below. This is easily explained by the fact that capital outflows from France in 1936 were a relatively small part of that country's Net National Product (NNP), but the increased inflows it represented (see Sweden, Finland, and Czechoslovakia) were fairly significant. The larger than predicted inflows for these three smaller countries could drive up the overall 1936 resid- uals. The reason 1933 is so underpredicted is that real exchange rates were calculated in this model on the basis of the bilateral dollar rate. The wholesale shift of real exchange rates for every country in the sample in 1933 may cause the negative change in capital flows to be much stronger than it should be for countries for which the dollar bilateral rate was not as important as the value of the pound, franc, or mark. Czechoslovakia, Denmark, Germany, and Japan are all countries whose changes in capital flows were all better than expected for 1933, possibly for this reason.

Finally, we should consider whether this discussion of political explanations of capital flows has added anything to a more traditional economic explanation. The combined model does account for a higher proportion of the explained

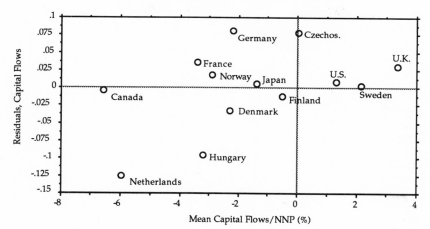

a. Residuals by Country

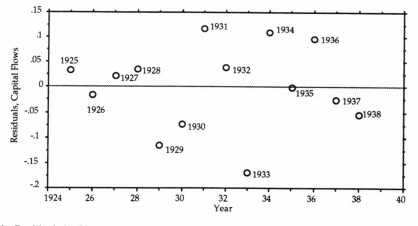

b. Residuals by Year

Figure 3.5: Residuals for Capital Flows (Political/Economic Model)

variance than either the political or economic models alone, but it is difficult to draw a firm conclusion since there are fewer observations and hence presumably less variance included in the combined model. Table 3.2 compares the ability of each of these models accurately to predict capital flows for each country: it shows that for seven countries the average absolute difference between the fitted and actual capital flows was smaller when political variables were used or were included in the model, compared to the pure economic model. For Canada, Czechoslovakia, Denmark, France, the Netherlands, Nor-

TABLE 3.2

Average Difference between Fitted Capital Flows
and Actual Capital Flows for Three Models

Country	Economic Model	Political/ Economic Model	Political Model
Canada	.136	**.116**	.145
Czechoslovakia	.148	.156	**.118**
Denmark	.126	.130	**.120**
France	.372	**.370**	**.370**
Finland	**.168**	.186	.202
Germany	**.231**	.291	.265
Hungary	**.169**	.189	.183
Japan	**.101**	.116	.105
Netherlands	.402	.382	**.364**
Norway	.162	.139	**.122**
Sweden	**.130**	.139	.145
United Kingdom	**.084**	.104	.101
United States	.084	.078	**.068**
Total Number of Best Models[a]	6	2	6
Average	.177	.186	.180

Method: For each country: | Fitted Y − Actual Y | / N; where *n* = number of fitted Y for each country. Boldface indicates the smallest average difference between fitted and actual capital flows.

[a]Including ties.

way, and the United States, the political or the combined model explanations generated better estimated capital flows than did the economic model alone.

THE CURRENT ACCOUNT

If political variables influence a government's credible commitment to a conservative monetary policy, as the above evidence suggests, then they should also contribute to a worsening current account, as inflation makes domestic goods increasingly expensive compared to imports. This section tests the relationship between regime type, influence of the Left, government stability, central bank independence, and labor unrest and the current account balance. The first section presents descriptive statistics on the current accounts of sixteen countries for the period under consideration. The second section presents a simple economic model of the current account, which emphasizes the importance of economic growth (at home and abroad), changes in the real exchange rate, and interest rates. The third section tests for the significance of five domestic political variables, and the final section compares the fitted values for the current account with the actual observed values and analyzes patterns in the residuals.

Once again, the impact of domestic politics on the current account is striking. The strongest and most consistent finding is that unstable governments are associated with deteriorating current account positions; greater Left representation and greater labor unrest were also associated with current account deficits. Central bank independence, associated with confidence in the tests above, is also correlated with better current account positions, but the differences were not statistically significant. Overall, *even when controlling for economic and foreign shocks*, three domestic variables are associated with current account deterioration. Over time, such deterioration would be inconsistent with the first norm of the gold standard.

Descriptive Statistics of Current Account Balances, 1923–1939

This section describes the distribution of yearly current account positions for seventeen countries between 1923 and 1939.[41] In total, statistics could only be found for 245 observations. The measure employed here is a country's balance of payments on current account relative to its NNP. More than three quarters of all observations (191) fell within the interval between -2 percent and $+2$ percent of NNP (figure 3.6). Austria experienced by far the most serious balance of payments deficits, averaging a deficit of over 5 percent of NNP during the interwar years as a whole (a whopping 14 percent of NNP in 1923). Hungary also performed significantly worse than the average, with a mean deficit of 2.1 percent. Other countries with worse than average deficits included Bulgaria, Italy, Japan, Norway, and Poland. On the other hand, Czechoslovakia and Finland had balance of payments *surpluses* that were significantly above the sample average. The greatest surplus in the sample was that of Finland in 1933 (7.4 percent of NNP). Canada, France, the Netherlands, Sweden, the United Kingdom, and the United States also had balances that were more positive than average, though not significantly so (figure 3.6a and table 3.3). In addition, there were wide differences in the degree of variation in balance of payments fluctuations among these countries. The United States and Italy had the least variability, while Finland, Canada, and Bulgaria had the most (figure 3.6b).

The worst average balance of payments for this sample was during the years

---

[41] Balance of payments statistics were not available for six countries in the original sample. They were Belgium, Greece, Spain, Romania, Switzerland, and Yugoslavia. Significant portions of the series are also missing for Germany (1926–1929), Hungary (early 1920s and late 1930s), and the Netherlands (1923–1929). Since we are concerned here with current account balance (goods, services, and interest payments), it is difficult to guess the current account position of Belgium and Switzerland (net creditors but with trade deficits) and Romania and Yugoslavia (net debtors but with trade surpluses). Greece and Spain's current accounts were probably unambiguously negative, since they were both net debtors and had balance of trade deficits.

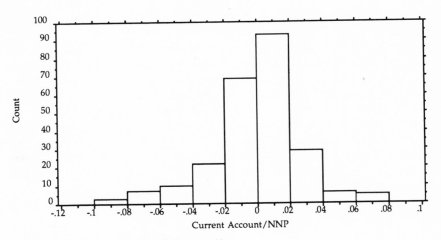

a. Frequency Distribution for all Country-Years

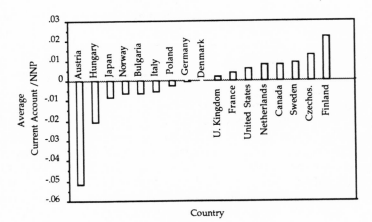

b. Average Current Account Balance, by Country

Figure 3.6: Current Account Balance/Net National Product, 1923–1939

in which most countries were on the gold standard. For the stabilization period (1923–1926), the average payments deficit was .5 percent of NNP, not significantly different than that for the interwar years as a whole. Deficits were much worse on average (1 percent of NNP; $p = .0009$) between 1927 and 1931, when most countries were on a gold standard. After 1931, the sample averaged a surplus of .6 percent of NNP, which was significantly better than the two decades taken as a whole ($p = .0001$). This pattern suggests that international

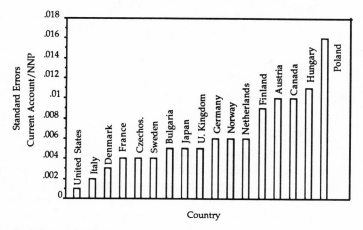

c. Standard Errors, by Country

Figure 3.6: (*Continued*)

TABLE 3.3
Current Account Position, by Country, 1923–1939

Country	Count	Mean	Std. Error	t statistic	Probability (2-tailed)
Austria	14	−.052	.01	−7.554	.0001
Hungary	12	−.021	.011	−2.505	.0129
Japan	17	−.009	.005	−1.215	.2256
Norway	17	−.007	.006	−.779	.4367
Bulgaria	13	−.007	.005	−.771	.4412
Italy	17	−.006	.002	−.722	.471
Poland	3	−.003	.016	−.126	.9002
Germany	11	−.001	.006	.079	.937
Denmark	17	−.0001	.014	.18	.8573
United Kingdom	17	.002	.005	.514	.6074
France	16	.004	.004	.81	.4189
United States	17	.006	.001	1.171	.2428
Netherlands	10	.008	.006	1.026	.306
Canada	17	.008	.01	1.445	.1496
Sweden	17	.009	.004	1.629	.1047
Czechoslovakia	13	.013	.004	1.941	.0535
Finland	17	.020	.039	3.579	.0004

Note: Arranged by mean deficit; probability refers to the two-tailed test that average current account of a given country is *not* significantly different from the sample as a whole.

adjustment was taking place during the early 1920s via the exchange rate, a mode of adjustment that was not available during the gold standard period.[42] The move toward greater surpluses in the 1930s reflects the collapse of agricultural prices and the desire to preserve home production during depression. The "periphery" (British Empire and Latin America, which are not included in this sample), rather than the center, was running the deficits in the 1930s.

A Simple Economic Model of the Current Account

The current account represents the difference between a country's total income and its total spending. It represents what is left of domestic output after consumption, investment, and government expenditures have been satisfied, plus net interest payments on past borrowing or lending. The most important economic determinants of a country's current account position are likely to include relative prices and relative demand (which will affect the balance of trade) and world interest rates (which affect net interest payments or earnings).[43]

Most simple models of the current account posit an import function that depends on national income: the greater the national income, the greater will be the demand for imports. Since exports are likely to be exogenously determined (e.g., by foreign growth and demand), as national income rises, we would expect to find a worsening balance of trade. The balance of trade is also influenced by the relationship between prices of domestic and foreign goods on the world market. Relative prices are best captured by real exchange rates,

[42] This interpretation is substantiated by the exchange rate data presented in Chapter 4: the years 1923–1926 had significantly more depreciation but better current account balance, while 1927–1931 had greater currency stability but significantly worse imbalance in external payments. The 1930s saw significantly more depreciation than for the period as a whole, and the sample was on average in surplus—evidence consistent with the proposition that adjustment was taking place through the exchange rate.

[43] The impact of interest rates will be ambiguous, however, since it will differ depending on whether or not a country was in a negative balance in the previous period. For cases in which the previous position was deficit, increased world interest rates have two effects. First, higher interest rates encourage savings over consumption (a substitution effect). For a country in deficit in the previous period, they also produce negative income effects, by raising the costs of debt service. Lower income reduces consumption and imports, improving a country's balance in the next period. It is not clear, however, whether or not the income effect will counterbalance the added burden of debt servicing to the current account balance. For cases of previous deficit, then, higher world interest rates will have an ambiguous effect on the current account in the next period. The expectations for countries in a surplus position in the previous period will likewise be ambiguous. As in deficit countries, higher interest rates encourage savings over investment, which should have a positive influence on the balance of payments. But unlike deficit countries, higher interest rates contribute positively to income, which is expected to increase consumption and worsen slightly the balance of payments. The effect of higher world interest rates on the balance of payments is therefore ambiguous for surplus countries; but to the extent that substitution effects dominate income effects, we might expect a small positive impact. Because of the ambiguity of the outcomes, no significant effects were in fact found with respect to interest rate changes. They were therefore excluded from the analysis.

which take domestic price ratios into account. When the real exchange rate increases (domestic prices are relatively high), we should expect a deterioration in the balance of trade and hence on the overall current account.

A simple model of the balance on current account would include real exchange rates, domestic growth rates,[44] and foreign growth rates. Since the autocorrelation functions for the current account balance for each country displayed significant evidence of one-period autocorrelation, a lagged dependent variable was included,[45] as were dummy variables for each country. Hence, the balance on current account is modeled as follows:

Current Account Balance = a + β_{1-14}(Country Dummies) + β_{15}(Current Account Balance[$t - 1$]) + β_{16}(%ΔReal Exchange Rates [$t - 1$]) + β_{17}(%ΔIndustrial Production[past 2 years]) + β_{18}(%ΔIndustrial Production, Trade Partner[$t - 1$]) + e

The results are reported in the first column of table 3.4. (Coefficients for dummies are found in the Appendix to Chapter 3.) These variables account for about two thirds of the variation for the balance of payments among these countries at this time. All three of our expectations are resoundingly confirmed. The strongest relationship was that between changes in domestic income and the current account. The results are unambiguous: higher real exchange rates worsen a country's balance on current account because its goods are simply too expensive compared to foreign alternatives. Higher domestic growth stimulates the demand for imports, and the obverse is true for higher growth among a country's major trade partners. Higher domestic growth therefore contributes to a deterioration in the current account, while foreign growth contributes to a surplus.

The Current Account and Domestic Politics

While all countries tend to borrow at times to smooth consumption, and while it is quite natural to run a deficit for short periods of time or under certain economic circumstances, this section points to domestic political conditions which have a *systematic* effect on a country's current account, due to inflationary pressures that build when a government's monetary commitments are incredible. This is a crucial finding because it throws into question the ability of governments to abide by Norm 1 under particular domestic political conditions. To test this interpretation of the current account, the five domestic political variables are used in conjunction with the economic variables (table 3.4).

[44] Changes in the index of industrial production were used to approximate domestic growth rates.

[45] I decided against testing the first difference of the dependent variable, since the lagged dependent variable in the following tests is almost certainly not 1 (it ranges in the following tests between .5 and .6).

TABLE 3.4
Five Models of the Current Account for 15 Countries[a], 1925–1939
(Nonstandardized Coefficients; Standard Errors)

Variable	Econ. Model	Domestic Political(1)	Domestic Political(2)	Political/ Economic	Pol./Econ. w/Inflation Control
Intercept	.00007	.004	.003	−.013	−.01
Current Account $(t-1)$	.6*** (.055)	.586*** (.061)	.587*** (.058)	.494*** (.06)	.496*** (.06)
%ΔReal Exchange Rate $(t-1)$	−.024*** (.01)	—	—	−.021** (.01)	−.022** (.01)
%ΔIndustrial Production (past 2 years)	−.035*** (.007)	—	—	−.042*** (.007)	−.045*** (.007)
%ΔIndustrial Production, Maj. Trade Partner $(t-1)$	.04*** (.012)	—	—	.051*** (.011)	.047*** (.012)
Democratic	—	−.0004 (.007)	—	—	—

%Left in Parliament (t − 1)	—	−.00036**	−.00036***	−.000394***	−.00044***
	—	(.00017)	(.00016)	(.00014)	(.000145)
Cabinet Turnover	—	−.003	−.003	−.007***	−.006***
	—	(.002)	(.002)	(.002)	(.002)
Labor Unrest	—	−.007*	−.007*	−.006*	−.006*
	—	(.004)	(.004)	(.003)	(.003)
Central Bank Independence (t − 1)	—	.005	.005	.009*	.009*
	—	(.005)	(.005)	(.004)	(.004)
ΔCost of Living (t − 1)	—	—	—	—	.044
	—	—	—	—	(.033)
N	173	176	176	146	146
SER	.016	.017	.017	.014	.014
adj. R^2	.636	.617	.62	.712	.714

Note: * = Significant at .10 level.   ** = Significant at .05 level.   *** = Significant at .025 level. These results include dummy variables for each country. See Appendix, Table 3.A. for complete results.

[a]Included countries: Austria, Canada, Czechoslovakia, Denmark, France, Finland, Germany, Hungary, Japan, Netherlands, Norway, Poland (two observations only), Sweden, United Kingdom, United States. Excludes Belgium, Bulgaria, Italy, Spain, Switzerland, Romania, and Yugoslavia, due to missing data.

Current Account Balance $= a + \beta_{1-14}$(Country Dummies) $+$
β_{15}(Current Account Balance$[t - 1]$) $+ \beta_{16}$(%ΔReal Exchange Rates
$[t - 1]$) $+ \beta_{17}$(%ΔIndustrial Production[past 2 years]) $+$
β_{18}(%ΔIndustrial Production, Trade Partner$[t - 1]$) $+ \beta_{19}$(Democracy)
$+ \beta_{20}$(%Left in Parliament$[t - 1]$) $+ \beta_{21}$(Cabinet Turnover) $+$
β_{22}(Labor Unrest) $+ \beta_{23}$(Central Bank Independence$[t - 1]$) $+ e$

The results of this equation and variations on it are also presented in table 3.4.
This model explains almost 70 percent of the variation in the current account for
some twelve to fifteen countries for most of the 1920s and 1930s. All of the
economic variables remain highly statistically significant in the expected direction, as are four out of five of the political variables.

The most consistent result across all versions of the model is that increased
representation of working-class parties in parliament contributed to a deterioration in the current account.[46] The results suggest that each percentage point
increase in left-wing representation in the parliament was associated with a
decrease in the current account of almost .04 percent of NNP. The influence of
left-wing representation was stable whether or not the democracy dummy was
included, which increases confidence that these results are not due to regime
type rather than the influence of the Left per se. These results support an
interpretation that associates the Left with a weakened current account in the
next period. One interpretation is that markets behave as though left-wing
governments are more concerned with domestic economic conditions than they
are with external balance. They anticipate attempts at domestic expansion,
causing inflation, and placing the current account under pressure.

Cabinet instability clearly contributed to current account deterioration in the
combined political/economic models. Whether or not we control inflation in
the previous period, an additional cabinet change in a year is associated with a
current account that is .7 of a percentage point less as a proportion of NNP. This
finding supports the credibility theory: markets believe that unstable governments will pursue inflationary policies (since they have no incentive to face the

[46] Standardized coefficients were as follows (political/economic model; country dummy variables are not reported):

Variable	Standardized Coefficient
Current account $(t - 1)$	.53
%ΔReal exchange rate $(t - 1)$	−.11
%ΔIIP (past two years)	−.35
%ΔIIP major trade partner $(t - 1)$	.24
%Left in parliament $(t - 1)$	−.19
Cabinet Δ	−.17
Labor unrest	−.09
Central bank independence $(t - 1)$	.77

negative short-term repercussions of retrenchment). Inflationary pressures build, with a predictable adverse impact on the current account.

Across all models, the effect of strike activity on the current account was negative. The greater the proportion of working days lost to strikes per population, the greater was the current account deficit. A 1 percent increase in this measure of labor unrest was associated with a .6 percent drop in the current account as a proportion of NNP. These results underscore the importance of conditions in the labor market in affecting a country's current account position. Strikes set off inflationary expectations (they also cut into production, which could reduce exports without reducing the demand for imports), which appears to have forced the current account toward deficit. The most vivid example of the damage to the current account caused by industrial unrest was the downward dive in the British current account in 1926, the year of the general strike.

The final domestic variable that appears to influence the current account is the independence of the central bank, although this variable meets standard tests of significance only in the two final versions of the model. The positive relationship fits our theoretical expectation: the more independent central banks tended to maintain price stability and external balance far more than did their politically controlled counterparts. Independent central banks' perceived willingness to place external balance above domestic economic conditions meant that they were better able to live up to the first norm of the gold standard.

The models tested here failed to confirm a statistically significant relationship between regime type and the current account. Whether or not a regime was democratic did not add anything to our estimate of the model, and this variable was removed in successive versions.

Once again it is important to note that the data presented here imply a specific direction of causation from political variables to current account deterioration. The inclusion of the lagged growth and inflation variables makes it unlikely that we would get these results if the political variable were the endogenous result of economic conditions prevailing in the previous year or two. Were this so, the political variables should have been weakened in the combined model with previous inflation controlled.[47] Instead, the combined model generally produced more convincing coefficients and smaller standard errors. These results make it very difficult to dismiss the critical impact of domestic politics on a country's external economic balance.

Fit between the Model and the Current Account

This model of the current account predicted almost 70 percent of the variance for the twelve countries in this sample between 1926 and 1939. Moreover, it explained this portion of the variation with a high degree of certainty (p

---

[47]Nearly identical results to those presented in the far-right-hand column were obtained when a two-year lag was used on the cost of living index.

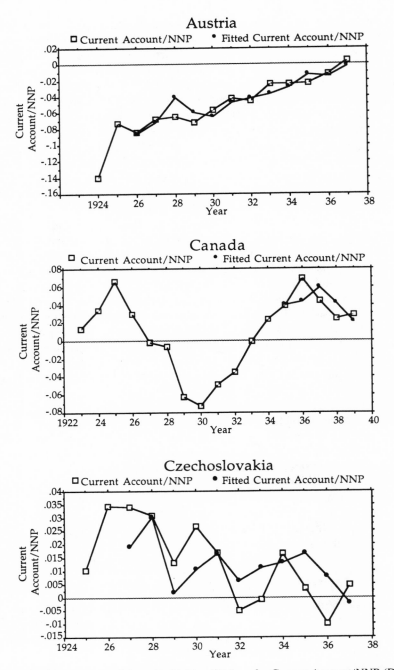

Figure 3.7: Comparison of Actual with Fitted Values for Current Account/NNP (Domestic Political Model 2)

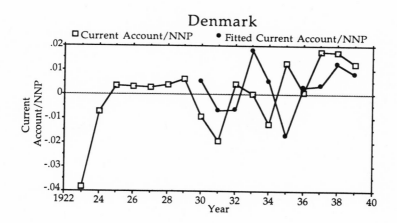

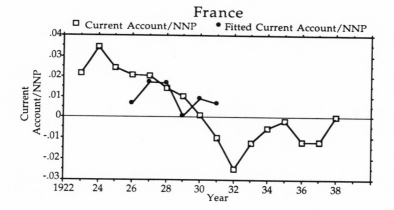

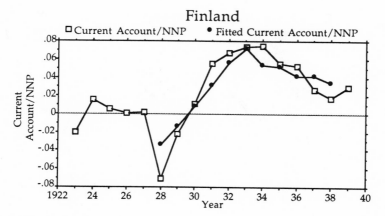

Figure 3.7: (*Continued*)

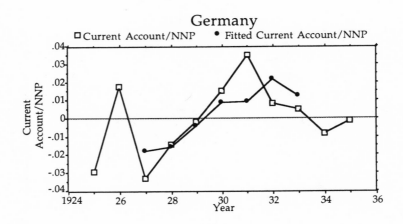

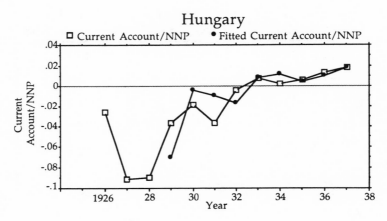

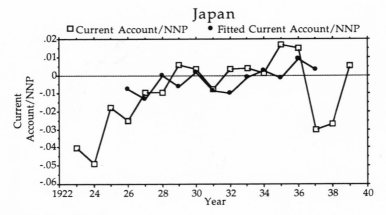

Figure 3.7: (*Continued*)
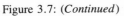

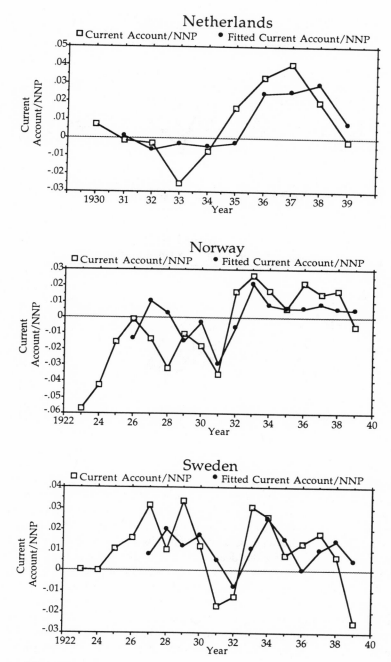

Figure 3.7: (*Continued*)

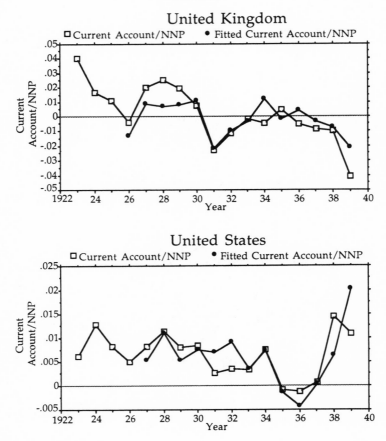

Figure 3.7: (*Continued*)

= .0001). Figure 3.7 shows just how well the model performed by comparing the fitted values with the actual observations of the dependent variable. The gradual current account improvement in Austria is captured almost precisely by the model, as is the more complex path of the British current account. The model has an impressive fit with Norway's external position, with the exception of missing the deep deficit in 1928. Both Germany and the Netherlands are tracked closely, except that Germany did better than expected in 1931 and not as well as expected in 1932, and the model misses the Netherlands' deep deficit in 1933. The model also does well in explaining the United States' current account, with the exception of 1938 and 1939. The model is much less successful in predicting the swings in the Swedish balance of payments in the 1920s and the Danish balance of payments between 1929 and 1934.

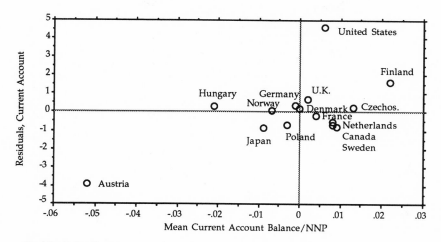

a. Residuals by Country

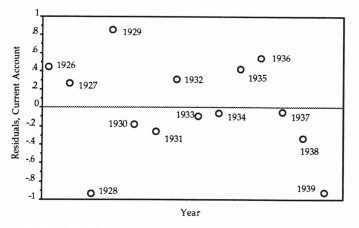

b. Residuals by Year

Figure 3.8: Residuals for Current Account (Domestic Political Model 2)

Figure 3.8 shows how the residuals are distributed on average by year and by country. If an important variable has been left out of the model, we should be able to discern a pattern in the clustering of the residuals in time or by economy type. Such a pattern is not obvious by year. (Note that Durbin-Watson statistics are not reported because of the inclusion of the lagged dependent variable.)

TABLE 3.5
Average Difference between Fitted Current Account
and Actual Current Acount for Three Models

Country	Economic Model	Political/ Economic Model	Political Model (2)
Austria	.009	**.008**	.011
Canada	.019	.013	**.012**
Czechoslovakia	**.010**	**.010**	.011
Denmark	.012	.013	**.009**
France	**.006**	.009	.008
Finland	**.013**	.014	.019
Germany	.014	**.010**	.016
Hungary	**.012**	**.012**	.021
Japan	**.010**	**.010**	.011
Netherlands	.012	**.010**	.013
Norway	.014	.013	**.011**
Sweden	.015	**.013**	**.013**
United Kingdom	.011	**.008**	.009
United States	.005	**.003**	.004
Total Number of Best Models[a]	5	9	4
Average	.009	.010	.012

Method: For each country: $\mid$ Fitted Y $-$ Actual Y $\mid$ / n; where $n =$ number of fitted Y for each country. Boldface indicates the smallest average difference between fitted and actual capital flows.

[a] Including ties.

Boom years and depression years fell both above and below the line.[48] Austria is strongly negative because the ratio of its current account deficit to NNP was so much larger than any other country to begin with that the sum of errors was bound to make that country an outlier. Overall, there are no egregious patterns in the distribution of average residuals, either by year or by country, which increases our confidence that relevant variables have not been omitted from the analysis.

Table 3.5 compares the average difference between the actual current account and the fitted values generated by the economic, the political/economic, and the pure political models. For most countries, the political/economic model produced fits that were closest to the actual current account. Only in the case of

[48] The overprediction of the model in 1928 is due almost entirely to larger than predicted deficits in two Nordic countries, Norway and Finland. Note that a Durbin Watson statistic would not be valid for this model since it includes a lagged dependent variable on the right-hand side of the equation.

France and Finland did the economic model clearly outperform the two others. The combined model performed best overall by this measure, generating fitted current account measures for nine countries that were as good or better than either contending model.

CONCLUSIONS

Economic and political theories are complementary in a study of the balance of payments. Economic explanations emphasize that real exchange rates, real interest rates, and growth rates should be the primary determinants of capital flows, while relative prices and relative demand should be the primary economic determinants of the current account. But there are also political influences on the balance of payments. I have argued that when governments' commitments to stabilize the currency are not credible, capital will flow out in anticipation of currency devaluation or depreciation, and inflationary pressure will lead to current account deterioration. Strategic interactions between a government that is motivated to try to stimulate growth and employment and a market that tries to anticipate these moves directly impacts on a country's external economic balance. Explanations as to why particular governments are perceived by economic agents as motivated to contrive an "inflationary surprise" are essentially political.

Three political variables that appear to affect a government's credibility with respect to monetary policy were critical in aggravating both capital outflows and current account deficits. The first and most significant was the political stability and expected longevity of the government. Unstable cabinets are perceived as having short time horizons, and are viewed as likely to accept inflation for short-term increases in growth and employment. The evidence is consistent with an interpretation that economic agents expect governments that are likely to have a short stay in office to be unable to implement monetary policies that might be painful in the short term. The implications of such a finding are profound: deficit countries that faced political turmoil at home were likely to lose the confidence of capital. Nor could they adjust their current consumption to compensate for these capital outflows, for the current account was likely to move into deficit as well.

A second explanation for external imbalance during the interwar years was the way markets reacted to politically manipulable central banks. The evidence presented here suggests that politically independent central banks were associated with capital inflows and with strong current account positions. Independent central banks apparently inspired market confidence that the money supply would not exceed the real demand for money, and that government spending would not be financed in an inflationary fashion. This is an effect that was significant only between 1925 and 1931, however. Central bank independence also had a strong positive association with the current account, indicative of the stronger banks' ability to place external balance above domestic economic conditions, as required by the first norm of the gold standard.

A third domestic political variable that contributed to both capital outflows and current account deficit was the extent of labor unrest, as reflected in strike activity. Strikes spark speculation that the government will be tempted to stimulate the economy to overcome increasing labor market distortions. Holders of liquid capital often bet that industrial conflict would put upward pressure on prices, which in turn would raise the risk of currency devaluation or depreciation. Governments facing industrial conflicts often simultaneously had to cope with capital flight and eventually with current account deterioration.

The role of the Left in governing only partially fitted our expectations. On the one hand, there was little evidence that the Left was subject to capital flight. However, the Left was clearly and convincingly associated with current account deterioration. The electoral bases of these socialist and labor parties encourages expansive macroeconomic policies; conversely, the task of retrenchment is pursued with greater vigor by center-right parties, whose upper- and middle-class electors are more likely to be creditors interested in price stability. This interpretation is consistent with much that has been written with respect to the differing macroeconomic preferences of the Left and Right. The implications for *international* monetary commitments are clear: to the extent that parties of the Left prefer expansion over deflation, they are likely to reject Norm 1 and tend to the needs of the domestic economy. It is no accident that all three of the major monetary powers jettisoned gold standard constraints during the watch of working-class parties.

The final domestic political variable that failed to show any effects was the difference between democratic and nondemocratic regimes. I hypothesized that since democracies are thought to have an "inflationary bias," they ought to be subject to greater capital outflows and to current account deficits. There was no evidence here to suggest that to be the case. Indeed, the inclusion of the regime type variable only disturbed the standard errors of other variables and lowered the overall explanatory power of the model in the case of capital flows. In the analysis of residuals, I noted that some of the nondemocratic regimes put stringent currency controls into place, which should be taken into account. It is not possible to say anything definitive about the effects of regime type based on the data in this chapter.

In national income accounting the current and the capital accounts must balance by definition. In reality, this balance is accomplished by gold movements (official settlements) or is fudged in "omissions and errors." This chapter has tested two separate components of the balance of payments, the current account (trade balance plus invisibles) and the capital account (the purchase of foreign assets). Independent data sets were used, with slightly different observations available for each. As expected, the overall negative correlation between the current account and capital flows is quite high ($-.7$). We would therefore suppose that the variables that are negatively correlated with the current account would tend to be positively correlated with capital movements. This is the case, for instance, with changes in growth in the previous period: higher growth attracts capital and causes the trade balance to deteriorate. But there are at least three political variables that cause the balance of trade to deteriorate *and* capital inflows to reverse. The first is cabinet instability. In every test performed, the result was that higher cabinet turnover had a negative effect on the current account (excessive absorption) and on the capital account (capital flight). The second is labor unrest. Widespread strikes encouraged inflationary expectations, sending the current account into deficit, and had a negative effect on capital flows. The third is political control of the central bank—an institutional arrangement that hardly inspired confidence. A summary of our findings so far is presented below.

	Effect on	
Variable	Current Account	Capital Movement
Regime type	$H_{0(-)}$	$H_{0(-)}$
Influence of the Left	−	$H_{0(-)}$
Labor unrest	−	−
Central bank independence	+	+
Cabinet instability	−	−

"H_0" means that due to high standard errors the alternative hypothesis could not be rejected. In the case of influence of the Left, the effect on the current account was strong and consistent, and the effect on capital movements was also negative, but did not pass traditional tests of significance.

The results so far point to an important conclusion: *domestic political conditions were often associated with current and capital account changes in the same directions*. When the trade balance and the capital account deteriorate together, the situation may not be sustainable for long. Economies headed by unstable cabinets, characterized by restless labor forces, governed by left-wing parties, and whose monetary policies were directed by politically controlled central banks would face the most serious difficulties in adjusting. They faced the greatest pressures to defect from the norms of the interwar gold standard regime. The following chapters examine who adjusted, and how.

TABLE 3.A
Five Models of the Current Account for 15 Countries, 1924–1939:
Report of Coefficients on Country Dummies
(Nonstandardized Coefficients; Standard Errors)

Country	Econ. Model	Domestic Political(1)	Domestic Political(2)	Political/ Economic	Pol./Econ. w/Infla.
Austria	−.01 (.006)	−.02* (.009)	−.019** (.09)	−.017** (.008)	−.02*** (.008)
Canada	.001 (.005)	.022* (.011)	.022* (.011)	.036*** (.01)	.036*** (.01)
Czechslovakia	.003 (.006)	.006 (.014)	.006 (.014)	.016 (.012)	.014 (.012)
Denmark	.003 (.006)	−.017 (.015)	−.017 (.015)	−.025* (.013)	−.026* (.013)
France	.003 (.007)	−.018 (.013)	−.018 (.013)	−.017 (.012)	−.023* (.013)
Finland	.018*** (.006)	.016 (.014)	.016 (.014)	.037*** (.013)	.036*** (.013)
Germany	.002 (.006)	−.013 (.014)	−.013 (.014)	−.019 (.012)	−.02 (.012)
Hungary	.011* (.006)	−.023* (.013)	−.023** (.011)	−.002 (.001)	−.004 (.01)
Japan	.001 (.006)	−.013 (.015)	−.013 (.015)	.004 (.013)	.001 (.013)
Netherlands	.003 (.006)	−.019 (.013)	−.019 (.013)	−.023** (.011)	−.025** (.011)
Norway	.002 (.005)	−.004 (.008)	−.004 (.008)	.001 (.007)	.0005 (.007)
Poland	−.006 (.018)	−.047*** (.021)	−.047*** (.02)	.006 (.019)	−.004 (.021)
Sweden	.005 (.005)	.001 (.007)	.0005 (.007)	.006 (.006)	.006 (.006)

(continued)

TABLE 3.A   (*Continued*)

Country	Econ. Model	Domestic Political(1)	Domestic Political(2)	Political/ Economic	Pol./Econ. w/Infla.
United Kingdom	−.001 (.005)	−.031 (.021)	−.031 (.021)	−.04** (.018)	−.042*** (.018)
United States (*n*th country)	—	—	—	—	—
N	173	176	176	146	146
SER	.016	.017	.017	.014	.014
adj. R^2	.636	.617	.62	.712	.714

Note: * = Significant at .10 level.   ** = Significant at .05 level.   *** = Significant at .025 level.

Chapter 4

DEVALUATION

THE PRIMARY obligation of each country on the gold standard was to maintain its national currency at a stable value relative to gold. This obligation was stressed in international forums and in the formal statutes of most central banks of Europe and North America. In 1922, the League of Nations emphasized that economic reconstruction of Europe depended on currency stabilization; that gold provided the only common standard upon which all countries could agree; that each country was responsible for determining and fixing the gold value of its monetary unit; and that each country had the responsibility for putting measures into place that would serve to maintain the international value of its currency at par.[1] Fixed gold parities were the accepted goal at the international conference of central bankers in 1927, and when German reparations were discussed in both 1924 and 1929. Exchange rate stabilization was a key concern of the delegates to the World Economic Conference in London in 1933, and it was the prime motivation for the Tripartite Agreement in 1936 between the United States, Britain, France, and the countries of the Gold Bloc. Currency stability was an ideal. Deviations from a country's established gold par was perceived as a threat to trading partners and potentially to the stability of the international monetary system as a whole. To devalue went against Norm 1. From the perspective of the interwar gold standard, devaluation was not a mode of economic adjustment that would be accepted with equanimity by other countries.[2] When deficit countries devalued unilaterally, the move was at best a desperate way to achieve external adjustment. When surplus countries did so (as the United States did in 1933), it only made it all the more difficult for those who remained on gold.

Yet, currency depreciation was a live option whenever countries suffered

[1] Cmd. 1667, 1922, Part II, "Report of the Second Commission (Finance)," and Cmd. 1650, "Resolutions Adopted by the Financial Commission of the 20th and 29th of April 1922," Resolutions 4, 5, 8 and 11(6).

[2] By contrast, post–World War II economic theory emphasizes not only the role of currency devaluation in restoring the balance between trading partners, but also the domestic expenditure switching effects of devaluation that channel resources into the traded-goods sector. Postwar conceptions view depreciation or devaluation as modes of economic adjustment with both internal and external distributive consequences. Devaluations are often advocated by the international financial community as part of a broader adjustment package both to improve the balance of trade and to channel investment toward the export sector. During the interwar years, only the French devaluation of 1936 approached international consensus on the need to devalue. I know of no other major case in which a *negotiated* devaluation took place.

severe balance of payments deficits, and it was often difficult to avoid in the face of surging capital outflows. To avoid depreciation would require a credible commitment to stabilize domestic prices via monetary stringency and a balanced government budget. The credibility of such a commitment was sensitive to domestic political conditions, as evidenced by the negative effects of political instability, labor unrest, politically controlled central banks, and left-wing participation in governance on capital flows and/or the current account. There is every reason to expect, therefore, that the ability and willingness to avoid devaluation—to make the domestic economic adjustments necessary to uphold the gold standard—depend on these political conditions. In this chapter, descriptive statistics on the incidence of currency depreciation across countries and years for the sample as a whole are presented. Second, characteristics associated with the probability that a country would be on the gold standard in any given year is examined. Third, a simple economic model of currency depreciation is presented, and the role of domestic politics and institutions is subsequently considered. Since international relations theory suggests structural or situational variables that may account for monetary cooperation, these are controlled in successive versions of the model. The results are strikingly consistent: unstable governments, those facing a higher degree of labor market turmoil, those governed by the Left, and those with politically controlled central banks did indeed allow their currencies to deteriorate more precipitously than did their opposites. An international understanding to abide by gold was especially vulnerable under this constellation of domestic political forces.

Descriptive Statistics: Currency Depreciation

Just how significant were currency depreciations during the interwar years? This section provides some idea of the frequency, size, and distribution of depreciation. Currency depreciation measures the percentage of change in the value of every national currency for each country-year in the sample (see Appendix I).[3] The years 1923 and 1924 were overwhelmingly affected by the German hyperinflation, and by extreme depreciation in Austria, Hungary, and Poland as well. But these accounted for only six country-years out of the 389 for which data were available. Figure 4.1 presents a yearly frequency distribution of changes in currency value for 23 countries. Only 35 percent of the cases were characterized by depreciation that exceeded 1 percent of the currency's value.

---

[3] "Country years" continue to be the unit of analysis, but since exchange rate data are far more readily available than balance of payments data, all twenty-three countries can be analyzed systematically. Belgium, Greece, Spain, Romania, Switzerland, and Yugoslavia are added to the analysis, except where missing data on the explanatory variables exclude them. Thirty cells are missing, yielding a possible 361 observations. I excluded the German hyperinflation of 1923–1924 from the sample, as well as the years 1938 and 1939 for countries that were no longer independent from Germany.

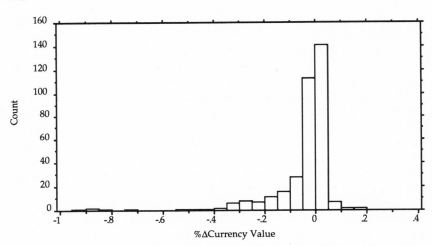

Figure 4.1: Frequency Distribution of Appreciations and Depreciations, 1923–1939

Most depreciations were fairly mild, but extreme depreciations are depicted in the long tail to the left.

Which countries depreciated the most? If the German hyperinflations are excluded, only Hungary and Spain (who never returned to the gold standard during this period) had mean changes in the value of their currencies that were significantly worse than the sample average. Hungary depreciated almost 12 percent per year and Spain slightly more than 11 percent. Bulgaria, Czechoslovakia, Germany, and Norway depreciated least (once the German hyperinflations are excluded, as they will be for the rest of this discussion; see figure 4.2 and table 4.1)

The interwar years were a time of uneven exchange rate behavior. From 1923 to 1926, many states were still in the process of stabilizing their currencies from wartime inflation and restrictions. During these years, many countries were removing wartime controls, building sufficient gold reserves to return to fixed rates, and trying to restore postwar budget equilibrium. In the early twenties, most countries in Europe allowed their currencies to float. The expectation of most monetary authorities was that this was a temporary state of affairs, a transitional period on the way back to the gold standard. By the mid to late 1920s, most of the countries in this sample participated in a fixed exchange rate regime based on the defense of legally established gold parities. The United States announced its intention immediately after World War I to maintain the dollar price of gold at its previous parity and to resume the free export of gold at $20.67 per ounce. Canada followed soon thereafter. By 1923 Austria had returned to fixed exchange rates, as did Germany in 1924. Several other countries stabilized in 1925 when Britain returned to gold, including the Nether-

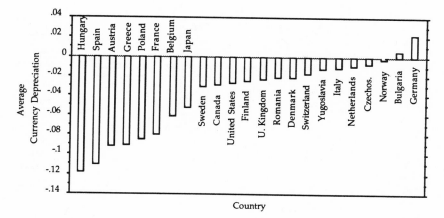

Figure 4.2: Average Currency Depreciation, by Country, 1923–1939

lands, Sweden, and Finland. Belgium, Denmark, and Poland stabilized their currencies by 1927, and Italy, France, Norway, and Greece finally stabilized de jure in 1928.

During the stabilization period (1923–1926), the average yearly depreciation was about 6 percent, while the average between 1927 and 1931 was only about .2 percent. The year 1927 marked the high point of the interwar gold exchange standard: every country in the sample was able to hold its currency virtually constant. The 1930s were almost as turbulent for currencies as was the stabilization period. Between 1932 and 1939, yearly depreciations averaged about 5.6 percent per country-year.[4]

Interwar currency values had much to do with the currency policies of the major economic powers. Figure 4.3 shows the relationship between the average change in the par value of all the currencies in our sample each year, compared to major currency policy *démarches* of Britain, France, and the United States. Average depreciation for the sample as a whole was clearly influenced by the

[4] The complete results of a two-tailed unpaired t test with 360 degrees of freedom for differences in currency depreciation between time periods were as follows:

Year	Count	Mean	Std. Dev.	Std. Error	t Stat.	Prob.
1923–1926	90	−.059	.225	.024	−1.48	.139
1927–1931	115	−.002	.09	.008	3.48	.0006
1932–1939	157	−.056	.101	.008	−1.94	.0537

Note that exchange rate variability was also much higher in the earlier period, as shown by a standard error that is almost three times as great. Again, these differences exclude the German hyperinflations of 1923 and 1924, which would make the contrast between the two periods even greater.

TABLE 4.1
Average Depreciation, by Country, 1923–1939

Country	Count	Mean	Std. Error	t statistic	Probability (2-tailed)
Hungary	16	−.119	.073	−2.297	.0222
Spain	16	−.111	.054	−2.056	.0405
Austria	13	−.093	.066	−1.386	.1666
Greece	16	−.092	.04	−1.51	.1324
Poland	16	−.086	.061	−1.353	.177
France	16	−.081	.038	−1.203	.2296
Belgium	16	−.062	.028	−.654	.5134
Japan	16	−.053	.034	−.394	.6936
Sweden	16	−.032	.018	.227	.8203
Canada	16	−.03	.015	.285	.7758
United States	16	−.028	.022	.343	.732
Finland	16	−.026	.028	.394	.6938
United Kingdom	16	−.024	.017	.444	.6572
Romania	16	−.022	.03	.503	.6156
Denmark	16	−.022	.033	.508	.6115
Switzerland	16	−.018	.016	.606	.545
Yugoslavia	15	−.013	.032	1.458	.1458
Italy	16	−.012	.031	.791	.4296
Netherlands	16	−.01	.009	.853	.394
Czechoslovakia	16	−.007	.008	.917	.3597
Norway	16	−.003	.035	1.049	.2951
Bulgaria	16	.006	.021	1.301	.1943
Germany[a]	14	.020	.030	1.127	.2603

Note: Arranged by mean depreciation; probability refers to the two-tailed test that average depreciation of a given country is *not* significantly different from the sample as a whole.

[a]Excluding hyperinflations of 1923 and 1924.

British devaluation of 1931, and to a lesser extent by the French devaluation and the collapse of the Gold Bloc in 1936. Table 4.2a shows the distribution of each country's major devaluations (those greater than 10 percent). Major devaluations occurred disproportionately in the stabilization period, especially in 1923 and 1924, before Britain returned to gold in 1925. A wave of devaluations (nine) occurred when Britain departed from gold; a secondary wave (six) occurred when the United States depreciated over the summer of 1933, and a third (five) occurred as the Gold Bloc finally crumbled in late 1936. However, contrary to what we might expect if these three powers were engaged in a ruthless game of retaliatory devaluations, *there is not one year between 1923 and 1938 in which any two of these three major economic powers devalued at the same time*. Indeed, there would seem to be a fairly important distinction

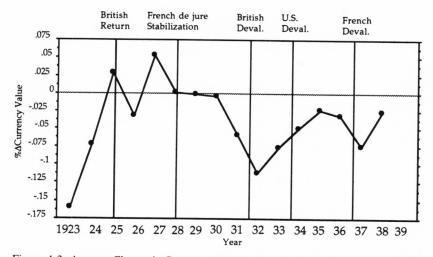

Figure 4.3: Average Change in Currency Value for the Sample as a Whole, in Relation to the Major Policy Changes of Britain, France, and the United States

TABLE 4.2
Currency Devaluations, 1923–1938
A. YEARLY NUMBER OF DEVALUATIONS GREATER THAN 10 PERCENT

Year	Count	Countries
1923	9	Austria, Belgium, Denmark, France, Germany, Greece, Hungary, Poland, Romania, Yugoslavia
1924	6	Belgium, Bulgaria, France, Germany, Hungary, Japan, Norway
1925	2	Greece, Hungary
1926	4	Belgium, France, Greece, Poland
1927	0	—
1928	0	—
1929	1	Spain
1930	1	Spain
1931	3	Austria, Italy, Spain
1932	9	Austria, Denmark, Finland, Greece, Japan, Norway, Spain, Sweden, United Kingdom
1933	6	Canada, Denmark, Greece, Japan, United States, Yugoslavia
1934	6	Canada, Czechoslavia, Denmark, Japan, Norway, Sweden
1935	1	Belgium
1936	3	Italy, Romania, Spain
1937	5	Czechoslovakia, France, Italy, Spain, Switzerland
1938	2	France, Netherlands

TABLE 4.2 (*Continued*)
Currency Devaluations, 1923–1938
B. NUMBER OF DEVALUATIONS GREATER THAN 10 PERCENT,
BY COUNTRY, 1923–1938

1	2	3	4	5–6
Bulgaria	Canada	Austria	Belgium	France
Finland	Czechoslovakia	Hungary	Denmark	Greece
Netherlands	Germany	Italy	Japan	Spain
Switzerland	Poland	Norway		
United Kingdom	Romania			
United States	Sweden			
	Yugoslavia			

between the French pattern of frequent devaluations of over 10 percent (five during the interwar years, concentrated in the early to mid twenties and late thirties), and the British and American pattern of one significant devaluation during the period as a whole. Table 4.2b indicates which countries most frequently took major devaluations of over 10 percent in a given year. It is interesting to note that Britain and the United States each devalued more than 10 percent only once during the period, while France did so more than any other country in the sample—and as frequently as did Spain, which never officially instituted a gold standard and was in the throes of civil war.

These data raise important questions. Why did some countries maintain the gold standard for several years, while others did so only briefly? What explains the pattern of devaluations? Does competitive retaliation suffice to explain the patterns that emerge? What characteristics are associated with currency stability versus depreciation over the period as a whole?

ON GOLD OR OFF?

Because of differing economic and political conditions in the countries in our sample, the period of currency stabilization was longer in some countries than in others (figure 4.4). By 1931, however, many had followed Britain's lead and abandoned their commitment to the gold standard, while some maintained their gold parities through 1936 and beyond. Table 4.3 shows how many years the countries in the sample remained on the gold standard. Switzerland, Belgium, and the Netherlands managed to stick to some form of the gold standard for a ten- to eleven-year stretch. The United States did so for fourteen years, albeit with a two-year lapse in 1933–1934. Despite the fact that France devalued frequently before 1927 and after 1935, for eight years the franc was maintained on a gold basis. The gold-based pound survived only six years. Yugoslavia and Japan had the fewest years on the gold standard, followed by Greece, Romania,

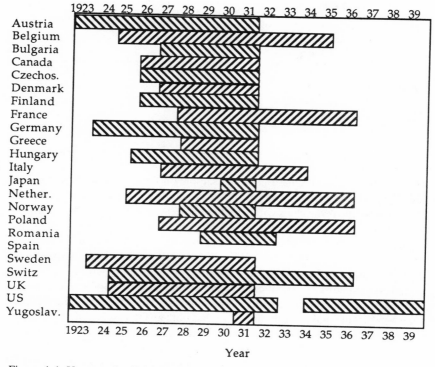

Figure 4.4: Years on the Gold Standard

and Norway. All three of the major economic powers—Britain, France, and the United States—are in different columns with respect to their time on gold.

What influences the probability that a country would be able and willing to maintain a commitment to gold? The previous chapter would lead us to suspect that cabinet instability, political control of the central bank, labor unrest, and left-wing participation in government—that is, those factors associated with either capital flight, current account deficit, or both—might make it more difficult to maintain a fixed commitment to gold. To test these explanations, let us consider whether or not a country was on the gold standard as a dichotomous dependent variable that takes on the value of *1* if the country is on a gold standard and *0* otherwise. We can analyze the probability of a country being on gold in any given year by using the cumulative normal distribution function corresponding to a probit model. In general, we would expect the variables that have been shown to influence external imbalance to affect the probability that a country would be able to maintain the gold standard during a given year. Certainly, such a model should take into account contagion effects of the gold standard across countries and in the previous time period; for this reason, the

TABLE 4.3
Number of Years a Country Remained on the Gold Standard, 1923–1939

0–3 Years	4–5 Years	6–7 Years	8–9 Years	10–14 Years
Spain (0)	Bulgaria (4)	United Kingdom (6)	Austria (8)	Belgium (10)
Yugoslavia (1)	Denmark (4)	Hungary (6)	France (8)	Netherlands (11)
Japan (1)	Czechoslovakia (5)	Italy (7)	Poland (9)	Switzerland (11)
Greece (3)	Canada (5)	Sweden (7)		United States (14)
Norway (3)	Finland (5)	Germany (7)		
Romania (3)				

average proportion of countries in the sample on the gold standard is inserted into the model as a crucial control. What we should expect to observe is that the domestic political variables with which we have been concerned have an important impact on the probability that a country will be on the gold standard for any given year: cabinet instability, greater left-wing participation in governance, rampant striking activity, and politically controlled central banks should decrease the probability of a country adopting or maintaining gold.

Several structural or situational variables may also be critical in explaining the length of commitment to the gold standard. Hegemonic stability theory suggests that the major economic power has both an interest in and the ability to provide international monetary stability. Hence, we might expect an economy's size to be positively associated with length of commitment to the gold standard.[5] In table 4.4, two alternative measures of size are tested: Net National Product, measured in constant 1929 U.S. dollars, and a country's share of world trade. If stable exchange rates are a public good, as Kindleberger implies, and if we assume that the larger power or powers have the greatest interest in providing this public good, then high scores on these variables should make it more likely that a country will be on gold. Similarly, I control for a country's net external investment position, following Jeff Frieden's suggestion that net external creditors should have a stronger interest than do net borrowers in maintaining exchange rate stability.[6]

The results of the probit analysis appear in tables 4.4a and b. Table 4.4a reports the probit coefficients, standard errors, and degree of statistical significance. Only three out of five domestic political variables had a statistically significant effect on the probability that a country would be on gold. Surprisingly, when considered in the context of our previous results, neither cabinet instability nor labor unrest had an important impact on this probability,

[5] Charles P. Kindleberger, *The World in Depression, 1929–1939* (Berkeley: University of California Press), 1986; Barry Eichengreen, "Hegemonic Stability Theories of the International Monetary System," in Eichengreen (ed.), *Elusive Stability*, (Cambridge: Cambridge University Press), 1990, chap. 11.

[6] Jeffrey A. Frieden, "Capital Politics: Creditors and the International Political Economy," *Journal of Public Policy* 8, Nos. 3/4, 1988, pp. 265–286.

TABLE 4.4
Probability of Being on the Gold Standard
a. PROBIT RESULTS: PROBABILITY OF BEING ON THE GOLD STANDARD

Variable	Probit Coefficient	Standard Error	t Statistic
Democratic	−.7411	.30435	−2.435***
%Left in Parliament	.01736	.00712	2.44***
Cabinet Turnover	.01076	.10842	0.099
Central Bank Independence	.2433	.0629	3.868***
Labor Unrest	−.1168	.3192	−.366
Share of World Trade	−.1221	.03923	−3.112***
NNP	.03466	.011611	2.985***
Net External Investment Position	1.1426	.27157	4.207***
Proportion of other States in Sample on Gold	4.4963	.41894	10.733***
Constant	−3.0879	.34228	−9.022***

Notes: Log likelihood (0) = −261.17.   Log likelihood function = −124.72.
Likelihood ratio test = 272.911 with 9 degrees of freedom.
Percentage of right predictions: 86%.
*** = Significant at .025 level.

although the direction of their influence was in the hypothesized direction. The strongest among the domestic political explanations turned out to be whether or not a regime was democratic, the independence of the central bank, and the extent of left-wing representation in governance. Table 4.4b interprets the strength of these effects for those variables that were statistically significant. Whether or not a country was a democracy had an important impact on the probability of its being on gold: when all other variables were held to their mean values, democracies had a probability of a little over half and nondemocracies had a probability of more than three quarters of being on the gold standard. This is a critical substantive finding, and it suggests that democracies were less able to withstand the domestic economic costs of maintaining gold. Nondemocratic countries, on the other hand, were better positioned to control domestic prices, quash labor demands, and put other policies in place that would allow the gold standard to be maintained, even at the price of domestic deflation.

It may be most interesting for the remainder of the discussion to concentrate on the impact of both the Left and the independence of the central bank *under democratic conditions*, and while holding the other variables at their mean

TABLE 4.4 (*Continued*)
Probability of Being on the Gold Standard
b. INTERPRETATION OF PROBIT RESULTS

	Democratic			Nondemocratic		
	Low	High	Difference	Low	High	Difference
% Left in Parliament	.389[a]	.628[a]	.239	—	—	—
Central Bank Independence	.333[a]	.680[a]	.347	.309[a]	.621[a]	.312
%World Trade	.560[b]	.270[b]	−.290	.890[b]	.560[b]	−.330
NNP	.386[b]	.738[b]	.352	.657[b]	.916[b]	.241
Net External Investment Position	.327[c]	.756[c]	.425	.615[c]	.924[c]	.309

Note: Numbers in the "High" and "Low" cells refer to the probability of a country being on the gold standard under the conditions specified, assuming all other included variables are held at their mean values.

The *"Difference"* column refers to the extent by which the probability of being on gold increases when the high value of the variable is considered, assuming all other included variables are held at their mean values.

The probability of a regime being on the gold standard was .509 for democratic and .778 for nondemocratic, assuming all other included variables are held at their mean values.

[a]Refers to a one standard deviation change in each direction from the mean observed value of the variable in the left-hand column.

[b]Minimum (low column) and maximum (high column) observed values for variable in left-hand column.

[c]Refers to net external debtor (low column) and net external creditor (high column).

values. Central bank independence clearly made it more likely, ceteris paribus, that a country would be on gold. A standard deviation interval of two around the mean in the independence of the central bank accounted for a jump in the probability of being on gold from about a third to more than two thirds (holding regime type constant). This provides reasonably compelling evidence that central bank independence contributed to a higher probability of a country's being on gold during this period. Independent central banks saw currency stability as their primary mandate. They were the domestic institutional seat of the international monetary regime based on gold.

The most surprising result in the context of the previous findings is that countries with higher left-wing representation in parliament had a higher probability of maintaining gold than those with less. Despite a tendency to have a deteriorating current account, left-wing influence did not translate into a diminished probability of being on gold in this probit model. On the contrary, for democracies, and holding all other variables at their mean values, a standard deviation shift of two in the value of left-wing representation around its mean shifted the probability of being on gold from .389 to .628, with the *higher* probability corresponding to the *higher* proportion of left-wing representation. This is hardly what we would have expected, given our argument regarding credibility and our earlier observation on the impact of the Left on the current account. The anomaly will be addressed below, where I develop a more general model of the determinants of currency depreciation. It will be shown that the Left supported the gold standard as long as the domestic economic costs were tolerable. During recession, however, the Left was clearly unwilling to crucify labor on a "cross of gold."

The three structural variables included in this model also proved crucial to the probability of being on gold. Larger traders were less likely to be on gold. Among democracies, the minimum observation on share of world trade is associated with a probability of being on gold of .560, while the value at one standard deviation above the mean is associated with a probability of only .270. This can be interpreted to mean that the dominant traders were less likely to maintain an overvalued currency, since the cost to exporters could severely impact the economy as a whole. On the other hand, size alone, as measured by NNP, was associated with a higher probability of being on gold. The .35 difference indicates that the larger, and possibly the more self-sufficient, economies were better able or were more willing than the smaller ones to maintain the gold standard. Finally, there is clear evidence that creditor countries were much more likely to be on gold. Among democracies, and with all other variables held at their means, net external debtors had a .327 probability of being on gold, while net external creditors had a .756 probability. Net external creditors were certainly more likely to remain on gold, which was clearly in their interest, since to devalue would degrade the value of their loans outstanding and undermine international confidence in their currency. Overall, two out of three of these structural variables speak to a hegemonic stability thesis based on the presupposition that international monetary stability is an international public good. Large economies (based on NNP) and creditors were far more likely than their counterparts to be on the gold standard. However, large traders displayed the opposite tendency, providing evidence that for those for whom trade was crucial, the gold standard could prove a straitjacket if the currency was over valued; they were more likely to reject the gold standard if an advantage could be had by devaluation. These results highlight just how sensitive any theory of hegemonic stability can be to the chosen measurement of "dominance."

This section has addressed a narrow but very important question: what is the correlation between the political variables we have been considering and the probability that a country was willing and able to maintain the gold standard? To be sure, two of the strongest influences appear to be structural: size, as measured by NNP, and creditor status appear crucial to making and maintaining this commitment. Dominance as an international trader worked in the opposite direction, however. Is this evidence of hegemonic leadership and an Olsonian example of the small, poor debtors taking advantage of the more "powerful" by jumping off the gold standard whenever it suited them to do so? Perhaps, but there is also strong evidence that domestic institutions—predominantly the central bank and the nature of the regime itself—greatly influence the probability of maintaining gold. Moreover, as will be shown in the next section, these structural explanations do not hold up when modeling variations in currency value for the period as a whole.

The greatest puzzle is why left-wing representation correlated with *more* years on gold. This seems at odds with what we know about the behavior of left-wing governments: in Britain, France, and the United States, parties of the Left put an end to the gold standard. Perhaps this is just an artifact of economic development: the advanced industrialized countries had politically integrated left-wing parties, and the smaller, more rural countries did not. Or perhaps left-wing governments play by the rules when the stakes are low. During depressions, they protect their constituencies and embrace currency depreciation, as the final section of this chapter will show.

Explaining Currency Depreciation

The previous section analyzed the influences on the probability that a country would be on the gold standard for any given year. But because the dependent variable was treated dichotomously, the probit model presented could not take full advantage of the information on the severity of depreciation available in this dataset. The probit model does not actually inform us how serious were the devaluations taken while a country was off gold. After all, it is not obvious that the countries with more gold standard observations also devalued the least. Austria devalued on average nearly 10 percent per year, while Norway devalued a fraction of 1 percent, yet the former was on gold for nine years and the latter for only four. France and Belgium both remained on gold for a fairly long period, but they also devalued quite frequently (see table 4.3). The United States remained on the gold standard much longer than Bulgaria (fourteen years compared to four), but the former actually depreciated over this period far more than did the latter (an average of 2.8 percent per year compared to virtually nothing for Bulgaria). It is clear, then, that any test of the influences on the probability of a country's commitment to gold is not the same as a full model of currency depreciation for this period.

This section uses pooled time-series cross-sectional multivariate analysis to estimate the impact of the variables we have been considering on currency depreciation.[7] To avoid circularity, I do not distinguish between exchange rate

---

[7] Since their numerical values would dominate the entire analysis, the depreciation levels of the German hyperinflation are excluded.

regimes, but treat the entire period as a whole. As in previous chapters, I begin with a simple economic interpretation, add the domestic political considerations, and finally test for the robustness of the explanation by adding structural variables to the analysis.

The Economic Determinants of the Currency Value

The economic model proposed here is kept to essentials: it says that the external value of a currency is influenced by the change in the differential between real home and world interest rates, changes in domestic wholesale prices, movements in the currency of a country's major trade partner, and the influence of past changes in the value of the currency itself. The elements of the basic model are spelled out below.

Real Interest Rate Differentials. In Chapter 3, I argued that the higher the real interest rate prevailing at home relative to that prevailing in the rest of the world, the larger would be the capital inflow. This analysis is now extended to predict that the value of the currency is a function of this real interest rate differential. Higher interest rates are expected to be associated with currency strength for two reasons. First, when capital is fairly mobile internationally, higher domestic interest rates attract capital from foreign sources and enhance demand for securities and other investments denominated in the domestic currency, increasing the overall demand for the domestic currency. Second, over the longer term, higher interest rates dampen domestic absorption and improve the current account balance. For these reasons, we would expect the real interest rate differential to be positively correlated with the value of the currency.[8]

Changes in the Value of Foreign Currencies. Under most circumstances, we would expect changes in the par value of a country's currency to be positively related to changes in the currencies of other countries in the international economic system.[9] Whether this is due to "competitive devaluation" or simply a form of loose pegging, there are strong reasons for the gold value of currencies on average to tend to move together rather than apart. Therefore, the model tested here takes into account the changes in the value of foreign currencies by including changes in the gold par value of the currency of the major trading partner in the same period. With the exception of those years in which fundamental currency realignments took place, currencies should tend to move to-

[8] As noted in the previous chapter, a complete series for comparable market interest rates is not available for many of the smaller countries in this series. Instead, I use the average bank rate of discount prevailing each year to construct real interest rate differentials.

[9] Note that I am referring to currencies' depreciation from a constant par value, and not a fluctuating bilateral currency relationship.

gether away from their previous gold pars. We expect a strong positive correlation between changes in the currency of the major trading partner and that of the country in question.

Changes in the Value of the Currency in the Previous Period.   Also included in this model is a lagged dependent variable. Currencies that are stable in the previous period are expected to remain stable, and those that have begun to depreciate are expected to continue to do so. This variable simply inserts an inertial element into the model. We expect a strong positive correlation between the value of the currency in the previous period and the present.

Changes in Wholesale Prices in the Previous Period.   Devaluation or depreciation can be induced by price shocks. Most typically, devaluation is associated with inflationary conditions: as domestic prices rise, goods become less competitive, leading to current account deficit and downward pressure on the currency. Inflation also dashes confidence in the currency, encouraging investors to sell domestically denominated assets in favor of those denominated in a stronger foreign currency. On the other hand, severe downward price shocks can also encourage depreciation if wages and other costs of production are not flexible downward, if unemployment swells, and if firms lie idle. Under these circumstances, severe price deflation may be countered by currency depreciation and monetary expansion.

To test these relationships, the following equation was used, and the results of the ordinary least squares are reported in table 4.5:

$\%\Delta$ Currency Value $= a + \beta_1(\%\Delta$ Currency Value$[t - 1]) +$

$\beta_2(\%\Delta$Currency of Major Trade Partner$) + \beta_3(\Delta$Real Interest Rate

Differentials$) + \beta_4(\%\Delta$Wholesale prices$[t - 1]) + e$

These variables account for over 30 percent of the variation in currency values for a sample of 267 observations. Three are highly significant in the expected direction; the price variable is also significant, but only at the 93 percent level of confidence. Of these four variables, the one with the greatest impact on changes in the value of the currency was changes in the currency value of the major trade partner, followed by the lagged dependent variable. According to these results, a change in the currency of the major trade partner was associated with a change of slightly more than half that size (.531) for the currency under consideration. Changes in the real interest rate differential also contributed to changes in currency value: as interest rates rose relative to world rates, the currency was strengthened, but falling relative domestic interest rates contributed to currency depreciation, as we would expect.

TABLE 4.5
Seven Models of Changes in Currency Value for 17 Countries[a] (Unstandardized Coefficients; Standard Errors)

Variable	Exp. Dir.	Econ. Model	Political Model 1	Pol./Econ. Model 2	Pol./Econ. Model 3 w/Infla.	Pol./Econ. Model 4 w/Dem.	Pol./Econ. Model 5 w/Strikes	Pol./Econ. Model 6 w/Controls
Intercept	—	-.005	-.167	-.088	-.091	-.069	-.088	-.079
%ΔCurrency Value $(t-1)$	+	.281*** (.06)	.195*** (.06)	.215*** (.058)	.241*** (.066)	.215*** (.058)	.217*** (.067)	.209*** (.060)
%ΔCurrency Major Trade Partner	+	.531*** (.081)	—	.357*** (.08)	.343*** (.081)	.357*** (.08)	.496*** (.099)	.354*** (.084)
Δ Real Interest Rate Differential	+	.004*** (.001)	—	.003*** (.001)	.004*** (.001)	.003*** (.001)	.003*** (.001)	.004*** (.001)
%ΔWholesale Prices $(t-1)$	+,-	.114* (.064)	—	—	.092 (.080)	—	—	—
Democracy	—	—	—	—	—	-.015 (.013)	—	—
Left-Wing Government (Dummy)	—	—	-.075*** (.015)	-.042*** (.014)	-.044*** (.002)	-.037*** (.015)	-.045*** (.014)	-.037*** (.015)
Left-Wing Government (Dummy) *%ΔIIP$(t-1)$	+	—	.655*** (.126)	.392*** (.127)	.38*** (.127)	.399*** (.127)	.298*** (.123)	.376*** (.134)

(continued)

TABLE 4.5 (Continued)

Variable	Exp. Dir.	Econ. Model	Political Model 1	Pol./Econ. Model 2	Pol./Econ. Model 3 w/Infla.	Pol./Econ. Model 4 w/Dem.	Pol./Econ. Model 5 w/Strikes	Pol./Econ. Model 6 w/Controls
%ΔIIP($t-1$)	+	—	—	.126** (.060)	.091 (.07)	.118* (.06)	.135** (.064)	.134** (.066)
Cabinet Δ	—	—	-.021*** (.007)	-.025*** (.08)	-.024*** (.008)	-.025*** (.008)	-.026*** (.008)	-.025*** (.009)
Central Bank Independence (1923–31)	+	—	.004*** (.001)	.005*** (.002)	.005*** (.002)	.005*** (.002)	.004** (.002)	.006*** (.002)
Labor Unrest	—	—	—	—	—	—	-.006 (.014)	—
Trade Dependence	?	—	—	—	—	—	—	-.001 (.033)
%World Trade	—	—	—	—	—	—	—	-.001 (.001)
NNP	+	—	—	—	—	—	—	-.00008 (.0004)
Net Investment	+	—	—	—	—	—	—	-.005 (.014)
N =		267	210	195	193	195	158	187
SER =		.083	.080	.070	.069	.07	.064	.071
adj.R^2 =		.303	.264	.41	.419	.411	.476	.403

Note: * = Significant at .10 level.   ** = Significant at .05 level.   *** = Significant at .025 level.

[a]Included countries: Austria, Belgium, Canada, Czechoslovakia, Denmark, France, Finland, Germany, Hungary, Italy, Japan, Netherlands, Norway, Poland, Sweden, United Kingdom, and the United States. Excluded countries: Bulgaria, Greece, Romania, Spain, Switzerland, and Yugoslavia, due to missing data.

The Political Correlates of Currency Value

The above analysis considered the effects of economic variables that are *not* under direct domestic political control. Real interest rate differentials, changes in the currency value of the major trade partner, the currency value in the previous period, and changes in wholesale prices were all shown to have a strong impact on currency value in the expected direction. Do political explanations add anything to this essentially economic explanation of depreciation?

Cabinet Instability.   In the previous chapter, cabinet instability was consistently and significantly associated with *both* capital flight and a deterioration in the current account. However, cabinet instability did not clearly impact the probability that a country would be on gold at any given time. There are good reasons, though, to expect that cabinet instability will have a strong negative effect on the value of the currency in this model. Since markets interpret instability as a sign of inflationary pressures to come, they are likely to sell the currency in question in favor of foreign assets. Moreover, it is likely to be very difficult to take internal adjustment measures to correct a deficit or to control inflation when cabinet life expectancy is low, and for this reason depreciation may be the path of least resistance for a government in no position to make hard choices. When markets anticipate devaluation, it often becomes a self-fulfilling prophecy.

Central Bank Independence.   The second variable treated here is the independence of the central bank from the government. So far we have shown that more independent central banks were associated with capital inflows, better current account positions, and a greater probability that a country would be on the gold standard. There are therefore strong reasons to expect more independent central banks to resist depreciation. As central bankers and financiers were wont to claim in the twenties, political independence was necessary to defend the currency; central banks under government control might be pressured to depreciate in order to avoid deflation, to boost employment, and to preserve a competitive edge in international trade. More independent central banks retain the freedom to carry out their primary mission: to protect the national currency from depreciation. If so, we would expect a positive relationship between central bank independence and the direction of currency change.

Left-Wing Representation.   In the previous chapter, the Left was associated with a strong deterioration in the current account, but there was little evidence that they were victims of capital flight. We were also surprised to discover in the probit model above that strong left-wing representation contributed positively to the probability of the country being on gold. Still, there are good reasons to suppose that parties of the Left are more concerned with maintaining domestic production and employment opportunities at home than they are with a strong currency, especially when recession threatens domestic jobs and the Left's social agenda. The Left is expected to make currency adjustments to avoid domestic deflation when economic downturn threatens the livelihood of workers. To test this modified hypothesis, I use an interaction term to specify the behavior of left-wing governments contingent on the direction of the business cycle in the previous period (Left Government*%Δ Index of Industrial Production[$t-1$]). If left-wing governments depreciate as recession sets in, we would expect a positive relationship between this interaction term and changes in the value of the currency,[10] but a negative relationship between left-wing government and depreciation otherwise.

Labor Unrest.   The next domestic political variable considered here is labor unrest. Strikes had a negative, statistically significant effect on both the current account and capital flows. High levels of labor unrest were also associated with fewer years on the gold standard. Because of its effects on production costs and continuity, as well as on capital flight, increased strike activity should depreciate the currency. The coefficient for labor unrest (working days lost per capita) should be negative.

Democracy.   In the previous chapters, it was shown that democracy had no statistically significant impact on the current account or capital movements. The probit model indicated, though, that being a democracy made it much less likely that a country would be on gold, other variables being held at their means. As a working hypothesis, let us therefore test the proposition that democracy is associated with a deterioration in the value of the currency. If this is so, we should expect a negative relationship between democracy and currency value.

CONTROL VARIABLES—STRUCTURAL CONSTRAINTS

In addition, four structural variables were taken into account. They were included primarily to ascertain that devaluation is not an artifact of some structural constraint or incentive—an economy's size, a country's trade dependence, its share of world trade, its domestic wealth, or its net external creditor position. As I mentioned above, public goods interpretations of the international monetary system suggest that actors (states) with disproportionate stakes in the stability of the system ought to be willing to pay the price of this stability by defending their currencies against depreciation. The probit model uncovered some evidence of such an influence for NNP and for creditor status, but found that the dominant traders were far less likely to maintain gold. Smaller coun-

---

[10] Left-wing government is a dummy variable with a major role for parties of the Left coded *1*. When multiplied by changes in the index of industrial production, a drop in the latter should also yield a drop in the value of the currency in the following period.

tries, more dominant traders, and poorer countries, on the other hand, are expected to adjust their currency in a way that best suits their national economic needs at the time.

DOMESTIC POLITICS AND CURRENCY DEPRECIATION: THE EVIDENCE

These domestic political and structural variables were tested while holding real interest rate differentials, price shocks, and foreign currency values constant. Versions of the following equation were estimated using ordinary least squares.

$\%\Delta$ Currency Value $= a + \beta_1(\%\Delta$ Currency Value$[t - 1]) +$
$\beta_2(\%\Delta$Currency of Major Trade Partner$) + \beta_3(\Delta$Real Interest Rate Differentials$) + \beta_4(\%\Delta$Wholesale Prices$[t - 1]) + \beta_5($Democracy$) +$
$\beta_6($Left Government Dummy$) + \beta_7($Left Government Dummy$*\%\Delta$IIP
$[t - 1]) + \beta_8(\%\Delta$IIP$[t - 1]) + \beta_9(\Delta$ Cabinet$) + \beta_{10}($Central Bank Independence$[23-31]) + \beta_{11}($Labor Unrest$) + \beta_{12}($Trade Dependence$)$
$+ \beta_{13}(\%$World Trade$) + \beta_{14}($NNP$) + \beta_{15}($Net Investment Position$)$
$+ e$

The results, reported in table 4.5, are strikingly consistent with our expectations. Three of the domestic political variables had statistically significant results in the expected direction in every version of the model tested. Cabinet instability, central bank independence, and left-wing government were all certainly related to changes in currency values during the interwar years, even when economic shocks, interest rate differentials, and changes in the currency value of the major trading partner are taken into account.

Cabinet instability had a strong negative impact on the external value of the currency across every model tested.[11] In these models, each additional cabinet turnover is correlated with a depreciation of about 2.5 percent. At this rate, cabinet turnover alone would have accounted for 10 percent depreciation in the

[11] The standardized coefficients were as follows (Political/Economic Model 2):

Variable	Standardized Coefficient
$\%\Delta$Currency value$(t - 1)$	.23
$\%\Delta$Currency value of the major trade partner	.28
ΔReal interest rate differential	.30
Left government (dummy)	$-.20$
Left government $*\%\Delta$IIP$(t - 1)$	.22
$\%\Delta$IIP$(t - 1)$	.14
Cabinet Δ	$-.17$
Central bank independence (1923–1931)	.13

French franc in 1938, in violation of the spirit of the Tripartite Agreement. (The actual depreciation that year was 28 percent.) This is an important independent political effect on currency depreciation that is statistically distinguishable from the effects of real interest rates, previous inflationary shocks (Political/ Economic Model 3), and changes in the currency of the major trade partner. This finding coincides with the evidence in the previous chapter: unstable governments are associated with deteriorating current accounts, capital flight, and, now we can conclude, currency depreciation.

These tests also show that the more politically dependent the central bank, the greater the depreciation of the currency, at least for the years between 1923 and 1931.[12] For this period, the difference between the least independent central banks (in Finland and Czechoslovakia) and the most independent (in the United Kingdom) could account for a difference of as much as 3.6 percent in currency value. Monetary institutional arrangements have consistently had a significant impact on the ability of a country to adjust internally and remain on gold in every test performed in this study. It is becoming clear why so much emphasis was placed on central bank independence by gold standard afficionados of the twenties and thirties.

Now we come to the puzzle of the effects and choices of left-wing governments. In the previous chapter the Left was associated with current account deterioration, but not significantly with capital flight. Furthermore, our previous analysis indicated that, surprisingly, higher left-wing participation in parliament was associated with a country's longer stay on the gold standard. But a long commitment to the gold standard was not incompatible with serious and frequent devaluation before and after the period of currency stability. The behavior of the left-wing government dummy and the left-wing/business cycle interaction term is very telling in this context. Considered independently of any other effects, left-wing governments *did* tend to depreciate their currencies more than governments in which there was little or no participation by the Left. The effect of a left-wing government in power was to depreciate the currency somewhere between 3.7 percent and 4.5 percent, even when economic conditions were taken into account. Moreover, the interaction term shows that recession was much more strongly associated with currency depreciation when left-wing governments were in power (the effects of Left government*%ΔIIP[$t - 1$] and %ΔIIP[$t - 1$]) than when they were not (%ΔIIP[$t - 1$] alone). *Left-wing governments not only depreciated on balance, but they were especially wont to depreciate in response to an economic slump.* A picture is emerging in which the Left was commited to gold only until the economic price of deflation

---

[12] The relationship between central bank independence and currency value is positive for the period as a whole, but the estimated effect is smaller, making central bank independence statistically insignificant when both decades are considered.

became intolerably incompatible with employment and other social goals. Whenever currency stability and domestic growth came into conflict, left-wing governments were more ready than were their center-right counterparts to choose growth and let the currency go.

Two domestic political variables had results that were in the expected directions, but were not statistically significant. Democracy had a negative coefficient (indicating that democracies depreciated more than did authoritarian regimes), but it does not pass traditional standards of significance. The inclusion of labor unrest eliminated more than thirty observations, and while it had the expected negative sign, it showed no significant relationship to currency depreciation.

None of the structural control variables bore any relationship with currency depreciation. These results seem to indicate that economic and domestic political conditions played a much greater role in the decision about whether or not to devalue than did structural constraints and incentives. In particular, there is no trace in these data of the "dominant power" upholding the norm of currency stability during the interwar years. There was no tendency for creditor countries to maintain their currency values, and no evidence that either the largest countries or the most important international traders stabilized their currencies any more than did their opposites. Far more convincing is a domestically driven explanation in which unstable governments depreciate because they do not have the ability to maintain gold commitments, and left-wing governments devalue because they will not tolerate the political and social costs of deflation, especially when a recession is already under way. Independent central banks, on the other hand, contributed to currency strength, though we can only be sure of this relationship between 1923 and 1932.

The issue of causation must be considered carefully in discussing this model of currency depreciation. The evidence presented here supports an interpretation that the *political* variables of interest influence economic outcomes rather more strongly than the other way around. For instance, cabinet instability remained statistically and substantively significant even when previous inflation (correlation $= -.102$), previous recession (correlation $= -.088$), and previous devaluations (correlation $= .114$) were taken into account. The weakness of these correlations suggests that the causal interpretation ascribed to the model is more than plausible. A similar stress should be laid on the causal role of left-wing governments. They were not simply epiphenomenon of the Depression. There is virtually no correlation between changes in the index of industrial production over the previous two years and the rise of a left-wing government for the sample as a whole; indeed, the direction of the correlation will not even support such an interpretation (correlation $= .035$). Since the political variables remain stable, significant, and in the hypothesized direction even when controlling for previous economic conditions, and since the simple correlations between these previous "shocks" and the political variables is low in any case, it is reasonable to assign an independent causal effect to the role of domestic politics on currency depreciation.

Fit between the Model and Actual Changes in Currency Values

Political/Economic Model 2 seems to be the most parsimonious explanation for changes in the value of the currency. Every variable in this model is extremely significant, and it explains about 40 percent of the variation in changes in currency values, which is quite good considering it contains no country dummies and considering the difficulty in predicting *changes* as opposed to levels.

Figure 4.5 depicts the goodness of fit between actual depreciation and depreciation predicted by Political/Economic Model 2. The model does very well in fitting changes in the value of the currency for Denmark, France, Finland, Hungary, Japan, Norway, Sweden, and the United States. The estimated values for Germany jump around much more than the actual value of the mark: there is evidence that Germany resisted depreciation in the early thirties, probably because of the system of exchange controls in place in that country. The Belgian pattern is well predicted up to 1934, but is off thereafter because Belgium devalued in 1935 without France (its major trade partner) and then resisted further devaluation in 1937 when the French franc continued to slide. The estimated impact of the major trade partner was evidently not as great for Belgium as it was for many countries in this sample. A similar pattern can be seen with movements in the pound: its devaluation in 1931–1932 is underestimated because the dollar was constant, but its fitted value in 1933 was overestimated because the dollar devalued without further downward movement of the pound.

Figures 4.6a and 4.6b show the distribution of residuals for all data points on average by country, and on average by year (no Durbin Watson statistic is reported because of the inclusion of the lagged dependent variable on the right-hand side of the equation). Negative residuals indicate depreciations greater than were generated from this model, while positive residuals indicate currency changes that are not as negative as those the model predicted. Countries for which average depreciation over the period was worse than expected include Denmark, Finland, and France. On the other hand, the currencies of Poland, Norway, and Hungary did better on average than the model predicted. Two of these countries had stringent currency controls in place for at least a portion of the period considered here: both the Hungarian pengö and the Polish zloti had only "nominal" rates (as opposed to market rates) from April 1933 to the end of the thirties.[13] The Norwegian krone's value on the other hand was determined

---

[13] Federal Reserve Board, *Banking and Monetary Statistics*, (Washington, D.C.: National Capitol Press), 1943, p. 665 and 672.

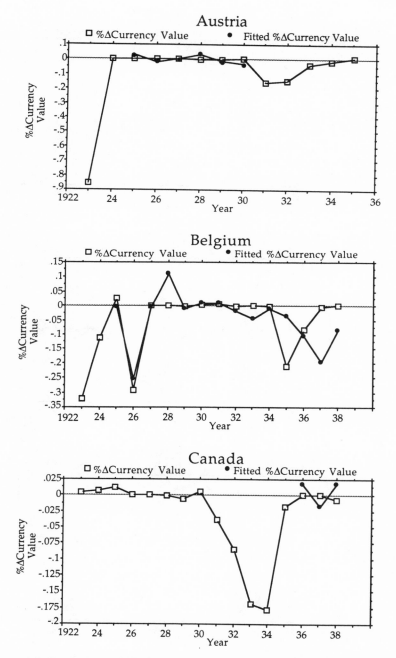

Figure 4.5: Comparison of Fitted and Actual Changes in Currency Value (Political/Economic Model 2)

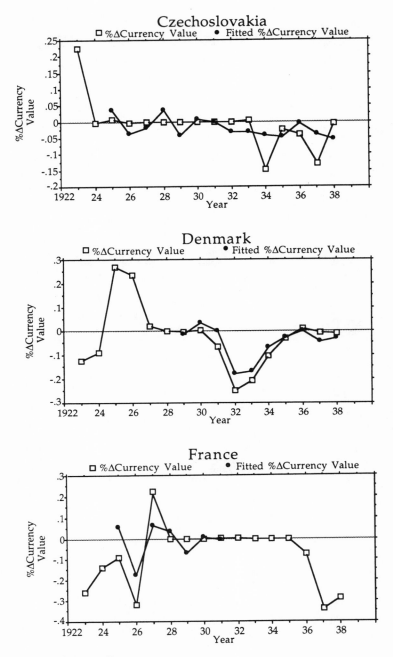

Figure 4.5: (*Continued*)

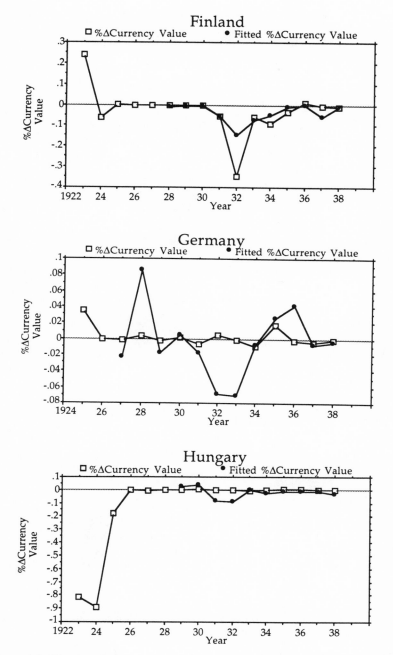

Figure 4.5: (*Continued*)

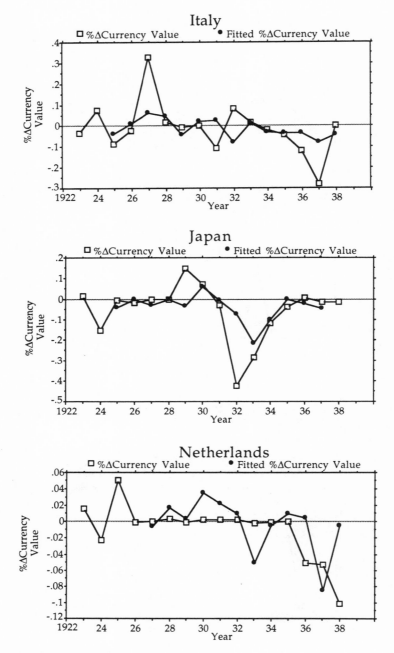

Figure 4.5: (*Continued*)

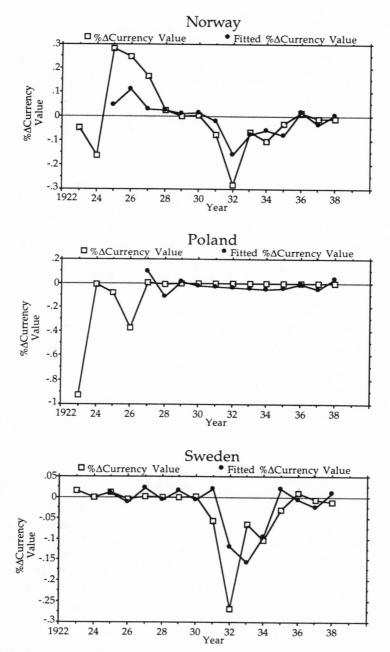

Figure 4.5: (*Continued*)

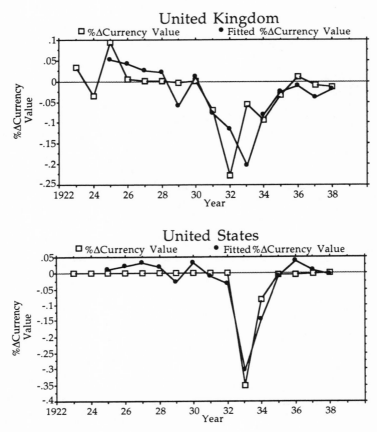

Figure 4.5: (*Continued*)

by the market for the period as a whole. Norway's residuals are positive largely because of the underprediction of the krone's appreciation between 1925 and 1927. The countries that had average residuals closest to zero were Italy (−.002), Austria (.001), Germany (.005), and Czechoslovakia and the United States (each −.005).

The model underpredicts depreciation to the greatest extent for 1932 (average residual of −.041), the year in which the effects of the British departure from gold show up in the yearly data. One reason the model underpredicts 1932 is that depreciation is modeled as a function of depreciation of the currency *of the major trade partner*, which underestimates the importance of the status of sterling as a reserve currency. In many cases, Germany may have been the major trade partner, but monetary conditions were much more influenced by the

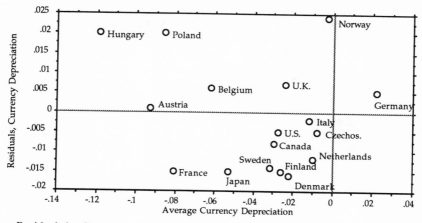

a. Residuals by Country

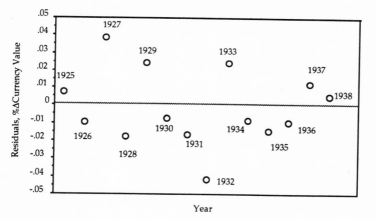

b. Residuals by Year

Figure 4.6: Residuals for Changes in Currency Value (Political/Economic Model 2)

pound. This explains why the model does so poorly for 1932.[14] Overall, though, the model generates an impressive fit with observed changes in the value of the currency for seventeen countries.

Table 4.6 compares the average difference between the actual change in

[14] A model that includes a 1932 dummy variable explained about 3 percent more of the variance, and the dummy proved highly significant. The inclusion of the dummy did not have a significant impact on our conclusions, however.

TABLE 4.6
Average Difference between Fitted Depreciation and Actual
Depreciation for Three Models

Country	Economic Model	Political/ Economic Model (2)	Political Model
Austria	**.013**	.023	.039
Belgium	.062	.054	**.051**
Canada	**.018**	.020	.045
Czechoslovakia	**.032**	.039	**.032**
Denmark	.049	**.032**	.044
France	.095	**.079**	.095
Finland	**.026**	.035	.056
Germany	**.016**	.028	.028
Hungary	.037	.033	**.025**
Italy	.083	**.077**	.084
Japan	**.056**	.064	.072
Netherlands	**.026**	.028	.026
Norway	.062	**.061**	.086
Poland	.034	.042	**.029**
Sweden	**.026**	.036	.046
United Kingdom	.047	**.039**	.041
United States	.042	.025	**.018**
Total number of best models[a]	8	5	6
Average	.047	.043	.049

Method: For each country: | Fitted Y − Actual Y | / N; where n = number of fitted Y for each country. Boldface indicates the smallest average difference between fitted and actual depreciation.

[a]Including ties.

currency value and the fitted values generated by the economic, political/economic, and pure political models. For nine countries out of seventeen, the political model or the combined political/economic model produced fits that were closest to actual currency changes. Only in the cases of Austria, Canada, Finland, Germany, Japan, and Sweden did the economic model clearly outperform the two others by this criterion. The combined model had the smallest overall average difference between the fitted and actual dependent variable.

CONCLUSIONS

This chapter has been concerned with the political and economic determinants of one adjustment option: currency depreciation or devaluation. The goal has been to discover whether or not, and to what extent, political variables systematically affected currency values during the interwar years. The presumptive norm during this period was that currencies should be fixed to gold. Deviations from this norm were viewed as disruptive to international trade and investment, and as a threat to the trade competitiveness of other countries. As Kenneth Oye has put it, to devalue a currency from its gold par was to "defect"[15] from the monetary norms of the period. This chapter shows that some of the strongest reasons for defecting had to do with domestic political conditions prevailing within each country.

The first part of this chapter concentrated on explaining the durability of a country's commitment to the gold standard. A probit model produced evidence that central bank independence contributed positively to the probability of being on gold, while democracies were much less likely to be able to make and maintain the gold commitment than nondemocracies. The one surprise that emerged from this test was that the higher the left-wing representation in parliament, the more likely a country was to be on gold. In addition, three structural variables influenced this probability: the largest economies and net external creditors were more likely to be on gold than their counterparts, but the dominant traders were not.

To understand currency fluctuations required a different analytical strategy, since the factors that influence the probability of being on the gold standard are not identical to those that explain devaluation (the patterns of France and Belgium provide examples). Therefore, a multivariate model was estimated that controlled for economic factors that we would expect to influence a currency's value: real interest rate differentials, price and business cycle shocks, changes in the value of the currency of the major trade partner, and the value of the currency itself in the previous period. When various combinations of these variables were controlled, three out of five of the original domestic political variables had a significant impact on the value of the currency in the expected direction, whether or not systemic variables were inserted as controls.

The results of the multivariate analysis help to resolve some of the ambiguities we had seen in the effect of the Left on the value of the currency. By separating the effects of the business cycle under left-wing governments and center-right governments, two things become clear. First, left-wing governments did depreciate their currencies overall, *independently* from the effects of the business cycle. But second, and crucially, left-wing governments were far more sensitive than their center-right counterparts to the Depression. Facing similar downturns, both left-wing and center-right governments tended to depreciate, but the Left did so on an order of magnitude that was three to four times greater than the center-right. This is powerful evidence that, under recessionary conditions, left-wing governments were far more likely to eschew deflation and let the currency value go than their counterparts. Left-wing governments could not put the currency above the condition of the domestic economy. They preferred to depreciate, especially under recessionary economic conditions.

The second strong result is the relationship between cabinet instability and depreciation. Depreciation was almost certainly greater when governments reshuffled cabinets repeatedly. Each additional cabinet turnover in a year was equivalent to about a 2.5 percent devaluation in this model. This is what we would expect given the strong relationship between cabinet turnover and deterioration of the current account and capital flight. Together, these findings lead to the conclusion that unstable governments were thought to be unlikely to take the long view necessary to stabilize an economy that was out of balance with the rest of the world. Markets reacted by selling the currency of a government that was likely to collapse.

Finally, political control of the central bank was associated with currency depreciation, at least between 1923 and 1931. This was true even when we controlled for net external creditor status and regime type, two factors that could plausibly have a confounding effect on the independence of the central bank. While the impact was not as strong as that of the Left or cabinet instability, it does remain highly significant across all versions of the basic model. This accords with our previous findings that more independent central banks had greater capital inflows and better current account balances. It also confirms what central bankers in England and the United States suspected in the twenties: the more independent a central bank from its government, the better its ability to defend the currency without the political interference for credit expansion or debt monetization. Domestic monetary institutions had a great deal to do with the ability and willingness of a country to live up to the norms of the gold standard.

The effects of labor unrest on the value of a currency were negative, though not very strong. In both the probit model and the ordinary least squares (OLS) model, labor unrest was in the expected direction, but was not statistically significant in either. Similarly, the probit analysis indicated that democracies were much less likely to be on gold than were authoritarian regimes, and the results of the OLS indicated that there was a slight tendency for democracies to depreciate somewhat more than authoritarian governments, but the difference was so insignificant that it may have been due to chance.

CUMULATIVE RESULTS

The natural result of a deteriorating current account and capital flight is downward selling pressure on a national currency. There is every reason to believe, therefore, that characteristics associated with these aspects of the balance of

TABLE 4.7
Cumulative Results: The Political Determinants of the Current Account,
Capital Movements, and Currency Value

Variable	Effect on		
	Current Account	Capital Movements	Currency Value
Regime type	$H_{0(-)}$	$H_{0(-)}$	$H_{0(-)}$
Influence of the Left	−	$H_{0(-)}$	−
Labor unrest	−	−	$H_{0(-)}$
Central bank independence	+	+	+
Cabinet instability	−	−	−
Control Variables			
Size (% world trade)	—	—	$H_{0(-)}$
Trade dependence	—	—	$H_{0(-)}$
Net investment position	—	—	$H_{0(-)}$
NNP	—	—	$H_{0(-)}$
Policy of major trade partner	—	—	+

payments should be associated with changes in the value of the currency in the same direction. This appears to be the case, despite the fact that datasets for the dependent variables are from different sources and cover slightly different observations. A summary of the findings so far is presented in table 4.7. "H_o" means that the null hypothesis could not be rejected at the 90 percent level of confidence. The direction of the estimated relationship is included in parentheses, nonetheless. With striking consistency, it seems clear that the conditions that undermined the current account and caused capital outflows were also implicated in currency devaluation. Thus, the economies headed by unstable governments, with significant left-wing participation in government and with politically controlled central banks, chose more often to devalue rather than to make fundamental adjustments that would halt current account deficits and encourage capital inflows. In short, the complexion of domestic politics made internal adjustment costly and incredible. The following chapter provides a case in point.

Chapter 5

FRANCE, 1924–1927

THE DESCRIPTION of conditions conducive to an imbalance of payments and depreciation bear an uncanny resemblance to those prevailing in France in the middle part of the twenties. While most countries had already returned to the gold standard, France's return was frustrated by a deteriorating (though still positive) current account, as well as by capital movements that worked against the stabilization of the franc. Figure 5.1 shows exactly where this case lies in terms of the two types of external pressures examined in Chapter 3. The current account balance was positive but deteriorating between 1924 and 1927. More importantly, capital fled for four years running. It is true that the current account continued to deteriorate up to 1932, but capital movements compensated for this shortfall. Not until 1935 and 1936 was there again a deterioration in *both* the capital and current accounts (a case that is taken up in Chapter 7).

Flight from the franc was the primary reason for its depreciation. During the six months between October 1923 and the beginning of March 1924, the franc lost about half its value, but rebounded dramatically in April. It deteriorated consistently over the next two years, before plunging to a low of 2.46 cents (U.S.) in July 1926. In 1928, the franc was legally stabilized at about 3.93 cents, and the idea of revalorization was eschewed, permanently and officially (figure 5.2).

The case of the devaluation and the stabilization of the French franc between 1923 and 1926 will provide an opportunity to observe the politics that underlie the quantitative relationships of the previous two chapters. The statistical results will also be used to interpret this episode; variables that would otherwise be difficult to evaluate in a single case setting can be better understood in the light of the multivariate causal models presented. Moreover, the French episode provides a good deal of variation on the explanatory factors we have examined. The first is the degree of cabinet instability. France in the early postwar years was a hotbed of political conflict. Several issues split the polity: how to pay for the war, the wisdom of the Ruhr occupation, the growing antagonism between bourgeois classes and the socialist or workers movement.[1] The most obvious manifestation of the fragility of the situation at this time was the sheer transience of cabinet government.[2] Ten different cabinet configura-

---

[1] David Thomson, *Democracy in France: The Third and Fourth Republics* (London: Oxford University Press), 1958, chap. 5.

[2] A complete official source on the makeup of French cabinets is found in a publication by the French Sénat, Services Législatifs, *Les Ministères de la France, 1871–1930 et 1930–1942* (Paris:

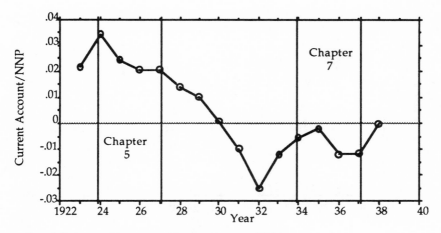

a. French Balance of Payments (Current Account/NNP)
Source: B. R. Mitchell, *European Historical Statistics.*

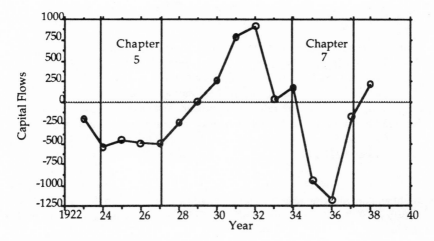

b. French Capital Movements
Source: United Nations, *International Capital Movements during the Interwar Years,* 1949, Table 1, pp. 10–12.

Figure 5.1: Defining the Case: Deterioration in the French Current Account and Worsening Capital Outflows

---

Sénat), 1930 and 1945. This paragraph draws entirely from the raw lists provided in this document, although party affiliations have been compiled from various other sources, including G. Bourgin et al., *Manuel des Parties Politiques en France* (Paris: Editions Rieder), 1928.

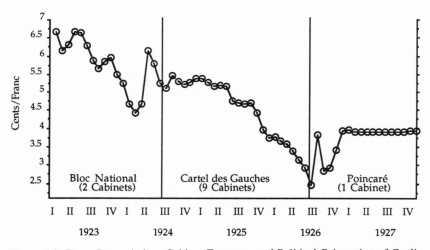

Figure 5.2: Franc Depreciation, Cabinet Turnover, and Political Orientation of Coalition in Power in France, 1923–1927
Source: Federal Reserve Board, *Banking and Monetary Statistics,* p. 670.

tions came and went between the beginning of 1924 and the end of 1926 alone. The political complexion of these cabinets gyrated from the Right under Raymond Poincaré and Frédéric François-Marsal through June 1924, to the Cartel des Gauches under Edouard Herriot, Paul Painlevé, and Aristide Briand up to July 1926, when Poincaré returned to power. The critical portfolio of finance bounced between nine different ministers from at least five different parties, while the average term for any one finance minister to serve uninterrupted at his post between 1922 and 1928 was about 239 days.[3] Two periods of relative calm (by the standards of the Third Republic) sandwiched this period of extremely high cabinet turnover, making it possible to examine the extent to which capital flight and devaluation resulted from the political turmoil. So the case of France between 1923 and 1926 will lend plausibility to the theory developed in the previous chapter that links domestic inflation, capital flight, a worsening current account, and ultimately currency depreciation with the market's perception of government instability. We should expect capital flight and franc deprecia-

---

[3] De Lasteyrie, 15 January 1922–29 March 1924, Fédération Républicaine de France; François-Marsal, 29 March 1924–9 June 1924, and again within another cabinet that lasted to 14 June 1924, Fédération Républicaine de France; Clémentel, 14 June 1924–17 April 1925 (party unknown); Caillaux, 17 April–29 October 1925, and again 23 June–19 July 1926, Parti Républicaine Radicale and Radicale Socialistes; Painlevé, 29 October–28 November 1925, Républicaine Socialistes and Socialiste Française; Loucheur, 28 November 1925–9 March 1926, Gauche Républicaine/Radicale; Peret, 9 March–23 June 1926 (party unknown); de Monzie, 19–23 July 1926 (party unknown); and finally, Poincaré, who lasted as finance minister a postwar record of 831 days, from 23 July 1926 to 11 November 1928, L'Alliance Républicaine Démocratique.

tion to correspond with the worst periods of cabinet instability, that is, the years of the Cartel des Gauches, which "ruled" from mid-1924 through mid-1926.

These years also provide variation on the political orientation of the party in power. The episode began under the Bloc National, a coalition of right-wing parties that included the Fédération Républicaine de France, the Parti Démocratic Populaire, and L'Alliance Républicaine Démocratique and was headed by Raymond Poincaré. The vicissitudes of the electoral system shifted power to the moderate Left in June 1924, and a series of governments were formed under various Radical Socialist leaders. (The far Left, including the French Socialists, usually withheld support.) Finally, a broad-based center-right government encompassing all elements save the extremes was formed once again under Poincaré. This Right/Left/center-right pattern provides some evidence on the relationship between political orientation of party in power and depreciation. However, in a single case study, the high covariance of instability and left-wing orientation makes it difficult to separate the effects of these on capital flight and the franc. This is where multivariate findings prove especially useful: the relationship between instability and capital flight is far more convincing than that between the presence of a left-wing government and the same outcome. In other words, we can now get better leverage on the variables of greatest causal importance in the French case by having had some experience with a more general model.

Third, the case addresses the issue of central bank credibility, and examines how the deterioration of credibility over time contributes to capital flight and depreciation.[4] At the same time, the case study allows us to dig deeper into the factors that can affect a monetary institution's credibility. In this case, the weakness of the Banque de France's leadership, as well as the high proportion of its assets that were government obligations (two plausible measures of independence for which it is difficult to find data), rendered the Banque somewhat more beholden to political manipulation. The Banque de France began with a reputation for independence, but this reputation dissolved when it was revealed that the Banque had obscured accounts to make it appear as though it had not cooperated with the government in monetization of the debt, when in fact it had. The reputation of the Banque was not restored until its leadership was replaced in June of 1926. As our previous findings would lead us to expect, this period of low credibility should be associated with capital flight, a worsening current account position, and ultimately currency depreciation.

Overall, between 1924 and 1926 France fit the description of a potential externalizer summarized at the end of the previous chapter. Unstable politics, left-wing government, and a reputationally impaired central bank all contributed to currency depreciation. Moreover, France's underlying structural position *permitted* externalization: very little of France's national economy depended on

---

[4] All previous analyses of central bank independence have been exclusively cross-sectional.

trade, and the financial sector was not highly internationalized, making it possible to tolerate currency swings. The French case corroborates the quantitative analysis. During the period of greatest instability, left-wing government, and political manipulation of the central bank, there was an important franc depreciation, and eventually stabilization at a fairly low level, a fact to which the rest of the world would simply have to adjust.

The chapter is organized as follows. The first section provides a general introduction to the condition of the French economy after the First World War. Growth, investment, employment, and productivity were all strong, especially compared to the countries that had undertaken systematic deflation. The second section discusses the conditions that sparked panic with respect to monetary inflation, which eventually led to a psychology of speculation against the franc. The failed Ruhr policy—and the realization that it was highly unlikely Germany could be forced to pay reparations on the scale that politicians had promised—piqued capital flight, but depreciation of the franc was arrested by a firm fiscal plan and a show of international financial support. The third section discusses why governments' credibility gap widened after the elections of May 1924. Cabinet instability, the stridency with which some elements of the Left were calling for punitive taxes on capital, and a central bank whose credibility was dashed upon the revelation of its intentional misrepresentation of advances to the government all encouraged capital flight, inflation, and depreciation. This section also discusses the shift in attitude within the governments and central banks of the United States and Britain, which led to a breakdown in international cooperation and further flight from the franc. In the absence of international institutions with clear responsibility for providing short-term bridging finance, the specter of hesitancy on the part of the central banks of the United States and Britain only furthered flight from the franc. The fourth section discusses the resolution to the crisis. With the defeat of the Left, Poincaré formed a coalition, the National Union, in 1926 and won immediate support for a credible fiscal program. But there was no drive to achieve prewar parity as there had been in Britain. The inflation itself had created winners and losers, ultimately making deflation and revalorization politically unpalatable. After years of depreciation and a loss of nearly four fifths of its value, the franc was stabilized at a low level, which complicated maintenance of the parities for those countries that had struggled back to their prewar values.[5]

[5] Several economic historians have noted that the stabilized franc was in fact undervalued. See, e.g., Alec Cairncross and Barry Eichengreen, *Sterling in Decline: The Devaluations of 1931, 1949, and 1967* (Oxford: Basil Blackwell), 1983, p. 44; Charles P. Kindleberger, *The World in Depression, 1929–1939* (Berkeley: University of California Press), 1986, p. 32; R. S. Sayers, "The Return to Gold, 1925," in Sidney Pollard (ed.), *The Gold Standard and Employment Policy Between the Wars* (London: Methuen), 1970, p. 93. For a statistical analysis based on cost of living indices and wholesale prices, which concludes that the franc was from 10 to 25 percent undervalued, see Pierre Sicsic, "Was the Franc Poincaré Deliberately Undervalued?" Unpublished essay, Harvard University, Department of Economics, November 1989.

THE REAL ECONOMY

In contrast to the cases of deficit in the 1930s, which will be discussed in Chapter 7, in the mid-twenties the French economy was booming.[6] Postwar reconstruction had elevated reindustrialization to the highest national priority and provided an opportunity for the country to modernize and rationalize to an extent unknown in French history and unparalleled in Europe.[7] The effect on the French industrial base was profound. By some accounts, French industry was far more efficient at this time than it had been before the war.[8] Between

---

[6] There are a number of books on the economic and political conditions of France in the interwar period. See Eleanor Lansing Dulles, *The Dollar, the Franc, and Inflation* (New York: Macmillan), 1933; James Harvey Rogers, *The Process of Inflation in France, 1914–1927* (New York: Columbia University Press), 1929; Martin Wolfe, *The French Franc Between the Wars, 1919–1939* (New York: Columbia University Press), 1951; Tom Kemp, *The French Economy 1913–1939: The History of a Decline* (New York: St. Martin's Press), 1972. A good contemporary French source is Georges La Chapelle, *Les Finances de la IIIème République*, Collection "L'Histoire" (Paris: Flammarion), 1937. For monetary conditions in Europe more generally at this time, see Charles P. Kindleberger, *A Financial History of Western Europe* (London: Allen and Unwin), 1984; D. T. Jack, *The Restoration of European Currencies* (London: P. S. King and Sons), 1927), especially chaps. 1 and 7; Derek H. Aldcroft, *From Versailles to Wall Street, 1919–1929* (London: Allen Lane), 1977, especially chap. 6. An excellent study taking into account the foreign policy dimension of French policy is Stephen A. Schuker, *The End of French Predominance in Europe: The Financial Crisis of 1924 and the Adoption of the Dawes Plan* (Chapel Hill: University of North Carolina Press), 1976. Shorter works include Jean-Claude Debeir, "Inflation et Stabilisation en France (1919–1928)," in *Revue Economique*, Vol. 31, No. 4, July 1980, pp. 622–647. The best memoirs on this period are those of Emile Moreau, *Souvenirs d'un Gouverneur de la Banque de France* (Paris: Librarie de Médicis), 1954.

[7] Despite the fact that the monetary value of the damage to industry was less than to nonindustrial sectors, industry received a disproportionately large share of reconstruction funds. According to a study by William McDonald, "By the end of 1920 advances to war-damaged mines and industries equalled 84% and 113%, respectively, based on their estimated damages in 1914 values whereas non-industrial damages received advances only equal to 22% of their estimated 1914 value, although such damages accounted for 78% of total losses." In francs, industrial *sinistrés* were given about 3.75 billion francs out of an eventual total of 6.6 billion. McDonald, *Reconstruction in France* (New York: Macmillan), 1922, p. 182. According to observers, exaggerated claims meant that some industries that were in a precarious position before the war were able to reconstruct two to three time over. Robert Stahl, *L'Organisation du Rélèvement Economique dans le nord Libéré* (Lille: Thesis), 1920, p. 39; F. Bidaux, "La Rôle de l'Etat et de l'initiative Privée dans la Reconstitution des Régions Devastées," Legal diss., Paris, 1922, p. 111.

[8] William F. Ogburn and William Jaffé, *The Economic Development of Post-War France: A Survey of Production* (New York: Columbia University Press), 1929, p. 120. D. W. Brogan, *France Under the Republic: The Development of Modern France (1870–1939)*, (New York: Harper & Brothers), 1940, chap. 4, pp. 599–622. According to a series of reports commissioned by the British Department of Overseas Trade, French industry was increasingly making use of advanced technology, concentrating, and utilizing resources much more efficiently. By 1925, it was feared that such policies and practices greatly enhanced France's productive capacity and competitive edge. J. R. Cahill, *Report on the Economic and Industrial Conditions in France* (London: His Majesty's Stationery Office), 1925, p. 20.

1921 and 1929 productivity per man hour rose an average of 5.5 percent a year.[9] As a result, France enjoyed relatively strong growth: by 1926 British and German industrial production still lagged at about 68 percent and 92 percent of their prewar levels, respectively, while the equivalent French rate was 126 percent (figure 5.3).[10]

One reason such growth was possible was that the inflation that had resulted from swollen postwar budgets was *unanticipated*. France had had no previous experience with inflation, and thus inflationary expectations were not well enough entrenched in wage contracts and pricing policies to contribute to general unemployment and economic slowdown. Wage agreements continued to lag behind commodity prices, which kept employment at around 3 percent, or nearly full levels.[11] Furthermore, creditors were willing to continue to extend reasonably cheap credit (a sign of the belief that inflation would be temporary). Industries profited greatly as their production costs fell while selling prices rose (figure 5.4).[12] Until market agents began to expect inflation from their government (around mid-decade), most people were willing to save a fairly normal proportion of their income. Under these conditions, investment expansion continued to be highly attractive, and economic growth remained strong despite the moderate inflation.[13]

The combination of higher productivity and declining real wages tended to keep imports and exports in rough balance.[14] Manufactures maintained a sur-

[9] Alfred Sauvy, *Histoire Economique de la France Entre les Deux Guerres*, Vol. 3 (Paris: Economica), 1984; also cited by Thomas W. Grabau, "Industrial Reconstruction in France After World War I." Ph.D. diss., Indiana University, 1976. p. 3.

[10] Sauvy, ibid., p. 323; Ingvor Svennilson, *Growth and Stagnation in the European Economy* (Geneva: United Nations), 1954, p. 29. For a comprehensive treatment of the comparison between France and Britain, including but not limited to the time period in question, see Charles P. Kindleberger, *Economic Growth in France and Britain, 1851–1950* (Cambridge: Harvard University Press), 1964.

[11] With the exception of a slight recession in 1924, which registered an unemployment rate of 5 percent. One reason wages generally failed to keep up with inflation was the fissiparous nature of union politics in the twenties. Ideological struggle within the labor movement seemed to dominate the agenda of the leadership, at the expense of serious collective negotiations for wage increases. Also note that the more marginal workers were foreign, and therefore voteless. Brogan, *France Under the Republic*, p. 635.

[12] The iron and steel industry was one of the few sectors that posted declines in real profits between 1919 and 1926. Max J. Wassermann, "Inflation and Enterprise in France, 1919–1926," *Journal of Political Economy*, Vol. 42, No. 2, April 1934, pp. 202–236.

[13] Ragnar Nurkse, *The Course and Control of Inflation*, (Geneva: League of Nations), 1946, chap. 7; Tom Kemp, *The French Economy 1913–1939*, pp. 82–99. Max J. Wasserman, "The Compression of French Wholesale Prices During Inflation, 1919–1926," *American Economic Review*, Vol. 26, No. 1, March 1936, pp. 62–73. On the general question of the stability of the franc prior to WWI, see Alain Prate, *La France et Sa Monnaie: Essai sur les Relations entre la Banque de France et les Gouvernements* (Paris: Julliard), 1987, especially chap. 4, pp. 63–79.

[14] Pierre Frayssinet, "La Politique Monétaire de la France (1924–1928)." Ph.D. diss., Department of Political Economy, University of Paris, 1928.

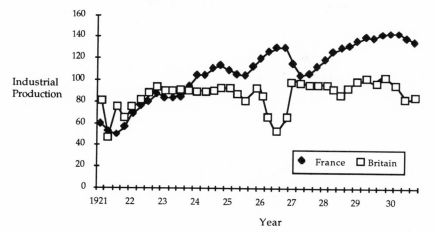

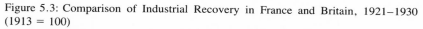

Figure 5.3: Comparison of Industrial Recovery in France and Britain, 1921–1930 (1913 = 100)
Source: Alfred Sauvy, *Histoire Economique,* pp. 315, table 1; 324, table 11; 325, table 12.

plus without a great increase in protectionism.[15] France had trade surpluses with Britain and Belgium, but between 1924 and 1926 it had a shrinking surplus with Germany and a growing deficit with the United States (figure 5.5). Yet the strength of the real economy[16] allowed governments to postpone resolving the problem of the public finances, and enabled the delusion to persist that Ger-

[15] According to indices compiled by the League of Nations, French tariffs on manufactured goods increased from 20 percent to 21 percent between 1913 and 1925, while American tariffs on manufactures increased from 25 percent in 1914 to 37 percent in 1925; Italy's went from 18 percent to 20 percent, Belgium's went from 9 percent to 15 percent, and the United Kingdom's went from no tariff to a 5 percent tariff on manufactured goods in 1925. League of Nations, *Tariff Level Indices: A Statistical Inquiry into the Level of Tariffs, in preparation for the World Economic Conference in April–May 1926* (Geneva: Economic and Financial Section; II Econ. & Fin. 1927.II.34), p. 15. Exports in the manufacturing sector were so strong that some proposed a tax on exports. See various issues of *La Journée Industrielle* between September and December 1926. See also the strong argument against the export tax by the Confédération Général de la Production Française, to the Président du Conseil, 26 January 1926, as well as Le Directeur des Affaires Commerciales et Industrielles, à Monsieur le Conseiller d'Etat, which is a summary of the barrage of protests the government had received from commercial and industrial groups regarding the export tax; 9 February 1926, F12 8805, National Archives, Paris. Jacques Duboin, *La Stabilisation du Franc* (Paris: Marcel Rivière), 1927, p. 104 (written in March 1926). Tourism was another sector that boomed, and angry Frenchmen mobbed buses of American tourists. One French contemporary noted, with not a little discomfiture, that unemployed Englishmen could come to France in the mid-1920s and get more from their unemployment checks than they could in their own country. Duboin, *La Stabilisation du Franc,* p. 33; also, La Chapelle, *Les Finances,* p. 130.

[16] Recall that in Chapter 3 it was shown that economic growth is usually associated with worsening current account deficits.

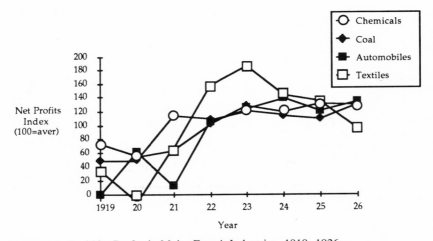

Figure 5.4: Real Net Profits in Major French Industries, 1919–1926
Source: Max I. Wasserman, pp. 202–236. "Inflation and Enterprise in France, 1919–1926."
Journal of Political Economy, 42, no. 2, 1934.

many would pay the reconstruction bill. Industrialists and traders encouraged this idea, since they gained handsomely from reconstruction funds and the stimulation of the mild unanticipated inflation.[17] The government officially defended France's inflation as "normal,"[18] and continued to borrow. But the precarious nature of the public finances shattered confidence and at certain flash points ignited a startling flight of capital on the part of speculators and, at the nadir of the crisis, the ordinary French petite bourgeoisie. The problem was not the debt's size,[19] but its short-term structure. Flight from the franc greatly depressed the market for government bonds—not a small problem for a govern-

[17] In 1923 industrial and commercial groups argued that the financial position of the government was not desperate, that tax receipts were increasing regularly, and that Germany's recovery made it more likely that it would pay reparations. These groups were vocal in their opposition to any type of tax on capital, profits, or revenues. The only type of tax they were willing to countenance was the traditional levy on "outward signs of wealth," for instance, use of electricity. But a tax on capital, it was argued, would encourage its flight, discourage repatriation, and contribute to the depreciation of the franc. Société pour la Défense du Commerce et de l'Industrie de Marseille, Séance de la Chambre Syndicale du 27 Février 1923, Report by J. B. Rocca, Files of the Ministry of Commerce, $F_{12}8167$, National Archives, Paris.

[18] "Le Problem de la Vie Chère," Comité Consultatif Supérieur du Commerce et de l'Industrie, 23 November 1923, Ministry of Commerce and Industry, F_{12} 8790, National Archives, Paris. The conclusion of this study was that "abnormal" price increases had totaled only 14 percent over a ten-year period, and that this compared favorably with most other European nations.

[19] Sauvy, *Histoire Economique*, pp. 16–17 (see especially fig. 17). Over the course of the decade, the government succeeded (in nominal terms, anyway) in reducing its debt relative to GNP first through inflationary measures, then through real increases in national production, and finally through amortizement beginning with Poincaré's regime. The result was that, as early as 1921, the public debt began to fall fairly consistently in relation to GNP.

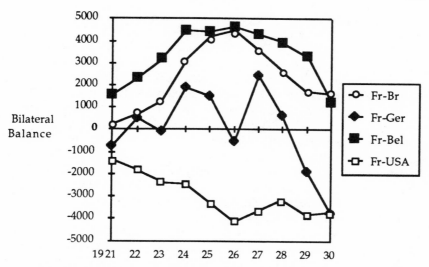

Figure 5.5: Bilateral Balance with France's Major Trading Partners, 1921–1930, in Millions of Francs
Source: Alfred Sauvy, *Histoire Economique,* Tables 4–6, pp. 341–345.

ment whose financial lifeblood flowed from obligations that matured every one, three, six, or twelve months. Crisis erupted every time a major flotation reached maturity. In the mid-1920s, repayments on mature short-term bonds reached 7 to 8 billion francs a month, and sometimes more.[20]

On a deeper level, inflation and depreciation had clearly benefited the industrial sector, at the expense of the rentier and real wages. Stabilization at a low real exchange rate reflected the ability of industry to consolidate the gains of the previous years.

CRACKS IN CREDIBILITY

The first episode of extreme franc instability was touched off by French foreign policy failure. By 1923, it had become increasingly clear that France was isolated on the issue of German reparations. British officials blamed France for forcing Germany into industrial disorganization and delaying the recovery of Europe, while American financiers refused to market a major loan in Europe

---

[20] D. T. Jack put the number of such bonds outstanding as totaling 58.4, 54.5, and 45.7 *billion* francs in 1922, 1925, and 1926, respectively. The decline in 1926 is made up for by an increase in advances from the Banque de France to the Trésor from 22.6 to 35.9 billions, and an increase in Treasury bills from 1.8 to 2.3 billion between 1925 and 1926, which indicates that during this time the government had mainly shifted its short-term borrowing from domestic investors to a rather pliant central bank. Jack, *The Restoration of European Currencies*, p. 117. The monthly figure is given by La Chapelle, *Les Finances*, p. 133.

unless there was a reasonable chance of German recovery. No longer was it obvious that the costs of reconstructing the French economy would be borne by the Germans. At the same time, the futility and costliness of the Ruhr occupation was becoming clear. A bear-market attack on the franc, which imperiled government finances by disrupting the sale of *bons de la défense nationale*, ensued in November of 1923. By the first quarter of 1924, the franc lost nearly half its value: it fell from about 6 cents in October to about 3.5 cents by early March.[21]

When the franc came under pressure in early January 1924, the Poincaré cabinet proposed strong fiscal measures to balance the government budget and reestablish confidence. These were generally in line with discussions that had taken place in banking and financial circles for some time. On the seventeenth of January, Poincaré proposed the *"double décime,"* which raised all existing taxes by 20 percent. It was simple and immediate, and was claimed to raise at least a billion francs a year. A series of measures were also proposed to improve tax collection, apprehend evaders, control foreign exchange operations, increase utility rates, and sell off unprofitable state enterprises. Poincaré also asked for the controversial authority to carry through administrative streamlining of government by decree for six months.[22]

These proposals immediately became mired in politics. The parliament debated for five wearisome weeks, while the franc continued to slide. Poincaré was working against a well-ingrained distrust of simple cross-the-board tax schemes based on earnings; even his own cabinet accepted the proposal unenthusiastically, fearing the voters' revenge at the general elections in May. Despite the urgency and international ramifications of the financial situation, the deputies debated with their characteristic parochialism.

The nemesis of the Bloc National proved to be the crucial position of the Radical Socialists, the moderate left wing of the coalition. Poincaré couldn't rule without them.[23] Prior to the war, they were the main governing party and had posed as the avatar of the "little man," opposed to an oppressive state, clericalism, and other ill-defined "predatory interests." In the financial debates of 1924, the Radical Socialists attempted to stake out political territory that was vaguely anticapitalist and sympathetic toward socialism (without, however, having a positive economic program).[24] Many deputies on the Left were convinced that reconstruction had served the selfish interests of industrial capitalists. In early 1924 many refused to vote for new taxes to pay for reconstruction

[21] Pierre Frayssinet, "La Politique Monétaire de la France (1924–1928)," p. 13; Schuker, *The End of French Predominance in Europe*, passim; Dulles, *The Dollar, the Franc, and Inflation*, chap. 5.

[22] Schuker, *The End of French Predominance in Europe*, p. 60.

[23] The Bloc had enough votes for passage of the tax package in the Chambre without the Radicals, but not in the Sénat.

[24] Peter J. Larmour, *The French Radical Party in the 1930s* (Stanford: Stanford University Press), 1964. I do not wish to imply that the extreme Left (Socialists) had a positive program to offer in 1924.

until some of these bloated payments were returned to the national coffers.[25] The difficulties of passing a program of heavy taxation under a coalitional government with a vexing left-wing flank proved to be insurmountable.

Poincaré tried to counter the Left and gain support for his financial package by invoking the national interest. As the debates wore on, he warned of the disastrous implications for the independence of French foreign policy. When this failed (many, after all, were highly critical of his "independent" foreign policy in the Ruhr), Poincaré pitched his appeal in terms of fairness. He told the parliament that "to defend the franc is above all to perform a service for the immense group of small investors, minor civil servants, humble pensioners, workers and employees, of all those living on fixed incomes. It is, above all, to come equally to the aid of all consumers, that is, of the entire nation."[26] Such an appeal attempted to seize the moral high ground (as well as the political center).

The parliamentary tax debates shaded into the campaign of 1924, in which the Left campaigned against the reckless borrowing of the Bloc National that had become necessary to fund the Ruhr occupation and maintain a high military profile.[27] The Cartel des Gauches criticized the Bloc's inability to sustain the franc and to control the soaring cost of living; it also criticized some of its social policies, which were branded as clearly antiunion. But when it came to the critical issue of taxation, the Left was a shambles. Herriot called for a capital levy, Painlevé "in principle" accepted a more moderate version of the double décime, and Vincent Auriol, representing the Socialists, was merely obstructionist.[28]

While the Chambre passed the tax legislation on 23 February, the Sénat continued to delay. The upper house was at this time perhaps slightly left of the Chambre in its orientation; moreover, it was piqued that the government was ramming its emergency legislation through. Delay was the legislative order of the day. Important senators such as Henry Bérenger and Paul Doumer insisted—without basis—that the United States and Britain would give France a large capital loan until Germany could be forced to pay reparations. By February, some senators had heard of the irregular advances of the Banque de

---

[25] They argued that much of what was paid as indemnities was based on grossly exaggerated estimates of damage, and that public monies were actually being used for industrial expansion. *Le Temps* 28 and 31 January and 1 February 1924.

[26] Quoted by Schuker, *The End of French Predominance*, pp. 63–64.

[27] Ibid., p. 64. See also Brian Chapman, *The Prefects and Provincial France* (London: Allen and Unwin), 1955, pp. 97–100.

[28] Socialists' arguments were far more rhetorical and self-consciously ideological than they were analytical. Though he spoke of closing the banks and locking up the bankers, Vincent Auriol (the Socialists' financial spokesman) basically favored the postponement of a fundamental change in fiscal policy. Indeed, he denied that fiscal policy had anything to do with franc depreciation. In 1924 he advocated defense of the franc through the requisition of foreign exchange from the banks and big industries. Socialists were more interested in connecting increased taxation with the failure of the Ruhr policy than with taking the long view on the nation's finances. Schuker, *The End of French Predominance*, pp. 76–77.

France to the Treasury, which eroded confidence on the right. The Treasury's position continued to deteriorate. By April, an attempted 3 billion franc long-term bond flotation through the Crédit National was woefully undersubscribed (the Radical Socialists opposed it in their popular press), and a certain degree of involuntary lending was foisted upon commercial banks and the Banque de France.[29] By the beginning of March, most foreign exchange specialists thought it too late to save the franc through taxation, and they advocated direct intervention.

Still, the Sénat hesitated to sanction the six-month emergency decree. The request for the power to streamline government imperiled the patronage value of local government sinecures, which were Radical Socialist party strong-holds.[30] Once again, party politics chipped away at the Bloc, as the wavering but necessary moderate Left withheld its sanction. The markets bolted; the franc took a deep dive at the beginning of March, and it reached a low of 123 francs to the pound and 28.9 francs to the dollar in New York on March 8.[31]

One of the most important reasons for the market's continued gamble against the franc was the central bank's known complicity in the government's financial morass. That political cooptation of the central bank endangers that institution's credibility—with serious consequences for capital flight, current account deterioration, and depreciation—is vividly illustrated by the market's reaction to the Banque de France's political pliancy in 1924 and 1925. Indeed, until the leadership shake-up of 1926 the bank accommodated the government whenever the latter had difficulty floating short-term bonds.[32] It did this mainly through the liberal rediscounting of treasury bills. As a result, the Banque de France had the highest ratio of claims on government as a percentage of its total earning assets of all countries surveyed by the League of Nations in 1926 (figure 5.6). With government assets looming so large in its portfolio, the Banque can hardly be said to have been above politics.

The Banque de France also accommodated the government by encouraging commercial banks to extend "extraordinary assistance" to the Treasury, and then rapidly reconstituted their liquidity with fresh money.[33] While legal, these

---

[29] Ibid., p. 87; La Chapelle, *Les Finances*, p. 163.

[30] For example, see Jacques Duboin (Radical party), Speech before the Chambre des Députies, *Journal Officiel*, 25 January 1924. For the Radical party's attack on the Ruhr occupation, see *Quotidien*, 28 January 1924.

[31] La Chapelle, *Les Finances*, pp. 114–121.

[32] Whenever there was a crisis of confidence, due to the inability of the government to renew subscription of its short term bonds, "the Trèsor inevitably found recourse, whether overt or masked, at the Banque de France." Prate, *La France et sa Monnaie*, p. 85. For a general review of the argument that France's inflation was due to accommodating monetary policy in the form of advances to the Trèsor, see Henry Miller, "The Franc in War and Reconstruction," *Quarterly Journal of Economics*, Vol. 44, No. 3, May 1930, pp. 523–538.

[33] Délibérations du Conseil Général, No. 112, Procès Verbal de la Séance du 6 Mars 1924, pp. 5–6, Archives of the Banque de France, Paris.

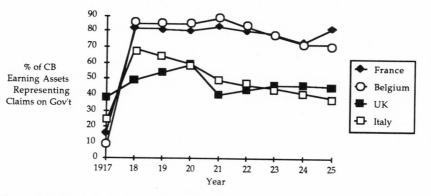

Figure 5.6: Central Banks' Claims on Their Governments, 1917–1925
Source: League of Nations, Memorandum on Currency and Central Banks, 1913–25, Vol. 1, Geneva, 1926, pp. 16–21.

operations had the same inflationary effect as if the Banque de France had made the advances itself.[34] The impact on the money supply was evident (table 5.1). While these operations were meant to improve the state's creditworthiness and help with bond marketability, they were disastrous for the reputation of the central bank itself. Furthermore, when it was discovered that central bank personnel, under Governor Robineau[35] (who was to lose his job in June of 1926), had manipulated the books of the bank to make it appear as though the money supply had not exceeded its legal limit, the Banque de France lost a tremendous amount of prestige. This revelation virtually dashed the central bank's ability to inspire public confidence or to speak as a credible voice for monetary conservatism.

The central bank also lost credibility when it hesitated to use two available policy levers to defend the franc.[36] First, it was far from aggressive in its use of

[34] Prate, *La France et sa Monnaie*, p. 89; Jean Bouvier, "The French Banks, Inflation, and the Economic Crisis, 1919–1939," *Journal of Economic History*, Vol. 13, 1984, p. 47.

[35] Governor Benjamin Strong of the Federal Reserve Bank of New York thought that Georges Robineau was virtually an agent of the Trèsor: "While I have always liked Robineau personally, he is a weak man and so far as I have been able to discover they have had no one in the Bank . . . who has been capable of resisting the Treasury, and in management the Bank has shrunk into being the instrument . . . of the Treasury." Memo, Strong to George Harrison, 5 July 1926, File C261.1, FRBNY. Most historical accounts agree that Robineau was a weak character who lacked the authority of his predecessors. Prate, *La France et Sa Monnaie*, p. 88; see also Jean-Denis Bredin, *Joseph Caillaux* (Paris: Hachette), 1980, and Jean-Joël Jeanneney, *François de Wendel en République: L'Argent et le Pouvoir, 1914–1940* (Paris: Editions du Seuil), 1976, pp. 181–183. Jeanneney makes the further point that much of the Conseil des Régents was composed of new personnel who in general were much weaker personalities than those they had replaced.

[36] Note that at this time the only instrument by which the central bank could keep control of the money market was through its discount rate. It did not have the legal power to perform open-market operations to affect the money supply.

TABLE 5.1

French Money Supply (Notes in Circulation), 1913–1926

Year	Index: Quantity of Money in Circulation	Annual Average Advances to the State (billions of francs)	% Bank Note Circ. Made Up of Advances to the State
1913	100	00.0	00
1919	332	23.4	67
1920	361	26.1	69
1921	356	25.3	68
1922	343	23.0	64
1923	353	23.1	62
1924	380	22.8	57
1925	421	26.5	60
1926	506	35.8	67

Source: William Ogburn and William Jaffé, *The Economic Development of Post-War France: A Survey of Production* (New York: Columbia University Press), 1929, pp. 56–59.

the discount rate. Every effort to tighten the money market widened the gap between market rates of interest and the return the government was willing to pay on the floating debt, compounding the government's financial difficulties by stimulating a flight from bonds to other more profitable investments. This dilemma persisted as long as the rate on the floating debt was fixed by the Treasury and not by the market.[37] Second, the central bank suffered self-inflicted paralysis by refusing to use one of its most important resources—its gold stock—to defend the national currency.[38] Defending the franc with gold was an option advocated by both the government and the financial community.[39] However, some of the Régents reasoned that shipping gold to defend the franc would actually cause more inflation by reducing the gold backing of the outstanding currency. Others who argued from a more nationalistic vantage were convinced that speculative maneuvers against the franc were part of Germany's plan to weaken France for the kill, and they thought that the shipment of gold would undermine France's longer term financial stability.[40] Overall, despite the central bank's formal independence, the deficit in leadership, the

[37] Memo: "Cross Currents in the Paris Market," Warren, 14 June 1926. File C261.1, FRBNY.

[38] According to the League of Nations' *Monthly Bulletin of Statistics*, the gold reserves of the Banque de France remained constant in absolute terms from the early 1920s through the various stabilization crises and their resolution. Total gold reserves were approximately 5.5 billion gold francs until the central bank began its gold-buying campaign in 1928.

[39] During the run that intensified in the first three months of 1924, the Conseil Général opposed a number of government schemes to raise stabilization loans using the gold stock of the central bank as collateral.

[40] Their alternative was to raise funds through a longer term bond issue whose earnings would be tax exempt. Edouard Rothschild, leader of the financial conservatives, and François de Wendel, industrialist, joined forces to oppose the use of the bank's gold stock.

dominance of government bonds in its own portfolio, and the hesitancy to use either the discount rate or the gold stock aggressively undermined its reputation for monetary stringency. The money supply burgeoned. The franc was defenseless against bear-market speculators who brought it to a historical low in the first week of 1924.

By February 1924 the monetary and financial morass drove French officials to seek stabilization assistance from abroad. Fundamental conflicts over reparations made it unlikely that succor would be forthcoming from the governments of Britain and the United States.[41] As the crisis worsened, French monetary authorities, urged by commercial banks whose assets were rapidly depreciating,[42] became increasingly convinced that a stabilization loan through private channels was their best hope. In early March negotiations began with J. P. Morgan and Company for a $100 million loan, which would be used to support the franc.[43] A deal was swiftly concluded that involved greater sums than French officials had requested, but with certain "conditions": the French government had to insist on the immediate passage of the tax package in the Sénat and to balance the budget; once the crisis subsided, the government had to agree to make no new appeals to domestic credit markets, except for purposes of consolidating the floating debt; and French officials had to agree to make a

---

[41] While British officials "welcomed" the franc's fall as a way to make France more pliant on reparations. Sir Otto Niemeyer (senior official in the British Treasury) wrote in early 1924: "The only thing likely to move the present French government towards a more reasonable reparations policy, apart from a slowly growing feeling of disquiet at French isolation amid the reprobation of a world horrified at starvation and ruin in Germany, is a fall in the French franc sufficiently serious to shake the confidence of the French peasant in his national securities." In February, Philip Snowden, Labour chancellor of the exchequer, noted that the franc was "the best weapon the English and ultimately also the Germans have against Poincaré." Prime Minister Ramsay MacDonald considered coordinated action against the franc to pressure France into accepting the report of the Experts' (Dawes) Committee on German reparations. But he told a group of German businessmen in April 1924 that "if we smash the franc to 150 or indeed 200 to the pound, we will get an increase in French competition and [domestic] unemployment." Though less vehement, American State Department officials also saw the international political advantages to the weak franc. In February, Arthur Young, their adviser to the Expert's Committee in Paris, wrote that "the franc has fallen very opportunely and the result has been a great increase of reasonableness in this country." The quotations in this paragraph are cited in Schuker, *The End of French Predominance*, p. 99–104.

[42] Squeezed between paying out high rates of interest on deposits in order to attract business, and the depreciating value of the assets they held, bankers and economists at Lazards Frères and Société Générale were particularly insistent that the franc should be defended. Their analogies were colorful, if (usefully) nationalistic: "Napoléon used his reserves at the decisive moment in order to win the battle. . . . In financial matters, it would be absurd to consider these reserves as fetishes, and one must be willing to engage them at the right moment. We are at a very psychological time. It is not enough to hold, we must counterattack. The means are there; won't we use them? It's a matter of hours." Quoted in Raymond Philippe, *Le Drame Financier de 1924–1928* (Paris), 1931, pp. 33–34. See also Jeanneney, *François de Wendel*, p. 187.

[43] Délibérations du Conseil Général, No. 112, Procès Verbal de la Séance Extraordinaire, du 7 Mars 1924, p. 10. Rothschild in particular inveighed against such expedients, but himself had approached Morgan for the railroad loan.

permanent commitment not to borrow anymore on the domestic market unless these loans could be serviced by new taxation. The Banque de France agreed reluctantly to pledge the shipment of gold in case of default.[44] Poincaré promised that the government would use all of its authority (which did not amount to much at this time) to bring the fiscal program to a rapid vote in the Sénat. He refused, however, to heed the Banque de France's recommendation that all expenditures to the devastated regions be halted.[45] Nonetheless, on 9 March 1924, the Conseil approved the sale of a maximum of 500 million francs worth of gold from the central bank's stockpile, and released a bland statement of official support.[46]

The effect of the Morgan loan on the market was immediate. Upon the announcement of the $100 million war chest on 12 March 1924, the franc made a spectacular and immediate recovery—before any resources were actually expended to defend it. This favorable psychology was reinforced when the government introduced a new plan for financial restoration on the fourteenth of March, along with a proposal that interest earned from short-term government bonds be tax-exempt. Within six weeks the franc regained almost half its value against sterling, going from 115.6 to 65.05 francs to the pound.

FROM A CRACK TO A GULF: JANUARY 1925–JULY 1926

The results of the May 1924 general election unraveled the return to confidence stimulated by the Morgan loan and Poincaré's fiscal regime. The elections marked the beginning of a period of uncertainty that would last until July 1926. The outcome of the vote did not represent a decisive defeat for Poincaré, nor did it provide the Left with an unassailable mandate for action. The Cartel and Socialists together received only about 3.39 million votes (not including votes for the Communists, whose support was withheld), and lost forty-nine seats,

[44] In a letter from Governor Robineau to the minister of finance it is abundantly clear the degree to which the Banque de France was reacting to, and failing to shape, policies for containment of the financial crisis. This letter—drafted within three hours of the government's request—gave complete authorization to pursue railroad loans, including an OK to contract funds for ten years, using the gold of the central bank as collateral. Reprinted in Délibérations du Conseil Général, No. 112, Procès Verbal de la Séance Extraordinaire, 7 March 1924, pp. 11–15.

[45] Letter from the Conseil Général to the Minister of Finance, Reprinted in Procès Verbal de la Séance Extraordinaire, 9 March 1924, pp. 15–16. The financial hard-liner Rothschild was the strongest voice on the Conseil Général pressing for the halting of all such expenditures, which he termed "economically and financially disastrous with a currency as depreciated as our own."

[46] The government's press release ran roughly as follows: "All measures necessary to the stabilization of the financial situation and the redress of the franc have been envisaged. The Government will insist, as it has said before, on a rapid vote in the Sénat on its financial plans and will restore the declarations made in the Chambre on the necessity of reducing expenditures and to put an end to the policy of borrowing. The Bank will continue to support the efforts of the government and will take all useful efforts to this end." Reprinted in Procès Verbal de la Séance Extraordinaire, 9 March 1924, p. 16. See also La Chapelle, Les Finances, p. 119.

while the array of opposition groups to the Right had received about 4.54 million votes. The new government, headed by the Radical Socialists, could only govern with the cooperation of the far Left—elusive at best—which contributed to the extreme ministerial volatility between 1924 and 1926.[47]

On top of a good deal of political instability, financial markets were nervous about the prospect of the Left in power at all. Conservative capitalists regarded Herriot, the new prime minister, with suspicion.[48] From the time Herriot's government came to power, French capital increasingly sought refuge outside the country by selling government *rentes* and *bons* and purchasing foreign securities. Exporters increasingly kept their earnings overseas. As inflation accelerated in 1925, the value of *rentes* fell precipitously while foreign securities had a constant tendency to appreciate. This largely reflected flight from the franc, which is estimated to have reached 20 billion francs in 1924–1925, and as much as 17 billion in 1926 alone.[49]

The Left simply could not present a coherent economic program. The major conundrum—how to raise revenues without increasing public borrowing, and thus bring public finances under control—was an issue upon which Cartel leaders themselves differed. While campaigning on the basis of progressive taxation, Herriot's wing of the party favored a "special contribution" from the wealthiest segments of society (i.e., a capital levy), while the more moderate wing led by Joseph Caillaux was against it.[50] An important segment of the left-wing coalition advocated "economizing" by cutting government employees in unspecified positions, by limiting undefined "waste," and by prosecuting fiscal fraud more diligently. It was not necessary, according to the moderate Left, to raise the overall tax burden.[51] The Cartel government made the tactical error of removing the 20 percent cross-the-board tax imposed in the last days of the Poincaré cabinet, but since no coherent replacement was adopted, the Treasury

[47] La Chapelle, *Les Finances*, p. 121.

[48] This conservative fear of socialist government is clearly portrayed in the communications between central bankers at this time. Leffingwell to Lamont, 8 May 1926; Strong to Mellon, 14 May 1926; C261.1, Federal Reserve Bank of New York Archives. It was also exploited baldly in the center-right French press. When Strong came to France in May of 1926, an influential editorialist, Pertinax, for *Echo de Paris*, wrote that the first question Strong put to French officials was "Can you give me the assurance that a Herriot government will not be formed?" (24 May 1926).

[49] La Chapelle, *Les Finances*, p. 131. For an estimate on capital flight, see P. Meynial, "La Balance des Comptes," *Revue d'Economie Politique*, Vol. 41, No. 2, March–April 1927, p. 127.

[50] Thus the 1925 party platform was conspicuously vague on the question of how the Cartel would distribute the burdens of increased taxation. Bourgin et al., *Manuel des Parties Politiques*, pp. 142–43. For a typical Radical party (Conservative Left) argument *against* tax on capital, see Duboin, *La Stabilisation du Franc*, pp. 40–49. The Radical party tended to favor an inheritance tax, which they claimed would have the beneficial redistributive effects of the capital tax, but without the wrenching economic effects. Ibid., pp. 75–76. Caillaux was the conservative voice on the Left, and he maintained a "useful ambiguity: the Left could not really be hostile to him, and the Right was now familiar with his reassuring orthodoxy." Bredin, *Joseph Caillaux*, p. 255.

[51] Duboin, *La Stabilisation du Franc*, pp. 61–71.

once again passed the hat in search of new advances from various credit institutions, who were in turn reimbursed by the central bank; and this contributed to a continual growth in money circulation. Fearful of the inflationary consequences, liquid capital took note, and took wing.

Paralyzed by divisions within his coalition, Herriot was incapable of facing the financial crisis aggravated by the flight of capital.[52] In April 1925 the situation grew critical, with the conservatives congealing around various versions of balancing the budget by indirect taxation, and the Radicals insisting on direct, heavy, and progressive taxes. The indecisive nature of these debates only aggravated the flight of capital, as "the man on the street joined the men in the Bourse" in rapidly converting money and money assets into foreign and real assets as quickly as possible.[53]

Divisions between the leadership of the Cartel continued into late 1925, and policy became more and more incoherent. Caillaux proposed the establishment of a Caisse d'Amortissement—a special independent body that would manage the floating debt through amortization and extension of maturity periods—which Herriot opposed publicly in the most vehement terms. In October 1925, a new cabinet headed by Paul Painlevé proposed the obligatory consolidation of the national debt (which would have forced public creditors into new terms and maturity dates), but this debate only stimulated demands for reimbursement of short-term bonds, encouraged further capital flight, and caused the franc to depreciate against foreign currencies. A month later Painlevé was out, and his plan for forced consolidation was disowned by his own party. Briand, the new prime minister, tried to pick up the pieces with a new proposal for raising indirect taxes. On the sixth of March 1926, this was turned down by a margin of 53 votes, and the Briand cabinet fell.[54]

It was during the reign of the Cartel that the corrupt practices of the Banque de France were fully revealed. Throughout this period, the central bank maintained its passive stance and clung to the fiction that it was "controlling" the money supply by remaining within the *plafond* (money supply ceiling). It is not altogether clear what role Herriot's government had in encouraging this fraud, but when it was brought to his attention in December 1924, an effort was made to obscure further the accounts rather than openly to lift the sacrosanct ceiling.

[52] There are numerous accounts of the Cartel's inability to come to terms with France's degenerating financial position. See, for instance, Frédérick Bon, *Les Elections en France: Histoire et Sociologie* (Paris: Editions du Seuil), 1978, chap. 3; Wolfe, *The French Franc*, chap. 3; Brogan, *France Under the Republic*, pp. 586–595.

[53] Wolfe, ibid., p. 39. D. W. Brogan notes that while the alliance between the Radicals (moderate Left) and the Socialists (further Left) was natural during an election, it was increasingly artificial in a governing situation, particularly when financial crisis threatened. The rift between these two parties was fundamental: the former did not at all favor increased government intervention in the economy or limitations on the rights of private property. The Socialists on the other hand tended to favor both and were contemptuous of the Radicals' simplicity and superficiality. Yet their cooperation in 1924 resulted in the election of over 100 socialist deputies. Brogan, ibid., p. 586.

[54] La Chapelle, *Les Finances*, p. 136, Brogan, ibid., pp. 592–594.

The money supply was out of control as long as the question of taxes languished in the parliament.[55]

Throughout the second half of 1924 and 1925 the Banque de France continued to stand by and watch advances to the state through commercial credit institutions grow and push up the money supply along with them. By January 1925 direct and indirect advances to the state reached 23.6 million francs, and the bills in circulation pierced the plafond, totaling 42.3 million francs. The governor of the Banque de France wrote to the president of the Conseil and the minister of finance on 5 February 1925, warning them that if they did not take some effective action, the legal limit would have to be raised.[56] This, of course, was an attempt to put the responsibility for "inflationary policy" back in the politicians' court. In April the plafond was legally raised to reflect the circulation figures, but it was also about this time that the opposition exposed the illegal means by which the Banque and the government were in fact concealing the true magnitude of the problem through false balance sheets. The Herriot cabinet fell, and the reputation of the Banque de France was at a historical low.

In the first half of 1926, the Banque de France and the Treasury continued to have conflicting approaches to the role of international financial assistance for the stabilization of the franc. Treasury officials were busy in May approaching both American and British central bankers for a credit secured by the French central bank's gold, a move that was opposed by right-wing demonstrators throughout the spring.[57] The governor of the Banque de France openly opposed such a credit, whether against gold or not.[58] Personnel from the French central bank continued to oppose outside assistance, even though the Comité des Experts favored a show of international support upon the conclusion of their report.[59]

[55] This fudging of the accounts was something that the governor of the central bank kept secret from even the regents. However, when Robineau approached Clémentel, then minister of finance, about authorizing an additional 2 billion francs to be added to the 41 billion ceiling, Clémentel flatly refused, saying he could not defend a "policy of inflation" before the parliament. Prate, *La France et sa Monnaie,* p. 90. In effect, the government was forcing the Banque de France to take the heat because it did not have the authority to present a reasonable and coherent economic package to the nation.

[56] La Chapelle, *Les Finances,* p. 127.

[57] Allen Douglas, "Georges Valois and the *Franc-Or:* A Right-Wing Reaction to Inflation," in Nathan Schmukler and Edward Marcus (eds.), *Inflation Through the Ages: Economic, Social, Psychological and Historical Aspects* (New York: Brooklyn College Press), 1983, pp. 226–245, p. 237. Right-wingers opposed the export of gold in defense of the franc because they saw it as stripping away the last metallic backing of the paper currency.

[58] Herman Harjes (J. P. Morgan's, Paris) to Benjamin Strong, 26 May 1926. File C261.1, FRBNY.

[59] Harjes to Strong, 7 June 1926, file C261.1, FRBNY. Only Picard of the Banque de France opposed an American credit. Other members of the Experts' Committee favored foreign assistance as "a gesture from abroad confirming that America also views with a favorable eye the change of policy of the government, the appointment of the Experts' Committee, etc., and also in order to strengthen the possibility of avoiding a renewed panic on the franc."

Meanwhile, the consensus that gradual revalorization could eventually be achieved was breaking down. A few Radical Socialist deputies began to warn the public of the devastating impact of revalorization. Armed with the example of the British and the Belgian deflations, an important segment of the Cartel began to argue that revalorization would harm all rentiers by immediately raising the debt of the state to totally unsustainable levels. Credit would be squeezed to the point of halting production entirely. And, they noted, as go the fortunes of production, so go the fortunes of the working class. In the emerging view, the price that such a policy of deflation had cost the British was about equivalent to that of reconstituting France's devastated regions. "To revalorize," wrote one proponent of this position, "is to try and make the French richer than they are. What folly!"[60] Proponents of this view noted explicitly that France did not have the same financial interest in revalorization as did the "City."[61] The government of the Left was beginning to lean toward de facto stabilization. This was the first time any government had publicly admitted that both inflation and deflation could cause economic catastrophe for the French economy.[62] Privately, Caillaux, the minister of finance, admitted to preferring to stabilize at 160–200 francs to the pound, which was recognized as being far from deflationary.[63]

Still, the Cartel could not reach consensus on policy. The tax issue, the ratification of the debt accords, and the issue of further foreign loans continued to prevent consensus.[64] One would have thought their work would have been simplified by the publication of the Comité des Experts' recommendations in July 1926. Supposedly above politics, this committee made a series of recommendations that might have been useful in galvanizing a consensus within the Cartel. Instead, it heightened the competition between Caillaux and Herriot. The committee recommended that the minister of finance be given "full

[60] Jacques Duboin, *La Stabilisation du Franc*. The chapter quoted was written in December 1925. Duboin was a member of the then ruling Radical Republican and Socialist Radical party. By 1925 this influential MP was criticizing his own Cartel government in legislative debates for pressing for revalorization, which he claimed was another form of destabilization. See his speech before the Chambre des Députies, 17 Feb. 1925, *Journal Officiel*. Another Radical politician who would gain influence in the future also thought that the economic impact of revaluation would be unsustainable. See Pierre Mendès-France, "Le Redressement Financier Français en 1926 et 1927," especially pp. 33–39.

[61] French MP Duboin noted that the reason Britain wanted to return to prewar parity was to retake its role as an international clearing house and compete with New York for business. This was a pressure France did not have. See his speech before the Chambre des Députies, *Journal Officiel*, 17 Feb. 1925.

[62] Comment by Piétri, budget discussion, *Journal Officiel*, 17 Feb. 1925. However, the minister of finance (Clémentel) continued to oppose official devaluation of the franc.

[63] Report of a conversation between Herman Harjes (Morgan, Harjes, France) and the French minister of finance, Joseph Caillaux. Harjes to J. P. Morgan New York, 26 June 1926. Also Harjes to Morgan, New York, 30 June 1926; File C261.1, FRBNY.

[64] Strong to Harrison, 8 July 1926, File C261.1, FRBNY.

powers" to hasten the program of financial restoration, which Caillaux did not hesitate to demand of the Chambre. He was, however, strenuously opposed by Herriot, who labeled him a "veritable dictator, threatening perhaps the freedom of the press, freedom to meet, and other personal freedoms."[65] This was truly the end of the Cartel. Herriot, who had provoked the crisis in the ruling party, could not even rustle up a willing minister of finance. General panic broke out on the Bourse. The franc fell to a record low of 290 to the pound, and the Cartel was given its walking papers on 19 July by a vote of 290 to 234.

French requests for international financial assistance were continually deflected during the reign of the Cartel. Though French financiers argued that a stabilization credit was an important symbol of international solidarity behind the franc and might make it possible for France to ratify the debt accords,[66] American officials tended to regard France's political and financial bouleversement as beyond the capacity of foreigners to calm. When Benjamin Strong, governor of the Federal Reserve Bank of New York (FRBNY), was approached by Jean Parmentier of the Ministry of Finance in early May of 1926 for a $100 million stabilization loan—to be secured by a deposit of the gold of the Banque de France—he refused, saying that such a loan would simply facilitate French flight from the franc. Strong and Alanson Houghton, the American ambassador to Paris, agreed that support of the franc was unjustifiable as long as the French themselves continued to trade their francs for foreign and real assets. They were also deeply suspicious that the Ministry of Finance's request for assistance was politically timed to bolster the franc just as the Chambre des Députies reconvened at the end of May.[67] In short, Strong judged that the tide of speculation against the franc was determined by the patent inability of the Cartel to implement a fiscal policy that would gain the confidence of holders of liquid capital. He also expressed reluctance to make a financial commitment to a teetering government of the Left.[68]

[65] Quoted by La Chapelle, *Les Finances*, p. 143 (my translation). Other biographers have noted Caillaux's "Bonapartist tendencies." See Bernard Oudin, *Aristide Briand, Biographie* (Paris: Editions Robert Laffont), 1987, p. 485. American officials were very much aware of this internal power struggle. Strong to Harrison, 18 July 1926, File C261.1, FRBNY.

[66] Harjes, at the Paris Branch of J. P. Morgan, thought that "a gesture of assistance" on the part of America would be advisable to help further confidence and make it possible for France to ratify the debt accords. Harjes to J. P. Morgan & Co., New York, 29 June 1926. Very much at stake, of course, was a desire on the part of Morgan's to retain its influence with the French government. See Strong to Harrison, 29 June 1926: "But Morgan may give Caillaux a credit so as not to sacrifice their position with the French Government." File C261.1, FRBNY.

[67] Cablegram, Strong to Mellon, 14 May 1926. File C261.1, FRBNY. Strong tried to influence the fiscal debate by pushing for a balanced budget and criticizing the unfairness of the French tax burden, from which, he claimed, agricultural profits and real estate were virtually exempt. Strong to Harrison, 28 June 1926. File C261.1, FRBNY.

[68] Strong to Harjes, 7 June 1926. File C261.1, FRBNY. Strong was explicit in his opposition to another Herriot government later in June: "If Herriot succeeds in forming a government how can one justify a credit to the French Government or to the Bank of France which may indeed be

Nor was Strong interested in assisting a central bank that he viewed as an arm of the French Treasury.[69] It was bad policy—as well as useless, Strong thought—to extend credit to a central bank that had shown itself incapable of monetary management. "Domestic management," he stated, "means a monetary and credit policy by the Bank of France which might conceivably bring it into conflict with what would superficially appear to be the interests of the Treasury. It might mean, for instance, high interest rates, a period of real deprivation, economy, and some unemployment for the French people." Strong backed actions that would help the central bank of issue get control of the money market. He inveighed against the legislative cap of 5 percent paid on national defense bonds, which precluded a serious squeeze on credit.[70]

American monetary officials and financiers were at least partially constrained by official American foreign policy. Several years prior, in March of 1922, the United States government had announced that all issuers of foreign loans to be sold to the American public were required to get State Department approval before commencing the transaction.[71] Up to 1924 the official right to review a foreign issue was rarely exercised negatively. But toward the end of 1923, France was increasingly the object of rancor in the United States Congress for having failed to fund its war debt to the United States. That Britain did so in December of 1923 only served to focus angry attention on the French. While the possibility of embargoing the Morgan loan of March 1924 had been discussed at the cabinet level, in 1924 "the relatively liberal position of the State Department prevailed," and Morgan was allowed to proceed.[72] But not so under the second Coolidge administration a year later. Once the controversy over the Ruhr occupation and the Dawes Loan had settled, the outstanding issue that drew public attention was that the French still had not agreed to pay their debts. This was the outcome that American officials wished to effectuate from 1925 on.

American central bankers seemed to assume that revalorization was not a realistic option for the franc. The FRBNY man on the scene, Robert Warren,

---

imposed upon the Bank by the Government and accepted by the bank unwillingly when the record of the former treatment of the Bank by Herriot's government is such as we know it to be?" Strong to Harrison, 20 June 1926. File C261.1, FRBNY.

[69] Harrison to Garrard (Under Secretary of the Treasury), 7 June 1926. File C261.1, FRBNY.

[70] J. P. Morgan (New York) to Harjes (Morgan, Harjes, Paris), 29 June 1926. File C261.1, FRBNY.

[71] There were different rationales for such a review process. Treasury Secretary Andrew Mellon thought it could be used to pressure the payment of official debts to the United States; Commerce Secretary Herbert Hoover thought there might be sound commercial reasons; and President Harding thought such pressure could be exerted as a measure for arms control. See Herbert Feis, *The Diplomacy of the Dollar: The First Era, 1919–1932* (Baltimore: Johns Hopkins University Press), 1950, pp. 7–14.

[72] Schuker, *The End of French Predominance*, p. 167.

thought that it would be possible on the basis of wages and prices to justify a somewhat higher rate than the 180 francs per pound sterling that was being discussed in the waning days of the Cartel, though, he wrote, it might not be economically desirable.[73] He thought that the weight of the internal debt would necessitate devaluation.[74] At any rate, the American central bankers seem to have understood the politics of the situation, for, as observed by Warren, "while [the French] were willing to pay lip service to 'stabilization,' they and their representatives shudder at the consequences."[75] Rather than a drive toward parity, the international financial community expected a return to the gold standard at the prevailing exchange rate at the time of the return.[76]

Under the circumstances, American monetary officials were cool to further stabilization assistance. In the end, the executive committee of the FRBNY opposed the proposed loan on the basis that the debt accords first had to be ratified and that France still had unused credits from the Morgan loan and a lot of gold—estimated at 40 percent of liabilities.[77] American central bankers claimed their hands were tied until France ratified the debt accords and came up with a comprehensive stabilization plan. Having been turned down by the Federal Reserve, Raoul Péret turned to the Bank of England. He was again refused assistance and for a similar set of reasons.[78] Another Morgan miracle would not be forthcoming. For similar reasons, a central bank credit was repeatedly denied. The policy of denial had proponents in both the United States government and the central bank, though for a different set of reasons: American government officials sought to pressure the French to fulfill their "obligations," while central bankers doubted whether loans or credits would in any case have fundamentally altered the crisis of the franc in the first half of 1926.

---

[73] Memo, "Experts' Plan," Robert Warren, 5 July 1926, File C261.1, FRBNY.

[74] Robert Warren (in Paris) to Governor Strong, 14 July 1926. File C261.1, FRBNY, "Special Conflicts." Warren, an official of the FRBNY and an observer of the French situation for several months, wrote: "I cannot wholly rid myself of the suspicion that the aim of an unknown number of influential persons is to let the franc go, get rid of the internal debt, plead bankruptcy, and get rid of the external debt, and as a compensation give up the whole reparations program with the end of effecting an economic cooperation of continental Europe, lightly taxed because free of public debts, and thereby able to compete effectively against England and the United States."

[75] Warren to Strong, 7 July 1926, File C261.1, FRBNY.

[76] J. P. Morgan Co., New York, to Harjes (Morgan Harjes Paris), 29 and 30 June 1926. File C261.1, FRBNY.

[77] Memo of a conversation between Governor Strong and Ambassador Houghton, London, 8 May 1926, prepared by Sprague. File C261.1, Federal Reserve Bank of New York Archives. Strong was also reluctant to risk the "odium" of taking the Banque de France's gold as security. Cablegram, Strong to Harrison, 8 May 1926. Cablegram, Harrison to Strong, 10 May 1926, File C261.1, FRBNY. At the same time, however, Strong feared that the intransigence of the American government on the issue of the signing of the debt accord could cause France's stabilization plans to collapse. Strong to Warren, 11 July 1926, File C261.1, FRBNY.

[78] Norman called Péret's trip to London to attempt to get central bank financing a "journey of a madman." Norman to Strong, 19 May 1926. File C261.1, FRBNY.

THE POLITICS OF CREDIBILITY

A drastic shift occurred in French politics in late July 1926. A discredited left-wing government ceded power under conditions of near-national emergency to a broad center-right coalition led by the former leader of the Bloc National. Poincaré returned to power that summer on such a broad basis of support that what opposition remained was isolated on the extreme left and extreme right. Not only with the support of the former Bloc National, but now with the contrite cooperation of the failed leaders on the moderate Left—including Herriot, Painlevé, and Briand—Poincaré took up the finance portfolio and was granted an array of powers that included the ability to make budget cuts by decree, to increase indirect taxes, and to raise taxes on transportation and tobacco.[79] Serious efforts were made to legislate increased revenues in August 1926. Taxes on incomes and securities were increased 50 percent, though the highest income brackets were spared so as to encourage the repatriation of capital.[80] For the first time since 1913, the French budget balanced in 1926.[81]

The effect of the Poincaré financial package on the exchange rate was almost immediate.[82] Speculators and others were further encouraged to buy francs when—consistent with our statistical findings that center-right parties are associated with currency strength—Poincaré announced his intention to the Chambre in November of letting the franc appreciate in order to lower the cost of living.[83] By late autumn a *pro*-franc panic seemed potentially worrisome. At

[79] La Chapelle, *Les Finances*, pp. 144–145. Why leaders of the Left agreed to give such powers to Poincaré can only be a matter for speculation. They may have been only too happy to escape the political confusion they had created and the financial confusion they did not fully understand. The only opposition to Poincaré was timid objection from the Socialists, who were not taken very seriously anyway.

[80] General income taxes in the highest brackets were cut from 60 percent to 30 percent to induce the repatriation of capital; taxes on the profits of industry and commercial enterprises were increased from 10 percent to 15 percent; taxes on wages and agricultural profits both were increased from 7.2 percent to 12 percent; land taxes increased from 12 percent to 18 percent; taxes on French securities rose from 12 percent to 18 percent; and some foreign securities were taxed at a rate as high as 25 percent. The overall impact of these tax increases was a tax rate increase of about 50 percent. Sauvy, *Histoire Economique*, pp. 388–389, tables 10 and 11 (all comparisons are as a result of the law of 3 August 1926). Brogan (*France Under the Republic*, p. 595) notes that there was nothing really new about these proposals; it was basically what the Committee of Experts had called for a few months earlier. But on the importance of Poincaré's credibility, see Thomas J. Sargent, "Stopping Moderate Inflations: The Methods of Poincaré and Thatcher," chap. 4, in Rudiger Dornbusch and Mario H. Simonsen (eds.), *Inflation, Debt, and Indexation* (Cambridge: MIT Press), 1984; Dulles, *The Dollar, the Franc, and Inflation*, 1929, pp. 197–199.

[81] Paul Einzig, *France's Crisis* (London: Macmillan), 1934, p. 18. Mendès-France claimed that the government was pursing a policy of budget surplus rather than equilibrium, noting that the Committee of Experts had called for 2.5 billion francs of new taxes in 1926 and 5 billion in 1927, whereas Poincaré proposed a rate in July 1926 that would yield between 9 and 11 billion (p. 31).

[82] Brogan, *France Under the Republic*, p. 596.

[83] Débats Parlementaires, Chambre, *Journal Officiel*, 14 November 1926. The subject was raised in reference to a question about raising salaries of government employees.

least the Banque de France and several important industrial interests thought so. When the pound bottomed out on 20 December at about 120 francs, the central bank succeeded in convincing Poincaré that emergency intervention was necessary. On the strong insistence of the Régents, Poincaré agreed to allow the issue of franc notes for use in exchange operations to halt the franc's appreciation.[84] There was still disagreement on exchange rate policy, however: by the end of December, Emile Moreau, Robineau's successor as governor of the Banque de France, had decided to cap the value of the franc at about 120 francs per pound, while Poincaré wanted to allow the franc to go to 100.[85]

Recession helped settle the issue. In the late months of 1927, the effects of appreciation were beginning to be felt in soft prices and declining orders. Especially hard hit were automobiles, leather shoes, metallurgy, and machinery. Textile orders in were down by a third in November 1926 compared to the average from May to June.[86] Between August 1926 and February 1927, the number of workers seeking unemployment assistance grew rapidly. Overall, the Conseil National Economique reported to the government an estimated 10–20 percent reduction in the number of workers in manufacturing.[87]

The recession, which coincided with the Poincaré fiscal program and franc appreciation, sparked off complaints among industrial and labor groups about the wisdom of revalorization. Local Chambers of Commerce openly complained.[88] Léon Jouhaux, general secretary of the Confédération Générale du

---

[84] Marcel Chaminade, *L'Expérience Financière de M. Poincaré* (Paris), 1927; Mendès-France, "Le Redressement Financier Français," pp. 56–58; Dulles, *The Dollar, the Franc, and Inflation,* 1929, p. 196.

[85] Moreau, *Souvenirs*, pp. 186–187.

[86] Mendès-France, "Le Redressement Financier Français," p. 198.

[87] "Rapport sur un Programme de Travaux Susceptibles de Parer Eventuellement à la Crise Chômage," Conseil National Economique, 24 January 1927, F 12.8801, National Archives, Paris. According to Mendès-France (pp. 212–213), unemployment in late 1926 and early 1927 was as follows:

Date	Unsatisfied Employment Requests	Unfilled Jobs	Unemployed Seeking Assistance
August 1926	8,597	11,449	—
September 1926	11,753	10,511	—
October 1926	11,759	8,077	—
November 1926	16,126	5,642	1,396*
December 1926	23,985	3,556	6,703
January 1927	75,506	4,751	17,178**
			45,222***
February 1927	96,670	6,303	79,689
March 1927	—	—	81,916

(* As of 8 Dec. 1926.   ** 6 Jan. 1927.   *** 22 Jan. 1927.)

[88] Moreau, *Souvenirs*, p. 163.

Travail (the country's major trade union federation), argued for stabilization at a relatively low level.[89] Heavy industry, represented by the Comité des Forges, met with Poincaré to complain of the distress caused by his monetary policies. Automobile manufactures made it clear to Poincaré in December that thousands of employees would be out of work if the appreciation of the franc persisted.[90] On December 14, the automobile manufacturers Citroën and Peugeot both approached the Banque de France for emergency credits.[91]

By February 1927 Poincaré was convinced that the economy was adapting with difficulty to the appreciating franc. He promised to maintain the present rate as long as possible "in a fashion that will allow industry to adapt . . . but above all in the interest of workers."[92] The economic crisis and the political constraints involved have been cited as the reason why Poincaré had to abandon revalorization, his preferred alternative, and accept stabilization at a fairly low level.[93]

Industry's opposition to revalorization was predictable, but what is more surprising was the concurrence of finance. The research department of the Banque de France came out in favor of stabilizing at a moderate level. Governor Moreau supported a reasonable middle ground between the diverse claims of various social and economic groups, and thought that Poincaré's policy of allowing further appreciation was dangerous.[94] While information on the preferences of the banking sector is sketchy, it is likely that on the whole they favored stabilization at present rates over a drive to revalorize. Most immediately, bankers feared that if pro-franc speculation got out of control, the bubble might burst and the franc would fall again to 200 to the pound.[95] Secondly, many banks themselves had bought foreign currencies during the flight from the franc, and those institutions were by late autumn of 1926 beginning to feel the squeeze when the pound fell drastically.[96] Finally, a

---

[89] Jacques Rueff, Preface, in Moreau, *Souvenirs*, p. viii.

[90] Mendès-France, "Le Redressement Financier Français," passim.

[91] Moreau, *Souvenirs*, pp. 175, 178–79.

[92] As reported in *Le Matin*, 10 February 1927.

[93] Mendès-France, "Le Redressement Financier Français," p. 61.

[94] Moreau, *Souvenirs*, p. 74. Pierre Quesnay, one of the most highly respected young economists in the Banque de France, concluded that the level of stabilization should be between 160 and 170 francs to the pound. At once an economic and political analysis, Quesnay's report concluded that while this rate still might prove a heavy burden on industry, another lower rate would prove too heavy a burden on the classes living on fixed incomes.

[95] Ibid., p. 153.

[96] Ibid., p. 177. Bouvier notes that the trend in foreign speculation in currencies had become much more important in the commercial bank's accounts in the interwar years compared to the prewar years. For the Banque de Paris et des Pays-Bas and the Banque de l'Union Parisienne, for example, the item "banks and correspondence" (probably currency speculation) had increased from 8.5 percent in 1923 to 20 percent in 1926–1930 (p. 40). Most of this speculation probably took place before the franc was stabilized, and much of it between 1923 and late 1926 was probably *against* the franc. In late 1926, therefore, these banks were likely holding depreciating foreign currencies.

number of important credit institutions may have been under direct pressure due to the impact of the appreciation on important industrial clients.[97] Industrial connections such as these may have sensitized the financial institutions to the economic hardships that would result from a high franc. Moreover, without a comparable key currency status and lacking an overwhelming stake in international finance,[98] there was no real benefit to the banking sector in striving for appreciation. And without the commitment of the French financial sector, the coalition for revaluation could be likened to an amorphous body without a head: the small and dispersed rentiers could—and did—call "foul"; but without a politically powerful sector with which to ally, these calls could eventually be downplayed, and ultimately set aside. Besides, by 1926 the adjustment to the loss of middle-class fortunes had largely been made, and in fact, by 1927, a part of these fortunes rebounded in an important upturn in the gold value of the stock of outstanding bonds.[99] According to one historian, "The small investors . . . were grateful that even four *sous* out of twenty [one fifth of the original parity] had been saved. That the French middle class had been rescued from complete ruin . . . was, from the point of view of the little man, so great a thing that it concealed from him the fact that France had at last paid for the war" through his savings.[100]

Those who still pressed for compensation for the decline in government securities and other values were by this time far outnumbered by those who

[97] One of the companies that suffered greatly from appreciation was Citroën. Both Lazard Frères and the Banque de France had lent heavily to Citroën in the 1920s. Bouvier, "The French Banks, Inflation and the Economic Crisis," *Journal of European Economic History*, Vol. 13, 1984, p. 66.

[98] For a scholarly account of the weakness of Paris as an international financial center, see Margaret Myers, *Paris as a Financial Center* (New York: Columbia University Press), 1936. The major reasons for its lack of international status was the underdevelopment of a short-term money market (pp. 1–5). This in turn may have been because France was a latecomer to international trade (pp. 157–158).

[99] The improvement in bond yields was as follows:

Type of Security	Rate in July 1926		Rate in July 1927		% Rise
	Nominal	Gold Value	Nominal	Gold Value	(Gold Value)
3%	44.2	4.65	55.6	11.28	141.5
4% (1917)	37.25	3.92	60.4	12.26	240.8
4% (1918)	36.5	3.84	59.4	12.05	213.9
5% (1920)	58.0	6.11	87.5	17.76	190.8
6% (1920)	51.25	5.40	85.9	17.44	222.9
4% (guar. rate, '25)	76.5	8.06	93.05	18.88	134.1
4% state RR	185	19.48	290	58.85	208.7
5% state RR	200	21.06	331	67.17	215.6

(Source: Mendès-France, "Le Redressement Financier Français," p. 242. Originally given by L' Association des Porteurs de Rentes.)

[100] Brogan, *France Under the Republic*, p. 598.

wished to gain regularity and predictability in exchange transactions. By and large, only a segment of the French Right was in favor of revaluation.[101] But with industry and commerce desirous of—and much of the middle class resigned to—legalized depreciation, this was a group without strong allies.

CONCLUSIONS

The case of the depreciation and stabilization of the franc highlights the centrality of credibility in monetary commitment, and corroborates the theoretical and statistical story presented above with evidence of a more qualitative, historically contextual sort. Rather than look for a "perfect fit" between quantative and qualitative data, the purpose of this case has been to show that the stories are compatible and indeed complementary. The case shows that some "exogenous" shock can raise initial questions regarding a credible fiscal and monetary policy—for example, the failure of the Ruhr policy in 1923 that caused holders of francs to begin to suspect that all was not well with French government finances—that certainly are not captured in our general model of credibility. But the case and the statistical evidence converge in suggesting that fears of inflation are fanned by political instability, distrust of the left-wing coalition, and the revelation of corrupt practices within the central bank. In the French case, the short-term structure of the government debt was to show just how vulnerable the government was to a *crise de confiance*. Only when these conditions were reversed in the summer of 1926 did capital repatriate and the franc stabilize, as would have been predicted by the direction of the coefficients presented in Chapters 3 and 4.

The case study is absolutely essential for understanding the sequencing of the various stages of currency crisis when credibility is slipping away. It therefore compensates for a serious shortcoming in the statistical analysis: *why* and *how* do we get from instability, left-wing governments, and politically controlled central banks to currency depreciation? Unfortunately, there is no way to conclude from this case study that France's path was in any way typical, even

[101] Dulles, *The Dollar, the Franc, and Inflation*, 1929, p. 483. In the Banque de France, de Wendel opposed buying gold currencies and Moreau's policy of keeping the franc down. Jeanneney, *François de Wendel*, pp. 316–354; Moreau, *Souvenirs*, pp. 65–66. See the Minority Opinion of the Technical Commission, written by Jean Coignet, "Revalorisation," in Octave Homberg, *La Stabilité Monétaire: Rapports, Travaux, et Comptes Rendus Voeux, et Résolutions de la Deuxième Semaine de la Monnaie* (Paris: Librarie Valois), 1927. Others continued to argue for a gradual yearly 4–5 percent revalorization. See "La Revalorisation et la Monnaie de Compte," by J. B. Rocca (president of the Society for the Defense of Trade and Industry for Marseille), ibid. Most informed observers by this time, however, were not convinced that the Banque de France could successfully manage a gentle revaluation and thought that appreciation would shackle the economy, lead to government budget deficits, hurt the balance of payments, and make France vulnerable to the whims of foreign capital. See Louis Pommery, presenting the majority opinion, "Rapport sur la Revalorisation," ibid. pp. 35–52.

though the explanatory variables and the outcome fit a very general model. The deterioration in France's external position was distinguished by three phases. In the first, the weakness of the French financial position was exposed by the costly, ineffectual, and isolating stance of French foreign policy. During the first quarter of 1924, cracks in the government's credibility opened up as the debate over fiscal reform met serious resistance in the Sénat. But the external financial assistance negotiated with Morgan, and the stringent fiscal regime implemented in the waning weeks of the Bloc National, had the immediate impact of reversing the negative market psychology and lofting the franc.

The second period coincided with the tenure of the Cartel des Gauches. Between April 1925 and July 1926, the crack in credibility widened into a deep divergence between the government's claimed macroeconomic policy and what the market expected. This period also coincided with an important change in American policy—the establishment of an embargo against countries that had not paid their war debts—as well as an increasing unwillingness by American and British central bankers to assist a financially mismanaged country in such a politically unstable situation. Capital flight accelerated, governments were constituted and fell at an alarming rate, and the franc plunged. Between August 1926 and June 1928, a drastic change in French politics was inaugurated by a broad and stable parliamentary majority able to enact serious fiscal measures. The role of external assistance and even influence was minimal, and the exchange rate chosen was ultimately determined by a balance of domestic social forces (particularly the interests of business, trade, and employment on the one hand and the rentiers on the other).

The stabilization of the franc fleshes out some of the findings of the previous chapters. Most striking is the relationship between the instability of the government and the flight of capital, which was eventually associated with the depreciation of the franc. While the first seeds of doubt were the result of the failed Ruhr policy, only a government in a fairly secure domestic political position, such as that enjoyed by Poincaré up to 1924, would have had the nerve to propose a 20 percent tax increase three months before an election. While Poincaré miscalculated the resistance he would get from the Radical Socialists (he even miscalculated the resistance he would get from his own cabinet), he had reasons to suppose that the prospects for continuing in office were good. The hesitance to pass taxes was clear in the parliament, however, and that hesitance was a signal to the market that the legislature was not ready to get serious about balancing the budget—the issue that had come to symbolize the commitment to control inflation.

It is also interesting to note the relative ease with which Poincaré's government secured external assistance; Poincaré evidently convinced foreign central bankers as well as holders of francs that he meant to arrest inflation and balance the budget. With Poincaré serving two years as president and commanding an overwhelming majority in the Chambre, potential creditors had good reason to believe that the bold fiscal reform would be successfully implemented. They were hugely impressed with the double décime. Such demonstrations of macroeconomic policy commitment fed an orgy of confidence, so much so that the market turned around *without* the use of the Morgan credit.

But herein lay the problem. Purveyors of extraordinary finance moved *with* the market instead of assisting to counter it. Poincaré's tax program would have improved the prospects for the franc without the Morgan loan, although the latter added to the rapid turnaround in the market psychology. The Cartel made the tactical error of repealing the double décime, and then could never form a coalition for a credible alternative. Factions within the Left disagreed where the greatest burden of taxation should fall. The parade of governments could never come down hard on domestic consumption: the devastated regions, benefits for farmers and veterans, public employment—none of these programs was the Left willing to cut, and no sector was it clearly willing to tax. The short-term costs were simply too high, and as the half-life of the succession of cabinets grew shorter and shorter, there was increasingly no point in paying them. In the end, no member of the Radical party would even agree to be minister of finance. The effect of this instability on the market was overwhelming, and the franc suffered the consequences.

In the interests of international economic stability, the Bank of England or the Federal Reserve Bank of New York might have extended credits to turn the market around. The lack of foreign assistance during this time was not for want of a request: finance ministers from the Cartel were repeatedly rebuffed in both London and New York. While American foreign policy imposed a clear constraint, the evidence suggests that foreign credits would not have been forthcoming in the absence of a credible French fiscal program. Hence, one of the weaknesses of the interwar monetary system was the lack of institutionalized channels and procedures (like today's International Monetary Fund, or the bridging loans provided by the Bank for International Settlements) for applying for emergency external assistance in the face of currency weakness and capital flight. Where foreign assistance was delayed or insufficient, markets redoubled their flight. A government whose credibility was weak lost the confidence not only of the market, but also of those who would provide foreign assistance. The problem with international cooperation was that it often reinforced rather than leaned against the prevailing market psychology, with predictable effects on international monetary stability.

It is difficult in this case to separate the effects of government instability from the effects of a left-wing coalition in power. It is clear that the Left did not inspire the confidence of capital with its calls for a capital levy and other fiscal measures that would penalize capital. But did the Cartel lose the confidence of franc holders because it was a left-wing government or because it was an unstable government? It is not possible to provide a definitive answer using case evidence; we do not have the luxury of exit polls for those who chose to convert their francs into foreign or real assets. The evidence does suggest that foreign central bankers were not enamored of the Cartel, but they may have been able to form a working relationship had a credible fiscal program received strong parliamentary support. In this case, the effects of political instability and the nature of the party in power are especially difficult to disentangle because when the center-right returned to power in July of 1926, cabinet stability was restored. This is where the multivariate analysis actually sheds light on the case: recall that there was scant evidence that left governments per se inspired capital flight any more than their center-right counterparts. In this light, the preponderance of statistical and historical evidence tends to prefer an interpretation that the Cartel's financial problems stemmed more from its instability than from its (rather mild) left-wing orientation.

What is more certain is that the weakness of the Banque de France contributed to the reputational difficulties experienced under the Cartel. The French central bank was a traditionally strong and independent institution[102] whose stature suffered greatly after the war and under the leadership of Robineau. This case study exposes a more qualitative element to central bank independence that cannot be captured by the formal, quantitative measure used in previous chapters. Yet the reputational effects of the suspected political pliability of the central bank had precisely the consequences demonstrated in the previous chapters. After the war, the heavy holdings of government bonds in the bank's portfolio made it very difficult to conduct an independent monetary policy. Moreover, the credibility of the central bank was clearly at a low point when the scandal of improper records on monetization of the debt was uncovered. The case study reminds us that the reputation of a central bank can change depending on the nature of the leadership; in this case, its credibility was greatly enhanced when the governorship passed to Emile Moreau. The fluctuation in the reputation of the central bank had an important impact on the mood of the market and contributed to shifts in the speculative tide. So important was this aspect of monetary credibility that American and British central bankers tried to link central bank credits and other longer term loans to institutional changes in the relationship between the Banque de France and the state. Greater central-bank independence was demanded whenever credits were discussed throughout the period. It was viewed as the most certain way of insulating the monetary authorities from political pressure to monetize the debt, of limiting inflation, and of convincing speculators that the franc was worth holding. Here, then, theory, history, and statistics all converge: during the twenties at least, markets

---

[102] According to my scale of structural independence, the Banque de France was rated 6, while the average for the sample as a whole was about 4.35 and the range was from 2 to 8. Thus, according to its statutes, the French central bank was one of the more independent in the group.

reacted incredulously to the promises of monetary stringency made by central banks who could be influenced by the state. The result was capital flight, a deteriorating current-account position, and ultimately currency depreciation.

The final phase of the French episode was the decision to stabilize the franc at a fairly low level. None of the theories or evidence presented prior to this chapter address this question of what determines the "political equilibrium" at which a currency will finally be stabilized. In France during the twenties, this was a decision that was almost exclusively based on national economic and social considerations.[103] Industrial groups were well aware of the advantages to them of a depreciated franc, and they benefited quietly from the government's disarray in financial matters and its generous reconstruction payments in the first half of the twenties. The real profits of the industrial sector burgeoned under the prevailing mild inflation. On the other hand, these gains were largely at the expense of bondholders and holders of other franc-denominated securities. Concern for the small saver (the government's creditors) prevented an early stabilization at realistic levels. For almost six years, the standoff between these social forces prevented a coherent fiscal policy and a realistic franc policy. Up to the middle of 1926, economic growth, new investment opportunities, and high employment levels allowed the conflict of interest between these two broad social/economic coalitions to be officially finessed for a number of years, much to the benefit of industry. In the summer of 1926, however, the strength of the franc and the ensuing recession highlighted the extent to which the bondholders' demands and those of industry could not be satisfied simultaneously. The appreciation of franc-denominated assets appeased the bondholders but made the demands of industry and labor more urgent. Then, too, the injuries from inflation and depreciation were sustained by a broad but disorganized group of small savers over an extended time period, making collective action difficult. The recession of the second half of 1926 and early 1927, by comparison, affected a concentrated and organized class of industrialists and workers. Nothing greater than one fifth of the prewar parity could be countenanced under the social and economic conditions prevailing in early 1927.

The fate of the franc was sealed when the Banque de France took the side of the industrialists. Its own economists produced studies that were extraordinarily sensitive to the needs of production and employment. Many of the régents had important industrial connections. In fact, in sharp contrast to the role played by the Bank of England, the Banque de France pleaded industry's case to the government in 1926–1927. It is crucial to recognize that the international as well as the domestic role of the Banque de France was altogether different from that of the Bank of England. With little to lose by way of a

---

[103] Neither the monetary authorities of the United States nor those of Britain made much of the issue of the value at which the franc should be stabilized, despite the complications the low rate presented for the latter. S.V.O. Clarke, *Central Bank Cooperation, 1924–1931* (New York: Federal Reserve Bank of New York), 1967, pp. 115–118.

leadership position in international finance, French banks sought domestic price stability over international prestige. From the perspective of France's economic decisionmakers, such an outcome represented a politically acceptable solution to the stabilization of the franc. It was a decision to which France's trading partners would simply have to adjust.

Chapter 6

TARIFF PROTECTION

FOR THE PAST CENTURY, trade barriers have been considered one of the most outwardly hostile ways to deal with balance of payments difficulties. Despite rampant protectionism during the interwar years, impediments to international trade were recognized as an immediate threat to trading partners' economic well-being, and as an eventual threat to the gold standard adjustment mechanism. At least six multilateral conferences and a plethora of bilateral negotiations aimed to reach accords on limiting and dismantling trade barriers during the interwar years. It was understood that such barriers simply externalized economic problems, while subsidizing the prevailing patterns of consumption and investment, and that they could eventually undermine adjustment between surplus and deficit countries.[1] The second norm of the gold standard system of adjustment was the preference for liberal trade policies rather than external controls. Trade barriers were—and are—viewed as a hostile means for a country to improve or preserve its balance of payments position.

This chapter describes and explains the incidence of tariffs in the twenties and thirties. I begin by showing which countries had the highest average tariffs, and point out that there was virtually no difference between deficit and surplus countries' tariff levels for the period as a whole. The remainder of the chapter deals with modeling first tariff *levels*, and then modeling *changes* in these levels. The evidence suggests that tariff *levels* are best explained by structural variables, especially an economy's size and degree of trade dependence. But *changes* in tariff levels are much more closely correlated with changes in economic and political conditions. As we would expect, tariff increases were associated with economic downturn. But somewhat surprisingly, given the position of labor on protection since the Second World War, greater left-wing representation in legislatures contributed to tariff decreases. Consistent with our findings in previous chapters, governments facing domestic political turmoil tended slightly to externalize by raising tariffs, while those that were more stable tended to reduce them. When we control for the impact of structural and economic variables, protection emerges as the choice of the center right, and of governments so precariously positioned that they were unable to absorb the costs of adjustment.

---

[1] Barry Eichengreen (ed.), *The Gold Standard in Theory and History* (New York: Methuen), 1985, p. 22.

Descriptive Statistics of Tariff Protection

Any measure of exactly how much a country is protecting its domestic producers from external competition is highly problematic. Protection can be achieved in a number of ways: through tariffs, quotas, excessive regulations, currency controls, bilateral clearing arrangements, and other creative means.[2] Many studies of the determinants of protectionist commercial policies explain the "demand for protection"[3] or "legislated tariff levels."[4] In this chapter, I am most concerned with actual tariff outcomes, and so I use the ratio of customs collected as a percentage of the total value of imports as the most widely available measure of tariff protection (see Appendix I). The higher this ratio, the higher the "tariff index" for any given country-year. This measure is appropriate since I am interested in comparing overall tariff levels across countries, rather than protection accorded various sectors within an economy.[5] Although this measure is obviously not a comprehensive measure of protection—it excludes import quotas, foreign exchange rationing, and other restrictions—it does give a very sensitive and complete series for one of the most important barriers to international trade at this time.[6]

Just how high were tariff barriers by this measure during the interwar years? Typically, customs revenues during this period ranged between 5 and 10 percent of the total value of imports. But the distribution is skewed to the left, with a tail of outliers, representing a very high tariff relative to imports, to the right. The average tariff index for the period as a whole was about 14 percent. Approximately 61 percent of all observations (205) were less than 10 percent (figure 6.1). Spain accounted for both of the extreme observations on the right. Coun-

[2] I do not try to explain why some countries chose to protect primarily through tariffs while others chose primarily import quotas, foreign exchange rationing, or other measures.

[3] Demand for protection (defined as *successful* escape clause petitions) is the dependent variable in Wendy E. Takacs, "Pressures for Protectionism: An Empirical Analysis," *Economic Inquiry*, Vol. 19, 1981, pp. 87–93; and in Cletus Coughlin, Joseph V. Terza, and Noor Aini Khalifah, "The Determinants of Escape Clause Petitions," *Review of Economics and Statistics*, Vol. 71, 1989, pp. 341–347; Helen V. Milner, *Resisting Protectionism: Global Industries and the Politics of International Trade* (Princeton: Princeton University Press), 1988.

[4] Legislated tariff levels are the dependent variable in Giulio Gallarotti, "Toward a Business-Cycle Model of Tariffs," *International Organization*, Vol. 39, 1985, pp. 155–187, and tariff rates are the dependent variable in Stephen Magee and Leslie Young, "Endogenous Protection in the United States, 1900–1984," in Robert M. Stern (ed.), *U.S. Trade Policies in a Changing World Economy* (Cambridge: MIT Press), 1987.

[5] There is a voluminous literature on the distribution of protection across sectors and industries. But I am concerned here with an overall tariff index comparable across countries, rather than an explanation of the sectoral distribution of protection.

[6] The data on customs revenues as a proportion of import values are available for every country in the sample except Yugoslavia and Japan. The only other countries that have more than one observation missing for the entire period are Hungary (1923–1926) and Spain (1936–1939). In all, of a theoretically possible 392 observations, 333 country-years could be assigned a tariff index, making this a fairly complete series.

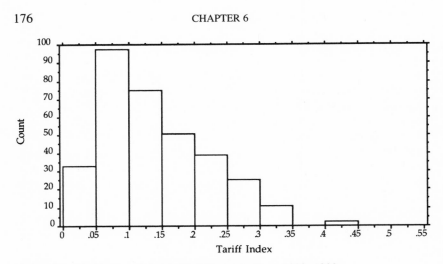

Figure 6.1: Distribution of Yearly Tariff Level Indices, 1923–1939

tries whose tariffs were significantly lower than the average for the period as a whole were Belgium, Czechoslovakia, Denmark, Hungary, the Netherlands, and Sweden ($p < .01$). Those whose tariffs were significantly higher were Bulgaria, Finland, Greece, and Spain ($p < .01$; table 6.1 and figure 6.2). All three of the major democratic economies—France, Britain, and the United States—had average tariffs very close to the distribution mean, and very close to one another.

Tariffs were much higher in the 1930s than in the 1920s. The average tariff index for the stabilization period (1923–1926) was about 11 percent; for the gold standard years (1927–1931), almost 13 percent; and for the remainder of the 1930s, about 17.6 percent. The probability of observing such significant differences between these time periods by chance is extremely small ($p < .01$).[7]

The time-series cross-sectional data are best appreciated by looking at each country's tariff index by year, compared to both the yearly average for the sample as a whole and compared to the tariff index of its major trading partner (figure 6.3). The general rise in protection is obvious between 1932 and 1936. Several countries, though, pursued tariff policies that were consistently less protectionist than those of both the sample average and their major trading

---

[7] The complete results of a two-tailed unpaired t test with 335 degrees of freedom for differences between time periods were as follows:

Year	Obs. #	Mean	Std. Dev.	Std. Error	t Stat.	Prob.
1923–26	78	.108	.074	.008	−4.27	.0001
1927–31	104	.128	.07	.007	−2.42	.0161
1932–39	155	.176	.1	.008	6.045	.0001

TABLE 6.1
Average Tariff Levels, by Country, 1923–1939
(Tariff Index = Customs Revenues/Total Value of Imports)

Country	Count	Mean	Std. Dev.	Std. Error	t stat	Prob. (t-tail)[a]
Austria	14	.119	.046	.012	−1.108	.2685
Belgium	17	.057	.027	.007	−4.234	.0001[a]
Bulgaria	17	.221	.029	.0007	3.574	.0004[b]
Canada	17	.141	.014	.003	−.222	.8242
Czechos.	15	.083	.02	.005	−2.752	.0063[a]
Denmark	17	.064	.014	.003	−3.883	.0001[a]
France	17	.154	.085	.021	.42	.6749
Germany	16	.189	.11	.028	1.974	.0492[b]
Greece	15	.242	.097	.025	4.331	.0001[b]
Hungary	13	.092	.021	.006	−2.181	.0299[a]
Italy	16	.123	.087	.022	−1.032	.303
Netherlands	17	.046	.027	.007	−4.786	.0001[a]
Norway	17	.114	.025	.006	−1.456	.1462
Poland	15	.122	.024	.006	−1.04	.300
Romania	16	.186	.072	.018	1.859	.0638
Spain	13	.328	.166	.046	8.092	.0001[b]
Sweden	17	.09	.015	.004	−2.6	.0097[a]
Switzerland	17	.14	.054	.013	−.239	.811
United Kingdom	17	.172	.081	.02	1.262	.208
United States	17	.162	.031	.007	.765	.4447

Note: Probabilities refer to the likelihood that the observed country mean is not significantly different from that for the sample as a whole. ($p < .05$)

[a] = Average tariff index is significantly *lower* than that of the sample as a whole.

[b] = Average tariff index is significantly *higher* than that of the sample as a whole.

partner. In the early to mid thirties, for instance, Belgium's tariff index was only about one third that of its major trading partner. Despite sharp upward shifts in tariffs imposed abroad, Denmark's and Sweden's tariff indices remained virtually constant over the period as a whole. A chasm between the policies of the Netherlands and its major trading partner opened up over the period. Norway followed both the average and its major trading partner until about 1931, when it broke with the rising tide and chose a relatively low tariff path. The tariff index of the United States is one of the most erratic, with big peaks in 1930, 1932, 1934, and 1938. The tariff index of Switzerland, on the other hand, seemed to mirror closely both the sample average and that of its major trading partner. Two countries' policies changed decidedly over the course of the two decades: Britain began the period with a very low tariff, but outstripped both the average and its major trading partner from 1933 to the end of the decade. Romania did the opposite: starting with an extremely high tariff index in the

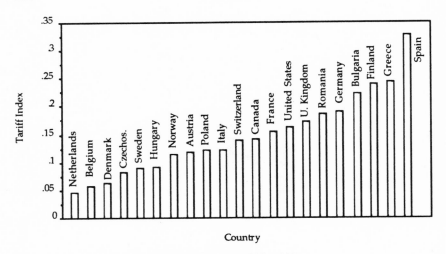

Figure 6.2: Average Tariff Level, by Country, 1923–1939

1920s, Romania progressively reduced customs, until by 1938 it had one of the lowest scores in the sample and a *differential* of almost 30 percent with its major trading partner.

Tariffs were also frequently used by surplus countries to frustrate international economic adjustment. While one might expect deficit countries to have chosen higher tariff levels (on the grounds that they were more likely to be characterized by uncompetitive producers who had a strong interest in being shielded from foreign competition), deficit and surplus countries on average maintained tariffs at about the same levels. Country-years characterized by strong surplus (the upper quartile range), had an average index of 13.4 percent in the following year, while country-years representing very weak payments (the lower quartile range) the corresponding index was 13.2 percent. These differences are statistically indistinguishable.[8]

EXPLAINING TARIFF LEVELS

What explains differences in tariff levels across countries during this time? It is important to understand the factors associated with high tariff levels, since such

[8] The complete results of a two-tailed unpaired *t* test with 110 degrees of freedom for differences between the upper and lower quartile ranges for balance of payments position with a one year lag were as follows:

Group	Obs. #	Mean	Std. Dev.	Std. Error	t Stat.	Prob.
Upper quart.	59	.134	.07	.009	.121	.9035
Lower quart.	53	.132	.056	.008		

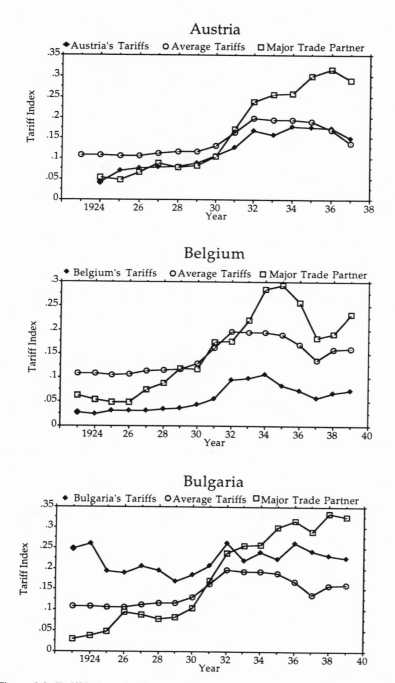

Figure 6.3: Tariff Indexes by Country, Compared to Sample Average and Major Trade Partner

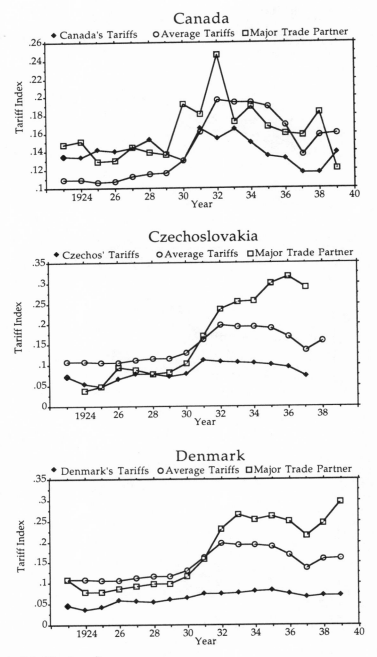

Figure 6.3: (*Continued*)

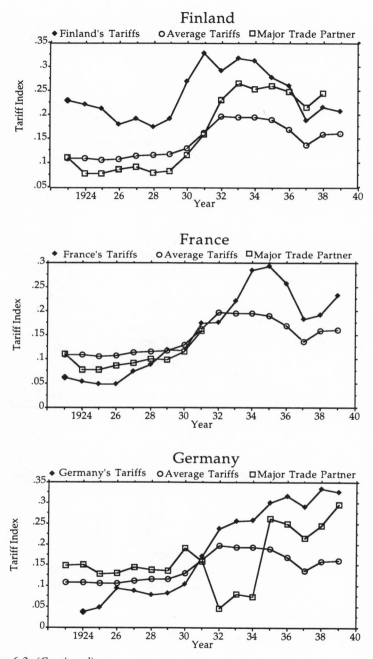

Figure 6.3: (*Continued*)

Greece

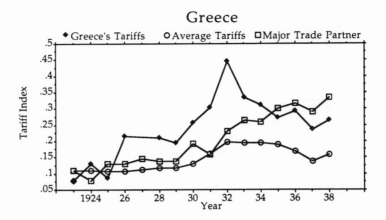

Hungary

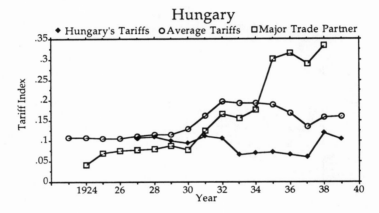

Italy

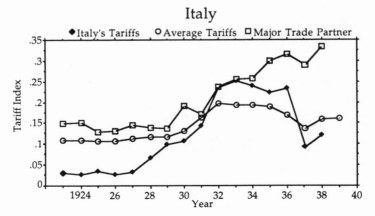

Figure 6.3: (*Continued*)

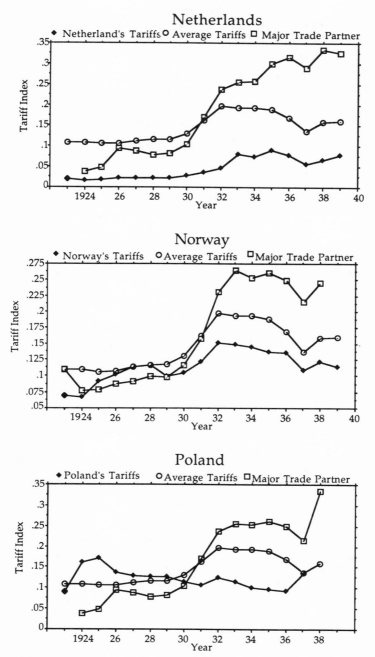

Figure 6.3: (*Continued*)

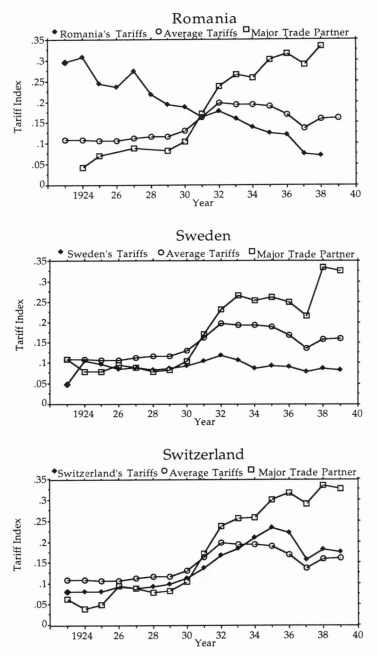

Figure 6.3: (*Continued*)

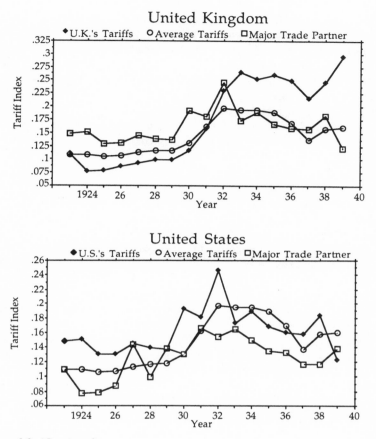

Figure 6.3: (*Continued*)

a policy seals off the economy from external pressures for adjustment. (Changes in tariff policy are treated below.) Three types of explanations for tariffs are often cited in the literature on protectionism and are examined here. The first is the level of economic development; the second is a country's international bargaining power; and the third looks at the domestic fiscal reasons for maintaining high tariff levels.

Protection and Economic Development. One of the most traditional explanations for tariff protection across countries relates to the economy's degree of industrial development. Traditional "infant industry" justifications claim that protection is justified at early stages of development, since producers have to begin on a small and inefficient scale, and are unable to meet the low costs of foreign competition. Because of the expected future gains from industrialization (acquiring and spreading knowledge and production techniques, developing infrastructure), developing countries have incentives to remove the competitive obstacles to industrial growth by protecting.[9] Since less developed countries can be expected to have a higher proportion of labor-intensive, low-skill industries, we should expect aggregate differences in tariff levels across countries according to their level of economic development.[10] Here, the level of economic development is approximated by per capita Net National Product, which correlates closely with a country's degree of industrialization.

International Systemic/Structural Variables and Tariff Levels. The international economic and international political economy literature emphasizes that a country's international bargaining position and its interest in free trade are influenced by its relative economic power. One way to measure such power is the sheer size of the economy. It is often presumed that larger economies have the leverage and bargaining power that enables them to implement policies unencumbered by external constraints. The problem remains in specifying the interests that large states have in particular commercial policies, and here the economic and political economy literature diverges. Economists emphasize that large economies can benefit from protection on terms of trade grounds.[11]

---

[9] Other means of nurturing infant industries—improving their access to capital markets, improving social investment—are theoretically possible and may be more efficient, but are more difficult to achieve and have a higher visible cost than tariffs.

[10] A. Maizels, *Industrial Growth and World Trade* (Cambridge: Cambridge University Press), 1971, pp. 141–144. The level of economic development has been shown to be important in explaining protection for various industries across developed and developing economies. A ten-country study by E. J. Ray found that average tariff levels across 225 commodity classifications were negatively related to labor and skill intensity, and to economies of scale. In the United States, industries with high levels of industrial concentration were also protected. E. J. Ray, "The Optimum Commodity Tariff and Tariff Rates in Developed and Less Developed Countries," *Review of Economics and Statistics*, Vol. 56, 1974, pp. 369–377; Ray, "Tariff and Non-Tariff Barriers in the United States and Abroad," *Review of Economics and Statistics*, Vol. 63, 1981, pp. 161–168. John A. C. Conybeare makes a case for the importance of level of economic development and tests it against three other explanations (national power and size, nature of the fiscal regime, and the ability of interest groups to take collective action). He concludes that the level of economic development (GDP per capita) is the most important determinant for differing average levels of tariff protection across thirty-five countries in 1971. "Tariff Protection in Developed and Developing Countries: A Cross-sectional and Longitudinal Analysis," *International Organization*, Vol. 37, 1983, pp. 441–463. A somewhat related argument, advanced by Jeffry A. Frieden, is that a country's net external investment position will be important to its trade policy choice. Frieden, "Capital Politics: Creditors and the International Political Economy," *Journal of Public Policy*, Vol. 8, Nos. 3/4 (1988), pp. 265–286.

[11] Theoretical discussion of the use of tariffs to improve the terms of trade is found in Charles P. Kindleberger, *International Economics* (Homewood, Ill.: Richard D. Irwin), 1968, chap. 7; Tibor Scitovsky, "A Reconsideration of the Theory of Tariffs," *Review of Economic Studies*, reprinted in American Economic Association, *Readings in the Theory of International Trade* (New York:

Tariffs effectively reduce a country's offer of exports for imports, with a portion of the difference going to the customs authorities. But for a country to be able to influence the relative price of its exports, it must have something resembling monopoly power, such that the demand for its goods is fairly inelastic. The more inelastic the demand for a country's goods, the more able it will be to improve its terms of trade through protection. Larger states are more likely to have monopoly power that could be used to implement a high optimal tariff.

A contending approach ascribes a more benign effect to size. According to public goods interpretations, larger and more powerful states are presumed to have an overwhelming interest in the stability and openness of the international trading system.[12] This depends on the assumption that larger states reap a disproportionate benefit from freer trade, and this in turn depends not only on size but also on a country's initial trade position and the elasticities of supply and demand for its products. Harry Johnson notes that "the strongest industrial power" (as defined by its initial trade position in industrial products) would increase its industrial exports more than its industrial imports under a system of universal free trade. He argues that there are clear reasons for the more powerful industrial states to exploit their economic leverage to encourage other states to open up their markets. This should result in lower tariffs for the more powerful traders, and possibly contribute to a more open trade system overall.[13]

McGraw-Hill), 1949, chap. 16. As an example of the asymmetric ability of larger states to reap welfare gains from tariffs, see Forrest Capie, *Depression and Protectionism: Britain between the Wars* (London: Allen and Unwin), 1983, p. 106, where he claims that Britain's national income was higher during the thirties than it would have been in the absence of the tariff; see also Giorgio Basevi, "The Restrictive Effect of the U.S. Tariff and Its Welfare Value," *American Economic Review*, Vol. 58, September 1968, pp. 840–849, which argues that the United States did realize some small welfare gains through its tariff.

[12] Stephen Krasner has tested the relationship between tariff levels and state power (relative size and economic development) and openness of the international trading system (lower tariff levels, higher proportions of trade to GNP, and less regionalism). He finds, generally, a positive relationship between state power and freer trade, but the interwar years are an important exception. "State Power and the Structure of International Trade," *World Politics*, Vol. 28, 1976, pp. 317–347. See also David A. Lake, *Power, Protectionism, and Free Trade: International Sources of U.S. Commercial Strategy, 1887–1939* (Ithaca: Cornell University Press), 1988.

[13] Harry G. Johnson, "An Economic Theory of Protectionism, Tariff Bargaining, and the Formation of Customs Unions," *Journal of Political Economy*, Vol. 73, 1965, pp. 256–283. Timothy McKeown has shown that in fact Great Britain did *not* use leverage to actively promote freer trade in the nineteenth century as this interpretation of the theory predicts. "Hegemonic Stability Theory and 19th-Century Tariff Levels in Europe," *International Organization*, Vol. 37, Winter 1983, pp. 73–91. "Hegemonic" theories of systemic economic openness add that world tariffs will tend to be bargained down when the leading industrial producer also happens to be a very large nation. Critiques of this theory can be found in John A. C. Conybeare, "Public Goods, Prisoner's Dilemmas, and the International Political Economy," *International Studies Quarterly*, Vol. 28, Spring 1984, pp. 5–22, and in Robert O. Keohane, *After Hegemony: Cooperation and Discord in the World Political Economy* (Princeton: Princeton University Press), 1984, pp. 31–46.

The strongest expectation is that overall tariff levels should be lower in a hegemonic system than in a more pluralist system. The logic is also used to explain tariff differentials across countries: since larger states are presumed to benefit disproportionately from freer trade, benign hegemonic theories would expect larger countries to choose lower tariffs.[14] By this interpretation, one might expect either NNP or share of world trade to be negatively associated with tariff protection.

A state's power as a trader, and hence its tariff structure, might have something to do with the dispersion of its trade among many partners. Conybeare argues that the diversification among trading partners may reduce the vulnerability of a country to retaliation, insofar as the costs of coordinated retaliation would be higher than if a country traded heavily with one or a few partners.[15] A country that depends heavily on a single market or a few markets is much more likely than its counterparts to be vulnerable to trade-partner pressure to keep tariffs low. Countries with a highly diversified trading "portfolio" may have much greater freedom of action. Higher concentration (measured here as the share of total trade that is accounted for by a country's top three trade partners) should therefore be associated with lower tariff levels.

Finally, trade dependence should have important implications for trade policy. High trade dependence makes it very costly for a country to raise the price of critical imported goods by adding tariffs. Tariffs raise the price of imported inputs and hence may make finished exports less competitive in the world market. Furthermore, tariffs might diminish the foreign exchange earnings of one's trade partners and end up reducing demand for one's own exports.[16] Most importantly, raising tariffs invites retaliation. In highly trade dependent countries, firms that need to export to survive are likely to form a strong coalition for a policy of relatively free trade. Overall, the high costs to highly trade dependent states of a breakdown in international trade overwhelm the potential benefits of implementing a restrictive tariff policy. The greater a state's dependence on trade, the more willing it will be to resist protection.[17] In our sample, the

[14] This proposition was tested across countries by Conybeare, "Tariff Protection," 1983. He found no significant relationship between several measures of size and power for tariff levels in 1971 for thirty-five countries.

[15] Conybeare, ibid., p. 448.

[16] W. M. Corden, *The Theory of Protection* (Oxford: Oxford University Press), 1971; Corden, *Trade Policy and Welfare* (Oxford: Oxford University Press), 1974.

[17] Few if any studies deal with this variable in a systematic way at the level of the national economy. Interestingly, while he mentions the importance of trade dependence in his study, Conybeare does not test its impact on trade policy in either a bivariate or a multivariate fashion. However, this notion of sensitivity and vulnerability was crucial in the interdependence literature that grew in the 1970s. Robert O. Keohane and Joseph S. Nye, *Power and Interdependence: World Politics in Transition* (Boston: Little, Brown), 1977. Peter J. Katzenstein argues that protection is not a strategy available to small countries, due the importance of trade to their economies and the risk of retaliation. *Small States in World Markets: Industrial Policy in Europe* (Ithaca: Cornell University Press), 1985. The importance of interdependence is developed systematically at the level of the firm and industry in the work of Helen V. Milner, *Resisting Protectionism*.

archetypes on each end of the spectrum are, on the one hand, Belgium, which was highly trade dependent and had a very liberal trade policy, and, on the other hand, the insulated and protectionist United States.

Tariffs and Domestic Economic Policy.   Finally, tariff levels may have been influenced by fiscal policy. For a number of countries, customs taxes still had a dual purpose during the interwar years. In addition to what today we would consider as serving the obvious function of sheltering domestic producers, tariffs were what many countries still depended on as their main source of government revenue. Switzerland, for instance, financed more than half its public budget through customs revenues. Canada, Greece, Norway, and Denmark were also heavily dependent on customs as a source of government revenue. Tariff levels may have been driven by the need to balance the public budget.[18] If so, we should expect a positive relationship between the tariff index and the proportion of tax revenues raised through tariffs.

Tariff Levels: The Evidence

The economics and international political economy literature suggests that tariff levels are likely to be driven by these developmental, international structural, and domestic policy-oriented policies. To test the relative weight of these explanations, the following equation was used:

$$\text{Tariff Index} = a + \beta_{1-19}(\text{Country Dummy}) + \beta_{20}(\text{Tariff Index } [t-1])$$
$$+ \beta_{21}(\% \text{ World Trade}) + \beta_{22}(\text{Trade Dependence}) + \beta_{23}(\text{Customs/Total}$$
$$\text{Taxes}) + \beta_{24}(\text{Net Investment Position}) + \beta_{25}(\text{Trade Concentration}) +$$
$$\beta_{26}(\text{NNP}) + \beta_{27}(\text{NNP/Capita}) + e$$

The results of combining various explanations appear in table 6.2. Dummy country variables and a lagged dependent variable were included on the right-hand side (see Appendix 6.A). Without a doubt, two of the most important substantive correlates of tariff levels have to do with the position and the exposure of a national economy to the international economic system. There is virtually no doubt that the more a country depends on trade as a portion of its NNP, the lower its tariff levels will be ($p < .0001$ in every version of the model). For every one percentage point increase in the degree of trade dependence, the tariff index was lower on average by about .15 of one percentage point. As an example of the substantive impact of high dependence on trade, according to the estimates generated by this model, trade dependence alone could account for almost nine percentage points difference in average tariff

---

[18] For an analysis of the fiscal constraint on tariff policy in the case of the United States, see John Mark Hansen, "Taxation and the Political Economy of the Tariff," *International Organization*, Vol. 44, No. 4, Autumn 1990, pp. 527–549.

TABLE 6.2
Five Models of Tariff Levels for 19 Countries[a], 1923–1939
(Nonstandardized Coefficients; Standard Errors)

Variable	Model 1	Model 2	Model 3	Model 4	Model 5
Intercept	.053	−.016	.031	.002	.036
Tariff Index	.523***	.633***	.667***	.669***	.557***
$(t - 1)$	(.039)	(.038)	(.038)	(.038)	(.04)
%World Trade	.005***	.004***	.004***	.004***	.005***
	(.001)	(.001)	(.001)	(.001)	(.001)
Trade Dependence	−.167***	−.155***	−.137***	−.135***	−.152***
	(.022)	(.025)	(.023)	(.023)	(.021)
Customs/Total	.267***	.201***	.152***	.154***	.219***
Taxes	(.041)	(.047)	(.046)	(.047)	(.041)
Net Investment	−.062***	—	—	—	−.004
Position	(.017)	—	—	—	(.039)
Trade Concentra-	—	.01	—	—	.026
tion	—	(.033)	—	—	(.028)
NNP	—	—	−.001	—	−.001
	—	—	(.001)	—	(.001)
NNP/Capita	—	—	—	−15.06	−11.83
	—	—	—	(28.69)	(31.98)
$N =$	300	309	297	297	282
SER $=$	.03	.034	.032	.032	.027
adj.$R^2 =$	.854	.859	.88	.88	.881

Note: These results include dummy variables for each country. See Appendix Table 6.A for complete results.
Note: * = Significant at .10 level.   ** = Significant at .05 level.   *** = Significant at .025 level.
[a]All models exclude Japan, Romania, and Yugoslavia, due to missing data. All models except Model 1 exclude Spain, due to missing data. Models including NNP variables exclude most of Poland and Greece 1923–1926, due to missing data.

levels between France and Belgium for the period as a whole. (The actual difference in these countries' tariff index for the interwar years was 9.7 percent.)

A second important substantive variable was a country's share of world trade. With a high degree of confidence and complete consistency across the four versions of the model, it appears that a one percentage point increase in a country's share of world trade was associated with a .4- to .5-point increase in its tariff index ($p < .0002$). This relationship would imply that the difference in their share of world trade alone might lead us to expect about a ten percentage point difference between Denmark's and Germany's tariff index (their average tariffs for the period as a whole were, respectively, .064 and .189). These analyses present strong evidence that larger traders had the monopolistic power to raise their tariffs in an asymmetrical fashion. Smaller traders behaved as though they feared retaliation. If these results speak to hegemonic theories, they are clearly in support of its more malign interpretations.[19]

There is also evidence that countries that depended on customs for tax revenues had higher tariffs as a proportion of imports. Across all runs, dependence on customs for tax revenues was strongly positively correlated with the tariff level. For every percentage point in the share of customs receipts in total taxes, the tariff index was on average higher by at least .15 of a point.

High tariff levels indicate a relatively inflexible antiadjustment economic policy. When we test for explanations of policy changes below, it is important to keep in mind that some of the tariff increases documented below may in fact be from very low overall levels. In particular, countries that were highly trade dependent kept tariffs much lower on average. On the other hand, large traders appeared to take advantage of their power to keep tariffs high, as did countries that depended on tariffs for tax revenues.[20] The picture that is emerging is not very surprising: the customs-revenue-dependent, rather insular economies had the highest tariff levels, as did the dominant traders in the sample. Countries with these characteristics are prime antiadjustment candidates. Let us now take up the question of what prompts a protectionist policy *change*.

Changes in Tariff Policy

The determinants of tariff levels were primarily structural explanations that were not expected to change drastically over the two decades, but which did differ significantly across countries. High tariffs made a liberal, macro-economically based adjustment strategy unlikely. Now we take up the problem of change in the tariff index from one year to the next. Change is much more erratic than overall levels, making it difficult to model accurately. Because of its wild fluctuations, the dependent variable is modeled as a two-year moving average.

What causes a shift in tariff protection from one year to the next? Major

---

[19] It is interesting, though, that while share of world trade was associated with tariff increases, absolute size of the economy (Net National Product) was not. Indeed, there was a tendency (though unstable across versions of the model) for larger economies to have lower tariff levels. This may be because of the strong correlation between these two measures of size (.673; adjusted R squared = .452; $p < .0001$).

[20] In bivariate tests, not replicated here, there was also an important relationship between tariff levels and the proportion of agriculture in Net National Product, and between tariffs and variability in the balance of payments. There is a positive correlation between agriculture as a proportion of NNP and the variability of the balance of payments of .479.

explanations include business cycle pressures, strategic international behavior, and a country's changing international position. Less conventionally, I also test for the influence of the domestic political conditions that have been implicated in the problems of external imbalance and currency devaluation. The decision to implement or raise tariffs is a policy of externalization with domestic distributional consequences. There are good reasons, therefore, to expect systematic differences in tariff policy change due to regime type, party in power, the stability of the policymaking environment, and, less directly, the nature and strength of monetary institutions. Each of these explanations for shifting tariff policy is discussed below.

Changing Economic Conditions.   Recession is associated with increased protectionism. This is one of the clearest lessons economists and international political economists have drawn from the experience of the interwar years. Falling industrial production and increased unemployment create a nearly irresistible impulse to protect jobs and domestic production and to try to maintain stable prices by excluding foreign goods. The value of protection to domestic producers is likely to be highest during periods of general economic distress. If one were to think of the problem in game theoretic terms, "Economic recessions exaggerate the Prisoner's Dilemma problem by raising the actors' marginal gains from predatory transfers."[21] When the economy is expanding, on the other hand, domestic producers may be more satisfied to share the buoyant demand for goods with foreign competitors.

Several studies have confirmed the negative relationship between the business cycle and the "demand" for protection, most frequently in the case of the United States.[22] These studies have found that protectionist pressures build and

[21] John A. C. Conybeare, "Trade Wars: A Comparative Study of Anglo-Hanse, Franco-Italian, and Smoot-Hawley Conflicts," *World Politics*, Vol. 38, No. 1, October 1985, p. 170.

[22] Wendy E. Takacs's research has demonstrated that protectionist pressures in the United States between 1949 and 1979 were related to the business cycle, but she also found that actual protection (defined as *successful* petitions) were not affected by the business cycle. Takacs, "Pressures for Protectionism," pp. 87–93. The work by Cletus Coughlin, Joseph V. Terza, and Noor Aini Khalifah has also found that the number of escape clause petitions filed in the United States between 1948 and 1984 increases during cyclical downturns. Coughlin et al., "The Determinants of Escape Clause Petitions," pp. 341–347. Giulio Gallarotti used historical data for Germany, the United States, and Great Britain to show that legislated tariff increases were more likely during periods of slow growth. Gallarotti, "Toward a Business-Cycle Model of Tariffs," pp. 155–187. Stephen Magee and Leslie Young argue that economic conditions such as the unemployment rate and the competitive position of the United States have had an important impact on the average tariff rate on U.S. imports across presidential administrations between 1900 and 1984. Magee and Young, "Endogenous Protection in the United States, 1900–1984," in Robert M. Stern (ed.), *U.S. Trade Policies in a Changing World Economy*, pp. 145–195. See also Timothy McKeown, "Firms and Tariff Regime Change," *World Politics*, Vol. 36, January 1984, pp. 215–233; James Cassing, Timothy McKeown, and Jack Ochs, "The Political Economy of the Tariff Cycle," *American Political Science Review*, Vol. 80, September 1986, pp. 843–862; Michael Wallerstein, "Unemployment, Collective Bar-

that average legislated tariff levels tend to be higher during economic down-turns. Since the demand for protection increases during recessionary periods, we would expect that on average the actual ratio of customs to imports should be higher as the economy slows.

Not all countries' commercial policies were equally sensitive to changes in economic conditions, however. Table 6.3 presents the results of separate cor-relations for each country in the sample between change in the index of indus-trial production and change in the tariff index the following year. A negative correlation indicates that as industrial conditions deteriorated, higher customs were collected on imported goods. The results show that the tariffs of Britain, Canada, and Norway were the most highly correlated with economic downturn in the previous period. Germany and Austria also had strong negative correla-tions, but higher standard errors rendered the relationship statistically insignifi-cant. The most surprising result in this chart is that the tariff index of the United States was significantly *positively* associated with changes in the industrial index, indicating that the United States tended to raise tariffs when economic conditions improved and to lower them when they deteriorated. A possible interpretation of the relationship between economic conditions and the tariff index by country helps to resolve the ambiguities surrounding the impact of size on the average tariff index: the *declining* hegemon most drastically used its monopoly power to protect itself from industrial decline, while the behavior of the *emerging* hegemon was apparently countercyclical. In short, the United States was a troublemaker for the international economic system in the twen-ties, but it tended to provide a more open market for goods after 1932.[23] In the multivariate analysis that follows, I use a lagged two-year moving average of changes in the index of industrial production to capture the direction of the business cycle.

Retaliation and Reciprocity.   One of the most important reasons for changes in the tariff index may be changes in the commercial policies of trading rivals.[24] Tariff policy may be externally strategically motivated. The work of Tibor Scitovsky provided an early analytical framework for understanding the impe-tus behind retaliatory tariff increases. In a two-country system, Scitovsky pos-tulated, an attempt by one country to gain a monopolistic advantage by raising its tariffs would lead the other to try and regain its losses by doing likewise.

---

gaining, and the Demand for Protection," *American Journal of Political Science*, Vol. 31, Novem-ber 1987, pp. 729–752.

[23] For a domestic political account of this shift, see Stephan Haggard, "The Institutional Founda-tions of Hegemony: Explaining the Reciprocal Trade Agreements Act of 1934," *International Organization*, Vol. 42, No. 1, Winter 1988, pp. 91–119.

[24] For a discussion of reciprocity and retaliation in tariff policy see John A. C. Conybeare, "Trade Wars," pp. 147–172.

TABLE 6.3

The Relationship between Change in the Tariff Index and Change in the Index
of Industrial Production, by Country[a]

Country	Count	Correlation	Adj. R^2	SE	Prob.
United Kingdom	15	−.598	.308	.023	.019
Canada	15	−.516	.21	.013	.049
Norway	15	−.493	.185	.014	.062
Germany	13	−.46	.14	.027	.113
Austria	13	−.455	.135	.016	.117
Netherlands	13	−.404	.087	.013	.171
Finland	12	−.38	.059	.041	.223
Czechoslovakia	13	−.364	.054	.014	.22
Belgium	15	−.309	.026	.014	.26
Italy	14	−.182	−.048	.051	.535
France	15	−.069	−.072	.037	.81
Romania	12	.058	−.096	.026	.858
Sweden	15	.14	−.056	.011	.62
Poland	11	.141	−.089	.017	.679
Denmark	11	.158	−.083	.005	.64
Greece	11	.388	.057	.089	.238
Hungary	11	.405	.072	.023	.216
United States	15	.469	.16	.033	.078

Note: Arranged by strength and direction of correlation.

[a]The equation for each country was: ΔTariff Index = a + β_1 (ΔIndustrial Production, [$t - 1$])
+ e.

"Countries that believe themselves to be sufficiently small to erect or raise
tariffs unpunished will do so as soon as they discover that they can thereby
increase their national welfare," he wrote.[25] This would lead to a spiral of tariffs
and tariff reprisals as each country attempted to maximize its welfare in the
short term, but it would lead ultimately to a situation in which each would be
worse off than before the tariff wars began.[26]

For our purposes, the welfare implications are not as central as whether or not
there is a clear relationship between movements of the tariff indices of trading
partners. While we can postulate that there might be a generally positive relationship, there is no reason that it should be identical across countries. Table 6.4
shows the correlation between yearly changes in the tariff index and changes in

[25] Tibor Scitovsky, "A Reconsideration of the Theory of Tariffs," in Ellis and Metzler (eds.),
Readings in the Theory of International Trade, p. 379.

[26] Subsequent work by Harry Johnson suggests that a country's welfare status after a round of
tariff increases depends on the elasticity of demand for that country's goods relative to those of its
trading partner. Harry G. Johnson, "Optimum Tariffs and Retaliation," *Review of Economic
Studies*, Vol. 21, 1954, p. 153. For applications to N-country and N-product settings, see Kiyoshi
Kuga, "Tariff Retaliation and Policy Equilibrium," *Journal of International Economics*, Vol. 3,
November 1983, pp. 351–366.

TABLE 6.4
Correlation between Changes in Tariff Index and Changes in the Tariff Index
of the Major Trade Partner

Country	Count	Correlation	Adj. R^2	SE	Prob.
Norway	15	.693	.44	.011	.004
Switzerland	16	.68	.424	.017	.0037
France	8	.651	.328	.019	.08
Romania	13	.515	.199	.023	.07
Austria	13	.498	.179	.015	.084
Italy	15	.454	.145	.045	.09
Czechoslovakia	14	.453	.139	.013	.104
Finland	15	.45	.141	.036	.09
Netherlands	16	.44	.136	.011	.088
Denmark	16	.434	.13	.006	.09
Bulgaria	16	.364	.071	.029	.165
Belgium	16	.361	.068	.013	.17
Hungary	12	.094	−.09	.04	.771
Sweden	16	.054	−.068	.018	.844
United Kingdom	16	.031	−.07	.03	.91
Spain	12	−.091	−.1	.085	.95
Greece	14	−.024	−.083	.091	.94
Poland	14	−.041	−.082	.027	.89
Germany	16	−.061	−.067	.029	.82
United States	16	−.18	−.037	.036	.50
Canada	16	−.472	.167	.013	.065

Note: Arranged by correlation.

the tariff index of the major trading partner for each country in the sample. As expected, most correlations were positive. In simple regressions, the correlations for Norway, Switzerland, France, Romania, Austria, Italy, Finland, the Netherlands, and Denmark were statistically significant at the .10 level. With the exceptions of France and Italy, many of the countries with the strongest positive correlations with changes in the tariff index of their major trading partner were the smaller and more highly industrialized states. While these countries kept their tariffs low overall, there does appear to be a higher degree of responsiveness in the tariff policies of the smaller industrial countries in the sample. Only one country, Canada, had a statistically significant negative correlation, which may be because of its ambiguous position between the United States and the sterling area. While the United States was Canada's major trading partner for the period as a whole, Canada's links to the system of imperial preferences may have pulled its policies much more toward Britain than the United States. As shown in table 6.3, Britain's and Canada's tariffs more closely reflected deteriorating industrial conditions, while those of the United States moved in the opposite direction.

Overall, a retaliatory model of tariff changes predicts a positive correlation between changes in the tariff index and similar changes abroad. I use a lagged two-year moving average of changes in the tariff index of the major trading partner to test the extent of responsiveness between a country's tariff index and that of its major trade partner.

Changing International Position.   There are strong theoretical reasons to suppose that as a country's position in the international trading system changes, its tariff policies will change as well. As discussed above, theories that emphasize the monopoly power of the larger traders would predict that as trade dominance increases, tariffs would increase as well, since it becomes easier to influence the terms of trade by raising tariffs. A benign hegemonic interpretation would make the opposite prediction: as a country's trade dominance increases, it should lower its tariffs because it has progressively more to gain from a relatively free trade regime. These propositions are tested by looking at the change in the lagged two-year moving average of a country's share of world trade. A positive association with change in the tariff index would support the exploitative interpretation, while a negative association would support a benign hegemonic interpretation.

Secondly, a country's vulnerability to changes in the commercial policies of trade partners is increased by its degree of trade dependence. Growing trade dependence is likely to lessen a country's leverage in international bargaining over commercial relations. Resisting the temptation to raise tariffs is likely to be viewed as the best way to avoid retaliation, which would be devastating for a country whose economy is sustained by trade. As a country's trade dependence increases, vulnerability to the policies of trade partners is heightened and tariff increases become more risky. The more open an economy becomes, the more likely it should be to lower rather than to raise its tariffs. I use a lagged two-year moving average for change in the degree of trade dependence to test this relationship. I expect a negative relationship between changes in trade dependence and changes in the tariff index the following period.

Domestic Political Conditions.   Changes in tariff policies were not merely dictated by the business cycle, nor were decisionmakers utterly constrained by their economy's size and its relationship to the international economy. Protection had to be decided upon in the context of larger macroeconomic questions and priorities, and the evidence presented in this study suggests that this context was sensitive to party preferences, government stability, and domestic monetary institutions. These conditions influenced a country's external economic imbalance and its decision about whether or not to jettison the gold standard and devalue. But if devaluation was deemed unacceptable, external economic imbalances could generate the domestic political pressure to protect. The decision whether or not to internalize the cost of adjustment, to partially externalize through devaluing or through protecting, or to externalize completely by devaluing *and* protecting is expected to be highly conditioned by domestic politics and institutions.

Consider first the role of the Left in shaping a country's adjustment strategy. The evidence presented in Chapter 4 indicates that the Left devalued much more significantly than did the center-right, and this was especially true during recession. The Left's core constituency was the working class, and interwar democratic, labor, and socialist parties were concerned with implementing policies that were expected to benefit this core constituency. The Left would simply not sacrifice labor to the deflation of the gold standard. This concern with the welfare of workers could have an important impact on tariff policy, too. One of the prime effects of tariffs in the interwar years was that they improved the return to capital in import-competing industries while raising the price of imported consumer goods to the working classes.[27] One left-wing party after another lowered tariffs when it came to power: the American Democrats reversed the high tariff policy of the Republicans after 1932, and the Front Populaire lowered tariffs in France in 1936. Even where they did not have the electoral power to block protection, parties of the Left were the voice of free trade. Hence, the British Labour party opposed the General Tariff of 1931; and Belgian Socialists inveighed against tariffs and quotas because of the effect these policies would have on the cost of living for workers. If these cases are representative, then we would expect parties of the Left to be associated with tariff reductions and parties of the center-right with tariff increases. Since tariffs are usually implemented legislatively, the equations below test the proposition that there is a negative relationship between the percentage of left-wing representation in parliament and change in the tariff index the following period.[28] To reduce the possibility of confounding the degree of left-wing representation with regime type, the democracy dummy variable is included in the equations that follow.[29]

---

[27] In general, tariff protection benefits the scarce factors of production and is a net cost to the relatively abundant factors of production. Wolfgang F. Stolper and Paul A. Samuelson, "Protection and Real Wages," *Review of Economic Studies*, Vol. 9, November 1941, pp. 138–151.

[28] The overall correlation between the percentage of the Left in parliament and tariff index is $-.247$. While I use percentage of the Left representation in parliament in these regressions, there is also evidence that governments in which the Left played a major role avoided tariff increases more frequently than did center-right governments. Governments in which left-wing parties played a significant role increased tariffs only thirty times, and decreased them twenty-nine times, when a random distribution of increases and decreases would have led us to expect more than thirty-five increases for the former and a little over twenty-three for the latter. A *chi*-square test suggests that these differences—an *under prediction* of tariff increases for the Left—are not due to chance ($p = .086$).

[29] While there is no basis for an a priori expectation about the degree of tariff protection and regime type, nondemocracies tended to have somewhat higher tariffs for the period as a whole and significantly higher tariffs before 1931. Results of the comparison of mean tariff levels for democra-

The effect of an independent central bank on tariff policy must only be thought of as indirect at best. The central bank itself will have nothing to do with tariff implementation, but it may create the conditions that indirectly influence policy choice. In the previous chapter, central bank independence was associated with currency strength. In some cases, currency stability could mean defending an *overvalued* currency, to the detriment of a country's own producers and exporters. The Bank of England has been accused, ex post facto, of engineering the revaluation of the pound sterling at too high a value, and defending that value even though it was perhaps inappropriately high for the British economy. When a currency is overvalued, exporters find it much harder to compete internationally, which can lead to pressures to protect producers. Politically controlled central banks, on the other hand, may be pressured by government to depreciate the currency, thus relieving the pressure to protect. Of course, this is only an indirect effect of the independence of the monetary institution, and it depends on our earlier observation that the more independent central banks were associated with currency appreciation/stability. While the effect will not likely be very strong, it does seem reasonable to expect that in the presence of an independent monetary authority whose top priority it is to ensure the integrity of the national currency, pressures for protection will build. If a portion of these are to be translated into actual tariff protection, we might expect central bank independence to be associated with somewhat higher tariff levels.

Finally, consider the impact of political and social turmoil on the propensity to raise tariffs. In every previous test, cabinet instability was clearly and significantly associated with external imbalance and currency depreciation, in contravention of the requirements of the gold standard. The reasons for hypothesizing such a relationship were that unstable governments in a precarious position would likely have a very low level of domestic authority, would take a very short term view of various policy options, and would ultimately choose the adjustment option that was most politically expedient. Unstable governments, I have argued, avoid hard choices; they tend to externalize in the short term, as

---

cies versus nondemocracies were as follows for the two periods (probability relates to the hypothesis that there is no significant difference between regime types with respect to tariff levels):

Years	Regime	Obs. #	Mean	Std. Dev.	Std. Error	t Stat.	Prob.
1923–31	Democratic	143	.109	.066	.006	−3.97	.0001
	Nondem.	39	.158	.08	.013		
1932–39	Democratic	104	.173	.109	.011	−.544	.585
	Nondem.	51	.182	.081	.011		

Note also that the standard error is the same for democratic and nondemocratic governments in the thirties, despite the fact that there are more than twice as many democratic observations.

their balance of payments position and currency policies have illustrated. This logic would predict political and social instability to be associated with higher rather than lower tariffs. In the short term, tariffs shift the costs of adjustment onto a country's trading partners. Moreover, it is far easier to tax foreigners than to raise taxes domestically, especially for a government whose local authority may be at its nadir. So, unstable governments are more likely to raise tariffs than to lower them because it allows them to externalize both the adjustment problem and the fiscal problem in the short term (which is all that matters for such a government). We should therefore expect a positive relationship between cabinet instability—and possibly labor unrest—and changes in tariff policy.

Economic, Structural, and Domestic Political Influences on Tariff Changes: The Evidence

To test these hypotheses, versions of the following equation were run, using ordinary least squares ("2MA" indicates that a two-year moving average was used):

$\%\Delta$Tariff Index [2MA] $= a + \beta_1$(1923–1930 Dummy) $+ \beta_2$ ($\%\Delta$ Index of Industrial Production[2MA, $t-1$]) $+ \beta_3$(Δ % World Trade [2MA, $t-1$]) $+ \beta_4$ (Δ Trade Dependence[2MA, $t-1$]) $+ \beta_5$ (% Left in Parliament [$t-1$]) $+ \beta_6$ (Democratic [t $-$ 1]) $+ \beta_7$ (Cabinet Δ) $+ \beta_8$ (Central Bank Independence [$t-1$]) $+ \beta_9$ (Labor Unrest [$t-1$]) $+ \beta_{10}$ ($\%\Delta$ Tariffs of the Major Trading Partner [2MA, $t-1$]) $+ e$

The results appear in table 6.5. Because changes in tariff levels gyrate much more than the levels themselves, this model explains only a small portion of the observed variation (adjusted R-squared approximately .20). As expected, changes in the business cycle were convincingly correlated with changes in tariffs. When economic conditions went sour, tariffs shot up to protect domestic producers and to keep prices from falling through the floor. A one-point drop in output was associated with a .65-point increase in the two-year average tariff index the following period, according to these models. Thus, we could expect the 12.5-point drop in Canada's index of industrial production in 1931 to contribute to a rise in the two-year average for tariffs in 1932 of about 7 percent. (The actual rise was about 14 percent.) Thus, that countries protected during recession is a substantively significant but hardly surprising finding.

What is more interesting for our purposes is the role that domestic political conditions played *even when controlling for the impact of the business cycle.* The strongest result from this set of regression equations is indeed eye-opening: the variable associated with the *strongest* downward turn in tariffs is representa-

TABLE 6.5
Five Models of Changes in Tariff Levels for 19 Countries[a], 1924–1938
(Two-year Moving Averages; Nonstandardized Coefficients; Standard Errors)

Variable	Model 1	Model 2	Model 3	Model 4	Model 5
Intercept	.134	.153	.131	−.008	.137
1923–1930 Dummy	−.106***	−.097***	−.095***	−.063***	−.091***
	(.024)	(.023)	(.025)	(.023)	(.025)
%ΔIndustrial	−.659***	−.707***	−.689***	−.437***	−.779***
Production	(.158)	(.161)	(.173)	(.16)	(.174)
$(2MA, t-1)$					
Δ%World Trade	.063***	.078***	.082***	.054**	.089***
$(2MA, t-1)$	(.024)	(.023)	(.024)	(.026)	(.024)
ΔTrade Dependence	−.609***	−.724***	−.758***	−.976***	−.529*
$(2MA, t-1)$	(.256)	(.233)	(.252)	(.326)	(.307)
%Left in Parliament	—	−.003***	−.004***	−.001	−.004***
$(t-1)$	—	(.001)	(.001)	(.001)	(.001)
Democratic $(t-1)$	—	.090***	.105**	.076*	.108***
	—	(.039)	(.048)	(.043)	(.047)
Cabinet Change	—	—	.012	.033**	.013
	—	—	(.016)	(.015)	(.017)
Central Bank Inde-	—	—	.004	.012*	.006
pendence $(t-1)$	—	—	(.007)	(.006)	(.007)
Labor Unrest	—	—	—	.011	—
$(t-1)$	—	—	—	(.03)	—
%ΔTariffs	.323	—	—	—	−.023
TP1$(2MA, t-1)$	(.336)	—	—	—	(.061)
N	247	247	226	173	208
SER	.176	.173	.177	.142	.166
adj.R^2	.175	.236	.245	.249	.265
D.W.	1.473	1.674	1.656	1.287	1.515

Note: * = Significant at .10 level.   ** = Significant at .05 level.   *** = Significant at .025 level.
[a]All models exclude Japan, Romania, Spain, Switzerland, and Yugoslavia, due to missing data. Only two observations are generated for Bulgaria and four for Poland, due to missing data. Models containing central bank independence exclude Canada before 1934, since its central bank was only created in that year. Models including labor unrest also exclude Belgium, Greece, Bulgaria, and Italy, due to missing data.

tion of left-wing parties in parliament.[30] An increase of one percentage point in left-wing representation was associated with a decrease in the two-year moving average tariff index of between .3 and .4 percent. This would mean, by way of example, that in a landslide as great as the 1932 election in the United States, where Democratic representation in Congress increased from 51 to 71 percent, we should expect to see a drop of four to ten percentage points in the tariff index. (The actual drop between 1933 and 1934 was approximately thirteen percentage points.) Tariff policies were clearly influenced by the constituency concerns of working-class parties. As left-wing representatives gained control of parliaments, they implemented tariff policies that they felt would reduce the cost of living for workers-cum-consumers. Furthermore, there is a slight negative correlation between previous recession and increased representation of the Left in parliament in the next period (correlation = − .073), but the direction of this correlation should increase our confidence that in fact the Left worked to lower tariffs, *despite the fact that they came to power under adverse economic conditions.*

The function of the democratic dummy was mainly intended to control for regime type while considering the impact of the Left. I did not advance a hypothesis regarding democratic versus nondemocratic forms of government and tariff policies. But the strong positive correlation between democracy and changes in the tariff index requires some (admittedly post hoc) discussion. The positive sign indicates that on average democratic governments raised tariffs to a greater extent than did nondemocratic ones. One reason for this result may be the effect of the central European (and largely nondemocratic) trade bloc that had developed around Germany by 1933. This bloc may have encouraged trade concentration while it reduced tariffs among its largely authoritarian adherents. A second reason for authoritarian regimes' association with decreasing tariffs might be the substitution of other modes of economic controls that made tariffs unnecessary. Thus, the strong currency controls in place in many of these countries (see Chapter 4) may have obviated the need for tariff protection. Since the democracies were loath to implement other forms of external controls, they maintained or increased tariffs. Thus, the positive coefficient for democracies may simply reflect a shift from one antiliberal instrument to another in the case of the authoritarian regimes. On the other hand, it may reflect the fact that democracies were indeed more sensitive to the demands of constituent producers who were to gain from protection.

[30] Standardized coefficients for Model 2 are as follows:

1923–1930 dummy	−.24
%ΔIndustrial Production (2MA, t − 1)	−.29
Δ%World trade (2MA, t − 1)	.20
ΔTrade Dependence (2MA, t − 1)	−.20
%Left in Parliament (t − 1)	−.30
Democratic (t − 1)	.18

Two other domestic political variables showed significant results in the latter versions of the model, although their coefficients and standard errors were not as stable as for the other variables tested. Cabinet turnover was positively associated with increased tariffs, although we can only be sure of this relationship in Model 4.[31] One additional cabinet change was associated with a 3.3 percent tariff increase. Since cabinet turnover does tend to be somewhat higher following a period of recession (correlation $= -.082$), there may be a mild degree of multicolinearity between these variables, but the relationship is not strong enough to undermine the plausibility of the hypothesis that when governments are unstable they tend to externalize; in this case, to raise tariffs rather than to deflate domestic prices or implement measures to improve their commercial competitiveness. (As we expected, labor unrest was also positively associated with tariff increases in the next period—further evidence of externalization in the presence of social unrest—but this did not approach statistical significance.)

As with cabinet instability, central bank independence was only statistically significant in the fourth model presented. This is hardly surprising, since the effects of the central bank on tariff policy can only be indirect. But the fourth model did provide evidence that the more independent central banks—those that were shown earlier to place a higher premium on currency strength—were associated with somewhat higher tariffs. A one-point increase along my eight-point scale was associated with tariff increases of about 1.2 percent on average. This is not a tremendous substantive impact, but it does indicate that central banks influence the macroeconomic setting in which commercial decisions take place. During the interwar years, their commitment to the currency provided a context for somewhat higher levels of protection.

Now we turn to the international structural variables included in this analysis. As the more predatory interpretation of economic power predicted, as countries gained more leverage in international trade (as their share of world trade increased) they became increasingly more protectionist. This is an important finding, since not only do large traders have significantly higher tariff levels, but as countries gained in their proportion of world trade they also tended to increase tariff levels further, suggesting that states respond to their growing economic power with higher tariffs rather readily. To the extent that the major power behaves as these statistics would indicate, this is strong evidence for the rent-seeking monopolistic hegemon, rather than a benign provider of public goods. Changes in the degree of trade dependence also contributed quite readily to a state's willingness to lower tariffs in the following period. As their

---

[31] This is not a function of holding strikes constant as much as a function of case attrition when labor unrest is included. When observations are restricted to only those cases included in Model 4, cabinet instability and central bank independence are both statistically significant in the expected directions whether or not strikes themselves are controlled. However, regressions using this truncated data set are not included because it would seem an arbitrary supression of the data.

economies became more open to international trade, governments were increasingly willing to reduce tariffs. Governments of increasingly insular economies, on the other hand, raised tariffs, as their self-sufficiency improved.

Perhaps the most pleasant surprise to come of this analysis is that, contrary to the expectations of a theory of retaliation, there was no statistically significant relationship between changes in the tariff index for one country and that of its major trade partner in the following year. (In fact, if one does not lag the tariff changes of the major trade partner, but instead considers them coterminously with a country's own tariff changes—not implausible if we posit an especially swift model of retaliation/reciprocity—the relationship is distinctly negative.) So, one of the most strongly held beliefs regarding international economic relations in the interwar years does not stand up to the aggregate data: there was only the weakest of evidence that tariff indices of major trading partners moved in the same direction with a year's lag. Of course, this does not rule out the rampant use of sectorally selective tit-for-tat behavior: a tariff increase on American wheat in retaliation for shutting Swiss watches out of the market, for example. Even less does it rule out tit-for-tat behavior that spilled over from tariff competition to import quotas or other exclusionary measures. Still, it is astounding that one of the most accepted explanations for protectionism during this period is washed away in the aggregate data by domestic political explanations, business cycles, and rent-seeking hegemonic behavior.

It is very difficult to capture the twists and turns in percent-change variables with a model as parsimonious as this one. Figure 6.4 shows how well Model 2 performed in this respect. It did very well in fitting tariff changes for Austria (after 1927), Belgium, Denmark, the Netherlands (to 1932), Norway, Sweden (after 1926), and the United Kingdom. The model reflects the shape of the curve for Czechoslovakia, but overestimates tariff increases every year except four. It did poorly in fitting values for Germany, Greece, Hungary, and Italy.

Figures 6.5a and b show how the residuals fell on average by year and by country. The model seemed somewhat to underpredict tariff increases during the 1920s (there were many years in which large positive residuals remained) and possibly to overpredict tariff increases for the thirties. In other words, according to this model, the thirties should have been more protectionist than they in fact were. Several countries reduced their tariffs more in 1937 than economic and other conditions might have warranted: Belgium, Denmark, France, Finland, Italy, the Netherlands, and Norway all reduced their tariff levels much more than the fitted values generated by the model. One reason for this unexpected dip in protectionism may have had to do with an institutional change that was not modeled in this chapter: the declaration of the Tripartite Agreement between France, Britain, and the United States, which tried to put an end to currency instability and reinstitute a modified "24-hour" gold standard. Despite the recession of 1937, the devaluation of the Gold Bloc and the signing of this agreement may have encouraged states to lower their barriers to

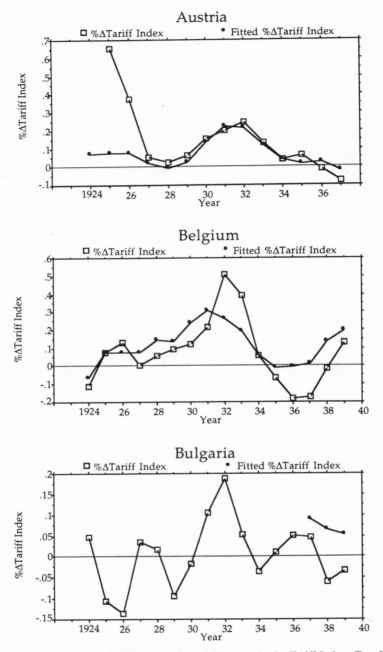

Figure 6.4: Comparison of Fitted and Actual Changes in the Tariff Index, Two-Year Moving Average (Model 2)

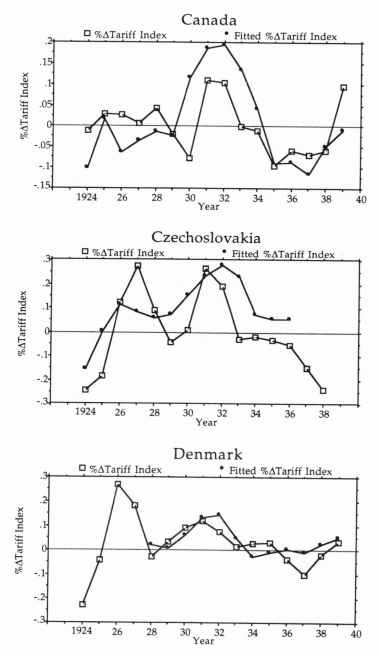

Figure 6.4: (*Continued*)

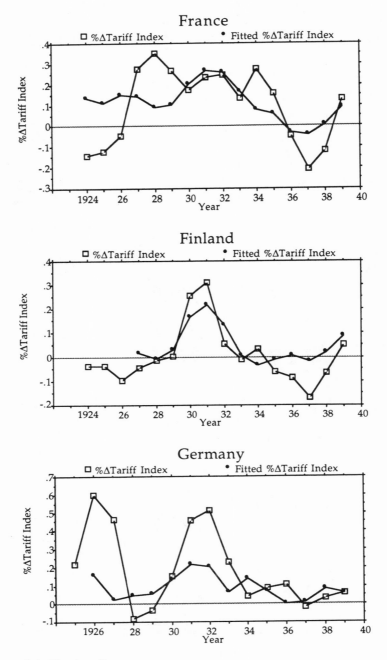

Figure 6.4: (*Continued*)

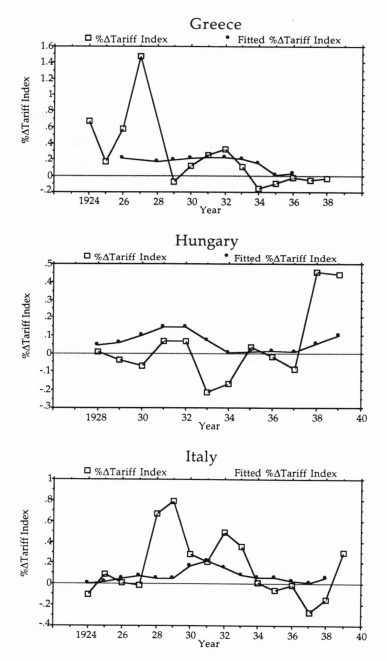

Figure 6.4: (*Continued*)

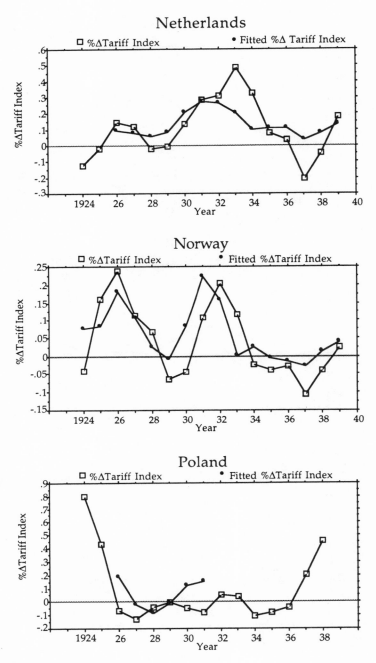

Figure 6.4: (*Continued*)

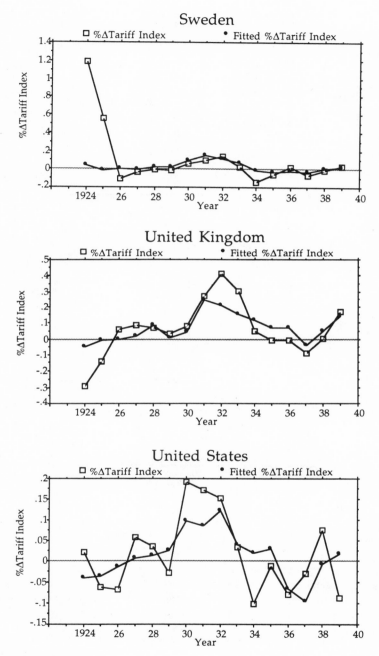

Figure 6.4: (*Continued*)

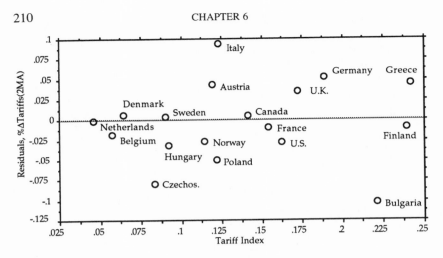

a. Residuals by Country

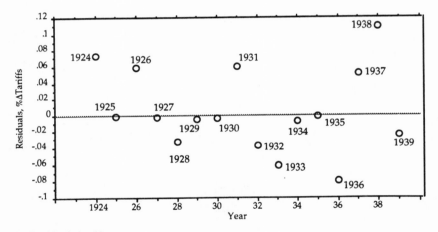

b. Residuals by Year

Figures 6.5: Residuals, Changes in the Tariff Index, Two-Year Moving Average (Model 2)

trade, since they were more secure in their expectations regarding currency markets.[32] Many of the countries that lowered their tariffs most were those which had been defending overvalued currencies as members of the Gold Bloc. When the bloc fell, the way was cleared for tariff reductions.

[32] The Tripartite Agreement in fact included language that called for the relaxing of barriers to trade, especially exchange controls and quota systems. The formal agreement of 25 September 1936 and statement of adherence by the associated powers can be found in the Documents of the Bank for International Settlements, Monetary and Economic Department, Basel, January 1937.

The residuals by country are fairly closely distributed around zero. The outliers are displayed in figure 6.5b. Bulgaria can be disregarded because only three residuals could be generated for the time period. Italy and Germany had much greater tariff increases than the model predicted, while Czechoslovakia and Poland reduced tariffs more than they "should" have. Overall, however, the model did remarkably well considering its degree of parsimony (five variables, one period dummy) and the difficult challenge of capturing changes over time and across countries with a single model.

Finally, we have to consider the contribution that the domestic political variables make to our understanding of the pressure to raise or the opportunities to lower tariffs. Table 6.6 compares the average difference between the fitted values and the actual values for tariff change for the first three models reported

TABLE 6.6
Average Difference between Fitted Tariff Changes
and Actual Tariff Changes for Three Models

Country	Economic Structural (Model 1)	Combined (Model 2)[a]	Combined (Model 3)
Austria	.097	.097	**.093**
Belgium	.100	**.092**	.099
Bulgaria	**.075**	.103	.106
Canada	**.072**	.088	.135
Czechoslovakia	**.113**	.117	.115
Denmark	**.042**	.043	.043
France	.140	**.132**	.139
Finland	**.081**	**.081**	.084
Germany	.115	.102	**.099**
Hungary	.194	.195	**.191**
Italy	.196	.198	**.195**
Netherlands	.114	.111	**.108**
Norway	.070	**.065**	.067
Poland	**.176**	.218	.219
Sweden	.102	.090	**.087**
United Kingdom	.099	**.089**	**.089**
United States	.118	.095	**.094**
Total number of best models[b]:	6.0	5.0	8.0
Average	.116	.114	.116

Note: Boldface indicates the smallest average difference between fitted and actual values among the three models.

Method: For each country: $| \text{Fitted } Y - \text{Actual } Y | / N$; where n = number of fitted Y for each country.

[a]Model for which graph of fitted versus actual dependent variable is presented (figure 6.4).
[b]Including ties.

in table 6.5. Only for six countries was the structural/economic/strategic model superior to models that include the domestic political variables explored in this chapter. But these six countries represented only about 11 percent of the total trade in this sample. The countries for which either Model 2 or Model 3 produced a better fit included the economic powerhouses (the United States, the United Kingdom, France, Germany, Italy, and Belgium) and accounted for an average of almost 89 percent of total international trade in this sample of countries for the period. The inclusion of these domestic political variables—chiefly, party in power and regime type, less significantly political instability and monetary institutional independence—can only be viewed as critical to an understanding of the changing pattern of tariff protection during the interwar years.

CONCLUSIONS

The establishment of high tariffs is one of the clearest examples of externalizing rather than adjusting to a deteriorating balance of payments position. Tariff barriers prevent adjustment by subsidizing current patterns of investment, production, and consumption. They also frustrate price adjustments as required by the gold standard. But this chapter has shown that the desire to protect through tariff barriers is not uniform across time and space, and has offered some explanations as to why this is so.

Structural factors are undeniably important in explaining both tariff index levels and changes in levels. Large trading countries were found to be much more likely than smaller countries to have high tariff indices. This finding is consistent with the theoretical economic literature, which emphasizes that more powerful trading countries have an incentive to raise tariffs to affect the terms of trade in their favor, and the political economic literature, which emphasizes the more exploitative aspects of hegemony. Moreover, the evidence was strong that as countries gained leverage (as their share of world trade increased), they raised their tariffs further. Across time and across countries, for tariff levels and for changes, a more dominant position in world trade was accompanied by greater tariff protection.

One reason for large states' readiness to collect high customs is very likely related to their insularity from the international trading system. Small states, on the other hand, are likely to be heavily dependent on international trade as a proportion of their total economic activity. Trade dependence is one of the most important correlates of tariff levels and policy change. The evidence presented here is unambiguous: the more a country depends on international trade as a proportion of its Net National Product, the lower its tariff level is likely to be; moreover, as trade dependence increases, tariff policies become more open. Graphs by country visually reinforce this impression: the small open economies of Belgium, Sweden, Denmark, and the Netherlands kept their tariffs much lower than the sample average and their major trading partner. They raised their tariffs in response to recession, but never eschewed a basically liberal policy stance.

High tariff levels were associated with a stronger dependence on tariff revenues as a proportion of total tax receipts. This suggests that one reason some countries kept tariffs high was due to a fiscal constraint. Countries whose tax structures were built around taxing foreign producers were likely to be less flexible in their ability to implement liberal tariff policies.

Even more important for the problem of external adjustment is the question of the conditions associated with tariff changes. One of the most strongly held beliefs found in the international political economy literature is that recession—and certainly depression—augurs ill for free trade. The models developed in this chapter support that conclusion, but it is somewhat surprising that at least one domestic political variable—party representation in parliament—has a greater impact on tariff changes than the direction of the business cycle.[33] Coefficients and standard errors for changes in the index of industrial production were quite robust across all trials, which should increase our confidence in these findings. Yet there were important differences across countries, with the United Kingdom, Canada, and Norway's tariffs showing the most sensitivity to changes in industrial production. Overall, depression does encourage protection, but large, insular countries with heavier center-right political orientation were likely to succumb to a much greater degree than their opposite numbers.

The Republicans have become known as the high tariff party in the nineteenth and early twentieth centuries, but these findings suggest that the phenomenon may be much more general than this. There were strong reasons for left-wing parties to support freer trade. They represented the "abundant resource" of labor that economists have noted is a net payer when it comes to protection. They had an interest in opposing tariffs that would raise the cost of living on many basic consumption items for the working class. When choosing between depreciation and protection, left-wing governments and more heavily left-wing dominated parliaments tended to choose the former over the latter.

Two other domestic political variables were in the hypothesized directions, but were not convincingly significant across all versions of the model. Evidence emerged that unstable governments tend to externalize through higher tariff increases, even when we control for previous recession. Countries with more independent central banks also had a slight tendency to raise tariffs, which is consistent with a greater demand for protection given their purported priority of currency strength. Finally, labor unrest was in the hypothesized direction, but was not statistically significant.

The most surprising result of this chapter is in fact a negative one: there was no evidence of tit-for-tat behavior in changes in aggregate tariff policy during

[33] As indicated by standard beta coefficient; for every model except Model 4.

the interwar years as a whole. In fact, in one version of the model, the relationship between changes in the tariff index of a country and that of its major trading partner was negative, although the standard error was too large to say anything definitive. In the simple regressions by country, the tariff indexes of only nine countries out of the sample had positive correlations with the tariff index of their major trading partner with a probability of .90; and only two, Norway and Switzerland, had positive correlations with probability of .95. It is likely, however, that this correlation is an epiphenomenon of a commonly experienced recession rather than tit-for-tat behavior: when changes in the index of industrial production were controlled in the multivariate analysis, the relationship vanished. This is not to claim that retaliation has no part in an explanation for particular commercial policies during the interwar years; it is only to point out the limits of such an explanation for the overall direction of tariff protection for the interwar years as a whole.

CUMULATIVE RESULTS

We are increasingly in a position to describe the conditions associated with a cooperative international economic policy stance during the years between the two world wars. We have been making our way toward an explanation of the conditions conducive to maintaining policies that could support currency stability and fairly liberal trade, two of the most important normative foundations of the international gold standard. Our findings are summarized in table 6.7. The first two columns—the current account and capital movement—indicate the likelihood that a given variable will be associated with a deteriorating external position. The third and fourth columns are policy responses that have normative implications in the context of the interwar gold standard. Adherence to the gold standard norms would require a positive sign (or at least the null hypothesis) in the currency value column, and a negative sign (or the null hypothesis) in the tariff policy column. Admittedly, this is only a partial analysis of the possible transgressions against the gold standard. It excludes options such as currency and capital controls, which the nondemocratic governments increasingly opted for in the thirties. But it does give an impression of the conditions associated with adherence versus defection for two important norms; namely, that currencies should remain stable (and preferably tied to and convertible into gold) and that markets should stay fairly open to international trade.

According to these results, the authoritarian governments appear more cooperative than do the democratic ones. This is because their tools of choice—strict capital and currency controls—are not handled here. The Left was associated with a deteriorating current account deficit and tended to try to remedy external imbalance by devaluing. But the Left also reduced tariffs more frequently than did right-wing governments. The policy mix chosen by represen-

TABLE 6.7
Cumulative Results: The Current Account, Capital Movements,
Currency Value, and Tariff Policy

Variable	Effect on			
	Current Account	Capital Movement	Currency Value	Tariff Policy
Regime type	$H_{0(-)}$	$H_{0(-)}$	$H_{0(-)}$	+
Influence of the Left	−	$H_{0(-)}$	−	−
Labor unrest	−	−	$H_{0(-)}$	$H_{0(+)}$
Central bank independence	+	+	+	$H_{0(+)}$
Cabinet instability	−	−	−	$H_{0(+)}$
Control Variables				
Size (%world trade)	H_0	H_0	H_0	+
Trade dependence	H_0	H_0	H_0	−
Net investment position	H_0	H_0	H_0	H_0
NNP/capita			H_0	H_0
Policy of major trade partner			+	H_0

tatives of the working class was to lower tariffs to reduce the cost of consumption and to let the currency go.

The results with respect to cases in which the central bank had a high degree of independence were neatly symmetrical but not quite as strong. When the central bank had a greater degree of independence, a country was less likely to be in deficit on either the current account or in terms of capital movements. And in exact opposition to what we saw when the Left had greater influence, independent central banks were associated with strong currencies and vaguely higher tariffs. What seems to be emerging is a conservative financially backed package, which favors the currency over the domestic consumer, and a working-class package, in which the opposite values appear to prevail.

Domestic turmoil seems to be associated with deficits and the externalization of these deficits. Cabinet instability and labor unrest had negative coefficients on both components of the balance of payments, and they had coefficients on both devaluation and tariff protection that were noncooperative. Admittedly, three out of four of these coefficients were so weak that the null hypothesis could not be rejected. But the direction of the coefficient lends credence to an interpretation that when domestic political conflict is high, it is easier to externalize rather than adjust to a balance of payments deficit.

Finally, we turn to the structural conditions associated with adjustment. The clearest result is the overwhelming support for the proposition that the smaller, more trade dependent countries tended to adhere most closely to the demands of the gold standard. The more trade dependent economies avoided either deficits or surpluses in their balance of payments overall,[34] and they kept their currencies reasonably stable and their tariffs low. Far from free-riding on the stabilizing efforts of others, the trade dependent economies were the unsung heroes of the interwar years. Despite the absence of any pressing balance of payments reason, large countries tended to have higher tariffs, although they did avoid strong currency depreciation.

A set of characteristics is emerging that was conducive to international economic cooperation during the interwar years. Highly trade dependent countries with stable governments and a quiescent labor force were most likely to avoid balance of payments deficits and to maintain policies in accordance with the norms of the gold standard. Additionally, governments of the Left tended to keep tariffs low, and politically independent central banks tended to defend the value of their currency. The final chapter explores the extent to which these characteristics match the policy mix chosen by Britain, Belgium, and France as they faced deficits and eventually departed from gold in the thirties.

---

[34] For simplicity, this result was not reported in Chapter 3. More exhaustive tests, including this result, can be found in chapters 2 and 3 of my Ph.D. dissertation, "Who Adjusts?" Harvard University, Department of Government, 1991.

TABLE 6.A
Five Models of Tariff Levels for 20 Countries, 1924–1939
(Nonstandardized Coefficients for Country Dummies; Standard Errors)

Country	Model 1	Model 2	Model 3	Model 4	Model 5
Austria	.007	.07***	.029	.059***	.018
	(.013)	(.021)	(.044)	(.024)	(.017)
Belgium	.107***	.104***	.057	.095***	.061
	(.019)	(.022)	(.042)	(.021)	(.048)
Bulgaria	.045***	.094***	.05	.079***	.047***
	(.011)	(.021)	(.044)	(.026)	(.016)
Canada	−.006	.055***	.019	.051***	−.0003
	(.014)	(.023)	(.042)	(.021)	(.02)
Czechoslovakia	.026**	.083***	.035	.065***	.029*
	(.012)	(.02)	(.043)	(.025)	(.016)
Denmark	−.001	.064***	.025	.059***	.004
	(.014)	(.024)	(.044)	(.022)	(.02)
France	.051***	.049***	.013	.041***	.011
	(.012)	(.013)	(.036)	(.016)	(.033)
Finland	.056***	.111***	.068	.098***	.061***
	(.018)	(.027)	(.046)	(.03)	(.02)
Germany	.01	.069***	.035	.059**	.034*
	(.013)	(.015)	(.033)	(.017)	(.019)
Greece	.034***	.087***	.061	.091***	.061***
	(.014)	(.023)	(.045)	(.028)	(.018)
Hungary	.011	.066***	.019	.049**	.012
	(.012)	(.021)	(.044)	(.025)	(.017)
Italy	.008	.063***	.02	.048**	.016
	(.011)	(.018)	(.04)	(.022)	(.016)
Netherlands	.076***	.077***	.032	.064***	.023
	(.017)	(.02)	(.043)	(.022)	(.039)
Norway	−.018	.051***	.014	.048**	−.003
	(.015)	(.023)	(.045)	(.023)	(.019)

(*continued*)

TABLE 6.A (*Continued*)

Country	Model 1	Model 2	Model 3	Model 4	Model 5
Poland	—	.057***	.008	.037	—
	—	(.019)	(.045)	(.028)	—
Spain	—	.138***	.093**	.122***	—
	—	(.021)	(.042)	(.024)	—
Sweden	.059***	.059***	.018	.051***	.009
	(.017)	(.02)	(.043)	(.02)	(.04)
Switzerland	−.023	.0004	−.023	.01	−.052
	(.025)	(.029)	(.048)	(.03)	(.044)
United Kingdom	.018	.024	−.004	.022	−.007
	(.013)	(.015)	(.031)	(.014)	(.031)
United States (nth country)	—	—	—	—	—
N =	300	309	297	297	282
SER =	.03	.034	.032	.032	.027
adj. R^2 =	.854	.859	.88	.88	.881

Note: * = Significant at .10 level.   ** = Significant at .05 level.   *** = Significant at .025 level.

Chapter 7

DEFICITS DURING DEPRESSION: BRITAIN, BELGIUM, AND FRANCE IN THE THIRTIES

THE 1930s posed a dilemma for deficit states that would remain on gold: deflation was extremely painful during business cycle downturns. This chapter presents qualitative evidence of the relationships we have uncovered to this point, by examining three cases of worsening external balance during depression. These cases were chosen to corroborate some of the key quantitative findings, so a major criteria was to choose cases that provide variance on the explanatory variables of concern. Hence, Belgium is the most highly trade dependent country in the sample, while Britain was much less so, and France was potentially self-sufficient. Britain was the largest trader for the period as a whole, while Belgium was a much smaller trader.

These cases also provide some variance on the domestic political conditions that have been tested over the last five chapters. France's governments were among the most unstable in the sample and were by far the most short-lived among these three countries. Britain and Belgium provide examples of stable democratic governments. All three countries began with highly independent central banks, but each central bank lost an important degree of independence in conducting monetary affairs by the end of the episode. Labor unrest was most serious in France, although comparisons will be impressionistic because aggregate data for the late thirties are missing for both Belgium and France. Political orientation of parties in power differed both among countries and within countries over time. Britain's episode began with a Labour government and was resolved under a conservative government of National Union. Belgium began with a conservative coalition and admitted Socialists to the coalition from March 1935. The French case began under a center-right government, but power shifted dramatically to the socialist Front Populaire. Overall, these cases provide good variance on a number of factors that have proved to be important in explaining the incidence of, and response to, balance of payments difficulties in previous chapters.

These specific cases were selected on the basis of a noticeable deterioration in the balance of payments occurring during the thirties. Emphatically, these cases were selected only on the basis of the pattern in the current account. They were not admitted or omitted because of the policies taken.[1] A conscious effort

---

[1] Hence, a very interesting story that is *not* included in this chapter is the "Roosevelt monetary experiment" of 1933, which led to the depreciation of the dollar (the balance of payments was not

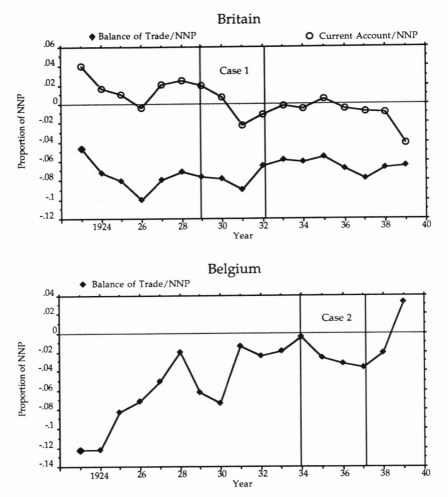

Figure 7.1: Cases of Deterioration of the Balance of Payments during Depression: Britain, Belgium, and France

was made to avoid selecting these cases on the basis of the dependent variable (the policy mix). Figure 7.1 displays the cases selected for each country. *Deterioration* in the balance of payments was a more important criterion than the absolute level of the deficit or surplus. This criterion is justified because I am

---

deteriorating). While this case is omitted, it should be noted that some of the patterns that emerge in this chapter are applicable to the American case: Democrats (like the British Labour party and the French Left) depreciated, but lowered tariffs.

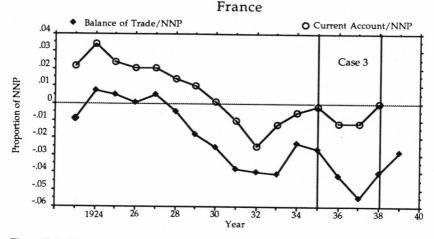

Figure 7.1: (*Continued*)

interested in how states responded to incipient imbalance, and the policy mix chosen to address the worsening situation. Furthermore, I gave no special weight to the current account over the balance of trade. They most often move together, and both the French and British cases could be justified by either measure. In the case of Belgium, balance of trade is the only available measure of external position.

The first case examined here is the deteriorating balance of payments that led to the British departure from gold in 1931. The second case is that of Belgium between 1933 and 1935. Despite the British devaluation four years earlier, Belgium did not devalue until 1935. The third case is the deficit that finally broke France's will to stay on gold. These cases provide an excellent opportunity to assess the usefulness of quantitative models in understanding the policy mix when countries faced deteriorating external positions under the depressed economic conditions of the thirties. To be sure, severe economic downturn encouraged all three of these countries to both devalue their currencies and to raise tariff protection. But the statistical evidence suggests that political and structural variables have a significant *independent* impact on the selection of a policy mix and the extent to which countries were willing to internalize rather than simply to externalize economic adjustment in the face of their deteriorating external position. First, since France was the most politically unstable, as well as the society that suffered the most serious degree of strikes and domestic unrest during its episode, we would expect it to have the greatest degree of externalization, especially currency depreciation. Second, we would expect depreciation for all three countries to be taken by governments in which left-wing parties participated (British Labour, Belgian Socialists, the French

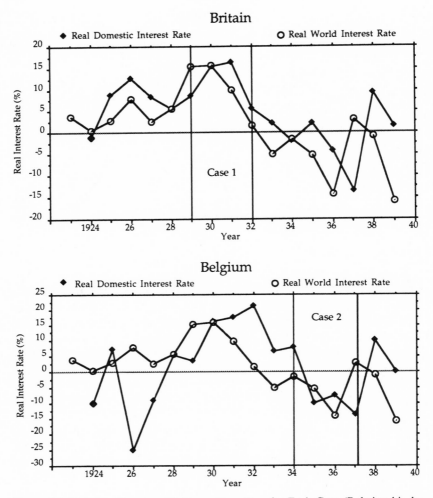

Figure 7.2: Relative Monetary Tightness Prevailing for Each Case (Relationship between Real Domestic Bank Rate and Real World Interest Rate)

Front Populaire.) Based on the influence of the Left, we might predict the sharpest devaluation as well as the strongest reduction in tariffs from the latter (both British Labour and Belgian Socialists were minor coalition partners during the period in question). Third, we would expect serious devaluation to take place once all of the relatively independent central banks of these countries had been shorn of their independent control of monetary and exchange rate policy. The creation of the British Exchange Equalization Account (early 1932) and the reform of the Banque de France under the Front Populaire (1936) should have

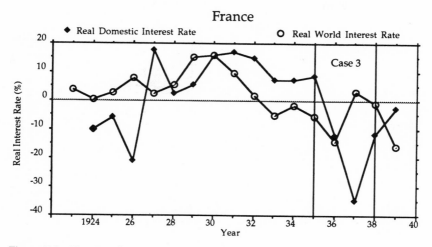

Figure 7.2: (*Continued*)

added to the currency depreciation of the pound and the franc. Finally, because of its extreme trade dependence, we should expect Belgium to raise tariffs the least, and because of its relative insularity, France should be expected to raise them most significantly. Britain, because of its preponderant share of world trade, could be expected to use its international leverage to keep tariffs high.

AGGREGATE INTRODUCTION TO THE CASES AND TO THE POLICY MIX

All three cases began with a commitment to gold. The gold standard required two types of macroeconomic policy adjustments on the part of countries going into deficit: budgetary stringency to reduce demand and tighter monetary policies to attract capital and compress prices. These policies were excruciating under the depressionary conditions of the thirties. Figures 7.2 and 7.3 give an impression of which countries bit the bullet as their current accounts slipped into deficit. The first figure deals with monetary policy. A strong effort to improve the balance of payments should be marked by a domestic bank rate that is higher than the prevailing world rate of interest, once differences in price level are taken into account (all rates in the graph are real). Britain kept its real bank rate only marginally above the world rate, and only for the last year of its balance of payments crisis. In the Belgian case, the domestic rate was higher than the world rate only in 1934 and 1936. The French case was preceded by consistently tight monetary policy, but under the Front Populaire the real bank rate fell strongly into negative territory, even as rates elsewhere rose. It is a clear pattern of giving up on deflation. All three cases were preceded by periods of

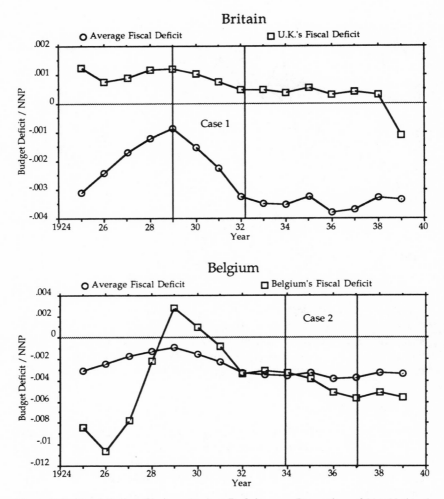

Figure 7.3: Fiscal Policy Choice: Budget Deficits as a Proportion of Net National Product for Britain, Belgium, and France Compared to Sample Average (Three-Year Moving Average)

relatively tight monetary policy. Britain's remained relatively restrictive, while Belgium's fluctuated and France's became extremely lax after 1936.

Britain also had the most restrictive fiscal stance of the three cases. It was the only country to be in budget surplus throughout its crisis, and the rate of deterioration was much less steep than that of the sample average (figure 7.3). Both Belgium and France ran budget deficits, although France's were larger and deterioration was much steeper than in Belgium's case. In terms of both mone-

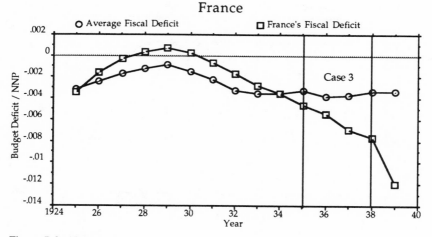

Figure 7.3: (*Continued*)

tary and fiscal policy, among these three countries Britain appears to have done the most to implement internal adjustment measures.

However, both Britain and France also externalized the burden of adjustment onto their major trading partners. Both of these countries devalued more than did Belgium (figure 7.4). While Belgium stabilized the franc within one year of devaluation, Britain refused to explicitly stabilize the pound until 1936. And the French franc continued to depreciate significantly for the rest of the decade, despite an explicit international commitment to stabilize.

Britain's tariff index did just about what one might expect of a large trading country facing a worsening balance of payments: it increased tariffs commensurately (figure 7.5). Britain began its crisis period with tariffs lower and ended up higher than the sample average. Belgium lowered its tariff protection every year in which its external balance worsened, and it always kept tariffs far below the sample average. France ran its tariffs up to a very high level prior to its crisis, but it reduced them sharply upon devaluation.

Table 7.1 summarizes the policy mix taken by each of the three countries during the period of their deteriorating balance of payments.[2] The sections that

[2] France and Belgium also had a system of import quotas, although Belgium's was quite lax. None of these three countries tried to implement anything but the lightest exchange controls for the briefest period of time.

	Years	*Import Quotas*	*Exchange Controls*
Britain	1929–1931	Negligible	None
Belgium	1934–1936	Increasing	Negligible
France	1935–1937	Increasing	None

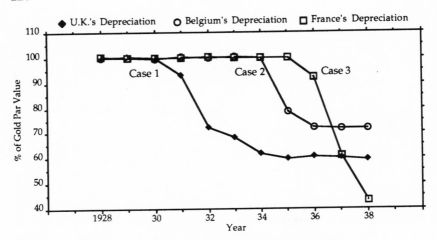

Figure 7.4: Departure from Gold Parity: Britain, Belgium, and France

follow discuss the policy mix for each case. Each begins with a description of the economic structure of the country and the economic conditions prevailing during the crisis episode. Policies of deflation, devaluation, and protection are discussed in turn.

THE CASE OF BRITAIN, 1929–1931

In 1931, Britain's balance of payments went into deficit for the first time in five years. In the late 1920s, Britain's current account surplus was insufficient to cover the deficit on capital account arising from long-term lending. To an unprecedented extent, Britain was dependent on short-term capital inflows to assist in financing the basic balance, which itself was deteriorating due to the overvaluation of the pound[3] and to the precipitous drop in the earnings of

---

(Data on import quotas come from the League of Nations, *World Economic Survey*, [Geneva: League of Nations, Economic Intelligence Service], various years. Data on exchange controls were gleaned from League of Nations, *International Currency Experience: Lessons of the Interwar Period* [Geneva: League of Nations, Economic and Financial Committee], 1944; and League of Nations, *Report on Exchange Controls* [Geneva: League of Nations, Committee on Exchange Controls], 9 July 1938.) The United Kingdom never had currency or capital controls as such; the only regulation was a loose embargo on foreign loan issues, enforced only by moral suasion, which was relaxed over the course of the thirties. Belgium only very briefly implemented a loose form of currency control in the second half of 1934, but it was rescinded shortly thereafter. France avoided exchange controls completely.

[3] See Norman's testimony before the Macmillan Committee, Sir Henry Clay, *Lord Norman* (London: Macmillan), 1957, pp. 160–162. For a statistical treatment of bilateral and weighted effective exchanges rates, which concludes that indeed the pound was significantly overvalued between 1925 and 1931 by a number of measures, see John Redmond, "Sterling Overvaluation in

invisibles (insurance, shipping, finance) in the first years of the Depression.[4] Two major changes in British foreign economic policy were inaugurated to stem the external deficit and improve employment at home. The first was the dramatic departure of sterling from the gold standard and the subsequent devaluation in September 1931. The second was the departure of the United Kingdom from its historic position of free trade with the implementation of a 10 percent ad valorem tariff on imports from nonempire countries.[5]

Economic Structure and Conditions

Britain was the largest trading country and the second largest economy in the world when it slid into balance of payments difficulties in the early 1930s. In 1930, the United Kingdom accounted for more than 21 percent of the aggregate trade that took place on the globe. For the interwar years as a whole, Britain accounted for about 17 percent of world trade. Less than 24 percent of its trade was with its top three trade partners, giving Britain the lowest degree of trade concentration of any country in this sample, and probably in the world.

Britain's international leverage was increased by its moderate trade dependence and its large passive trade balance.[6] The United Kingdom was in the middle of the pack (tenth out of twenty-one countries in this sample) in terms of trade dependence: total trade accounted for an average of only about 34 percent of its NNP for the period as a whole. Table 7.2 gives an indication of the importance of exports to particular British industries.[7] Because Britain imported far more from other countries than it exported to them, it was in a very

---

1925: A Multilateral Approach," *Economic History Review*, 2d Series, Vol. 37, No. 4, November 1984, pp. 520–532.

[4] For an excellent treatment of the evolution of the British balance of payments, see Alec Cairncross and Barry Eichengreen, *Sterling in Decline: The Devaluations of 1931, 1949, and 1967* (London: Basil Blackwell), 1983, pp. 33–38, 56–57.

[5] In 1914, Britain had no protective tariffs. The "McKenna Duties" imposed during the First World War were a flat 33.5 percent rate on luxury goods that took up valuable cargo space. The "Key Industries Duties" (Safeguarding of Industries Act, 1921) covered only a small number of strategically important industrial goods, with duties between 33.5 and 50 percent. In 1931, dutiable goods amounted to 2 to 3 percent of British imports. Forrest Capie, "The British Tariff and Industrial Protection in the 1930s," reprinted as chap. 4, in Charles H. Feinstein (ed.), *The Managed Economy: Essays in British Economic Policy and Performance Since 1929*, (Oxford: Oxford University Press), 1983, p. 95. For an exhaustive recitation of British trade law, see A. S. Harvey, *The General Tariff of the United Kingdom: Law and Regulation* (London: Sir Isaac Pitman and Sons), 1933. On the significance of the tariff as a policy reversal, see Edwin Fitch, *Britain's New Tariff* (Ill.: Freeport), 1932.

[6] For an account of how this leverage was used to secure widespread and unreciprocated concessions in foreign markets, see T.J.T. Rooth, "Limits of Leverage: The Anglo-Danish Trade Agreement of 1933," *Economic History Review*, Vol. 37, No. 2, May 1984, pp. 211–228.

[7] Forrest Capie, "The British Tariff and Industrial Protection in the 1930s," in Feinstein, *The Managed Economy*, p. 104.

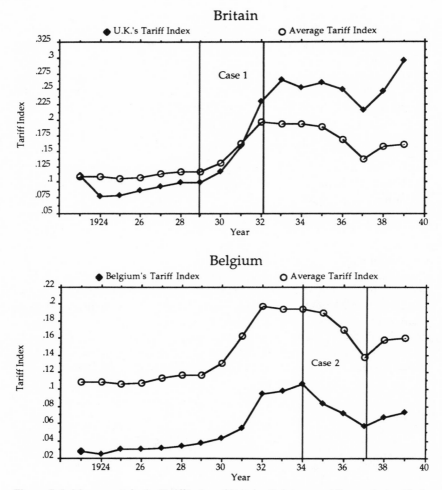

Figure 7.5: Movements in the Tariff Index of Britain, Belgium, and France during Each Crisis

strong position to impose trade restrictions unilaterally and use this position of strength in subsequent negotiations.[8]

The story of British industrial decline is well known.[9] It is only necessary to point out here that the traditional industries emerged from the war relatively

[8] League of Nations, *Quantitative Trade Controls: Their Cause and Nature* (Geneva: League of Nations, Economic, Financial and Transit Department), 1943, p. 32.

[9] David S. Landes, *The Unbound Prometheus: Technical Change and Economic Development in Western Europe from 1750 to the Present* (Cambridge: Cambridge University Press), 1969, chaps. 5 and 6; Donald N. McCloskey, "Did Victorian Britain Fail?" *Economic History Review*, Vol. 23, No. 3, December 1970, pp. 446–459.

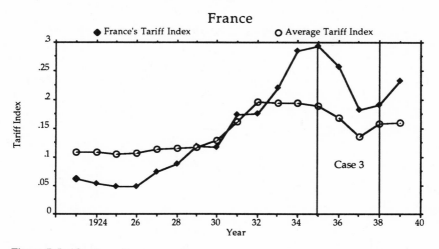

Figure 7.5: (*Continued*)

neglected and greatly disadvantaged compared to the reconstructed industrial sectors of the Continent.[10] Britain's external position was severely weakened by loss of competitiveness in British industry and the loss of income from overseas investments.[11] Compared to many other nations that prospered in the twenties, Britain stagnated.[12] Coal, steel, textiles, and shipping experienced the most serious recession, while sectors employing new technologies (chemicals, automobiles, and electricity) experienced respectable growth.[13] Unem-

[10] British industry came out of the postwar boom in terrible financial condition. Industry was overcapitalized and had excess capacity; its credit condition was very low and so could hardly attract new capital for investment. A. E. Kahn, *Great Britain in the World Economy* (New York: Columbia University Press), 1946, pp. 75–76.

[11] "Twenty years were needed, Norman thought, to recoup the missing income from investments and to restore the competitive prowess of British industries. In the meantime, Britain's balance of payments problem could only be resolved by the cooperation of central banks, meaning in this context: support for sterling as well as for other shaky currencies." Melchior Palyi, *The Twilight of Gold, 1914–1936* (Chicago: Henry Regnery), 1972, pp. 139–140.

[12] Charles P. Kindleberger, *The World in Depression, 1929–1939* (Berkeley: University of California Press), 1986, p. 41. Countries of Western Europe that performed much better than Britain were Sweden, Belgium, France, and Germany; countries of Eastern Europe that had much better growth were Hungary, Romania, and Czechoslovakia. Both Denmark and Norway suffered from gold parity deflation, as Britain had. See Derek H. Aldcroft, "Economic Growth in Britain in the Interwar Years: A Reassessment, *Economic History Review*, August 1977, pp. 200–212; W. Arthur Lewis, *Economic Survey, 1919–1939*, (Philadelphia: Blakiston Company), 1950, p. 41; J. M. Letiche, "Differential Rates of Productivity Growth and International Imbalance," *Quarterly Journal of Economics*, Vol. 63, No. 3, 1955, p. 377; Derek A. Aldcroft, "Economic Growth in Britain in the Interwar Years," *Economic History Review*, August 1967.

[13] R. S. Sayers, "The Springs of Technological Progress in Britain, 1919–1939," *Economic Journal*, Vol. 60, No. 238, June 1950, pp. 275–291.

TABLE 7.1
Summary of the Policy Mix during Period of Worsening Deficits: Britain, Belgium, and France

Country	Years	Monetary Policy	Fiscal Policy	Devaluation	Tariff Index
Britain	1929–1932	Tightening	Tight	Large (no stabilization)	Low to High
Belgium	1934–1937	Erratic	Moderate	Moderate (stabilization)	Low to Moderate
France	1935–1938	Loosening	Loosening	Large (further depr.)	High to Moderate

ployment was much higher than elsewhere: Britain's average unemployment from 1926 to 1929 was 11.4 percent, while the comparable figure for the United States was 3.25 percent and that for France (1928–1931) was 4.5 percent.[14]

The Policy of Deflation

Between 1928 and 1931, Britain's current account surplus of £104 million evaporated into a deficit of £114 million. To stem the pressure on the pound caused by the deteriorating current account, much more emphasis was given to fiscal orthodoxy than to monetary stringency. The Bank of England appeared to have given up on the use of the bank rate to defend the pound, but budget orthodoxy was implemented with puritanical devotion, a policy combination somewhat surprising given the independence of the Bank of England and the Labour orientation of the prime minister and the chancellor of the exchequer at the time.

The use of the bank rate to control the deteriorating external position was erratic throughout this episode. Several of the classic accounts of the period suggest that even the most independent of central banks, the Bank of England, was not exempt from political pressure to refrain from draconian credit policies.[15] In 1927, when the bank experienced its first serious difficulty defending

[14] For studies that focus on the unemployment problem in Britain, see Michael Beenstock and Peter Warburton, "The Market for Labour in Interwar Britain," CPER Discussion Paper No. 105, April 1986; D. Benjamin and L. Kochin, "Searching for an Explanation of Unemployment in Interwar Britain," *Journal of Political Economy*, Vol. 87, No. 3, June 1979; K. J. Hancock, "The Reduction of Unemployment as a Problem of Public Policy, 1920–1929," *Economic History Review*, Vol. 15, No. 2, December 1962; Sidney Pollard (ed.), *The Gold Standard and Employment Policy Between the Wars* (London: Methuen), 1970, pp. 1–26.

[15] One reason may have been the severe labor unrest in the wake of the restrictive conditions surrounding the return to gold in 1925. The general strike of 1926 politicized the gold issue and aroused mass public sentiments against a supposed conspiracy of international bankers. Palyi, *The*

TABLE 7.2

The Importance of Exports to Various British Industries, Late 1920s, Early 1930s

Industry	% Exported	Industry	% Exported
Cotton and silk	41	Electrical engineering	14
Wollen, worsted	33	China/earthenware	13
Nonferrous metals	25	Motor vehicles	12
Chemicals	22	Lace	11
Shipbuilding	23	Soap, candles, perfume	10
Iron & steel	18	Building materials	4
Rubber	17	Timber trades	1

the pound, then Chancellor of the exchequer Winston Churchill seems to have prevailed upon the governor of the Bank of England, Montagu Norman, not to raise the rate.[16] In the end, rates in 1927 were raised only moderately.[17]

Sterling weakened again over the summer of 1928, largely due to the pull of capital toward the booming American stock market. This time the bank rate was not raised at all, but remained at 4.5 percent throughout the year. Sluggish economic conditions made it preferable to intervene directly in the foreign exchange market rather than raise the bank rate.[18] Gold drains forced a one-point rate increase in February 1929, but this move was probably too little too late. The Bank of England lost some £27 million in gold in the third quarter of 1929, yet it did not raise the bank rate all summer. The rate was increased one point to 6.5 percent in September, and then gradually reduced to 2.5 percent,

---

Twilight of Gold, p. 102. Ernest Bevin, a union leader, blamed the return to gold for the general strike of 1926. See Bevin's testimony before the Macmillan Committee: Macmillan Committee Report, Cmd. 3897, London, HMSO, 1931. Keynes called the miners "the victims of the Economic Juggernaut. They represent in the flesh the fundamental adjustments engineered by the Treasury and the Bank of England to satisfy the impatience of the City fathers to bridge the 'moderate gap' between 4.40 dollars and 4.86 dollars." See Andrew Boyle, *Montague Norman* (London: Cassell), 1967, p. 207.

[16] In conversations with Moreau, Norman indicated the extent to which it would be politically difficult to counter the effects of the French sales of pounds by raising the bank rate. See Emile Moreau, *Souvenirs d'un Gouverneur de la Banque de France* (Paris: Librarie de Médicis), 1954, p. 324–325.

[17] S.V.O. Clarke, *Central Bank Cooperation, 1924–1931* (New York: Federal Reserve Bank of New York), 1967, p. 128. A moderate increase may have sufficed since the Federal Reserve Bank of New York had agreed to relax its own rate somewhat. Palyi, *The Twilight of Gold*, p. 144.

[18] Norman also went to New York to try and secure a sharp increase in the American discount rate in order to break the speculative fever, to be followed by interest rate reductions. Norman could not secure agreement on this point. According to Cairncross and Eichengreen, the Bank of England used its "secret" reserves rather than those held by the Issue Department to defend the pound. Cairncross and Eichengreen, *Sterling in Decline*, pp. 47–49; see also Clay, *Lord Norman*, p. 238.

not to rise again until almost three months into the Continental banking crisis of 1931. In late July, the Bank of England finally raised its rate to 3.5 percent and, a week later, to 4.5 percent. No further increases in the bank rate took place, a fact that has led historians of the episode to speculate that the bank was under pressure to not sacrifice industry for the sake of the pound.[19] Instead, the bank used foreign credits and hidden reserves to defend the pound. Overall, it is difficult to draw the conclusion that the bank rate was used aggressively either to defend the pound or to accomplish fundamental price adjustments during the balance of payments crisis.

Fiscal policy provides a contrast. With the exception of the rift between factions of the Labour party in 1930 and 1931, there was a high degree of consensus in Britain on the necessity of debt reduction and budget balance. In contrast to France, Britain had undertaken a credible program of debt amortization, and there was a generally high level of acceptance of high taxes to do so. The British people were paying perhaps a quarter of their taxes toward retiring the public debt (the comparable figure for Germany was 2 percent).[20] As a result, repayment of the long-term government debt was proceeding apace.[21]

Annual budgets throughout the crisis period were consistently deflationary. In fact, they were *more* deflationary under the Labour government, with Philip Snowden as chancellor of the exchequer, than they had been under the Conservatives, with Winston Churchill at the financial helm.[22] The prime motive for the Labour leadership's conservative approach to the budget was its obsession with business and financial confidence. Snowden agreed with the assessment of the Colwyn Committee (1927), which concluded that "a determined and consistent policy of debt reduction would doubtless have so largely inspired confidence as to enable debt interest rates to be lowered."[23] Balanced budgets were viewed as key to confidence, which in turn was essential to maintaining the parity of the pound. Such, in any case, was the view of Snowden, the Treasury, the Bank of England, and the financial sector—all of those concerned, perhaps,

[19] Cairncross and Eichengreen, ibid., p. 63; Palyi, *The Twilight of Gold*, p. 171.

[20] Alan T. Peacock and Jack Wiseman, *The Growth of Expenditures in the United Kingdom* (Princeton: Princeton University Press), 1961.

[21] See the table on U.K. net debt position, 1914–1934: House of Commons papers, reprinted in Palyi, *The Twilight of Gold*, p. 99

[22] Ursula K. Hicks, *The Finance of British Governments, 1920–1936* (London: Oxford University Press), 1938, pp. 7–8. She notes that the contradiction between budgetary policies and the gold standard commenced under Churchill; the Labour party under the budget control of Snowden was, by contrast, "Victorian." It is interesting, though, that the Labour party was most suspect as far as the international financial community was concerned. Thus in May 1927, Poincaré warned Moreau that a British *Labour* government might give up the gold standard. Moreau, *Souvenirs*, p. 319.

[23] "Report of the Colwyn Committee, 1927" (Cmd. 2800), pp. 967–972, as cited by Joseph Sykes, *British Public Expenditure, 1921–1931* (London: P. S. King & Son), 1933, p. 7. Thus in 1930, the income tax, supertax, estate duties, and beer duties were all raised. Hicks, *The Finance of British Governments*, p. 12.

with the exception of the more radical wing of the Labour party and the Liberals.[24]

Labour's left flank, led by Oswald Mosley, and backed by Ernest Bevin and Walter Citrine of the Trades Union Congress, demanded more liberal unemployment benefits. To satisfy this wing of the party, in January 1930 dependents' benefits were raised and qualifying requirements relaxed.[25] But the cost of doing so was to push the budget toward deficit. Benefits to the now 2.5 million unemployed Britons accounted for a deficit of £70 million in 1930 and an expected deficit of £100 million for 1931. The "dole" became the market's gauge of how far Britain would go in taking internal adjustment measures.[26] Labour's willingness to sacrifice its own sons became the measure of its faith—and the crucial determinant of the market's confidence in the pound sterling.

Despite an awareness that the budget—and in particular the commitment to unemployment compensation—had become the symbol of the government's credibility, the issue was so sensitive for the Labour government that it was avoided until July 1931. In the meantime, £70 million had been frozen in German banks and the Report of the Committee on National Expenditure had been made public.[27] Both were disasters for confidence in the pound.[28] Ultimately, cuts in unemployment insurance were the price to be paid, not only for market confidence but also for central bank credits from Paris and New York. A final blow to confidence occurred on 16 September, when elements of the Royal Navy went out on strike over wages. The symbolic impact of the protest was much greater than its substantive impact, and capital exports accelerated.[29]

[24] The Liberals had a "reflationary" program for addressing the unemployment problem. In 1929, David Lloyd George outlined a plan that called for maintenance of the gold standard and free trade, as well as advocating loan-financed public works. See his pamphlet, *We Can Conquer Unemployment* (London: Liberal Party), 1929, p. 7. George claimed his program could reduce unemployment by up to half.

[25] Walter A. Morton, *British Finance, 1930–1940* (Madison: University of Wisconsin Press), 1943, p. 62.

[26] In the words of Frederic C. Benham, *Go Back to Gold* (London: Faber and Faber), 1931, p. 23; "The recent 10 percent cut is not important because of the relief it gives to our national expenditure. . . . The cut is important because the dole is a support and a symbol of our lack of flexibility and our blind *resistance* to change."

[27] In its report, which was made public on 31 July 1931, the May Committee predicted that the government's budget deficit would approach £120 million in 1933.

[28] In a memo to Snowden on the day he saw the report, Sir Richard Hopkins wrote: "The first thing foreigners will look at is the budgetary position. Whether it is reasonable that they should do so may be open to debate. That they do is beyond question. When on Monday the Governor sounds J. P. Morgan as to the possibility of an American loan to support the pound, the first question the latter will ask, in my belief is, 'Will steps first be taken about the dole and the budgetary position?'" Quoted in Cairncross and Eichengreen, *Sterling in Decline*, p. 64.

[29] According to Lord Vansittart, "Europe thought that revolution had started, that troops were unpaid, and mobs starving." Lord Robert Vansittart, *The Mist Procession: The Autobiography of Lord Vansittart* (London: Hutchison), 1958, p. 425.

Under these conditions, the Labour cabinet resigned and a national government took over on the twenty-fourth of August.[30] In exchange for new cuts, the government was awarded credits of $200 million in the Paris and New York markets. "Once more, Snowden emerged as the champion of the most puritanical economy."[31] But when the government revealed its fiscal plan two weeks into its tenure, the markets remained unconvinced.

Whether *any* budget could plausibly have stemmed the tide of speculation against the pound by September 1931 is an open question. What is clear, though, is that after devaluing, the British never abandoned fiscal orthodoxy. Well after the sterling crisis had passed, budget orthodoxy continued as an integral part of the Conservative recovery program. The budget remained in surplus and taxes were raised, as table 7.3 shows.[32] Expenditure cuts made in September 1931 saved £70 million in 1932–1933. Severe fiscal tightening, achieved mainly through the raising of taxes in relation to total GNP, continued almost unabated until 1934.[33]

The main reasons for avoiding budget deficits were to prevent inflation[34] and further depreciation of the pound, and to establish the confidence necessary for the orderly conversion of the public debt to a lower rate of interest, which was undertaken in 1932.[35] Few in Britain—and fewer still in policymaking circles in the Treasury—were convinced that deficits would stimulate the economy.[36]

[30] The new national government was composed of four Labour, four Conservative, and two Liberal cabinet members.

[31] Hicks, *The Finance of British Governments*, p.14.

[32] H. W. Richardson, "Fiscal Policy in the 1930s," chap. 3 in Charles H. Feinstein (ed.), *The Managed Economy: Essays in British Economic Policy and Performance Since 1929* (Oxford: Oxford University Press), 1983, p. 75.

[33] Roger Middleton, "The Constant Employment Budget Balance and British Budgetary Policy, 1929–1939," *Economic History Review*, 2d Series, Vol. 34, No. 2, May 1981, pp. 266–286, especially p. 281. But for an estimate of the degree of fiscal tightening that takes price level and fiscal "leverage" into account, and concludes that fiscal policies were not as tight as Middleton implies, see S. N. Broadberry, "Fiscal Policy in Britain During the 1930s," *Economic History Review*, Vol. 37, No. 1, February 1984, pp. 95–102.

[34] Philip Snowden wrote in his autobiography, "It is one thing to go off the Gold Standard with an unbalanced budget and uncontrollable inflation, but it is far less serious to take this measure, not because of internal financial difficulties, but because of excessive withdrawal of borrowed money. We have balanced our budget and therefore removed the danger of having to print paper, which leads to uncontrolled inflation." *An Autobiography*, Vol. 2, (London: Nicholson and Watson), 1934, p. 1055.

[35] Sykes, *British Public Expenditure*, p. 376.

[36] The "Treasury View" can be summarized as follows: "very little additional employment and no permanent employment" can be created by loan-financed public works. Statement of the chancellor of the exchequer, Winston Churchill, Hansard (Commons), 5th series, 227, 15 April 1929, col. 54. G. C. Peden argues that the Treasury View was not simply based on dogmatic attachment to inappropriate economic theories, but that they were concerned about the impact of fiscal experimentation on capital flight. G. C. Peden, "The 'Treasury View' on Public Works and Employment in the Interwar Period," *Economic History Review*, 2d Series, Vol. 38, No. 2, May 1984, pp. 167–181, especially p. 179. See also H. W. Arnt, *The Economic Lessons of the Nineteen Thirties*, (London: Frank Cass), 1944, p. 129; Hicks, *The Finance of British Government*, p. 15.

TABLE 7.3

Public Revenues and Expenditures in Britain, 1929–1932

(Millions of Pounds Sterling)

Year	Gross Income	Gross Public Expenditures	Surplus or Deficit	Tax Rate (Shillings/£)
1929–30	815.0	781.7	33.3	4.0
1930–31	857.8	814.2	43.6	4.5
1931–32	851.5	818.6	32.9	5.0

Source: H. W. Richardson, "Fiscal Policy in the 1930s," chap. 3, p. 75, in Charles H. Feinstein (ed.), *The Managed Economy: Essays in British Economic Policy and Performance Since 1929* (Oxford: Oxford University Press), 1983.

Instead, Britain used its newfound freedom from the gold standard to loosen its monetary stance. The high interest rates that had been necessary to defend the pound up to September 1931 were gradually relaxed, giving the Treasury an opportunity to carry out large-scale conversions of the public debt in June 1932. "Cheap money"—but not deficit financing—became the chief avenue to British recovery.[37]

The Decision to Devalue

By most accounts, devaluation was not a planned policy, but resulted from the gradual deterioration in the balance of payments combined with specific events and policies that undermined confidence in the government's ability and willingness to defend the pound. The government's desire to remain on gold at the existing parity was in fact strong enough for it to attempt deflation, even as Britain's unemployment crept toward 20 percent. Devaluation, it was believed (most ardently by the Conservatives, but by others as well), would have three serious consequences. First, it would cause inflation as investors tried to unload pounds and the price of imported goods rose in the local currency.[38] Second, it would raise the cost (in pounds) of servicing the war debt owed to the United States and diminish inter-Allied debt receipts and receipts on other foreign investments (denominated mostly in sterling). This would have no small impact on the current account, for "when both public and private assets were considered, perhaps half of Britain's foreign investment income was denominated in

[37] Donald Winch, "Britain in the Thirties: A Managed Economy?" in C. H. Feinstein, *The Managed Economy: Essays in British Economic Policy and Performance Since 1929* (Oxford: Oxford University Press), 1983, pp. 51–52.

[38] Too great a depreciation, it was argued, would unleash excessive wage demands in the face of a sharp rise in the cost of living. Domestic inflation would undermine the beneficial trade effects of the original devaluation, since rising domestic prices would destroy the initial price advantage of devaluation.

sterling."[39] Third, and most serious, devaluation would create uncertainty, further disrupt international trade, and undermine London's position as an international financial center and the pound's centrality as a vehicle and reserve currency. There was a widespread sense that devaluation would irrevocably alter London's position in the international economic system.[40]

Few called for devaluation as a means either to redress the balance of payments or to improve the domestic employment situation. When the Macmillan Committee published its report, the only voices that did not express a visceral fear of devaluation were those of organized labor.[41] Ernest Bevin, the general secretary of the Transport and General Workers Union, was one of the few to suggest that in fact the prevailing gold parity was not sacred.[42] While the Federation of British Industry vented its concerns about overvalued sterling, it did not make a specific policy recommendation. As late as August 1931, the federation appeared committed to the international gold standard.[43]

The devaluation was a policy "choice" only in the sense that it was the inevitable result of the lack of confidence that stemmed from a series of preceding choices and values. Confidence waned when it was unclear whether or not the central bank would have the nerve to raise the bank rate during the depression; it vanished when a labor government hesitated to cut financial support for the unemployed. Once the pound was devalued, however, there was a conscious decision not to return to a gold standard, but to "manage" the pound as might best suit the national interest. In 1932, an Exchange Equalization Account was established that enabled British monetary authorities (the Treasury) to manipulate the pound toward domestic economic objectives by intervening in gold and foreign exchange markets.[44] Britain wanted the freedom to pursue

[39] Barry Eichengreen, "Sterling and the Tariff, 1929–1932," *Princeton Studies in International Finance*, No. 48 (Princeton: Princeton University Press), 1981, p. 27. The Treasury, more than anyone else, was obsessed with the cost of servicing Britain's external debt, even though by 1931 it was becoming less and less likely that the United States would collect its interallied war debts.

[40] Ibid., p. 9. Despite the fact that he had opposed a return to gold at the prewar parity in 1925, Keynes himself argued that devaluation was not the best way to address the balance of payments difficulties facing the country. Arguing that the gold standard was the linchpin of the international financial system—from which Britain's banking and service sector benefited greatly—Keynes noted that devaluation would create uncertainty and further disrupt international trade, which in turn would have a negative impact on the already depressed export industries. Thus, despite the fact that he had earlier opposed tariffs, Keynes argued that an emergency tariff was the only way to solve the unemployment problem that was consistent with maintenance of the gold standard. He also thought that a tariff would improve Britain's terms of trade and contribute to the balancing of the budget.

[41] See Macmillan Committee Report, Addendum I and reservations to Addendum I.

[42] Cairncross and Eichengreen, *Sterling in Decline*, p. 60.

[43] R. F. Holland, "The Federation of British Industries and the International Economy, 1929–1939," *Economic History Review*, 2d Series, Vol. 34, No. 2, May 1981, pp. 287–300, especially pp. 288, 291. The FBI essentially reflected the views of the traditional export sectors: iron and steel, shipbuilding, and engineering.

[44] While the EEA was formally supposed to iron out fluctuations in the value of the pound, it appears to have been designed with the purpose in mind of keeping the pound down. Susan

its easy money policy and engineer its own recovery without serious external constraints. It was not until September 1936 that Britain would make a highly conditioned agreement to stabilize its managed currency.

Commercial Policy

Trade protection was an issue that had historically divided Britain along partisan lines. Since the turn of the century, the Conservative party had actively advocated tariff protection.[45] As Britain's external position began to deteriorate, the Conservatives advocated the tariff as a means of defending the currency. Yet it was months after the devaluation that a tariff act was actually voted. In other words, the establishment of a tariff could not be construed as an emergency measure, but as a conscious act of policy.

Traditionally, two justifications were advanced for tariff protection: first, it could be used as a policy lever to reorganize agriculture and industry;[46] and second, it would help solidify the empire through a system of preferences. To these traditional arguments the crisis of 1929–1931 added three new justifications: improvement in the balance of payments, maintenance of the gold standard, and the preservation and stimulation of employment.

Liberals and some elements of the Labour party opposed higher tariffs as vehemently as the Conservatives supported them. Liberals cited traditional trade theory to substantiate their opposition. Labour leaders opposed tariffs on the grounds that they would raise the price of food and hence the overall cost of living for the working class.[47] Free trade was also justified by the Labour party on vaguer, more "internationalist" grounds, and as late as 1930 Willie Graham,

---

Howson, *Sterling's Managed Float: The Operations of the Exchange Equalization Account, 1932–39, Princeton Studies in International Finance*, No. 46 (Princeton: Princeton University Press), 1980, p. 9; See also Leonard Waight, *The History and Mechanism of the Exchange Equalisation Account* (Cambridge: Cambridge University Press), 1939; F. W. Paish, "The British Equalization Fund," *Economica*, Vol. 2, February 1935, pp. 61–74; N. F. Hall, *The Exchange Equalisation Account* (London: Macmillan), 1935.

[45] For which they were roundly defeated in the 1906 and again in the 1924 elections. S. H. Beer, *British Politics in the Collectivist Age* (New York: Alfred A. Knopf), 1965, p. 288; Sean Glynn and John Oxborrow, *Interwar Britain: A Social and Economic History* (London: Allen and Unwin), 1956, p. 135; A. J. Marrison, "Businessmen, Industries, and Tariff Reform in Great Britain, 1903–1930," in R.P.T. Davenport-Hines (ed.), *Business in the Age of Depression and War* (London: Frank Cass), 1990, pp. 91–121; Morton, *British Finance*, p. 76. On the defeat in the 1923–24 elections, see Keith Middlemas and John Barnes, *Baldwin: A Biography* (London: Weidenfeld and Nicolson), 1969.

[46] Donald Winch, "Britain in the Thirties: A Managed Economy?" p. 52; Ian Drummond, *British Economic Policy and the Empire, 1919–1939* (London: Allen and Unwin), 1972; I. Drummond, *Imperial Economic Policy, 1917–1939* (London: Allen and Unwin), 1974.

[47] Snowden, in particular, argued to the bitter end that higher tariffs were not in the interest of the working class. See his pamphlets, *The Menace of Protection* and *The Truth About Protection—the Worker Pays*, (London: Labour Party), both 1930. See also Glynn and Oxborrow, *Interwar Britain*, p. 137.

president of the Board of Trade, submitted a proposal to the League of Nations for a two-year tariff moratorium, followed by negotiated reductions. But deteriorating economic conditions overseas meant that there was little interest in this approach among Britain's trading partners.[48]

Soaring joblessness led some who opposed tariffs under "normal" conditions to concede that since wages were so rigid, a general tariff might be useful in reducing unemployment.[49] This shift was evident in the debates of the Economic Advisory Council (EAC), which had been established by Labour Prime Minister Ramsay MacDonald in February 1930. By the summer of 1930, the EAC was coming around to the conclusion that it would be best to promote "a new orientation in our economic life in which the export trade plays a smaller part and production for the home market a larger part."[50] Moreover, the tariff appeared to be the one policy option that was also compatible with maintaining the gold parity of sterling. Increasingly, a tariff was emerging as the only politically feasible means of stimulating domestic growth in a fixed-currency framework.

Despite the debate over the effects of a tariff on British employment, the Labour cabinet refused fully to embrace protectionism. Free trade continued to symbolize the government's commitment to international solutions to Britain's problems. Snowden was a vehement opponent of the tariff, and found allies among the Liberal members of the House of Commons. Labour and Liberal parliamentary groups began to cooperate over the course of 1930, with the latter giving the government support in exchange for promises of electoral reform and continued opposition to the tariff. Yet, there were undeniable signs of defection to the protectionist camp. The prime minister extended qualified support for a 10 percent duty in January 1930. Oswald Mosley resigned from the Labour government following its rejection of his proposal for a system of import controls (May 1930). John Maynard Keynes's public announcement in March of 1931 of his support for a 10 percent tariff sent the remaining free traders reeling.[51] Finally, the publication in July 1931 of the Macmillan Report, which made the case for a general tariff as a means of reducing unemployment, put free traders distinctly on the defensive.

Defections from the free trade alliance were also mounting in industries that

[48] League of Nations, *Commercial Policy in the Interwar Years* (Geneva: League of Nations), 1942.

[49] William Beveridge, recognized at the time as the foremost British expert on unemployment, thought that the spread of collective bargaining and unemployment insurance contributed to wage rigidity.

[50] This is from the summary of the EAC in response to questions posed by the prime minister, as quoted by Eichengreen, "Sterling and the Tariff," p. 10. Keynes essentially agreed with this conclusion. While the EAC was moving toward the tariff solution, there was still disagreement over the wisdom of protectionism. Ibid., p. 11.

[51] See his article in *New Statesman and Nation*, 7 March 1930, pp. 53–54.

had previously opposed protectionism. During the second half of the year, a consensus was beginning to form in the Federation of British Industries (FBI) that a tariff was in the interest of the bulk of its members. Automakers especially became vocal for protection. The FBI entered the campaign for the tariff, arguing that it would raise employment opportunities in Britain's industrial sectors.[52] Yet, as late as December 1930, the FBI steered a moderate course: its Memorandum on Industrial Policy stressed that tariffs were at best an expedient response to the crisis, and that their long-term viability was in doubt.[53]

Further, Labour party defections from free trade must be understood in light of the alternatives. As the financial crisis gathered and the unemployment problem temporarily receded by comparison, the government was faced with the dilemma of how to balance the budget in order to restore confidence. Conservatives were demanding reductions in unemployment. Ordinarily, tariffs would have been unacceptable to both the Trades Union Congress and Labour MPs. They were accepted grudgingly, in hopes of stemming cuts in unemployment insurance.[54]

As the financial crisis gained momentum in the first weeks of August, organized labor saw fewer alternatives for adjustment. It was clear that something had to be done to raise revenue and to address the external imbalance. Faced with a choice between making substantial cuts in unemployment insurance and accepting an external tariff, the government found the latter alternative more and more palatable. But there was still no consensus within the cabinet. Labour was caught between two undesirable choices: to defend the currency through protection or to purchase credibility by cutting unemployment benefits by 10 percent.

The issue was not resolved before the pound left gold. In theory, the balance of payments "problem" was solved by the managed pound, but the question of protection did not go away. Conservatives came out of the 1931 elections in a much stronger electoral position, and were rewarded with much stronger representation in both the government and the House of Commons. They dominated the new National Government; Snowden and three Liberals were the sole surviving free traders. The Conservatives saw this as an opportunity to implement the commercial policy that they had pressed for in the elections of 1906 and 1923. Snowden was replaced at the Exchequer by the Conservative Neville Chamberlain. Over the objections of the remaining Labour representatives, the Trades Union Congress, and the trades-oriented press, the National Government passed on November 17, 1931, the Abnormal Importations Act, which gave the Board of Trade temporary power to impose duties of up to 100 percent on imports entering the country in abnormal quantities. In January 1932, a 10

---

[52] Holland, "The Federation of British Industries," p. 289.
[53] Ibid., p. 290.
[54] Eichengreen, "Sterling and the Tariff," p. 20.

percent general tax was proposed as a means of reducing imports and balancing the budget. It was introduced as the Imports Duty Bill into the Commons on 4 February 1932. With very little consideration for the possible retaliatory effects, tariffs were heaped upon devaluation, possibly to achieve that traditional Conservative goal of Imperial preference (meant to solidify the British Empire),[55] or possibly to guard against hyperinflation that the twenties had "shown" was associated with floating exchange rates.[56] In either case, it was a clear Conservative victory, opposed by Labour, whose members were skeptical of the employment benefits and certain of who would bear the costs.

The Policy Mix

In Britain there was generally broad support for the policies needed to uphold the gold standard. The polity had accepted high taxation with relative docility, permitting Britain to run budget surpluses for most of the thirties.[57] Fiscal policy remained tight, but as the external position deteriorated, the market groped for some signal that Britain could adjust.[58] Unemployment insurance became the ultimate litmus test of the nation's flexibility and the monetary authorities' credibility. The reputation of the Bank of England contributed to confidence in the pound, as our quantitative results would predict, but at times the bank's inaction sent disconcerting signals to the market. When the market

[55] The Conservative justification, according to Chamberlain, was to strengthen empire ties through Imperial Preference, improve Britain's bargaining position with other countries, raise revenue, improve employment, improve the balance of payments, and ensure against a rise in the cost of living that would attend devaluation. Chamberlain, Hansard (Commons), 5th series, CCLXI (1931–32), cols. 289–290.

[56] A consideration of the effects of foreign retaliation played a very minor role in the tariff debate, possibly because most nations already had tariffs of their own. Despite the fact that most economists saw the negative impact of the tariff on employment, conservatives continued to view the tariff as a way to reach external balance and halt the "cycle" of inflation and depreciation. This was the basis of the conservative pro-tariff arguments made in the parliament at the end of 1931. Eichengreen, "Sterling and the Tariffs," p. 33.

[57] Susan K. Howson, *Domestic Monetary Management in Britain, 1919–38* (Cambridge: Cambridge University Press), 1975, chaps. 4–5; Donald Winch, *Economics and Policy: A Historical Study* (New York: Walker), 1972, chap. 10.

[58] The realization that too much political and social resistance had built up may have been key to the loss of confidence in the ability to stay on gold. See Palyi's description: "The refusal of private enterprise, especially in the case of the depressed older industries, to meet the requirements of the day through aggressive modernization; the rigidity and belligerency of labor, which opposed changes and all temporary sacrifices; the activities of intellectuals and politicians, supported by powerful newspapers, in representing Britain's ills as the result of a conspiracy of 'reactionaries' and 'international capitalists'—all these forces combined to prevent Britain from regaining her prewar economic position." Palyi, *The Twilight of Gold*, p. 69. According to Palyi, the most vocal critic of the gold standard was organized labor. "Politically, the most significant factor was the resistance of organized labor to the alleged or real impact of the monetary 'mechanism' on wages and employment." Ibid., p. 102.

needed a strong indication that the central bank would defend the pound at all costs, it was thrice disappointed: once in the summer of 1929, again at the outbreak of the Continental banking crisis, and finally in the waning weeks of the gold standard. Overall, the market judged that a left-wing government would not tolerate the deflation needed to stay on gold. Capital outflows and depreciation were the result, in accordance with the findings of our more general models.

What is interesting about the British case is not simply the devaluation, but the addition of the General Tariff. The tariff was clearly the progeny of Conservative campaigns predating the First World War. After the devaluation, the Conservatives also argued that it was a device for keeping the pound from further devaluation. The tariff was opposed by Labour, which saw it as a consumption tax and not as a domestic employment measure. This parallels the pattern that emerged strongly in the quantitative models of tariff increases: the Left was champion of freer trade across Europe during these decades. Of course, in Britain, the depression added weight to the traditional conservative impulse to protect, and there were defectors from Britain's traditional policy of free trade. As the largest trader in the world, Britain could well afford to indulge such impulses—a result that, once again, shines through clearly in the quantitative analysis. As the next case highlights, this was not an option open to highly trade dependent countries.

The Case of Belgium, 1934–1936

The smaller, more trade dependent countries were the most ready to adjust. Belgium is an example. Although Belgium eventually went off the gold standard, it did so only after all reasonable efforts to alter its internal prices had been made. Belgium resisted protection and quickly restabilized its currency at a lower level. The policy mix remained relatively liberal, but ended in a mild devaluation due to the prominence of the traded goods sector and the conflicts between labor and capitalists over how the burden of deflation should be shared between them.

Economic Structure and Conditions

The most striking feature of the Belgian economy in the first half of the 1930s was its extreme openness. Of the twenty-one countries examined in the previous chapters, Belgium had by far the highest proportion of total trade to Net National Product, at nearly 80 percent.[59] Belgium's foreign trade per capita was

---

[59] Note that this figure is for import plus exports over NNP. For Belgium, total trade also includes gold shipments, which could not be separated from the aggregate, but is likely to be small compared to other trade.

about twice that of Great Britain's.[60] At least eighteen major industrial sectors
depended on exports for more than 50 percent of their earnings.[61] As domestic
agriculture produced only about 60 percent of the country's food consumption,
Belgium was a net importer of agricultural and raw materials and an exporter of
manufactured and semifinished products (table 7.4).[62] Approximately 67 percent of Belgium's imports could be considered necessities for the Belgian
population and the economic life of the country, while Belgium's exports were
mostly manufactured goods facing stiff competition from other industrialized
countries, notably the United States and Britain. The importance of Belgium in
international trade was much greater in the interwar years than it is today:
Belgium was the world's fifth largest trader, behind the United Kingdom, the
United States, France, and Germany.[63]

Belgium was in fairly deep depression by the early thirties. At the end of
November 1930, the number of workers completely and partially unemployed
totaled 113,483; one month later this figure had leapt to 180,752, of which
62,568 persons were completely without work.[64] Unemployment was spread
unevenly among Belgian industries: by 1933, more than 57 percent of the
unemployed in Belgium were in three sectors: metallurgy, textiles, and building. The first two of these had been directly disrupted by the fall in world
demand for Belgian exports, illustrative of how the country's welfare depended

[60] RG 151 (U.S. Department of Commerce, Bureau of Foreign and Domestic Commerce),
Belgium 1934, Box No. 44: 9 April 1934. National Archives. Henceforth, RG 151/44, 9 April
1934; NA.

[61] The following Belgian industries exported more than 50 percent of their entire production in
the early thirties:

Artificial cement	57%	Iron and steel	61%
Nickel	91%	Agricultural machinery	66%
Wire and nails	82%	Plate and window glass	90%
Chemical fertilizers	56%	Paints and varnishes	54%
Glue and gelatine	91%	Matches	69%
Stearine, candles, etc.	76%	Cotton cloth and covers	60%
Rayon	66%	Zinc	71%
Linen	70%	Wool yarn and cloth	60%
Paper and cardboard	68%	Playing cards & bookbinding	67%

These figures are based on ten-year averages. "Annual Economic Report—Belgium." RG 151/ 44,
30 January 1934; NA.

[62] RG 151/44, 30 January 1934; NA.

[63] There is a real discrepancy in the available data on this point. Statistics compiled by the
Commerce Department suggest that Belgium was seventh, not fifth, in percentage of world trade,
and that Belgium's trade increased in the thirties—to 3.2 percent as compared to 2.6 percent in
1926. RG 151/44, 30 January 1934; NA. Arthur Banks's cross-polity time-series data show a
precipitous drop in Belgium's position in the 1930s. It is so steep (from about 14 percent to 4
percent) that one suspects an error.

[64] RG 151 /42, 23 February 1931; NA.

TABLE 7.4

Belgium's Proportion of Imports and Exports,
Various Sectors, Early 1930s

	% of Total	
	Imports	Exports
Foodstuffs and beverages	21.76	6.8
Raw and semimanufactured materials	45.84	37.56
Manufactured products	29.25	53.09
Live animals, precious metals, etc.	3.15	2.56

on continued trade. Unemployment compensation totaled about 7 percent of the entire state budget by 1932. As in other countries, the Depression reduced government resources just as demands for expenditures were at their strongest.

Devaluation of the pound and the dollar complicated the problem for Belgium of achieving price competitiveness at the current franc parity.[65] While the depreciation of these currencies greatly reduced Belgium's foreign debt,[66] it made the problem of deflating to meet foreign competition especially frustrating. As Prime Minister Paul Van Zeeland wrote, "Our real aim was to adjust Belgian selling prices to sterling prices but each time this adjustment reached another stage, a new drop in the pound made it necessary to start all over again. It was impossible to say where this futile pursuit of an elusive shadow would end."[67] It finally ended with the decision to devalue the Belgian franc in March 1935.

Since Belgium's domestic prices were out of line with those of her most important trade competitors, the only solution was to lower them. Belgium first tried to accomplish this through deflation. Well past the point where the costs of deflation had exceeded the apparent benefit, the policy shifted to reducing relative prices through devaluation. Technically, Belgium had the resources to

[65] The value of the depreciated currencies (the pound and the dollar) were much more important to Belgium's external position than were any of the currencies in the Gold Bloc. Alfred Braunthal, "The New Economic Policy in Belgium," *International Labour Review*, Vol. 33, No. 6, June 1936, pp. 762–789; H. Van der Wee and K. Tavernier, *La Banque Nationale de Belgique et L'Histoire Monétaire entre les Deux Guerres Mondiale* (Brussels: Banque Nationale de Belgique), 1975, p. 258.

[66] Due to the dollar's depreciation, the debt owed to the United States government decreased by about 5.2 billion francs, and the debt due the British government fell by about 506 million francs. Ordinary dollar loans were reduced by 2 billion francs, and ordinary sterling loans by about 640 million francs. With an additional decrease of 30 million francs due to the devaluation of the Swedish crown, the total reduction of Belgium's debt due to depreciation was about 8.34 billion francs, which brought the Belgian government's total indebtedness to about 49 billion francs. RG 151/43, 13 July 1933; NA.

[67] Paul Van Zeeland, *The Van Zeeland Experiment* (New York: Morteus Press), 1943, p. 30.

defend the franc. But there was no point in a highly trade dependent economy of strangling national production to save the currency. Devaluation was prompt, avoiding all but the briefest interlude of currency control, and the franc was rapidly stabilized. Belgium avoided excessive protectionism for the entire episode.

Private Sector Adjustment: Wage Compression

Belgium had to trade to survive. By 1934 costs in Belgium were so much higher than abroad that most export industries that were still operating were doing so at a loss, with some government support. Much stress was placed on lowering production costs in key export industries, which meant, first and foremost, reducing wages.[68] In 1932 efforts to reduce wages in coal mining had touched off limited but worrisome strikes, but did not drastically reduce wages.[69] Disagreements over pay motivated strikes in January 1934 in the wool and spinning industries of Ghent, and again in the coal industry that spring.[70]

Yet there seemed no alternative to deflation, given the country's imperative to compete. On 19 April 1934, a meeting was held among the ministers of finance, labor, and industry, the governor of the central bank, and representatives of the Société Générale, at which consensus formed around the need for more deflation, with the aim of at least a 15 percent reduction in production costs. None doubted that the most important part of this reduction would have to come from further wage cuts, with which the government officially urged unions to comply.[71] Textile workers accepted pay cuts of about 6 percent in the

---

[68] As early as the beginning of 1931, employers in coal, metallurgy, and textiles tried to put though salary cuts ranging from 5 to 10 percent. RG 151/42, 5 January 1931; NA.

[69] In July 1932, a four-day strike, involving 65,000 workers in the Charleroi region, prompted clashes between workers and state police and two infantry companies. The strike was contained, but not before some 120,000 out of 150,000 coal miners had walked out. The results of the strike were inconclusive, though: employers agreed only to implement no new wage cuts for the next three months, and to suspend the last round of cuts. RG 151/42, 11 July 1932; 20 July 1932. Estimation on the number of workers involved in coal mine strikes during July and August is that of the Belgian Bureau of Mines, as reported in RG151/42, 16 August 1932; NA.

[70] RG 151/44, 9 March 1934; NA

[71] RG 151/44, 26 April 1934; NA. According to the American commercial attaché, "The Government is definitely encouraging any movement to cut production costs, and considers that Belgian industry must adjust itself to new conditions and that labor must even lower its standard of living if Belgian foreign trade is to be maintained." He doubted, however, that significantly more deflation was socially feasible. RG 151/44, 21 and 24 April 1934; NA. As part of its campaign to reduce the costs of production, industrial management was also firmly opposed to the forty-hour workweek, even though the government had signed an international accord to adopt the shorter week. The Comité Central Industriel de Belgique, an organized group of manufacturers, met on May 23 and denounced the adhesion of Belgium to the forty-hour week proposed by the International Bureau of Labor. The Comité argued that the forty-hour week was contrary to the government's position on deflation and proposed that if the government found it impossible to rescind its

spring of 1934, while in May union workers in the steel, mechanical, and construction industries voted to accept 5 percent wage cuts without striking.[72] Wool workers gave in to all demands on the thirtieth of July after spending 16 million francs to support the strike in vain.[73] Coal miners had to be handled gingerly, since a strike in that strategic sector would have drawn a "turbulent population" out of work and onto the streets, and it would have forced up the price of coal at a time when industry was trying to reduce production costs.[74] While there was some unrest in isolated areas, strikes were fairly well contained.[75] As it turned out, coal miners absorbed their share of wage cuts as well.

Overall, industrial deflation had accomplished wage reductions of 15 to 20 percent by the end of 1934, but this was still not enough to make Belgian goods competitive, especially since the pound continued to fluctuate. Despite the tremendous cost to labor and industry, Belgium opted for several years to internalize the costs of adjustment. Highly dependent on the good will of foreign commercial authorities, policymakers in Belgium thought that any other course posed far too great a risk.

Public Sector Adjustment

Recession wiped out the budget surpluses that Belgium had enjoyed during the boom of the late twenties.[76] The best way for the government to contribute to price compression was thought to be through balancing the budget and financial orthodoxy. Memories of the inflation associated with the floating debt after the Great War heightened the resistance to short-term borrowing[77] and increased

---

adhesion to this international accord, it should at least make its assent contingent on the adoption of the forty-hour week by all the European governments of countries that were serious industrial competitors of Belgium. RG 151/44, 31 May 1934; NA.

[72] RG 151/44, 25 May 1934; NA.

[73] The deflationists had won, but it was a pyrrhic victory, since one of Belgium's most important wool markets, Germany, was practically closed on account of foreign exchange difficulties. RG 151/44, 6 August 1934; NA.

[74] RG 151/44, 30 April 1934; NA.

[75] In one mine, 400 miners walked out demanding a 10 percent wage increase. In another mine 1,000 workers went on strike because they were not granted a day of mourning for 56 miners who had perished in a mine explosion the previous week. RG 151/44, 24 May 1934; NA.

[76] From 1927 to 1929, revenues had exceeded expenditures by about 4.1 billion francs, but this was diminished in the early thirties by deficits of 1.7 billion in 1930 and 2.5 billion in 1931. By far the largest increase in the budget was for unemployment relief and old age pensions (750 million and 1.05 billion francs, respectively). Budgeting in 1932 was further complicated by the moratorium on German reparations, which would ordinarily have supplied 425 million francs per year. Including about 750 million for unemployment relief, the total 1932 deficit was expected to reach almost 2.8 billion francs. RG 151/42, 5 September 1932; NA.

[77] There was pressure in the summer of 1932 to borrow at short-term rates, because on October 1 the government had to meet maturing ten-year obligations totaling about 770 million francs. Belgium ended up borrowing 800 million French francs in the Paris market, so as to reserve the

the nation's willingness to cover expenditures with new taxes, even though Belgian taxes were already quite high by international standards.[78]

In the winter of 1933 a conservative government (ruling by decree) imposed cuts and raised taxes by about 1.45 billion francs.[79] Belgians were called upon to pay higher income taxes, taxes on entertainment, make a National Crisis Contribution based on income, and pay higher stamp taxes, turnover taxes, and certain consumption taxes. The consumption taxes were particularly galling to the Socialists, who claimed that the working classes were being forced to bear an unfair portion of the burden. They argued that the working classes alone would have to pay some 300 million francs, or about 20 percent of the total new taxation, even as they became the victims of reductions in unemployment subsidies and wage cuts.[80] But without the support of the Christian Democrats or the Catholic party, the possibility of a parliamentary remedy was slim.[81] Nor did the Socialists wish to prompt a general strike under the present conditions.[82]

Higher taxes still would not balance the budget. Once again, in 1933, the government asked for a three-month period in which to rule on budgetary matters without the consent of parliament.[83] The Socialists objected, knowing that unemployment and other social expenditures were at stake. But when the Christian Democrats agreed to support the government, the way was cleared for a three-month rule by decree in budgetary matters.[84] The government imme-

---

domestic market for future borrowing. The French banking consortium that took up the Belgian loan included the Banque de Paris et des Pays-Bas, Crédit Lyonnais, Société Générale de Crédit Industriel et Commercial, Banque de l'Union Parisienne, Crédit Commercial de France, and Banque Nationale pour le Commerce et l'Industrie. RG 151/42, 11 July 1932; NA. The Telephone and Telegraph Monopoly also got a 250 million franc loan from Swiss and Dutch financial groups. RG 151/42, 19 September 1932; NA. This approach was criticized as not sufficiently "far-reaching" by the Liberal party members of the ruling coalition, and the cabinet was forced to resign. RG 151/42, 17 October 1932; NA.

[78] RG 151/42, 1 August 1932; NA.

[79] Henri Jaspar, an arch-conservative and former prime minister, became minister of finance, and Emile Francqui of the central bank was appointed to the Comité du Trèsor, ensuring a very orthodox approach to fiscal policy. RG 151/42, 7 November 1932, NA; RG 151/42, 25 October 1932, NA; RG 151/42, 19 and 27 December 1932, NA; RG 151/43, 27 February 1933, NA.

[80] RG 151/43, 20 March 1933; RG 151/43, 16 January 1933. The Socialists protested various consumption taxes, especially those on sugar, coffee, margarine, matches, and tobacco.

[81] A government crisis was narrowly averted on 22 March as a result of Christian Democrat pressure for more liberal unemployment benefits. However, a compromise was arranged, and the vote of confidence on the subject was sustained by 99 to 82. RG 151/43, 27 March 1933.

[82] RG 151/43, 25 January and 27 February 1933. The Socialists did propose, in the autumn of 1933, a plan to restructure the Belgian economy through extensive programs for public works, the nationalization of credit, and other "mixed economy" strategies. H. Van der Wee and K. Tavernier, *La Banque Nationale de Belgique*, pp. 257 and 269.

[83] RG 151/43, 22 May 1933. The bill also gave the government the authority to take any measures for the purpose of preventing and repressing all acts of a nature to weaken the credit of the state.

[84] RG 151/43, 11 May 1933. According to the American commercial attaché in Brussels, conservatives favored the "cabinet dictatorship," while the Socialists appeared merely to be "grand-

diately instituted new penal measures to prevent fiscal fraud; it withheld about 20 percent of all subsidies paid out by the government (with the exception of salaries); it impounded about 10 percent of the current allotment for government supplies and travel; and it began a process for the review of employees' salaries. It also lowered from 10,000 to 2,000 francs the ceiling for which special authorization would have to be granted for expenditures.[85] Pension and unemployment allowances were cut, government salaries trimmed by 5 percent, and the National Crisis Tax raised. Along with other economies, the government estimated a savings of about 800 million francs.[86]

Over continuing objections from the Socialists, the compression of public expenditures went fairly smoothly, and the government agreed to reconvene parliament earlier than required by law. The previous year's new taxes were maintained and collection of them increasingly tightened.[87] Confidence in the franc and in the country's finances returned, and an internal loan of 1.5 billion francs was fully subscribed by the Belgian public in one day.[88] At the end of 1933, the overall budget was in a worse position than the year before, but in a fairly favorable position compared to most other European nations.[89]

Nonetheless, it was becoming increasingly difficult for Belgians to see the rewards for all the deflationary efforts to date. A weak coalition government could not continue to deflate the economy by decree indefinitely. After all, the central government controlled only a small corner of the economy. It refused to dictate prices and wages to the private sector, or to force the involuntary conversion of the public debt, as Mussolini had done in Italy. If deflation were to be accomplished in Belgium, it would have to be through voluntarism, not compulsion.[90] The best that could possibly be hoped for was an additional 5 percent compression—still a far cry from the necessary 15 percent that would

---

standing" in their opposition without a serious programmatic alternative. RG 151/43, 15 May 1933. The Chambre des Députes passed the bill on 12 May (96 to 83) and the Sénat on May 17 (91 to 63).

[85] RG 151/43, 24 May 1933.

[86] RG 151/43, 9 June 1933. The government still had to arrange external finance to meet its urgent budget obligations. In June 1933 it began to negotiate a loan with French and Dutch bankers for 250 million Belgian francs, to be placed in the form of Treasury bonds. The loan was necessary to meet the immediate needs of the government for the month of July (salaries and debt servicing). RG 151/43, 13 June 1933.

[87] RG 151/43, 7 September 1933.

[88] RG 151/43, 4 October 1933. American commercial attachés thought the Belgian government was making a good-faith effort to correctly forecast and balance its budget.

[89] RG 151/43, 5 December 1933. While the ordinary budget was nearly balanced, the extraordinary budget, which was almost exclusively devoted to public works and national defense, could only be covered through such borrowing. RG 151/43, 9 November 1933.

[90] The government called for the *voluntary* conversion of the public debt; the government *desired* that banks reduce their interest rates; and the government *appealed* to the provincial and communal authorities to reduce their taxes and expenditures and *requested* public utilities to reduce their rates. Finally it *appealed* to professionals to reduce their charges for service and to the working classes to adapt their wage expectations to the cost of living. RG 151/44, 22 May 1934.

make Belgian products competitive on the world markets. As long as the government did not have control over wages—which it had no intention of taking[91]—deflation by decree was hopeless. It was also becoming politically costly. A dissatisfied parliament overthrew the conservative cabinet on 6 June 1934.[92] Still, no clear alternative program emerged to supplant the deflationists, and the new cabinet was very similar to the old one, a signal that there would be no substantive change in policy.[93] Deflation would continue, and the franc would be defended.[94] Whether this policy could be implemented by a government as unpopular and a coalition as weak as those that ruled Belgium in the late spring of 1934 remained to be seen.

Commercial Policy

Despite the plunge in its exports, Belgium avoided protectionism on the scale practiced elsewhere.[95] When trade was controlled, Belgian policymakers tended to select quotas rather than tariffs.[96] As an emergency measure, quotas

[91] RG 151/44, 21 June 1934.

[92] Some denounced the deflationary policy as completely misguided, and others criticized it as not stringent enough. RG 151/44, 7 June 1934.

[93] RG 151/44, 11 June 1934. Jaspar, the previous finance minister who was very unpopular by this time, was moved to the Ministry of Foreign Affairs, where he could exert his rather strong character in the pursuit of Belgium's external interests.

[94] RG 151/44, 18 and 21 June 1934.

[95] For a general comparison of Belgium's trade policies with the rest of Europe, see H. Liepmann, *Tariff Levels and the Economic Unity of Europe: An Examination of Tariff Policy, Export Movements, and the Economic Integration of Europe, 1913–1931* (London: Allen and Unwin), 1938, pp. 74–76, 134–136, and 264–269.

[96] Below is a complete schedule of import quotas in existence from January 1934:

Quotas Applied by the Ministry of Agriculture

Live cattle, sheep, hogs	May 1932	Cream & milk	Jan. 1933
Beef, mutton, pork	May 1932	Fruits & vegs. (8 var.)	July 1933
Sausage, canned & prepared meats	May 1932	Eggs	July 1933
Butter	May 1932	Rye & rye flour	Oct. 1933
Cut flowers	May 1932	Cheese	Oct. 1932

Quotas Applied by the Ministry of Industry and Labor

Corn by-products	July 1932	Silk & rayon	Sept. 1933
Coal	Oct. 1931	Rubber shoes	Sept. 1933
Sugar	Aug. 1932	Mine props	Nov. 1933
Nitrogen products	Aug. 1931	Clothing	Nov. 1933
Wool felt	Oct. 1932	Salt	Dec. 1933
Silk knitted-wear	June 1932	Leather shoes	Mar. 1932

Quotas Applied by the Ministry of Transports

Fish	July 1932	Furniture	Dec. 1933

were less likely to result in retaliation because foreign exporters who were granted licenses were "permitted to share in the spoils" of unearned profits and hence were less likely to lobby their own government for retaliation.[97] When Belgium increased protection, it was usually for use as a negotiating tool.[98] Protection was not favored as an overall trade policy.[99] In fact, most industries were so export-oriented that they would hardly have benefited from a protected domestic market. Belgium began to negotiate the dismantling of its quota structure as soon as the franc was devalued, in contrast to the continued high tariff posture of Britain after 1931, and it remained one of the countries most strongly committed to free trade throughout the interwar years. It had almost nothing to gain—and much to lose—by erecting walls around its economy.

Quotas in Belgium were late, light and lax. Despite the early susceptibility of quotas to the international Depression, the first quota law was implemented in August 1932 (a full year after France began implementing its quota system).[100] In general, these limitations allowed for imports to levels of up to 100 percent of imports from the previous year.[101] Quota enforcement was fairly lax as well. In the summer of 1932, the Belgian government implemented an automobile quota, which Americans admitted had almost no effect on the importation of American automobiles.[102]

One reason quotas were not prosecuted with greater vigor was that they were

---

[97] League of Nations, *Quantitative Trade Controls*, p. 33.

[98] Belgium was extremely active in negotiating agreements to lower trade barriers. An example is the Ouchy agreement with Holland (February 20, 1933), whereby the two countries would reduce import duties on each other's products by 10 percent per year, until the prevailing rates were halved. According to the agreement, any other country willing to sign on would be accepted on the same basis, effectively providing for reciprocal unconditional and unlimited MFN treatment between Belgium and the Netherlands. RG 151/43, 24 February 1933. Belgium also negotiated tariff reductions with New Zealand (5 December 1933) and Argentina (January 1934). Reportedly, the increase in Belgium's trade barriers just prior to the World Economic Conference was designed to give it some bargaining leverage to encourage tariff reductions in other countries. RG 151/43, 26 June 1933. Within the Gold Bloc, Belgium pressured France to widen the bloc's sphere to include a reciprocal trade area, but France resisted. Henry L. Shepherd, *The Monetary Experience of Belgium, 1914–1936* (Princeton: Princeton University Press), 1936, p. 197.

[99] Which incidentally may be another reason Belgium implemented quotas instead of tariffs: they were administered and would not have to be debated before the parliament.

[100] On France's first quotas, see Frank A. Haight, *A History of French Commercial Policy* (New York: Macmillan), 1941, pp. 162–163.

[101] It was reported by the American commercial attaché to be enforced very liberally. RG 151/42, 26 August 1932. The American commercial attaché reported that these quotas affected trade with America to only a very slight extent, though they could be "inconvenient and unfair to particular firms."

[102] Indeed, the Ministry of Industry was unprepared to protect: imports of parts were to be limited to the amounts imported in the previous year, but no one had counted the previous year's imports, so the ministry was unable to say definitively how many car parts could be imported. RG 151/42, 19 and 26 September 1932. The lack of effect of these quotas on trade is a consistent theme of the American commercial attaché at this time.

so unpopular.[103] The greatest opposition came from exporters who feared retaliation. Coal quotas were opposed by importers as well as by shipping interests.[104] The government often refused to grant restrictive coal quotas on the grounds that these could undermine broader beneficial trade arrangements.[105] When Belgium did cut quotas on industrial goods, compensation was usually negotiated in some other sector to compensate for the trade partner's loss.[106]

Quotas on necessities such as foodstuffs were politically sensitive, and were opposed by both export industries and the Socialists, who argued that they raised the cost of living for the working class. One government was alleged to have collapsed at least in part due to its proposal to limit butter imports.[107] Belgian manufacturers were the most bitter critics of an emerging policy of agricultural quotas: nothing caused greater worry among producers of cement, automobile parts, glass, and chemicals than a threat—such as that issued by the Dutch in 1933–1934—that continued agricultural quotas would be cause for retaliation against Belgian manufactures.[108]

Overall, Belgium's system of quotas was mild. By 1937, the percentage of total value of imports subject to restrictions (quotas or licensing) was about 24 percent; and it should be kept in mind that "subject to restrictions" did not always mean these restrictions were avidly enforced. This figure compared

[103] RG 151/42, 8 August 1932.

[104] The proposed quota was for 30 percent of 1930 levels. RG 151/42, 6 September 1932. Representatives of the ports of Antwerp and Ghent approached the government demanding the modification of coal import quotas. They argued that unemployment increased in the ports proportionately with the decrease in coal imports. They argued that in 1929, when about 1.7 million tons of coal were imported overseas and 1.1 million tons by inland waterways, that only 220 dockers were unemployed, whereas in 1932, only 1.1 million tons *total* were imported and 1,406 dockers were unemployed. RG 151/43, 3 October 1933.

[105] Belgian coal interests wanted to scrap the Belgo-German trade agreement of 1926 and replace it with a stringent system of quotas, but the Belgian Ministry of Foreign Affairs refused on the grounds that this treaty was a great advantage to other branches of Belgian industry. RG 151/43, 12 May 1933. Quotas were also turned down in the spring of 1933 on the grounds that Belgium had unconditionally accepted the tariff truce proposed by the United States and was barred from a general system of quotas.

As a further example of the political power of exporters for freer trade, powerful iron and steel interests, which had a lucrative market in Japan, successfully opposed moves to exclude inexpensive Japanese bicycles, electrical appliances, and other fixtures from penetrating the Belgian market, despite much publicity to the so-called "Japanese trade menace." RG 151/44, 24 January 1933. Belgian iron and steel exports to Japan totaled 226 million francs for the first three quarters of 1933 and constituted 86 percent of total Belgian sales to Japan during that period.

[106] Following negotiations with Germany, Belgium announced in August that it would reduce its coal quota from 55 to 45 percent of the 1931 levels, but it was also agreed that Germany would be compensated with a promise of machinery purchases. RG 151/42, 25 August 1932. Imports of coal were to be reduced in exchange for an agreement that the Belgian National Railways would place special machinery orders in Germany. RG 151/42, 5 October 1932

[107] RG 151/42, 17 October 1932.

[108] RG 151/44, 1 February 1934.

favorably with that of many other countries: almost all of Italy's and Poland's, more than half of Austria's, and a substantial portion of Czechoslovakia's and Greece's imports were subject to control by this time. Among the democracies, the comparable figure for France was 58 percent; for Switzerland, 52 percent; for the Netherlands, 26 percent; for Norway, 12 percent; and for the United Kingdom, 8 percent.[109] (Recall, however, that Britain's tariffs were much higher than those in Belgium.)

As for tariff policy, duties began to increase noticeably in 1932, often in order to meet the fiscal needs of the state.[110] The increased import duty on car parts was an example of a revenue-inspired duty.[111] For purposes of balancing the 1933 budget, the transmission tax, the gasoline import duty and excise tax, and the import duty on automobiles were expected to be among the principal items to be increased.[112] Duties on coffee, tea, and cocoa—which were nearly doubled in early 1933—were also considered fiscal measures.[113] As in the case of quotas, these tariffs were widely criticized. Customs officers—who never did approve of the new duties—were hardly cooperating with their own government in their collection, in an effort to discredit the Ministry of Industry officials who drew up the plan.[114]

As the Depression deepened in the Gold Bloc countries, Belgian policymakers were increasingly subject to pressure from particular industries to be more aggressive in protecting their economic interests. An import tax on coal and the import quota restriction on clothing imposed in late 1933 were the results of such pressure.[115] These pressures were building toward a reorientation of Belgium's trade policy in the direction of "unilateralism when necessary" and "negotiation to improve free trade whenever possible."[116] Most-favored-nation status was suppressed for any country whose commercial

[109] Margaret S. Gordon, *Barriers to World Trade* (New York: Macmillan), 1941, pp. 244–253; League of Nations, *World Economic Survey*, p. 189.

[110] A law of June 16, 1932, authorized the government to increase the transmission tax on imports from certain countries, but France was excepted and a similar exception was being negotiated with Canada. RG 151/42, 7 July and 1 August 1932. Duties on radios were increased during the first half of October 1932. RG 151/42, 24 September 1932. The American commercial attaché, in his review of the budget situation, immediately warned the Commerce Department that revenue requirements would be behind higher Belgian tariff rates before the end of the year. RG 151/42, 24 September 1932.

[111] The commercial attaché wrote, "While we have many factors in favor of maintaining a reasonable rate of duty on automobiles, the Belgian Government is unfortunately hard pressed for funds, and because of this element there is still a possibility that the rates on car parts may be materially increased." RG 151/42, 14 November 1932.

[112] RG 151/42, 26 December 1932.

[113] RG 151/43, 23 January 1933.

[114] RG 151/43, 20 March 1933.

[115] RG 151/43, 7 December 1933.

[116] RG 151/43, 6 November 1933. Skepticism of the use of import quotas as a bargaining chip was also expressed by the Ministry of Foreign Affairs, which supported only the most cautious and limited use of quotas. RG 151/44, 5 March 1934.

policies were unfavorable to Belgium.[117] To give added flexibility to trade
policy, the Belgian government was authorized to make any changes in the
import duty schedule that it saw fit.[118] The impact of industrial pressure for
protection was beginning to have a significant effect on trade policy: by the
beginning of 1934, nearly fifty import quotas were in force.[119]

Despite the new "aggressive" reorientation, Belgian trade policy was still
fairly moderate. The country's major trading partners generally interpreted the
new stance as an effort to open up foreign markets, not to shut down the Belgian
market to trade.[120] Belgium's "new commercial policy" was really no more
than an explicit policy of negotiation. Fundamentally, the Belgian government
remained in favor of free trade, or, at most, moderately protective tariffs.[121]
Aside from a few marginal changes, Belgian tariff policy had been altered little
since the general 15 percent increase in tariffs put through in late 1932.[122]

As the spring of 1934 passed, it had become increasingly apparent that
Belgium's policy of bargaining had had very little effect.[123] The options were
narrowing. Neither deflation nor the mild program of protection could restore
profitability to Belgium's exporters. Increasingly, enlightened opinion began to
converge around the unthinkable.

The Decision to Devalue

The decision to devalue the franc stemmed from the realization that it would be
politically impossible to deflate the economy the remaining 15 percent required

[117] RG 151/43, 7 December 1933.

[118] The new law required the government immediately to seek legislative confirmation of its
decision, and if it were to be refused, reimbursement was required for whatever duty had been
collected in excess of normal rates. RG 151/44, 4 January 1934.

[119] RG 151/44, 8 January 1934.

[120] RG 151/43, 9 November 1933. The American commercial attaché noted that despite industrial demands, a policy of protection "is not very efficacious in the case of a country which depends
largely on export markets for its prosperity." The American commercial attaché also noted that
Belgian prosperity depended on foreign trade more than on any other one factor, and that foreign
barriers to trade were Belgium's chief worry. They interpreted Belgium's new defensive commercial policy as a response to foreign barriers. RG 151/44, 26 March 1934.

[121] RG 151/44, 8 January 1934. This theme of free trade through bargaining was central to the
speech of Emile Francqui, governor of the Société Générale de Belgique, to the stockholders of that
institution in early 1934. RG 151/44, 28 February 1934.

[122] Some changes included the February 1933 increase in the duty on automobile parts, an
increase in the duty on plywood, and a decrease in the duty on cheddar cheese. On February 12,
1934, import duties were increased slightly, coincident with disappointing tax returns for January,
which were 63 million francs less than for the same month a year before. RG 151/44, 9 March
1934.

[123] On May 16, Jaspar addressed the country by radio, calling for an even tougher commercial
policy that would be more energetic against dumping, would try to organize Belgian producers to
protect their interests, and would reciprocate trade bilaterally. RG 151/44, 22 May 1934.

to preserve trade. There was increasing recognition that the piecemeal policy of protectionism was costly, politically unpopular, and not achieving the desired results. But devaluation would be politically risky as well. As elsewhere on the Continent, the popular mind associated devaluation with inflation. It was a policy of last resort.[124]

In contrast to the devaluation of the pound, it would have been technically feasible in the spring of 1935 to defend the Belgian franc. Indeed, the position of the Banque Nationale was strong. In May 1933 its gold holdings totaled about 13.4 billion francs, compared to about 12 billion francs at the beginning of the year.[125] Gold cover was at a record 69.4 percent and remained that high into 1935. Belgium was "pushed" off gold not by its inability to defend the franc, but by unsustainable price differentials.[126]

By the spring of 1934, holders of capital began to place their bets that the policy of deflation could not succeed. Confidence was on the decline, as expressed in financial institutions' increasingly short-term lending patterns.[127] Confidence was shaken by worse than projected tax takes, despite the government's effort to speed up collection.[128] Signals from semiofficial circles began to point toward the possibility of devaluation. One of the vice governors of the Banque Nationale in April 1934 compared his country's effort to maintain the gold standard to a battle, in which a wise general always had a second line of defense. Many took this to mean that if continued deflation led to spreading strikes in textiles and coal mining, the government would be ready to drop the value of the franc perhaps 15 percent and immediately restabilize at a lower level.[129]

By the summer of 1934 further deflation seemed impossible. As for the budget, the minister of finance and the minister of labor could not even agree on a common position for decreasing the unemployment dole.[130] The appeal to workers to accept further wage reductions and to utility companies to reduce their charges had had practically no result whatsoever.[131] Manufacturers con-

---

[124] Charles Roger, "New Deal for Belgium," *Foreign Affairs*, Vol. 13, No. 4, July 1935, pp. 625–637. On the degree of consensus in Belgium regarding the need to maintain the gold standard through 1934, see H. Van der Wee and K. Tavernier, *La Banque Nationale de Belgique*, p. 255.

[125] RG 151/43, 11 May 1933.

[126] RG 151/44, 26 March 1934; Roger, "New Deal for Belgium," pp. 9–34. The central bank was publicly opposed to any departure from the gold standard, and Belgium had earned a reputation as an outstanding advocate of currency stability. RG 151/44, 3 April 1934. Governor Franck of the Banque Nationale continued to insist, through the spring of 1935, that the central bank had sufficient resources to maintain the franc's gold parity. Van der Wee and Tavernier, *La Banque Nationale de Belgique*, p. 280.

[127] RG 151/44, 3 and 5 April 1934.

[128] RG 151/44, 5 April 1934.

[129] RG 151/44, 24 April 1934.

[130] RG 151/44, 7 May 1934.

[131] RG 151/44, 4 June 1934.

tinued to complain that production costs were too high, and insisted that the deflation program be pushed through rapidly.

By June 1934, many influential Belgians, particularly those near the trading centers such as Antwerp, were voicing support for a switch to inflation.[132] Trade had come to a standstill, and the defense of the gold-based franc was increasingly fingered as the culprit.[133] In July 1934, Charles de Broqueville, Belgium's prime minister, seemed to waver in his insistence on guaranteeing the franc's value before the Chambre.[134] In September 1934, credit policy was eased, allegedly to lower the costs of production, but in effect this signaled the end of deflation.[135] The combination of worsening trade conditions and the possibility that the government might devalue made it more difficult for the government to market its bonds, despite returns of up to 6 percent.[136] The more difficult it became to borrow, the more desperate the government became to protect its creditworthiness. In December 1934, it forbade the circulation of any information that might be harmful to the credit of the state, even if the author of the information did not understand the consequences of releasing such information.[137] Such measures only served to stir up dissent within the cabinet, and within days the government collapsed. An unsuccessful attempt to constitute a new cabinet caused increased exports of capital, and the central bank lost about 400 million franc's worth of gold trying to defend the parity. A new cabinet, under the leadership of Georges Theunis and an American advance of $25 million against gold shipments en route helped to stem the drop in the franc's value. The crisis was averted for the time being by the public confirmation of a large government loan placed in Holland.[138]

Meanwhile, Belgium's effort to deflate was further frustrated by fluctuations in the value of the pound, which depreciated 5.7 percent against the dollar between August 1934 and March 1935.[139] Sterling depreciation shifted selling pressure to the franc and effectively nullified Belgium's effort to deflate. Influential businessmen and economists began openly to speak of devaluation as inevitable, which intensified the run on gold.[140]

---

[132] RG 151/44, 25 June 1934.

[133] RG 151/44, 13 November 1934.

[134] RG 151/44, 2 July 1934.

[135] Van Zeeland, *The Van Zeeland Experiment*, p. 32.

[136] RG 151/44, 13 November 1934.

[137] RG 151/44, 4 December 1934.

[138] RG 151/44, 10 December 1934.

[139] Shepherd, *The Monetary Experience of Belgium*, p. 200.

[140] In September 1934, Professor Fernand Baudhuin of the University of Louvain, on a consulting stint to the Ministry of Finance, suggested that further deflation was useless and that devaluation ought to be considered. Yet his recommendation made no visible impact on the government. Before a meeting of the Catholic party in November, Baudhuin said devaluation was "inevitable" unless Belgium could somehow deflate another 15 percent. The theme was picked up by his colleagues, and soon a prodevaluation "Louvain School" was publishing widely on the need for devaluation.

By the beginning of 1935, discontent over wages, working conditions, and unemployment was so rampant that frightened politicians began to abandon plans for further wage cuts for public employees. In February, the government told parliament that workers' salaries would not be touched, and under threat of a new miners' strike, agreed to a minimum wage for coal miners. When Theunis admitted before the parliament that the "period of deflation was over in Belgium," this added to the capital flight. Losses from the central bank between the beginning of the year and the sixteenth of March totaled more than 4 billion francs' worth of gold.[141] The Theunis government implemented emergency exchange controls, and resigned.

A new government was formed, headed by Paul Van Zeeland of the Catholic party. His "Government of National Renovation" admitted Socialist ministers (who had been excluded under previous governments) according to their representation in parliament.[142] The new government devalued about 28 percent, and stabilized the franc within days.[143] On the British model, an Exchange Equalization Account was established under the control of the Finance Ministry to maintain the stability of the franc at the new rate.[144]

Conclusions on the Policy Mix

Belgium's imperative was to compete in international trade. There can be little doubt that Belgium made a serious effort to deflate domestic prices in order to regain the competitiveness that was lost with the successive devaluations of the pound and the dollar.[145] Wages were reduced some 20 percent, in some cases

---

Then in the late winter of 1935, when the professor publicly termed devaluation "imminent," a run on the reserves of the central bank led within days to losses totaling 2 billion francs worth of gold and foreign currencies. For further comment on the academic critique of deflation, see H. Van der Wee and K. Tavernier, *La Banque Nationale de Belgique*, pp. 269–270.

[141] Fernand Baudhuin, *Dévaluation du Franc Belge* (Brussels: Edition Universelles), 1935, p. 82. There was still plenty of gold in the central bank to defend the franc. Moreover, the Banque de France had offered exchange facilities to help support the franc, but these had been rejected by the Theunis government because they would not have changed the fundamental problem of an overvalued franc for Belgium's trade. Van Zeeland, *The Van Zeeland Experiment*, p. 34; Van der Wee and Tavernier, ibid., p. 278.

[142] The Chamber of Deputies was composed of 79 Catholics, 73 Socialists, 24 Liberals, and 11 extremists of various descriptions. Four of the Socialist ministers held the following portfolios: Justice; Public Works and Unemployment; Labor; and Radio and Transport. One was also admitted without portfolio. Jaspar, the former finance minister and leader of the Right, thought that the new cabinet had "been composed in defiance of good sense." *New York Times*, 28 March 1935.

[143] This rate was made the legal one by 28 May 1936.

[144] The Belgian Exchange Equalization Account did not intervene much on behalf of the franc because it firmed quite readily around the second of April—days after the devaluation.

[145] Even foreign observers agreed that Belgium was doing everything within its power to make internal price adjustments. On the compression of wages, the American commercial attaché wrote: "The situation as it stands is that labor is working under conditions which must necessarily breed

without prolonged industrial strife. Taxes were raised, and the public budget was cut sufficiently to keep the Treasury out of serious trouble.

What eventually drove Belgium to devalue was the realization that it was sacrificing a great deal only to take aim at a moving target—the price of the pound. It would have been technically feasible to defend the franc (the Banque Nationale had sufficient gold to do so), but defending the parity would not solve the fundamental problem of the price disparity. And the problem of the international price disparity would not resolve itself without serious social and economic disruption: as our more general statistical model predicted, strikes to resist further wage compression only stimulated capital flight and added downward pressure to the franc. It was simply futile to go on deflating. Belgium devalued moderately, and stabilized the franc with reasonable haste.

Belgium avoided excessive protection, a result predicted by the model developed in Chapter 6. All efforts to improve exports were taken with the risks of retaliation kept well in mind.[146] After devaluation, Belgian producers avoided overexporting in favor of earning larger profits on the same volume of exported goods.[147] Belgian export and transportation industries could be counted on to oppose any move toward protectionism. And as in Britain, workers' parties opposed tariffs and quotas as taxes on consumption that would raise the cost of living for the working class. When Socialists entered the government coalition, the currency was devalued and trade restrictions relaxed, consonant with the models proposed in previous chapters. A similar mix was selected by the French Socialists, although the continuing political instability prevented France from ever truly stabilizing its franc, as the following section shows.

THE CASE OF FRANCE, 1935–1937

From 1931, and certainly after 1933, France faced a worsening balance of payments position. The balance of payments went into very deep deficit (2.5 percent of Net National Product) in 1932, and improved but remained negative for several years thereafter. Prices in France were some 15 to 20 percent higher than those in Britain, which placed France's traded goods sector under severe external pressure.[148] Despite the expansion in world trade that occurred be-

---

discontent and trouble, while employers and the Government have already gone the limit in aiding labor." RG 151/42, 27 July 1932; 4 August 1932; NA. He also thought that the government had shown "considerable courage and decision" . . . in trying to adjust internally. RG 151/44, 22 May 1934. But while giving the government credit for its courageous efforts to avoid devaluation, the American commercial attaché, for one, thought that circumstances would eventually force the devaluation of the franc. RG 151/44, 30 April 1934.

[146] Van Zeeland, *The Van Zeeland Experiment*, pp. 71–73.

[147] Ibid., pp. 72–74.

[148] See Alfred Sauvy, *Histoire Economique de la France Entre les Deux Guerres*, Vol. 2, 1931–1939 (Paris: Economica), 1967, pp. 400–401 and 508–509. This price differential partly explains

tween 1932 and 1935, French exports fell from 1.5 billion to 1.3 billion francs. During these years, exports were only 66 percent of imports, whereas before the Great War they had been on average 80 to 85 percent of imports.[149]

The first response was trade protection, the second was domestic deflation, and the third was a devaluation negotiated with Britain and the United States. The political power of the French agricultural sector and the relatively low dependence of the French economy on trade made protection seem a low-risk choice. In contrast to Belgium, France had no strong internationalist export sector that could be counted on to defend free trade. Prolonged deflation was possible because of the marginalization of the urban working classes and their representatives from macroeconomic decisionmaking until 1936. In contrast to the United States, labor and agriculture never united behind devaluation and demand stimulation. When devaluation was finally chosen (by a Socialist government), it was dressed up as "international adjustment" whereby both Britain and the United States agreed not to undercut the French franc's depreciation. As in the case of Britain and Belgium, it was not until a working-class party took power that France moved toward devaluation.

The Policy of Deflation

Like the Belgian currency, the French franc was overvalued after the sterling and dollar depreciations, making French exports uncompetitive on world markets. As in Belgium, the solution was to drive down French wages and prices. Every French government from 1932 to June 1936 proposed some combination

---

the widening gap in exports between Britain and France, as the following index figures for exports indicate (1929 = 100):

Year	Britain	France
1929	100	100
1930	81.9	89.5
1931	62.7	76.1
1932	62.9	58.7
1933	64.2	59.7
1934	69.1	59.9

Calculated by M. Filippi, Inspecteur des Finances, Rapport sur "La Crise des Exportations Françaises," 25 June 1935; $F_{12}8793$; AN/P. The overvaluation of the franc also put the tourist industry—traditionally an important part of the French balance of payments—into a coma. In 1935 tourist expenditures in France were estimated at only about 750 million francs, compared to 8 billion annually between 1926 and 1931 and 2.5 billion in 1934. Institut Scientifique de Recherches Economique et Sociales, L'Evolution de l'Economie Française, 1910–1937 (Paris: Recueil Sirey), 1937, table 19.

[149] "Rémarque sur la balance des comptes de la France," 29 November 1932; B32.318; MF/P. Of the French deficit over 1924–1932, sixty-nine percent was with the United States.

of higher taxes, lower government expenditures, and lower wages. The lesson of the Poincaré years was that the financial health of the country depended on a large gold reserve, a stable franc, and balanced budgets. Budget deficits were the prime suspect in causing franc instability in the twenties.[150] Fiscal equilibrium was thought to be the only way to prevent franc instability, as the balance of payments deteriorated in 1932.

In contrast to both Britain and Belgium, France made little headway in budget balancing from 1932 to 1933. The instability that followed the success of the moderate Left in the 1932 election was reminiscent of the Cartel of the twenties: the fiscally conservative Radical Socialists needed the Socialists (who opposed deflation) to form a government majority, but, as in 1924, this support was withheld more often than it was given.[151] As in the twenties, the result was extreme cabinet instability (table 7.5). During 1933, governments had to resort to provisional monthly budgets five separate times, and in 1933, the public debt rose from 291 to 302 billion francs—the first important increase since 1928.[152]

One of the first efforts to cut government expenses was taken by the Herriot government in September 1932. The Radical Socialists presided over a significant involuntary conversion of the public debt to lower rates of interest (from 6–7 percent to 4.5 percent), which saved the government some billion and a half francs. Bondholders were furious. Herriot's expenditure cuts foundered in the Chambre when they ran aground of powerful groups such as veterans organizations, civil servants, and agriculture.[153] The government was defeated in December when it proposed to pay the upcoming installment of the war debt to the United States at a time when it had very little political capital in the bank.[154] The ministries that followed proposed a series of more or less drastic plans to balance the budget, only to have austerity measures repeatedly thrown out by the Chambre.

The events of early 1934 put an end to the indecision—and nearly to parliamentary government itself. In February, violent street riots broke out in Paris,

[150] Kenneth Mouré, *Managing the Franc Poincaré*, (Cambridge: Cambridge University Press), 1991.

[151] The Radical Socialists actually were quite eclectic in their economic policies. While the party frequently inveighed against large-scale industry, "money powers," "trusts," and large-scale capital, it generally had very little experience in fiscal matters. To compensate, Herriot appointed the extremely orthodox Louis Germain-Martin as minister of finance in 1932. But between 1932 and 1934, there was almost complete unanimity within the party on the primacy of a balanced budget. Peter J. Larmour, *The French Radical Party in the 1930s* (Stanford: Stanford University Press), 1964, pp. 71–75.

[152] Martin Wolfe, *The French Franc Between the Wars, 1919–1939* (New York: Columbia University Press), 1951, pp. 106–8.

[153] Alain Prate, *La France et sa Monnaie: Essai sur les Relations entre la Banque de France et les Gouvernements* (Paris: Julliard), 1987, p. 124.

[154] Maurice Baumont, *La Faillité de la Paix, 1918–1939* (Paris: Presses Universitaires de France), 1946, pp. 469–470.

TABLE 7.5
Government Heads and Ministers of Finance in France,
June 1932–June 1936

Government Head	Took Office	Minister of Finance
Herriot	4 June 1932	Germain-Martin
Paul-Boncour	18 December 1932	Chéron
Daladier	31 January 1933	Georges Bonnet
Sarraut	26 October 1933	Georges Bonnet
Chautemps	26 November 1933	Georges Bonnet
Daladier	30 January 1934	Piétri
Doumergue	9 February 1934	Germain-Martin
Flandin	9 November 1935	—
Bouisson	1 June 1935	—
Laval	7 June 1935	Régnier
Sarraut	24 January 1936	—

involving discontented masses as well as political extremists. The riot reflected general dissatisfaction with the political corruption, indecision, and ineffectiveness of the preceding three years.[155] Within days, the Confédération Générale du Travail called for a general strike to protest the growing threat from the Right.[156] Capital fled: during the week ending February 9 alone the reserves of the Banque de France fell by 2 billion francs.[157] The parliament was galvanized under the social and political tensions of February 1934 to allow a "Cabinet of National Union" under Gaston Doumergue to press through a series of deflationary measures.[158] A balanced budget was seen as the only way to reestablish confidence in politically turbulent times, and this reform was presented as being critical to supporting the franc. Doumergue was granted the right to rule by decree, and he began by cutting the salaries of all government employees by 10 percent, with the more highly paid employees levied an additional 10 to 15 percent. Government pensions were cut 3 percent, and 30,000 *fonctionnaires* were to be discharged from government payrolls. Doumergue insisted that his program be passed en bloc, which avoided the drawn-out conflict of the previous year.

[155] The *New York Times* reported that the riots could be traced to bitterness over taxes, economic stress, parliamentary wrangling, policy toward Germany, and graft in high places. *New York Times*, 7 February 1934, p. 2, col. 8. Reportedly, 10 were killed and 500 were injured. Ibid., p. 1, col. 8. Rioting groups included the right-wing quasi-military group, the Croix de Feu, the National Union of Veterans, Fascists, Royalists, university students, and Communists. Ibid., p. 2, col. 5.

[156] The general strike was held on February 13, and some 75 percent of all workers were reported out and 600 were arrested. *New York Times*, 14 February 1934.

[157] *Le Temps Financier*, 19 February 1934.

[158] The Socialists were invited to join the cabinet, but refused because they continued to be opposed to the policy of deflation. *New York Times*, 9 February 1934, p. 1, col. 4.

Still, expenditures outstripped taxes in both 1933 and 1934. The costs for public debt service, national defense, and unemployment assistance proved resistant to compression. Meanwhile, the Trèsor's new bond issues could barely keep pace with those falling due. When Doumergue's power to rule by degree expired, he threatened to dissolve the Chambre des Députies without the consent of the Sénat. Amid cries of "dictatorship," his government fell and another led by P. E. Flandin took over.

The economy was given the barest of reprieves from deflation under the Flandin government. Moved perhaps by the demonstrations of public employee unions and the Left's campaign against Doumergue's "Famine Plan," Flandin promised that he would not permit a devaluation, and that he would continue to work for budget equilibrium, but that there would be no further cuts in governmental expenditures.[159] He would borrow. This prompted a sharp protest of "reflation" from the Banque de France, which felt the emphasis must continue to be placed on budget cuts. Indeed, the Banque argued that the only way to ease the money market was to tighten up fiscal policy.

A number of things transpired over the course of 1935 to complicate the policy of deflation. Belgium's departure from its gold parity in March 1935 stimulated speculation that the French franc would be the next domino to fall. Adding to the unsettled conditions were the successes of the Communist party in several municipal elections. Capital flight ensued. During the third week of May the gold reserve of the Banque de France fell by some 3.5 billion francs.[160] In June, the Flandin government fell. Another attempt at forming a government was made by Fernand Bouisson, but this government lasted only seven days, and within a week Pierre Laval became Président du Conseil.

Laval's administration gave deflationary policies a new lease on life. He asked for and got the cooperation of the Banque de France and the parliament, which handed him power to rule by decree for about four months, during which time 549 "decree-laws" were enacted that touched every sector of the French government and economy. Every wage under government control, all administrative budgets (except those relating to national security and unemployment), the price of bread, utilities and rents (public and private), even interest payments on government bonds were all reduced 10 percent. A second and third round of economies took place in August and October. Despite these efforts, expenditures were reduced by only 5 billion francs from 1933 levels, and were still 6 billion francs higher than in 1928. The Trèsor turned increasingly to the money market, where uneasiness over the fiscal situation drove up medium- and long-term interest rates. Discount rates at the Banque de France had been

---

[159] He also took action to cartelize the textile industry to reduce costs, cut the government wheat subsidy, and raised the compulsory education age to 14 to reduce unemployment, all of which were still consistent with a policy of deflation. Wolfe, *The French Franc*, p. 113.

[160] Conseil Générale, Séance Extraordinaire, 25 May 1935, Banque de France Archives, Paris.

pushed up to stem the gold outflow in the wake of the Belgian devaluation, making borrowing more and more difficult.

Working class parties consistently opposed deflation, and withheld their parliamentary support.[161] The Socialists campaigned vigorously against the obsession with budget balancing and proposed that the government take the more positive role of stimulating economic demand.[162] Their platform was anything but deflationary: they called for the restoration of purchasing power as a response to the deflationary policies of all governments since Doumergue's. They demanded a repeal of Laval's decree laws and asked for a reduction in the workweek to forty hours without a corresponding reduction in wages. They also wanted national unemployment insurance and an extensive program of public works.[163] Union leaders were also opposed to deflation. Léon Jouhaux, secretary of the Confédération Générale du Travail, denounced the policy of deflation at that organization's annual meeting in September 1935.[164] Reflationists existed, but prior to June 1936 they were not at the wheel of fiscal and monetary policymaking authority.

By the end of 1935, it was evident that deflation was not succeeding. The financial distress of the Trèsor was such that the Banque de France changed its long-standing policy and agreed to discount treasury bonds in unlimited quantities, which the government sold to private banks and the Caisse des Dépôts et Consignations. In this way, 13.8 billion francs were eventually raised, or about three quarters of the value of all bonds outstanding when the Socialists took over in 1936. With the 1936 elections on the horizon and the far Left predicted to make large gains, further fiscal and monetary measures were postponed. If devaluation were to take place, it became increasingly likely to occur under a Socialist government.

As expected, the first act of the Socialist government was to bury the policy of deflation: it required employers to sign the Matignon Agreement, which

---

[161] The Socialists had broken with the Radicals in 1933 when the latter had tried to economize by firing government employees. *Le Populaire*, 28 January 1933. It should be noted that the Socialist party was offered cabinet participation during most of the years of the deflationary policy, but declined that participation. The Socialist party had a fairly strong constituency among "fonctionnaires," making it politically impossible for it to support economies involving layoffs. Nathaniel Greene, *From Versailles to Vichy, The Third French Republic, 1919–1940* (New York: Thomas Y. Crowell), 1970, p. 65; D. W. Brogan, *France Under the Republic: The Development of Modern France, 1870–1939* (New York: Harper & Brothers), 1940, p. 651. According to Brogan, "[T]he Socialists were the party of the *fonctionnaires* just as much as the Radicals were the party of the small businessman and the Communists of the proletariat." Ibid., p. 651.

[162] Blum said it was necessary to "breath life into the economic organism hurt by the depression and bled by deflation." Joel Colton, *Léon Blum: Humanist in Politics* (Cambridge: MIT Press), 1974, p. 124.

[163] Ibid., p. 112.

[164] Herbert Burton, "France and the Depression," *Economic Record*, Vol. 12, No. 22, 1936, p. 24.

guaranteed higher wages, a three-week annual holiday with pay, and the forty-hour workweek. Devaluation was now more than likely; it was inevitable.

Commercial Policy

France was unabashedly protectionist in the 1930s. The average level of the tariff index was not much different from those of Britain and the United States for the interwar years as a whole, but in France extreme reliance was placed on import quotas rather than customs duties—a choice shaped by previous tariff agreements. Quotas were originally designed as temporary measures meant to protect a select group of national producers against what was thought to be a brief period of falling prices.[165] In the early to mid thirties, however, they became a fairly permanent fixture of French commercial policy that could be used to compartmentalize trade by sector and by trading partner.[166]

Thanks to France's large but inefficient agricultural sector, a system of primary produce quotas was inaugurated in 1931. For the interwar years as a whole, agriculture made a much larger contribution to France's Net National Product (22 percent) than was the case for most other Western European countries.[167] Throughout the thirties, French agriculture enjoyed almost complete insulation from external competition. Figure 7.6, based on internal Ministère du Commerce calculations, shows how protection for agricultural goods increased during the first half of the thirties. From 1931 to 1936, government policy was aimed explicitly at preserving the domestic equilibrium in the supply and demand of agricultural products by the systematic exclusion of all or nearly all foreign agricultural products.[168] The cumulative effect of these policies was to spare French agriculture the worst of the price declines suffered by the rest of the world's primary producers: prices of agricultural goods in France

[165] Haight, *A History of French Commercial Policy*, pp. 141–147.

[166] A report of the Conseil Nationale Economique in 1930 expressed this stance quite clearly. Rather than a regime of free trade, the CNE advocated a commercial policy that would direct business toward countries with which France had negotiated special trade agreements. France's goal should be to establish a system of "reciprocal and rigorous loyalty and clarity in tariff protection." Questionnaire Rélatif à une Actione Economique Concertée Transmis au Gouvernement Français par la Société des Nations; Rapport du Conseil Nationale Economique, 26 August 1930; $F_{12}8802$; AN/P. For an official justification of this policy, see Rapport Présenté par M. Boissard, Inspecteur des Finances, sur "Les Echanges Internationaux et la Politique Douanière Française au Cours de la Crise Economique", November 1930, $F_{12}8802$; AN/P.

[167] The corresponding figure for the United Kingdom was 4 percent; the Netherlands, 7 percent; Switzerland, 12 percent; Norway, 14 percent; Germany, 15 percent; and Denmark, 17 percent. B. R. Mitchell, *European Historical Statistics, 1750–1970* (London: Macmillan), 1975.

[168] A. Tardieu, Ministre d'Agriculture, Direction de l'Agriculture, Office de Renseignments Agricoles, No. 5.462/0, 4 November 1931, $F_{12}8794$; AN/P. See also Burton, "France and the Depression," p. 19.

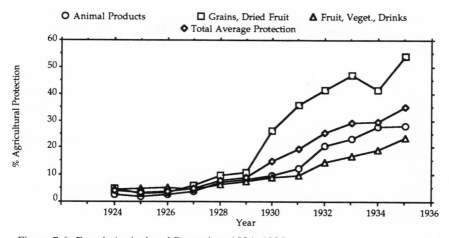

Figure 7.6: French Agricultural Protection, 1924–1935
Source: "Statistiques Indiquant le Pourcentage des Produits Agricoles, de 1924 à 1935" (unattributed), F_{12} 8794; AN/P.

fell only 14 percent from 1931to 1932, while prices of industrial goods fell by 19 percent.[169]

If agriculture received the bulk of the protection, industry was not neglected. By early 1933, quotas covered more than 1,200 goods, or about one sixth of all classes of goods and one third of the total value of imports. These restrictions covered goods that accounted for about one third of the value of imports into France, including many food and beverage items, forest products, iron products, leather, furniture, some textiles, certain machines, and glassware. In addition, in 1933 France extended quantitative controls over some thirty new industrial products imported from Germany, after the Germans had abrogated the tariff structure on agricultural products that had been established in the Franco-German agreement of 1927.[170] Thus, by the opening of the World Economic Conference in London in spring 1933, France had erected a highly complicated protectionist structure covering agricultural and manufactured articles.

It can hardly be surprising that France was unenthusiastic about the Roosevelt administration's proposed "tariff truce" for the duration of the London conference. In the absence of American and British commitments to stabilize their currencies, France opposed any commitment to freeze its commercial

[169] "Production et Commerce: La Valeur de la Production Agricole Française," 25 January 1934, F_{12}8794; AN/P.
[170] League of Nations, *World Economic Survey, 1932–33* (Geneva: League of Nations), Economic Intelligence Service, 1933, p. 202.

policy.[171] Moreover, agricultural associations were exerting the utmost political pressure to preserve the protective mantel to which they had grown accus-
tomed since 1930. Piqued that it had not been explicitly represented on the
delegation to the conference, the Confédération Nationale des Associations
Agricoles met in April 1933 to reinforce its demand that its protection not be
bargained away at the World Economic Conference.[172] In late May, local
Chambres d'Agricoles overwhelmingly voted resolutions demanding reinforced tariff protection, rejecting the American tariff truce, renouncing agreements on agricultural products, and calling for the maintenance of quotas. Their
petitions flooded the Ministry of Commerce, claiming that to reduce protection
would cause the ruin of agriculture and endanger French rural society as a
whole.[173]

The French delegation to the London conference was anxious to avoid the
whole issue of trade liberalization. First, it tried to keep commercial policy out
of the multilateral forum altogether, preferring to negotiate trade agreements
bilaterally or regionally.[174] Second, France took the position that monetary
stabilization (still quite a ways off) would have to precede significant trade
liberalization.[175] Third, France raised tariffs in anticipation that they might
have to be negotiated away.[176] When the conference failed, France tried to

[171] France submitted a list of reservations to the proposed tariff truce, including new conditions
created by devaluation of the dollar, seasonally justified agricultural quotas, and taxes of a fiscal
character. Le Ministre des Affaires Etrangères à le Ministre des Finances, 21 April 1933, B32.321;
MF/P.

[172] "Les Agriculteurs et la Conférénce Mondiale de Londres," Confédération Nationale des
Associations Agricoles, 12 April 1933, B32.317; MF/P. See also a letter from the CNAA calling
for resistance to any concessions at all to American agriculture, and demanding that no agricultural
goods be sold in France at less than the prevailing national prices. 13 April 1933, B32.317; MF/P.
For a strong plea for the maintenance of import quotas, see CNAA, "Observations Presentées au
Nom de L'Agriculture Française au Gouvernement et à M. le Président Herriot," 12 April 1933,
B32.317; MF/P.

[173] See the series of resolutions and questionnaires turned in by various locai French chambers of
agriculture, B 32.321; MF/P.

[174] Record of a telephone conversation with Charles Rist, 9 January 1933, B32.317; MF/P.

[175] "Note des Experts à la Commission Préparatoire de la Conférence Economique Mondiale sur
la Deuxième Session de la Commission," 9 to 20 January, 1933, B32.317; MF/P; "Stabilisation des
Monnaies," 12 May 1933, B32.320; MF/P. The French were also convaincu that it would be
useless to convene the World Economic Conference at all as long as the dollar and pound were not
stabilized. See "Projet Américan de Fonds de Stabilisation Tripartite," 12 Mai 1933, B32.318;
MF/P; and Ministre des Affaires Etrangères à Ministre des Finances, 24 April 1933, B32.320;
MF/P. There was also parliamentary pressure not to participate in the World Economic Conference
unless the dollar and pound were definitively stabilized. See speech of Pierre-Etienne Flandin,
Journel Officiel, Vol. 17, 1933, p. 2488.

[176] "Compte-rendu de la 2ème séance de la Commission Interministérielle chargée de Préciser la
position de la France à l'égard des questions inscrites au programme de la Conférence Economique

solidify the Gold Bloc through offers of trade liberalization, but bloc preferences were difficult to negotiate, and often boiled down to very little.[177] After 1935, the Ministère des Finances tried with modest success to reorient Gold Bloc protection away from quotas and toward less restrictive tariff duties.[178] Overall, France chose both to deflate and to protect domestic producers through tariffs, though this policy mix proved insufficient by early 1936.

A few weeks after devaluation, Léon Blum's Socialist government suspended quota restrictions on about 100 industrial articles and reduced customs by 15 to 20 percent on goods that were not subject to quotas. License taxes were lowered by about 20 percent for agricultural goods. The decree also provided for the creation of a Commission de Révision Douanière, which was charged with making up a new tariff schedule with an eye to disassembling the welter of quotas. The Blum government also agreed with the British that a study be conducted by Paul Van Zeeland, prime minister of Belgium, about undertaking an "inquiry into the possibility of obtaining a general reduction of quotas and other obstacles to international trade."[179] Whether it is attributable directly to the policies of the Blum government or to the release of pressure afforded by devaluation, the tariff index did dip significantly in 1936 and 1937.[180]

International Negotiations and the Decision to Devalue

One of the most remarkable aspects of the decision to devalue the French franc in October 1936 was that it had been delayed so long. In France, much more so than in Britain or Belgium, a fanatical importance was attached to maintaining the value of the franc Poincaré.[181] Opposition developed to deflation, but no

---

Mondiale," 8 April 1933, B32.317; MF/P; "Commission Economique pour la Preparation de la Conférence Mondiale," 8 April 1933, B32.317; MF/P.

[177] Chambre de Commerce de Marseilles, "Conclusion entre les pays ayant conservé l'etalon-or de Traités basis sur les principes d'Ouchy," 12 July 1934, B32.323; MF/P; "Compte-rendu de la Commission Réunis à la Direction des Accords Commerciaux le 29 Septembre 1934," B32.323; MF/P. The effort to improve trade within the Gold Bloc was supported by French trade organizations such as the Chambre de Commerce de Paris. "Examen des Mesures Economiques envisagés par les Pays du Bloc-Or à la Suite de la Conférence de Bruxelles," 16 January 1935, B32.323; MF/P.

[178] "Note sur un Projet de Politique du Bloc-Or," 12 March 1935, B23.323; MF/P.

[179] Haight, A History of French Commercial Policy, pp. 181–183.

[180] Some of these protective measures were restored in late 1937, when France's balance of payments troubles were renewed. After the devaluation of the franc, France raised certain quota restrictions, but in view of the continuing strain on the franc and the continuing unfavorable balance of trade, in 1937 it raised tariffs to the previous levels. In April 1938 France restricted the quota on coal imports. League of Nations, World Economic Survey, 1937–38 (Geneva: League of Nations, Economic Intelligence Service), 1938, p. 166–167.

[181] This is a major theme of Kenneth Mouré, Managing the Franc Poincaré.

group or party proposed devaluation as an alternative. Only isolated individuals—
and they could be counted on the fingers of one hand—thought that devaluation
of the franc was a viable and necessary policy option.[182]

France deflated and protected to try to maintain the gold-based franc. It also
tried to avoid devaluation by influencing the price and monetary policies of
Britain and the United States. In 1933, France backed a plan for coordinated
reflation, but differed significantly from Britain and the United States on how
this might be accomplished. France rejected the "monetary methods" of America's devaluation and Britain's policy of cheap money[183] and advocated a policy
of coordinated production (supply manipulation) to raise world prices.[184] If
world prices rose, France's deflation could be much less drastic.[185]

A second, less ambitious approach to international price coordination was
for France to secure agreement from Britain and the United States that the franc
would not be put under further pressure by further devaluation of the currencies
of those countries.[186] In February 1935, the French prime minister himself went
to London to try and gain assurances of the pound's stabilization. These were
not forthcoming.[187] Failing in their direct attempt to secure stabilization of the

[182] The only person on the moderate Left who recommended devaluation of the franc for most of
the mid thirties was Raymond Patenôtre, the under secretary of the economy. By 1935 Socialists
Paul Reynaud and Marcel Déat also advocated devaluation. *Journel Officiel Débats* (Chambre),
1935, pp. 2240–2243. Despite their opposition to deflation, neither the Socialists nor the Communists favored devaluation.

[183] Two things stood in the way of a cheap money policy in France, according to French officials:
first, it would permit excessive Treasury flotations and undercut efforts to balance the budget; and
second, it would shake confidence and induce hoarding. "Note sur la Situation de la France à la
Conférence Economique Mondiale," 1 March 1933, B32.317; MF/P. The French thought that the
threat of monetary instability undercut the confidence necessary to make medium- or long-term
investment. Memo, "Position Française à la Conférence de Londres (Questions monétaires et
financières)," 8 June 1933, B32.319; MF/P. For the French critique of the British position on gold
distribution, see "Note sur les Thèses Britanniques dans l'Ordre Monétaire," 8 June 1933,
B32.319; MF/P.

[184] Note from the French ambassador in Washington to the Ministère des Affaires Etrangères, 27
February 1933; MF/P.

[185] Speech of Pierre-Etienne Flandin, *Journel Officiel*, Vol. 17, 1933, p. 2488.

[186] Memo, unattributed, 27 February 1933, B32.317; MF/P; L'Attaché Financier à l'Ambassade
de France, Londres, à Monsieur le Ministre des Finances, 24 May 1933, B32.319; MF/P.

[187] Sir Frederick Leith-Ross, chief economic adviser to the British government, responded that
the pound's weakness was due to a decline in British exports to the Continent, which in turn was due
to the Gold Bloc's defensive trade policies. Under the circumstances, he told the French prime
minister, the British government had no desire to commit sterling to a particular value. With the fate
of the franc uncertain, and with the power to raise or lower the gold content of the U.S. dollar in the
hands of an unpredictable American president, the British position on stabilization was to wait for
some definitive development before making a commitment. Even international consultations were
discouraged throughout 1935 and the first half of 1936. By March 1935 some in the British
Treasury, including Sir Ronald Lindsay (British ambassador to Washington) and Leith-Ross (chief
economic adviser to the British government), began to feel that perhaps the British policy was a

pound, the French next sought American support for this goal. In the spring of 1935, the Banque de France approached American authorities in the hopes of arranging a joint loan to Britain to stabilize the pound. Henry Morgenthau, the U.S. secretary of the treasury, was opposed to this plan,[188] but he did stave off the effects of a panic sale of francs when the French government fell by agreeing to make available through earmark $150 million of its gold in Paris.[189]

French opinion still resisted the idea of devaluation. Although prices were higher in France than in Britain, they were not "absolutely incompressible". If the currency were to be devalued, on the other hand, the devaluation was expected to be followed by an immediate rise in the cost of living and increasing salaries. Any minimal export gain to be had was expected to be annulled immediately by increases in foreign protection. There was also the hope that world prices would rise sufficiently to ease the problem of deflating at home.[190] All of these arguments were summoned by decisionmakers, who were firmly convinced that the French public opposed devaluation, and hence that devaluation was politically infeasible.

Over the course of 1935 and early 1936, the permanent Treasury staff were reported to be increasingly receptive to the idea of devaluation: any stimulus to business activity would increase revenue from taxation and encourage the dishoarding of gold and currency and the repatriation of capital, while the profits of devaluation could be used to relieve the Treasury's position, which

---

little too standoffish. These officers suggested that the British and American stabilization funds at least exchange information on their operations so as not to work at cross-purposes. There was talk on this idea in the American embassy in London, but Chamberlain (then chancellor of the exchequer) remained unconvinced and scotched such ideas in May 1935. See S.V.O. Clarke, "Exchange-Rate Stabilization in the Mid-1930s: Negotiating the Tripartite Agreement," Princeton Studies in International Finance, No. 41 (Princeton: International Finance Section, Department of Economics, Princeton University, 1977), pp. 19–21.

[188] Henry Morgenthau thought this idea futile: the British had not requested such a loan, and probably would not accept it. J. E. Crane (deputy governor, FRBNY), notes on a conversation with Charles Cariguel (director of the Foreign Department, Bank of France), George Harrison, and Harrison's conversation with Morgenthau, 6 March 1935, File 2012.5, Harrison Papers, Federal Reserve Bank of New York [hereinafter, HP, FRBNY]. According to Crane's notes, the French also thought it likely that the British would refuse this loan, but thought that at least this would place the responsibility for continuing disequilibrium squarely on Britain, "where it belonged." See also Crane notes, 12 March 1935, File 20215.5, HP, FRBNY.

[189] However, Harrison and others at the FRBNY thought that some program for stabilization should be prepared. He tried to persuade Morgenthau that the United States ought to be considering steps to secure greater exchange stability. "The Secretary said that the President and he were definitely determined not to approach the British or to take any initiative. [Harrison] took the position that we might find out what the plans of the British are or whether there was anything we could do in conjunction with them." Harrison's notes on a conversation with Morgenthau, 9 March 1935, File 20215.5, HP, FRBNY.

[190] Emmanuel Monick to the Ministre des Finances, 8 June 1935, B32.325; MF/P.

had by this time become desperate.[191] By the spring of 1935, foreign observers viewed a devaluation of the franc as inevitable.[192]

But it was not until 1936 that the urgency to adjust the value of the franc was really apparent. France's gold reserves were dwindling rapidly, so that by the time the Front Populaire came to power, some 30 billion francs' worth of gold had already left the country.[193] Domestic political unrest and crippling strikes had erupted.[194] The threat of German rearmament had recrudesced. The Blum government thought it might be able to blunt domestic criticism if it could embed the franc's devaluation in a multilateral agreement of broader scope. To save face, Vincent Auriol, France's Socialist minister of finance, proposed a multilateral agreement that would revalue and stabilize currencies in accordance with world prices. This would avoid singling out the franc for devaluation and would legitimize the move through an international agreement.[195] Negotiations began with Britain and the United States in June of 1936. The three major powers agreed that a devaluation of 25–30 percent was to be expected.[196] After twelve conservative governments had tried to engineer four years of more or less stringent deflation, which had led to recurrent episodes of bloody street riots and three months of widespread strikes, the franc Poincaré was finally devalued one third by a Socialist coalition on 25 October 1936.

[191] Memo, "The French Franc," 11 February 1936, File 260, FRBNY. *The Economist*, 8 February 1936, p. 308; 22 February 1936, p. 416. A loan for £40 million (the equivalent of approximately 3 billion francs) was floated in London at 3 percent interest—a rate much lower than could be found in the extremely tight Paris money market in 1935–36. For a very good analysis of the French financial position and how it was perceived to be related to the prospects for devaluation, see memo, "Discussion on a Devaluation of the Franc," 21 March 1936, File 260, FRBNY.

[192] The British financial press had virtually accused France of having left the gold standard, because the tangle of fragmented expedients implemented to prevent devaluation had practically shut down the operation of the gold standard mechanism. Views from Britain were transmitted from the French ambassador to the Ministre des Affaires Etrangères, 6 June 1935, B32.324; MF/P.

[193] Kindleberger, *The World in Depression*, p. 252.

[194] Partial strikes were under way in nearly every industry by late May, and by June had spread to the building trades, transportation, coal mines, textiles, and services (especially hotels). *New York Times*, 4 June 1936, p. 1, col. 4. By one estimate, 95 percent of metallurgy factories were occupied by strikers in early June. Philippe Bourdrel, *Le Mur de l'argent: Les gouvernement de gauche face au capital* (Paris: Editions Noël), 1985, p. 105.

[195] S.V.O. Clarke, "Exchange-Rate Stabilization," p. 25.

[196] Morgenthau was outnumbered in his proposal that the devaluation should be limited to 15 percent. Harrison emphasized that the British should have guaranteed access to U.S. gold in exchange for U.S. dollars in order to facilitate the stabilization of the pound. The group was clear that the least desired outcome would be a French embargo on gold without devaluation. Harrison memo of a conversation with Morgenthau, 4 June 1936; notes on a meeting at Morgenthau's home, 9 June 1936, File 2012.06, HP, FRBNY. Over the summer, the general outlines of a stabilization agreement were hammered out in secret between the Treasuries of France, Britain, and the United States. Various French proposals for a fairly rigid exchange rate regime were set aside by the Anglo-Americans. The French had wanted the three governments to agree to specified fixed margins within which their exchange rates would fluctuate. Such an explicit commitment was adamantly opposed by the British. The French had proposed aligning currencies according to some combina-

Conclusions: The French Policy Mix

Deflation was a disaster in France. Until June of 1936, a series of governments had tried with more or less commitment to engineer a policy for which the social consensus simply did not exist. French politics were too polarized and too unstable to support a policy of wage reductions and reduced government expenditures. Yet the fanatical commitment to the franc Poincaré prevented an objective assessment of the chances of success for such a policy. Almost no one advocated devaluation, yet the polity could not sustain deflation. The policy limped along for as long as it did because of the commitment of the Radicals to the interests of the rentier.[197] These creditors had a strong institutional base of support in the Banque de France and the financial community. The financial press also campaigned for a balanced budget and maintenance of the gold standard.[198] But, emphatically, these forces did not command the social unity necessary to compress consumption. The far Left (the Socialists and Communists) would not implicate themselves in supporting deflation. They championed the cause of public employees, whose positions and salaries were threatened by budget cuts, and workers, who demanded minimum wages and a maximum workweek. Under these conditions, there was very little progress toward budget equilibrium or wage compression. In addition to industrial strife, French political life was increasingly polarized between Communists and Fascists who took their bloody rivalry to the streets. In accordance with the findings in Chapter 3, social unrest and political instability spurred liquid capital increasingly to seek safe haven in Britain and the United States.

One reason France could limp along without significant deflation and with an overvalued currency was that the French economy was so much more insulated from the world economy than that of Britain and certainly Belgium. Protection

tion of world prices, with the view to eventually returning to the gold standard. Roosevelt, not wishing to be associated too closely with the gold standard (an idea itself too closely associated with the "New York banking crowd"), scratched out both of these ideas and replaced them with references to improved living standards. Finally, the French had wanted all three governments to sign a single declaration, but even this posed problems for Britain and the United States, both of which wished to retain maximum flexibility. Memo, Harrison conversation with Morgenthau, 24 September 1936, File 2012.6, HP, FRBNY.

[197] "French politicians between 1933 and 1936 were more concerned with protecting the purchasing power of their constituents' investments than with correcting the strangulating effect of the overvalued franc." Wolfe, *The French Franc*, p. 134. See also Herbert Burton, "France and the Depression," pp. 15–27, especially p. 24.

[198] Typical were the words of *Le Temps Financier*, 24 April 1933: "France . . . will maintain the gold standard. In the midst of universal upheaval she will cling to the solid ground offered by monetary order and her money will show other nations the sole road to follow and the sole goal to aim at in order for the world to recover normal activity and future security with sane currencies."

supported the Radical Socialists' half-baked deflation as much as it did their primary constituents in agrarian France.[199] During the Radicals' tenure, import quotas shifted from temporary expedients to quasi-permanent trade barriers. When the Front Populaire came to power, this edifice of protection was given critical review. As was the case for the Labour party in Britain and the Socialists in Belgium, Léon Blum's government was actually much more in favor of free trade than the conservatives and moderate Left, which had presided over the tariff buildup of the early thirties. Protection was reduced significantly in 1937, providing historical, contextual corroboration to the statistical findings of Chapter 6.

Fundamentally, however, France could afford to be protectionist because she was relatively self-sufficient.[200] With an economy much less open than that of Belgium or even Britain, protecting domestic producers from foreign competition was a relatively low-risk strategy for France. It was also the strategy that best preserved the illusion that the franc Poincaré could outlast the French people's patience with deflation.

CONCLUSIONS

Britain, Belgium, and France all experienced deteriorating balance of payments positions under depressionary economic conditions. All three countries tried to deflate their economies in order to improve their competitive position and defend the value of their national currency. All three eventually failed. Devaluation is neither the beginning nor the end of the story, however. It is only one aspect of the policy mix and one element in a sequence of efforts to adjust the domestic economy to achieve external equilibrium. The mix differed among these countries in ways that were broadly consistent with the aggregate data analyzed in Chapters 3 through 6.

---

[199] The agricultural sector—along with small traders—was the backbone of the Radical Socialists' political support. "The Radicals represented rural provincial France. . . . By the 1930s, [they] had ceased appealing to the working classes." Larmour, *The French Radical Party*, pp. 18–19. This preoccupation with agriculture is reflected in "Production et Commerce: La Valeur de la Production Agricole Française," 25 January 1934, $F_{12}8794$; AN/P. In this document, the author argued that the structure of the French economy was essentially agricultural, and that many more people were employed in agriculture in France than in Britain or the United States. He also argued that the position of agriculture was much more predominate after the war than before, although the franc statistics used may be inflated because they are neither a real value nor a percentage of national production.

[200] The CNE noted that France was both industrial and agricultural, and was "the country which would suffer the least if forced to make it on its own." Questionnaire Rélatif à une Actione Economique Concertée Transmis au Gouvernement Français par la Société des Nations, Report of the Conseil Nationale Economique, 26 August 1930, $F_{12}8802$; AN/P.

Deflation

Deflation requires price and wage reductions that are very difficult to achieve in the presence of domestic political conflict or a left-wing government that is committed to easing the hardships associated with wage cuts and unemployment. These cases flesh out the findings of the previous chapters that left-wing governments, labor unrest, and cabinet instability are associated with deterioration in the current account and with capital flight. In Britain, the Labour party's decision in 1930 to expand unemployment benefits became the issue on which capital delivered the Labour government a vote of no confidence. In France, the Blum government's first act was to defy deflation by pushing though the Matignon accords, which immediately lifted wages and cut working hours. In Belgium, deflation was pursued over Socialist opposition, and ended when the Socialists were brought into the Van Zeeland cabinet. In all three cases, deflation was opposed by the Left and, in the case of France and Belgium, was abandoned when the Left assumed a greater voice in governance. Even in Britain, an important wing of the Labour party opposed deflation, causing a cabinet and party crisis that opened the way for a Conservative electoral victory and policy domination after September 1931.

These cases highlight the problem of credibility of a deflationary policy for a left-wing government, a result that did not prove to be statistically significant in our model of capital flight but did show up in the current account balance and the eventual decision to devalue/depreciate. Britain's Labour government met with capital flight even when the budgets were balanced and despite the fact that Snowden's budgets were more deflationary than Churchill's had been. In France, capital was exported when the Communists won ground in local elections in 1935 and exited en masse when it became evident that the Front Populaire would win the 1936 election. Despite the fact that the French Socialist/Communist coalition government pledged its opposition to devaluation, markets anticipated the inflationary effect of the Front's social policy, and acted accordingly.

Labor and social unrest was a most serious problem in France, and somewhat less so in Britain. Labor unrest signals resistance to wage reductions to the market. In Belgium, there were pockets of resistance to lower wages, but in numerous instances wage reductions were achieved without prolonged social strife, which contributed to a nominal wage compression of some 20 percent. In Britain, the general strike of 1926 had led to huge capital outflows, even though workers were soundly defeated. Strikes were far fewer in the crisis period, but the symbolism surrounding the Royal Navy "mutiny" served to undermine confidence and complicate the defense of the pound. Serious social unrest racked the French polity, most violently during the street riots of February 1934, and culminated in widespread strikes in the industrial and service sectors in the spring of 1936. Resistance to wage reductions undermined the policy of deflation and helped to destabilize the franc. As Chapter 3 suggested, labor unrest contributed to both capital flight and current account deficit, though the evidence of a direct relationship with depreciation was somewhat weak.

These cases also point up the difficulty of deflating when governments do not enjoy stable parliamentary support. The French case is exemplary. Various governments were formed and fell before any serious effort could be made to raise taxes or cut public expenditures. The high turnover rate was reflective of a deeper political division: the Radical Socialists wanted to deflate to protect bondholders and the petite bourgeoisie, while the Socialists wanted to protect public employees and move toward demand stimulus. There existed no stable coalition for deflation. Every statistical finding presented predicts worsening external economic imbalance under unstable political conditions. External deterioration was only slowed under the suspension of parliamentary government (rule by decree).

Protection and Devaluation

The cases examined here are consistent with the finding of Chapter 6: the larger the trader, and the less trade dependent a country is, the more likely it is to resort to protectionism. British policymakers were especially cognizant that they were in a position to influence the international terms of trade and to bargain from a position of strength if tariffs were raised. It was recognized that the domestic market was large and diversified enough that Britain could afford to forgo a portion of its international trade if necessary. Similarly, as French officials were wont to note, of the industrial countries of Europe, France would have the least to lose from a reduction in international trade, since its domestic economy was balanced between industrial and agricultural production. Belgium was in a fundamentally different position. It had to compete to eat. As the most highly trade dependent country in our sample, Belgium's welfare depended on its ability to sell its products—at a profit if possible, but with government subsidies as a last resort—to the rest of the world.

Size and trade dependence had serious consequences for the policy mix. Britain had some of the highest tariffs of any country in the sample for the thirties, while France implemented high tariffs and a formidable system of import quotas. Belgium raised tariffs in 1932 and did have a weak system of quotas, but neither tariffs nor quotas were on the scale of the larger powers. Even representatives of Belgium's trading partners commented on how lax the system of protection was. These case studies also illustrate the pressures that lead to freer trade: in Belgium, industries in the highly trade dependent export sector and in shipping were able to convince policymakers (should any convincing be necessary) that free trade benefited the country as a whole and that the risk of retaliation was not worth the added protection. No such free trade coalition existed in France. Rather, protests from powerful agricultural groups prevented a fundamental reassessment of the country's commercial policy.

One of the most interesting themes of these three cases is that left-wing parties were opposed to protectionism and center-right parties were its champion—a result predicted in the earlier statistical analysis.[201] As a result, in Britain, where the reins of political power began with the Labour government and shifted to the Conservatives, tariffs began lower than the sample average and ended higher. In France and Belgium, the power shift was in the opposite direction: from Conservatives to the Left. In both of these countries, tariffs began at high levels and were reduced. In all three cases, working-class parties argued that tariffs constituted a consumption tax and raised the cost of living for workers.

In Britain, there was a prevalent belief in the Labour party that a tariff would not contribute to employment. Despite the fact that devaluation relieved the balance of payments problem, Conservatives thought a tariff would solidify the empire and spare the pound a further downward slide. In Belgium and France, Socialists echoed the complaint that tariffs were taxes on consumption. Furthermore, while it is difficult to quantify, there was a vague feeling in each of the left-wing parties that tariffs were an anathema to the general internationalist stance with which they wished to be identified. The British Labour government made a serious attempt as late as 1930 to get international agreement to a tariff truce.[202] The French were not at all receptive until Blum's Socialist government came to power. These instances render plausibility to the aggregate findings that the Left was more willing than the center-right to lower barriers to international trade.

The cases are also useful in analyzing the trade-offs made between the various adjustment options. As one of the two most important financial centers in the world, Britain implemented a reasonably credible program of monetary and fiscal deflation. The general tariff was added by the Conservatives to defend the pound and cement the empire. Britain's size as a trader and its passive trade balance meant that Britain had more to gain than lose from its departure from free trade. Belgium could not endure a prolonged disequilibrium between domestic and international prices. Belgium avoided excessive protection, deflated resolutely to the point where it was clear the economy could not be deflated any further, and then just as decisively devalued, reduced tariffs, and restabilized. This mix reflects the strategy of an economy that cannot afford to disengage from the world economy. In France, political instability and domestic conflict, combined with a blind attachment to the franc Poincaré, were

---

[201] The same pattern held for the United States, where Republicans were the party of the high tariff and the Democratic Roosevelt administration worked toward freer trade with the implementation of a series of bilateral reciprocal trade agreements commencing in 1934.

[202] As did the Democratic Roosevelt administration prior to and during the London Economic Conference (1933).

destined to take France further and further away from equilibrium with the rest of the world. A dense regime of protection (the luxury of a large and self-sufficient economy) only obscured the fundamental contradiction and delayed adjustment of a society that wanted to remain on gold but could not deflate. Devaluation encouraged a degree of trade liberalization, but the gains of 1937 were largely lost by 1938, and the French franc continued to slide.

Chapter 8

CONCLUSIONS

THE INTERWAR years have been described as among the most conflictual in modern international economic history. Traditional explanations for economic conflict in the twenties and thirties have centered on the shock of the Great Depression, the lack of a willing leader to shoulder the cost of maintaining order and openness, and, of course, raw nationalism that grew out of the conflicts of World War I and the vindictive nature of the peace.

This study does not overturn these traditional culprits of conflict and collapse. But it does show that they must not be used as catchall explanations for every beggar-thy-neighbor policy implemented between the two world wars. Economic externalization was associated with specific political and institutional conditions, and these conditions were often of as great or greater importance in explaining the tendency to defect from recognized norms of international economic policy as are the more traditional explanations.

The focus of this study has been on the behavior expected of all countries that aspired to maintain a gold standard. I have argued that three norms supported this regime: first, that priority must be given to external economic balance above economic conditions at home, and to exchange rate stability over domestic price stability; second, that liberal external economic policies were to be preferred over external controls; and third, that supplementary international finance should be provided in cases of balance of payments or currency crises. The first of these norms applied asymmetrically to deficit countries, but the second was meant to apply to deficit and surplus countries alike. The third was an extension of practices that had developed toward the end of the nineteenth century. In short, the ideal adherent to the interwar gold standard was expected to adjust its domestic economy in such a way as to maintain rough external equilibrium, to defend the currency, and to minimize barriers to trade. The reality, as we know, differed dramatically from this ideal. Nonetheless, these norms defined the content for exemplary international economic cooperation during the interwar years. My purpose has been to specify the conditions under which a cooperative adjustment regime could be built. Who adjusted internally as the gold standard required, and who externalized by devaluing (or allowing the currency to depreciate) and by protecting? Propositions have been advanced using a time-inconsistency/rational expectations model of capital flows, the current account, and currency depreciation; and a theory of relative economic power, trade dependence, and political party preferences for understanding patterns of trade protection. The resort to various theoretical traditions is crucial in understanding the pressures to devalue and to protect, since the logic for externalizing in each case is distinct. Theoretical pluralism is not only useful, it is critical for understanding why it is that a country may choose one form of externalization over another.

THE ARGUMENT

Any theory that purports to explain why states select strategies of internal over external adjustment must develop an explanation of the political pressures and incentives to externalize. Devaluation resulted from pressures to run a current account deficit or to experience sudden and significant capital flight. These pressures are in turn linked to political conditions that make it painful to deflate the economy and hence hard to make a credible commitment that inflation will be avoided. I have argued that the temptation to devalue is greatest when the political costs of cutting consumption and deflating prices are highest, and when the government's commitment to Norm 1 is least credible.

The interwar years were a fertile testing ground for theories of commitment and credibility and their impact on macroeconomic policy choice and hence gold standard adjustment. The newly politicized labor movement provided an opportunity to test the extent to which parties of the Left were associated with overexpansion and capital flight due to the *belief* that they would inflate rather than tolerate a high level of unemployment, with the result that the higher the representation of the Left in the governing structure, the greater the inflationary pressure, the capital flight, and the deterioration in the current account as prices and domestic demand soars. Anticipating the electorally based macroeconomic imperative of the Left, the commitment to avoid monetary inflation was likely to be incredible to market participants and especially holders of liquid capital. Hence, the Left was expected to be linked both to a worsening balance of payments and to a strong downward pressure on the currency.

A similar rationale would link unstable political conditions with capital flight, current account deterioration, and currency depreciation. The tendency to accommodate rather than to rein in inflation, like the decision to overborrow, has a good deal to do with the security and expected duration of a government's political control. Markets have good reasons to expect unstable governments to be less willing to deflate and to be the most likely to give in to short-term political pressures for expansive monetary and fiscal policies. They expect unstable governments to discount the future highly; hence, a government whose position is tenuous will not be able to make a credible commitment to maintain a "responsible" monetary policy. The costs, which are concentrated in the present, far exceed the benefits to be realized in the highly discounted future. Political instability was hypothesized to cause both capital flight and current account deterioration. Unstable governments were expected to be prime candidates for currency devaluation.

Other forms of political and economic conflict were expected to contribute to balance of payments difficulties as well. Specifically, demands for better wages (whether or not these demands were actually met) could convince markets of impending inflationary pressures emanating from the labor market. The expectation of inflation due to wage pressures could cause market actors to account for this possibility in their new contracts and portfolio composition, and could easily convince capital to flee—in itself raising domestic prices and contributing to a deterioration in the balance of payments. Thus, countries experiencing a high degree of labor unrest are expected to face pressures to devalue, in clear contravention of the norms of the gold standard.

Finally, politically independent central banks should be better able to avoid inflationary debt monetization and to implement more restrictive credit policies than banks under more direct government control. Central bank independence is expected to assure markets that promises of monetary stringency would actually be fulfilled; that tight monetary and credit policies would in fact be used to damp down domestic demand (improving the current account) and to help attract capital (strengthening the currency). In accordance with the accepted wisdom of the twenties, I hypothesized that greater central bank independence would contribute to currency strength and adherence to the first norm of gold standard adjustment.

A second ideal of the international gold standard was that liberal external economic policies were to be preferred over policies of control and exclusion. The most common—though by far not the only—departure from the principle of liberal external economic relations was tariff protection. Theories of protection are distinct from theories of devaluation: while both have the effect of raising the price of foreign goods compared to those prevailing in the home market, the pressure and logic for each policy is very different. In the case of protection, structural arguments are much more relevant than those pertaining to credibility. Traditional economic theories emphasize the ability of large traders to alter the terms of trade in their favor through tariff protection; hence, I expected the larger traders to be the quickest to protect and the least likely to adjust. Similarly, since highly trade dependent countries need open international markets to survive and have a great deal to lose should a trade partner retaliate, I hypothesized that the higher the degree of trade dependence, the lower tariffs would be.

Yet, there is no reason to assume that these structural constraints dominate the decision to protect. As in any question of taxation, it is necessary to ask who is expected to benefit and who to pay when tariffs are increased. The incidence of the tax is likely to be a highly charged domestic political issue. The net payer of higher customs duties during the interwar years was believed to be the working class. Levies on the necessities of life—food, beverages, matches, and tobacco—were viewed as taxes on consumption that would be borne disproportionately by workers. The commitment to the cheap loaf became as much an ideological as a strictly economic rationale for the Left's opposition to protection. As representation of the Left increases in commercial policymaking arenas, tariff reductions ought to prevail.

Major Findings

These domestic political accounts of the incentives governments faced to defect either through devaluation or through tariff protection were forced to compete with the more entrenched explanations such as the direction of the business cycle, structural constraints and opportunities (size, trade dependence, net creditor position), and patterns of behavior predicted by reciprocity/retaliation. The result has been to enrich greatly our understanding of the sources of stress on the adjustment norms of the interwar years. The first set of important findings suggests that specific political and institutional conditions made it difficult for a country to maintain the gold standard because they contributed to unsustainable external economic imbalance. Table 8.1 summarizes the major findings with respect to the political determinants of crises in the balance of payments during the interwar years. The diagonal formed by the upper-right and lower-left cells indicates patterns in the current account and capital flows that may be considered "normal" or "sustainable" for creditor countries in a surplus trade position (upper right) and for debtor countries in a deficit trade position (lower left). These patterns pose no serious problem for a country that would maintain the gold standard; surplus countries are simply financing the current account position of deficit countries, as one would expect to be the case under normal circumstances (recall that capital flows and current account changes are highly negatively correlated at about $-.7$). However, four domestic political variables contributed to *both capital flight and current account deterioration* during the interwar years—a combination that was ultimately disastrous for a country that would remain on gold and resist external economic controls. Where governments were unstable and labor was restive, where parties of the Left had input into economic policymaking, and where governments could manipulate the policies of the central bank, it was impossible for a country to maintain a credible commitment to keep domestic prices and demand under control, resulting in an unsustainable spiral of both capital flight and current account deterioration. These conditions also discouraged surplus countries from extending exceptional finance, which compromised the third gold standard norm. As France discovered between 1924 and 1926, and as the British Labour party discovered in 1931, foreign assistance during a balance of payments or currency crisis was unlikely to be forthcoming under the conditions listed in the lower-right-hand cell.

Just how a government decided to deal with impending balance of payments difficulties, however, differed significantly according to its degree of political instability, the ideological and coalitional commitments of the party in power,

TABLE 8.1
Summary of Results: Influences on the Balance of Payments

	Capital Inflows	Capital Outflows
Current Account Improvement	Stable Governments[a] No Labor Unrest[b] Center-Right Government[c] Indep. Central Bank[a] CONDITIONS CONSISTENT WITH NORM 1	SURPLUS/CREDITOR PATTERN CONSISTENT WITH NORMS 1 AND 3
Current Account Deterioration	DEFICIT/DEBTOR PATTERN CONSISTENT WITH NORMS 1 AND 3	Unstable Governments[a] Labor Unrest[b] Left-wing Government[c] Politically Dep. Cent. Bank[a] CONDITIONS INCONSISTENT WITH NORMS 1 AND 3

[a]Statistically significant and stable for most models for capital flows; significant in the indicated direction for at least one model for current account.

[b]Statistically significant and stable across most models for both capital flows and current account.

[c]Statistically significant and stable across most models for current account; in the indicated direction, but not significant for capital flows.

and the institutional design of its monetary institutions. Table 8.2 summarizes the major findings. Each cell contains the characteristics associated with the policy mix indicated along the top and to the left. (There is no implication that the conditions listed within each cell must be found together.) The characteristics that were most consistently associated with the willingness and ability to internalize the burden of adjustment according to Norms 1 and 2 are indicated in the upper-left-hand corner. The evidence suggests that for the interwar years, the countries that adjusted in the most cooperative fashion were politically stable and, with less certainty, were not plagued by widespread strikes or, one suspects, other forms of social unrest. Stability enhanced a country's ability and willingness to internalize the costs of adjustment. Notice, too, that the smaller, more highly trade dependent countries were likely to adopt cooperative trade policies, although the same cannot be said of their currency policies. These states did not erupt in unbridled conflict each time distributive issues came to the fore; the pressures of openness were likely responsible, as Peter Katzenstein has noted, for the development of flexible domestic structures for containing conflict and compensating losers and for external policies of competing fiercely

TABLE 8.2
Summary of Results: Influences on the Policy Mix

	Defend Currency	Devalue/Depreciate
Reduce Tariffs	Stable Governments[b] No Labor Unrest[d] INTERNALIZER	Left-wing Government[a] Politically Dep. Cent. Bank[b] Small, Trade Dependent[c] (PROGRESSIVE NORM SELECTION) MONETARY EXTERNALIZER
Raise Tariffs	Right-wing Government[a] Indep. Central Bank[b] Large, Insular Economy[c] (CONSERVATIVE NORM SELECTION) TRADE EXTERNALIZER	Unstable Governments[b] Labor Unrest[d] EXTERNALIZER

[a]Statistically significant and stable across most models for both currency and trade.

[b]Statistically significant and stable across most models for currency; significant in the indicated direction for at least one model for trade.

[c]Statistically significant and stable across most models for trade; in the indicated direction, but not significant for currency.

[d]Indicated direction, but not statistically significant for either currency or trade.

but fairly in international markets.[1] Extreme openness also discouraged a dogmatic attachment to a given currency parity in the face of untenable price distortion, as was evident in the Belgian case. This study leaves little room for doubt that the roots of "flexible adjustment" discussed in Katzenstein's analysis of small, highly trade dependent states had their genesis in the interwar years.

Table 8.2 also profiles the characteristics associated with trade and currency defection (lower-right-hand cell). Externalization was most strongly associated with domestic political turmoil, most especially government instability. Countries experiencing internal conflicts had clear incentives to export their problems rather than to solve them. Moreover, the international system was highly permissive of externalizing via tariffs for economies that depended very little on international trade for domestic prosperity. Countries with these characteristics used the international economy as a dumping ground for all the negative externalities that were too costly to absorb at home. There were times when France fell into this category, with very negative consequences for the international economic system as a whole.

---

[1] Peter Katzenstein, *Small States in World Markets: Industrial Policy in Europe* (Ithaca: Cornell University Press) 1985.

Finally, there are two hybrid policy mixes that represent selective norm implementation. One of the most novel aspects of this research has been to confirm an often unarticulated intuition that right-wing conservative polities indeed have different adjustment preferences than do left-wing progressive polities. It is no accident that all three devaluations among the major democratic economies—Britain in 1931, the United States in 1933, and France in 1936— occurred *not* in rapid succession, as a theory of reciprocity or tit for tat would have predicted, but *only* in the presence of left-wing governments for which the costs of deflation were intolerable. It is no accident that the British general tariff was implemented *only* after the Liberal/Labour coalition had been beaten back to three free traders in the cabinet of the Government of National Union; that it was the Roosevelt administration and not that of Hoover that took the initiative for the Reciprocal Trade Agreements; that the Socialists in Belgium decried tariffs; and that the Front Populaire moved to dismantle France's armor of quotas as one of its first items on the agenda of international economic relations.

The other side of the coin is equally telling. Obsessed with the fortunes of creditors and the upper classes, center-right governments were more likely than were left-wing governments to defend the currency, possibly at the expense of growth and employment. Their task was greatly facilitated when a strong, independent central banking institution provided the wherewithal and the credibility needed to deflate and defend. On the other hand, the Conservatives were quite willing to protect, sometimes for a set of independent reasons, and sometimes as a way to vouchsafe that the currency would not depreciate due to current account difficulties. Both rationales were advanced, for instance, by British Conservatives, who saw 1931 as an opportunity to solidify the empire and prevent the pound from further depreciating by implementing the general tariff—over the strong objections of the Labour party.

What is remarkable is that these domestic political explanations have an important impact on the balance of payments and the choice of adjustment strategies *even when economic conditions and structural constraints are controlled*. This was especially true of devaluation. Certainly, devaluation was influenced by economic stagnation and by changes in the currency of a country's major trade partner, results that were underlined in the case of Belgium in the first half of the thirties. But even so, governments of the Left were far more likely than those of the center-right to devalue, *especially* under recessionary conditions. Stable governments and politically insulated monetary authorities were associated with strong currencies even when such structural conditions as net investment position, wealth per capita, size, and trade dependence (none of which could be shown to be convincingly related to curency depreciation) were taken into account. It is true that changes in tariff policies were influenced by a country's size and degree of trade dependence, but *significant* changes in policy were associated with the degree of political influence of the Left. Finally, an important negative finding was the lack of evidence of tit-for-tat behavior between a country and its major trading partner in the implementation of tariffs.

In short, external economic imbalance and the policy mix selected to address it are profoundly influenced by countries' willingness and ability to internalize, which in turn depends as much or more on their domestic politics and institutions than on structural variables or tit-for-tat behavior.

IMPLICATIONS FOR INTERNATIONAL COOPERATION

The cases and the evidence presented here help to demonstrate why international economic cooperation was so weak during the interwar years. Unless a deficit country happened to be a "natural internalizer," there was always the risk that its trade partners would pay an important part of the costs of its adjustment. The absence of a system of collective economic security meant that surplus countries—or individual firms within those countries—had to assess the risks and benefits of facilitating gold standard adherence by other states in the system. Two of the cases presented in Chapters 5 and 7 provide striking evidence that ad hoc surplus/deficit negotiations were fraught with difficulties and sometimes led to unintended negative consequences. External financial assistance was sporadic at best, and often *reflected* rather than *countered* market sentiments. Thus, international financial assistance in the form of a stabilization credit from Morgan *coincided* with strong fiscal policy measures that might alone have helped to reverse the market's bearish speculation against the franc. But when France was unable to implement a credible fiscal and monetary program, central banks and private firms both hesitated, signaling the market that all bets were off with respect to the franc. This refusal to facilitate the defense of the franc again *coincided* with speculators' pressures; it hardly allayed their fears. International cooperation was easy when the chances of success were already high: when a conservative and relatively secure government had the political backing to implement stringent fiscal reforms. Unfortunately, international capitalists were not willing to provide support in the harder cases: those in which the domestic constellation of political forces rendered the government's policies incredible to the market. Thus, finance was denied to an unstable left-wing government at a moment when a show of international solidarity might have saved the franc and prevented its undervaluation later in 1928. The problem was that ad hoc international assistance acted more *like* the market than it served to *counter* the market.

A similar problem arose during the 1931 pound crisis. The conditions required by the Banque de France and the Federal Reserve Bank of New York for further credits were so stringent—they demanded nothing less than the elimination of unemployment insurance from the Labour government's budget—that they broke the Labour party's unity, felled the government, and dealt sterling a fatal psychological blow. If the central banks of America and France would not come to the aid of the Bank of England, this could be the end of Western monetary civilization. Once again, surplus assistance reinforced rather than countered the prevailing market sentiment, demanding that unless Labour cut unemployment insurance there could be no succor.

As a result, in the absence of international institutions designed to provide emergency finance to stem currency crises, there was no certainty that international cooperation would be forthcoming in a fashion that could convince markets of the community of nations' commitment to stability. The certainty that the major powers would close ranks to stem bear-market speculation had vanished. There was undoubtedly a strong element of national jealousy in the decision to withhold cooperative assistance. But there is another element that is rarely mentioned in the literature on this period: assistance was often deterred because of a low expectation that it would work. When the weak-currency country fit the description of a monetary externalizer (left-wing government, politically controlled central bank, unstable government facing high labor unrest), providers of extraordinary nonmarket assistance balked like the speculators. Cooperation itself had become incredible. The impact on the stability of the monetary system was evident.

IMPLICATIONS FOR INTERNATIONAL POLITICAL ECONOMY

The trend since the early 1980s has been to understand conflict and cooperation in the international political economy as a result of structurally and strategically defined interactions between states, whose preferences and payoff structures are assumed rather than documented. In the last few years, however, there has been some backlash against imputed values and the assumption of the dominance of systemic influences. Those who approach politics from a more comparative perspective have proposed that a second game is in progress at the domestic level.[2] The result of this insight has been exactly what the game theorists have dreaded: an increasingly unwieldy game structure and an almost endless list of domestic conditions, institutions, bargaining tactics, personalities, and factors that might "matter." One reels at the problem of comparing and ordering these influences. Even those who are sympathetic with the research agenda may be forgiven for not knowing where to begin. The conclusion drawn by those who place a high premium on parsimony has been that "[n]ot much successful theorizing from any methodological standpoint about the effects of domestic politics has been accomplished in international relations—simply because domestic factors add complications that are currently impossible to deal with."[3]

The findings of this study are far more optimistic for the future convergence of comparative and international politics. Two highly generalizable concepts

[2] Robert D. Putnam, "The Logic of Two Level Games," *International Organization*, Vol. 42, Spring 1988, pp. 427–460

[3] Christopher H. Achen and Duncan Snidal, "Rational Deterrence Theory and Comparative Case Studies," *World Politics*, Vol. 41, No. 2, January 1989, p. 155.

emerge from this research that span the international and domestic settings and that are consonant with some of the most powerful insights game theory itself has generated to date. The first of these is credibility. The second is the time horizon.

Credibility. Credibility is the ability to make a believable commitment to fulfill a promise in the absence of an enforceable contract. Countries that have difficulty establishing their credibility are likely to have tremendous problems in realizing mutual gains with their counterparts in the international system. I have argued that a breakdown in credibility was responsible for a country's difficulty in abiding by the norms of the interwar gold standard, and that credibility actually influenced the possibilities for reaching cooperative international agreements to stabilize the interwar gold exchange standard. In the monetary issue area, it is relatively straightforward to hypothesize about the conditions that undermine the ability of a government to make a believable commitment to implement a noninflationary macroeconomic policy. This study suggests that four domestic political variables affected a government's ability to make credible commitments during the interwar years: its degree of political stability, the degree of social or labor unrest within the polity, the political orientation of the government, and the independence of the central bank from political control.

The concept of credibility has rich possibilities for uniting domestic and international politics across a number of issue areas. One of the most promising areas has been in international financial and debt negotiations in the presence of sovereign risk. In the absence of unenforceable contracts, the inability of a government to make credible commitments to "responsible" macroeconomic policies and to limit future borrowing results in international agreements that are much less optimal (for both lenders and borrowers) than if the government had been able to make a credible commitment in the first place. The dynamic contracting literature has exploited the notion of credibility to explain why the inability to make believable commitments can lead to suboptimal patterns of lending: too little capital lent at too high a rate for too short a term to governments that face incentives to pursue unprofitable projects, to overborrow, and, in the extreme, to default.[4]

[4] Jeffrey Sachs and Daniel Cohen, "LDC Borrowing with Default Risk," NBER Working Paper No. 925 (Cambridge, Mass.: NBER), July 1982; Richard Cooper and Jeffrey Sachs, "Borrowing Abroad: The Debtors Perspective," in Gorden W. Smith and John T. Cuddington (eds.), *International Debt and the Developing Countries* (Washington, D.C.: World Bank), 1985, pp. 21–60; Kenneth M. Kletzer, "Asymmetries of Information and LDC Borrowing with Sovereign Risk," *Economic Journal*, Vol. 94, No. 374, June 1984, pp. 287–307. Credit rationing is another response to uncertainty and risk. See D. Jaffee and T. Russell, "Imperfect Information, Uncertainty, and Credit Rationing," *Quarterly Journal of Economics*, Vol. 90, November 1976, pp. 651–666; J. Stiglitz and A. Weiss, "Credit Rationing in Markets with Imperfect Information," *American Economic Review*, Vol. 71, June 1981, pp. 393–411. Jonathan Eaton and Mark Gersovitz, "Debt

Credibility may help order an inquiry into domestic and international bargaining across a broad number of issue areas. The central empirical inquiry should probe into the conditions that shatter or bolster credibility in a specific issue area. Many of these are likely to be domestic political conditions, as was the case for monetary cooperation in the interwar years. To focus on the conditions that make commitments believable sets aside the sometimes sterile argument over system versus domestic influences, and focuses attention instead on factors from any source that affect the likelihood that a country will be able to carry through on its promises.

Time Horizons. One of the central contributions of game theoretic analyses has been to point out the importance for rational choice of the value players place on future streams of benefits. If players will not be in the game for long, they have no reason to bear high present costs, and their opponents-cum-partners know this. This is precisely the problem that game theorists have taken up in their analysis of the Prisoner's Dilemma: a strategy of defection dominates one of cooperation in one-shot play because there are no expected long-term benefits from future cooperation. Where the players put a high value on future benefits, reciprocity and cooperation are the most rational—and the most collectively stable—strategies.[5] These insights, which inform the literature on international economic cooperation, emphasize frequent, intensive, transparent, and, particularly, long-term interactions as crucial to understanding cooperation.[6] However, the obverse is equally telling: "if the other player is unlikely to be around much longer because of apparent weakness, then the perceived value of w [the discount rate] falls and the reciprocity of TIT-FOR-TAT is no longer stable."[7] We can hypothesize that governments with low time horizons will prefer to deviate least from their present course. They will defect, and cooperation will be difficult.

The empirical issue then becomes, What conditions influence the discount

---

with Potential Repudiation: Theoretical and Empirical Analysis," *Review of Economic Studies*, Vol. 48, April 1981, pp. 289–310. For an excellent review of the dynamic contracting literature, see Vincent Crawford, "International Lending, Long-term Credit Relationships, and Dynamic Contracting Theory," Discussion Paper, University of California, San Diego, Department of Economics, August 1984.

[5] Michael Taylor, *Anarchy and Cooperation* (New York: Wiley) 1976; Robert Axelrod, *The Evolution of Cooperation* (New York: Basic Books), 1984, chap. 3. Another excellent discussion on the notion of discount rate and its implication for rational choice is found in Jon Elster, *Ulysses and the Sirens* (Cambridge: Cambridge University Press), 1979.

[6] Robert O. Keohane, *After Hegemony: Cooperation and Discord in the World Political Economy* (Princeton: Princeton University Press), 1984; see also the special edition of *World Politics*, Vol. 38, No. 1, October 1985. For a theoretical and empirical refutation of this approach for the study of international relations, see Joseph M. Grieco, *Cooperation Among Nations* (Ithaca: Cornell University Press), 1990.

[7] Axelrod, *The Evolution of Cooperation*, p. 59.

rate? The systemic literature has concentrated on describing international institutional arrangements and stable strategies that draw the future out *between* states. Yet it is sometimes difficult to account for moves in which governments behave as if there were no tomorrow. In fact, this might be the case. It is perfectly consistent—indeed, logically required—to extend the analysis of players' discount rates to their chances of remaining in the game. The lame duck has been standard fare in American politics for decades. Yet it remains conspicuously absent from analyses of the game at the international table.

Seizing on time horizons as a way to explore the linkup between the domestic game and the international game not only has the advantage of logical consistency, but it is also testable. This study has shown that the quintessential economic externalizers were countries whose domestic politics were highly unstable, and whose prospects for remaining in office were hence not bright. This finding could be extended to a consideration of the domestic institutional arrangements that foster instability: party fractionalization, electoral systems that habitually produce minority governments, even social and distributive conditions that cut short a government's life expectancy. Focusing on the domestic influences on the discount rate will help to prioritize the morass of possible domestic level influences on cooperation.[8] Variables can then be inserted into the analysis, not because they are "systemic" or "domestic," but precisely because they affect the time horizon. The unifying notion of the discount rate avoids the ad hoc effect of simultaneously wanting to say that everything matters at once. This concept does enjoy a sort of logical priority, for *nothing* matters if the future does not. Short time horizons are associated with policy choices that follow a predictable path of least resistance; that is, no policy change and no cooperation, *the essence of which is change*.[9]

Parting Words

In conclusion, I would like to make a few observations on the interwar years, which have provided the richest of settings for understanding the nexus between domestic and international politics. These two decades were more than an interregnum between systems of hegemonic dominance; they were years in

---

[8] Work has already been done in this area in international debt negotiations. Theoretical work linking the default decision to political instability include Joshua Aizeman, "External Debt, Planning Horizon, and Distorted Credit Markets," NBER Working Paper No. 2662 (Cambridge, Mass.: NBER), July 1988. Default and political polarization are explored in Alberto Alesina and Guido Tabellini, "External Debt, Capital Flight, and Political Risk," NBER Working Paper No. 2610 (Cambridge, Mass.: NBER), June 1988. Models that draw attention to the link between default and fiscal incapacities include Homi J. Kharas, "Constrained Optimal Borrowing by LDCs," *Domestic Finance Study* No. 75 (Washington, D.C.: World Bank), 1981.

[9] I recognize that domestic time horizon is only likely to account for a small part of the overall variance in a cooperative outcome, since a large proportion of cases will surely be stable ones, and stable governments will nevertheless vary greatly in their willingness and ability to cooperate.

which domestic polities themselves were making a revolutionary transition from the elite politics of the nineteenth century to the mass politics of the twentieth. This transition affected each state's ability to abide by the traditional norms of accepted international economic behavior. Of Britain, Palyi has written,

> When, in the very center of the international credit system, labor refused to tolerate even minor or temporary hardships and obsolete business was determined to hold its own . . . the message should have been clear that one could no longer play the gold standard "game" by its classical rules. The welfare state's determination to bypass the "automatism" resulted in making the gold standard very nearly unworkable. In the century before 1914 the gold standard survived and flourished because it had never before been exposed to such chronic strains as now appeared in the interwar era.[10]

The problems the British experienced were even greater elsewhere: the rise of the Left, a proliferation of political parties and realignments, unprecedented conflicts between unions and industry management, tensions between agricultural and industrial sectors, struggles over the very nature of the regime for governance—all of these complicated leaders' bids to maintain power. In a very real sense, the "twenty years' crisis" was a double entendre.

The domestic political and international conditions upon which stable economic relations depended were at a crossroads. The ways in which these conflicts were played out at the domestic level had clear consequences for adherence to traditional norms of international adjustment. Polities dominated by the agenda of the conservative Right clung to currency stability at the price of ever-mounting protection, while in those polities dominated by the progressive Left, parities were dethroned and protective mantles were gradually disassembled. For countries in neither camp, which oscillated between unstable political coalitions and experienced the highest degree of turmoil, the solution was to not adjust at all but to externalize. The primary concern for leaders riding a domestic political maelstrom was to maintain some semblance of control over fissiparous political conditions. Where international cooperation facilitated that task, it was engaged with equanimity. Where it posed greater short-term costs than a government could ever expect to recover, the choice was clear.

[10] Melchior Palyi, *The Twilight of Gold, 1914–1936* (Chicago: Henry Regnery), 1972, p. 104.

GENERAL DATA APPENDIX

This appendix provides sources and commentary on the economic, political, and structural data analyzed in the quantitative sections of this book. Dependent variables are presented first, followed by explanatory economic variables, domestic political variables, and structural variables.

DEPENDENT VARIABLES

Current Account Balance/Net National Product

Both numerator and denominator were expressed in national currency at current value. The numerator is the net balance on current account for each country-year. Source: B. R. Mitchell, *European Historical Statistics, 1750–1975* (New York: Facts on File), 2d rev. ed., 1980, Table K3, pp. 858–868. In some cases, Net National Product (NNP) figures had to be estimated from Gross National Product (GNP) figures, which are generally 5 to 10 percent higher than NNP ones because they do not include capital depreciation. Where gaps in the data exist, as in the cases of Belgium and Switzerland, the NNP has been interpolated based on available observations. Where NNP data were available only in constant prices, as in the case of France and Czechoslovakia, these were converted to current prices using yearly price ratios. For countries for which *only* GNP data were available—Austria, Czechoslovakia, Italy, Japan, Norway, Sweden—GNP figures were multiplied by .925 to get an approximate NNP. The NNP for Finland may be questionable because of the currency unit used.

The major source for NNP was B. R. Mitchell, *European Historical Statistics, 1750–1975*. In an effort to locate comparable net figures, supplementary data were gathered and comparisons made with the following country statistics:

Britain: B. R. Mitchell, *Abstract of British Historical Statistics* (Cambridge: Cambridge University Press), 1962. Canada: M. C. Urquhart and K. A. Buckley, *Historical Statistics of Canada* (Cambridge: Cambridge University Press), 1965. (For part of this series [1927–1939] I had to estimate a conversion from NNP expressed in factor shares to one expressed in current market prices.) Denmark: Kjeld Bjerke, "The National Product of Denmark," in *Income and Wealth*, Series 5 (Cambridge: Bowes and Bowes), 1955, pp. 123–151, Table 10. France: constant NNP was converted into current prices using the price indices supplied by Alfred Sauvy, *Histoire Economique de la France Entre les Deux Guerres* (Paris: Economica), 1984, Vol. 3, Tableau VIII.1, p. 347. Japan:

Shigeto Tsuru and Kazushi Ohkawa, "Long Term Changes in the National Product of Japan Since 1878," in *Income and Wealth*, Series 3 (Cambridge: Bowes and Bowes), 1953, pp. 19–44. United States: United States Department of Commerce/Bureau of the Census, *Statistical Abstract of the United States* (Washington, D.C.: Government Printing Office), various issues. Yugoslavia: Ivo Vinski, "National Product and Fixed Assets in the Territory of Yugoslavia, 1909–1959," in *Income and Wealth*, Series 9 (London: Bowes and Bowes), 1961, pp. 206–233.

Capital Flows

All data on capital flows are taken from United Nations Secretariat, *International Capital Movements During the Interwar Years* (Lake Success, N.Y.: United Nations), 1949, Table 1, pp. 10–12. The original data are expressed in millions of U.S. dollars. A negative sign refers to a capital outflow and a positive sign to a capital inflow. These flows were estimated by the UN from data on the current account as well as from gold movements. For comparability in a time-series cross-sectional context, I have standardized the data in two ways. First, to facilitate comparisons across countries, capital flows are standardized relative to Net National Product. Second, each observation is scaled relative to total sample volume per year. The yearly standardization is justified since I am not interested in explaining the contraction or expansion in the overall volume of flows but rather the shifting of flows *among* economies. The result is an indicator of changes in the flow of capital, which should not be dominated by the largest economies, nor by contractions in the total volume of lending, which were substantial in the late twenties and thirties.

Currency Depreciation

Ideally, depreciation must be measured against some constant, such as gold. However, most countries changed their gold basis one or more times during this period, so it is difficult to obtain an uninterrupted series for every country for the whole time period. The League of Nations' *Monthly Bulletin of Statistics*, for example, publishes an interrupted series that begins with the deviation of a currency from its prewar gold parity for the 1920s, but then switches to the 1929 gold parity of the currency as a benchmark from which depreciation occurred in the 1930s. Exchange rates are more readily available, but are sensitive to change in the currency selected as yardstick. Since the United States dollar was stable up to 1933, I have used the ratio of U.S. cents/national currency published in the Federal Reserve's *Banking and Monetary Statistics* up to 1930, and used percent change from 1929 gold parity for the remainder of the period. "Depreciation" and "appreciation" are always used here in references to this combined series. Depreciation = [Exch.rate(t) − Exch.rate(t − 1)] /

Exch.rate($t - 1$). In a few cases (e.g., the French and Belgian stabilizations in the late 1920s), de jure stabilizations make it appear as though there were large discrete jumps in the currency value when in fact these were only legal redefinitions. In these cases, the change both before the stabilization and afterwards were averaged excluding the changed stabilization rate itself, since it is not evidence of market depreciation. Finally, many currencies were inconvertible in the 1930s, and so had no free-market gold value, which should be kept in mind when analyzing their "stability" during that period.

Tariff Index

The tariff index is the ratio of the monetary value of customs collected as a share of total value of imported goods. Both the numerator and denominator of this ratio are expressed in local currency at prevailing prices. Source: B. R. Mitchell, *European Historical Statistics, 1750–1970* (London: Macmillan Press), 1975; numerator: series H-5, pp. 716–726; denominator: Series F-1, pp. 493–497. The level of this index and the percent change in the index from year to year are tested: [Tariff Index(t) − Tariff Index($t - 1$)]/Tariff Index($t - 1$).

Explanatory Economic Variables

Cost of Living Index

The cost of living index with base year 1929 = 100. For several countries, the index applies only to a major or capital city, e.g., Warsaw for Poland, Prague for Czechoslovakia, Budapest for Hungary, Madrid for Spain. Where cost of living indices are not available, an index of consumer (retail) prices has been used instead. Source: B. R. Mitchell, *European Historical Statistics, 1750–1975*, Table I2, pp. 745–746.

Wholesale Price Index

The index for wholesale prices for each country with base year 1929 = 100, as recorded in B. R. Mitchell, *European Historical Statistics, 1750–1975*, Table I1, pp. 738–739.

Real Interest Rate Differentials

Market interest rates are difficult to document for all the countries in this sample. Due to data limitations, I had to use central bank discount rates in lieu of local market rates (League of Nations, *Monthly Bulletin of Statistics*, various issues). United States three-month Treasury bill yields were used as a proxy for world interest rates (in the case of the United States, three-month British

Treasury bill yields were used as the world rate). All rates are real; that is, the rate of inflation or deflation was subtracted from the nominal rate of interest. Local price changes were those of the cost of living index, while world price changes were an index based on British, American, French, and German cost of living indices, weighted by their share in world trade. The ratio of these prices was therefore 17 (Britain): 12.3 (United States): 8.2 (France): 7.3 (Germany). For each of these four countries, the world price it faced was calculated as the ratio of the remaining three (its own prices were excluded in calculating the world price). Cost of living indices are described above. On the assumption that the effects of changes in domestic and foreign interest rates are of equal importance, the differential between world and local prices was taken, and the variable tested was the change in this differential from the previous period.

Real Exchange Rates

Real exchange rates were calculated on the basis of the bilateral rate with the United States dollar. This nominal rate was multiplied by the ratio of foreign to domestic price changes, on the basis of the cost of living index cited above. This variable is tested as percent change in real exchange rates from the prior to the present year. Bilateral exchange rates were taken from yearly averages published by the Governors of the Federal Reserve Board, *Banking and Monetary Statistics* (Washington, D.C.: GPO), 1943, pp. 662–682. Consumer price indices were used to get the real rates (see Cost of Living Index above). The formula for calculating real rates was ($/foreign currency)($P^*/P$). Foreign prices ($P^*$) are the trade-weighted average of those for Germany, France, Britain, and the United States based on their average share of world trade for the period as a whole, as follows: 17 (Britain): 12.3 (United States): 8.3 (France): 7.2 (Germany). For each of these countries, foreign prices were the weighted average of the other three. The calculation for percent change in the real exchange rate was $[\text{RER}(t + 1) - \text{RER}(t)] / \text{RER}(t)$.

Output (Domestic Growth Rates, Index of Industrial Production)

Output is measured by percent changes in the index of industrial production for each country from year to year (1937 = 100). The index of industrial production is that published in B. R. Mitchell, *European Historical Statistics, 1750–1975*, Table E1, pp. 356–357.

Foreign Output (Foreign Growth Rates, Foreign Index of Industrial Production)

Foreign output growth is measured by the change in the index of industrial production of the major trading partner for each country each year. The major trading partner was the one with which total trade value (imports plus exports) was greatest in any given year, according to B. R. Mitchell, *European Historical Statistics, 1750–1975*, Table F2, pp. 503–576. Source and calculation of output (growth rate) are as above for the domestic index of industrial production.

Currency Value of the Major Trading Partner

This variable is based on the currency depreciation (see definition and sources cited above) of a country's major trading partner (as defined under Foreign Output above).

EXPLANATORY DOMESTIC POLITICAL VARIABLES

Democratic Governments

The criterion used for judging a country democratic was that it held reasonably competitive elections. Countries were admitted as democracies if they excluded extreme parties, but not if widespread party suppression was prevalent. Countries that remained democratic for the entire period were Belgium, Canada, Denmark, France, Finland, the Netherlands, Norway, Sweden, Switzerland, the United Kingdom, and the United States. Countries that were considered democratic for a portion of the period were Austria (to 1934), Bulgaria (1926–1931), Czechoslovakia (to 1938), Germany (to 1933), Japan (1924–1933), Poland (to 1927), Spain (1930–1935), and Yugoslavia (to 1928). Countries that were never rated democratic during the period were Hungary, Italy, and Romania. Democratic regimes were coded *1* and nondemocratic regimes were coded *0*. Sources: Gregory M. Leubbert, "Social Foundations of Political Order in Interwar Europe," in *World Politics*, Vol. 39, No. 4, July 1987, pp. 449–478; Vincent E. McHale and Sharon Skowronski (eds.), *Political Parties of Europe* (Westport, Conn.: Greenwood Historical Encyclopedia of the World Political Parties), 1983.

Left-Wing Government (Democracies Only)

The influence of the Left is measured by the degree of left-wing participation in government. I distinguished between cases of no or minor left-wing participation (as a small supporting member of the government coalition), major-left-wing participation (coalition leader), and only left-wing leadership. The former were coded *0* and the latter coded *1*. Data on left-wing participation in government were collected for the following democratic cases: Austria (to 1932), Belgium, Denmark, Finland, France, Germany (to 1933), the Netherlands, Norway, Sweden, and the United Kingdom. Source: Peter Flora, *State, Economy, and Society in Western Europe, 1815–1975* (Frankfurt am Main: Campus Verlag), 1983, pp. 153–189. Sources also included Richard Rose (ed.), *Elec-*

toral Behavior: A Comparative Handbook (New York: Free Press), 1974; and Vincent E. McHale and Sharon Skowronski (eds.), *Political Parties of Europe*. Data on cabinet composition were also found in Berthold Spuler, *Regenten und Regierung der Welt: Minister-Ploetz*, Teil 2 (Würzburg: A. G. Ploetz, Verlag), 1964. For this sample during this period, only democratic regimes had left-wing participation in government. The Left was suppressed or marginalized in most nondemocratic regimes during this time. To lessen the possibility of confounding regime effects with left-wing participation, I consider the impact of left-wing governments among democracies only (using an interaction term for democracy and left-wing participation).

Influence of the Left in Parliament

Sources for determining which parties were left-wing include Chris Cook and John Paxton, *European Political Facts, 1918–1973* (New York: St. Martin's Press), 1975; Richard Rose (ed.), *Electoral Behavior*; Stefano Bartolini, "The European Left Since World War One: Size, Composition, and Patterns of Electoral Development," in Hans Daalder and Peter Maier, *Western European Party Systems: Continuity and Change* (Beverly Hills, Calif.: Sage), 1983, pp. 139–178. United States Democrats and Canadian Liberals were classified as "left-wing" on the basis of their relative position in the political spectrum of those countries. The statistic used is the percentage of left-wing representation in parliament each year.

Cabinet Instability (Turnover, Change)

This is defined by the number of times each year in which at least 50 percent of the cabinet changed, or else the prime minister was replaced, as recorded by Arthur S. Banks, *Cross-Polity Time-Series Data* (Cambridge: MIT Press), Segment 1, Field M. This was compared to data collected in Berthold Spuler, *Regenten und Regierung der Welt*, and for very complicated cases, national sources, including, for France, *Les Ministères de la France, 1871–1930 et 1930–1942* (Paris: Sénat, Services Legislatifs), 1930 and 1945.

Labor Unrest

Labor unrest is measured by the number of total working days lost each year per capita. Source: B. R. Mitchell, *European Historical Statistics*, Series C3, pp. 181–190. Data are missing for Belgium, Bulgaria, and Greece.

Central Bank Independence

An eight-point scale was devised, combining two dimensions of formal central bank independence: (1) the degree of political control over appointments and

(2) the degree of political supervision of the bank's activities. The higher the rating of the central bank, the more independent it was from formal political control (according to its statutes or constitution). The following criteria were used:

For appointments:

1 = government appointed the chief executive officer of the bank and the governing board.

2 = government appointed *either* the executive officer *or* the board only.

3 = government could either select from a slate of non-governmentally proposed candidates, or else could propose candidates only, or else could select only a minority of the governing board.

4 = government input was either nonexistent or trivial.

For degree of political supervision (central bank supervision/policy control):

1 = continuous and formal state (executive) supervision/intervention
2 = executive branch has nonvoting policy input
3 = parliamentary supervision
4 = reporting requirement only

Sources included C. H. Kisch and W. A. Elkin, *Central Banks: A Study of the Constitutions of Banks of Issue* (London: Macmillan), 1928; Hans Aufricht, *Central Banking Legislation: A Collection of Central Banking, Monetary, and Banking Laws* (Washington, D.C.: International Monetary Fund), 1961; M. H. de Kock, *Central Banking* (New York: John de Graff, Inc.), 3d ed., 1954; Edmond Ulrich, *Les Principes de la Réorganisation des Banques Centrales après la Guerre* (Paris: Librarie du Recueil Sirey), 1931; Columbia University School of Business, *Scandinavian Banking Laws: A Translation of the Act and Regulations Governing the Central Banks* (New York: Columbia University Press), 1926; Paul Singer (ed.), *Monetary and Central Bank Laws* (Geneva: League of Nations, Economic Intelligence Service), 1932; Gianni Toniolo (ed.), *Central Banks' Independence in Historical Perspective* (New York: Walter de Guyter), 1988 (various essays); Germone Clifford, *The Independence of the Federal Reserve System* (Philadelphia: University of Pennsylvania Press), 1965; Harold James, *The Reichsbank and Public Finance in Germany, 1924–1933* (Frankfurt: Knapp), 1985; R. S. Sayers (ed.), *Banking in Western Europe* (Oxford: Clarendon Press), 1962 (various essays); National Bank of Czechoslovakia, *Ten Years of the National Bank of Czechoslovakia* (Prague: Orbis), 1937.

Majority Status of Government (N.B.: not included in a multiple regression)

Sources for Austria, Belgium, Denmark, Finland, Germany, the Netherlands, Norway, Sweden, and the United Kingdom: Peter Flora, *State, Economy, and Society in Western Europe*, chap. 4, pp. 153–189. The majority status of French governments reflects their status at elections only and does not capture the frequent cooperation and defection of other parties as well as party splintering, which was characteristic of the Third Republic. Sources for Bulgaria, Czechoslovakia, Greece, Hungary, Poland (one observation only), Romania, and Yugoslavia were based on the coalition information and the seat distributions listed in Vincent E. McHale and Sharon Skowronski (eds.), *Political Parties of Europe*; for Canada, Robert J. Jackson and Doreen Jackson, *Politics in Canada: Culture, Institutions, Behavior, and Public Policy* (Toronto: Prentice-Hall), 1986, p. 433. A number of cases of dictatorship are missing because they were either not available or irrelevant. These included Austria (1933–1937), Bulgaria (1932–1939), Czechoslovakia (1933–1938), Germany (1932–1939), Greece (1923–1925), Yugoslavia (1929–1932), Italy, Japan, Poland, and Spain. Switzerland was omitted because no statistics could be found, probably due to its unusual formulation for selecting an executive.

Explanatory Structural Variables

Net National Product (Size)

For comparability across countries and to account for changes in currency values, NNP is expressed in constant 1929 U.S. dollars. Several of the smaller countries are missing data on NNP: Greece (1923–1926), Poland (1923–1925 and 1930–1937), Romania, Spain (1936–1939), and Yugoslavia. Where one or two data points were missing in a country series, they were estimated through interpolation or extrapolation, taking into account the trend in trade volume. (See notes on NNP under Current Account Balance/Net National Product above.)

Share of World Trade (Size)

Data on share of world trade are from Arthur Banks, *Cross-Polity Time-Series Data*, Segment 5, Field D. Sections of the series for Austria, Bulgaria, Czechoslovakia, Hungary, Germany, Romania, and Yugoslavia have been estimated from those countries' total trade figures in the following way: total U.S. trade was taken as the "base" for establishing total world trade; total trade figures for each country were converted to dollars at the prevailing rate for each missing year; country trade expressed in U.S. dollars was divided by total trade in U.S. dollars to get a preliminary estimate. This preliminary estimate was compared with the available data and for each country a conversion factor was established for overlapping values. This conversion factor was used to correct the preliminary estimates.

Net Investment Position

Net investment position is measured here as a dummy variable that separates debtors from creditors for the period as a whole. Hence, there is no variation in this net creditor status over time; only across countries. Because the net investment of a country is expected to change only slowly, this is not a dangerous oversimplification. Countries that were classified as net creditors for the period as a whole were Belgium, France, the Netherlands, Sweden, Switzerland, the United Kingdom, and the United States. All others were considered net debtors (except for Spain, for which no data could be found). Sources: League of Nations, *World Economic Survey, 1931–32* (Geneva: Economic Intelligence Unit), 1932, pp. 39–40; United Nations Secretariat, *International Capital Movements During the Interwar Period*, pp. 10–12 and 18–20.

Trade Concentration

Trade concentration is the share of total trade that is accounted for by a country's top three trade partners. Numerator and denominator include imports plus exports (B. R. Mitchell, *European Historical Statistics*, Table F1, pp. 493–497). The top three trade partners are determined by their total value of trade with the country in question (ibid., Table F2, pp. 503–576).

Trade Dependence

Trade dependence is total trade (imports plus exports) as a proportion of NNP (see explanation of NNP given above). Source: B. R. Mitchell, *European Historical Statistics, 1750–1975*, Table F1, pp. 493–497.

NNP/Capita

For numerator, see explanation of NNP given above. The denominator is total population (usually estimated between censuses) in thousands. Source: Arthur Banks, *Cross-Polity Time-Series Data*, Segment 1, Field B.

Customs Revenue/Total Taxes

The numerator is total customs revenue per year; the denominator is total ordinary government revenue exclusive of loan receipts. For some countries, total revenues include receipts from public enterprises. Source: B. R. Mitchell, *European Historical Statistics, 1750–1975*, Table H5, pp. 716–726. Both numerator and denominator were originally expressed in millions of units of national currency at current prices.

Tariff Index of the Major Trade Partner

See source and definition for Tariff Index and explanation of Major Trade Partner discussed in the section on Foreign Output above.

CENTRAL BANK INDEPENDENCE DATA

CENTRAL BANK APPOINTMENTS

Key:

1 = government appointed the chief executive officer of the bank and the governing board
2 = government appointed *either* the executive officer *or* the board only
3 = government *either* selected from a slate of non-governmentally proposed candidates, *or* proposed candidates only, *or* selected only a minority of the governing board
4 = government input was nonexistent or trivial

Austria	2	The chairman was appointed by the federal president on the nomination by the federal government. The vice chairman was elected by the board of directors, whose members in turn were elected by the general meeting of stockholders (with restrictions on representation by sector).
Belgium	4	The governor was nominated and dismissed by the Crown. The board of directors, regents, and censors were elected by a general meeting of stockholders.
Bulgaria	1	The governor, deputy governor, and board of directors were nominated by royal decree on the recommendation of the minister of finance. Both executive officers could be dismissed by the Sobranié (parliament) on recommendation of the minister of finance.
Czechoslovakia	1	The governor was appointed by the president of the Republic, and could be suspended or dismissed by the president on a motion of the government. The government appointed three members of the board of directors, and six were appointed by shareholders. The vice governor was appointed from among the six appointed by the president of the Republic.

Denmark	3	Fifteen directors were appointed by shareholders and two by the king; four or five managers were appointed by shareholders and two by the Ministry of Trade. The directors elected the chairman.
Finland	1	The chairman of the board and the members of the board of management were appointed by the president of the Republic.
France	2	The governor and two deputy governors were appointed by the president on the proposal of the Ministry of Finance. The general council comprised the above officers plus fifteen regents, who were elected from a general assembly of the largest 200 shareholders.
Germany	3	1923–30: The president was elected by the General Council (half German and half foreign); German members were elected by the shareholders and foreigners from among the remaining foreigners on the General Council. The board was approved by the General Council and was appointed by the president of the Reichsbank. (The government had veto over the selection of a president twice, but was forced to accept the third choice.)
	2	1930–32: Conditions of the Young Plan enabled the German government to regain permanent veto over the selection of president.
	1	1933–39: Reichsbank appointments were made by the Führer.
Greece	2	The governor and deputy governor were elected by a general meeting of shareholders; the governor then had to be approved by the government.
Hungary	1	1920–24: The bank was essentially run by the Ministry of Finance.
	2	1925–?: The governor was nominated by the minister of finance and appointed by the head of state. The board of directors was elected by the general assembly of shareholders, and the deputy governor was elected by the board from among its own members.

Italy	?	No data were available prior to 1926.
	2	1926–?: The director general and the deputy director general were elected by the administrative council (most of whom were elected by shareholders) and had to be approved by the government.
Japan	1	The governor and vice governor were appointed by the government with Imperial approval. Four directors were appointed by the Ministry of finance from among eight candidates submitted by the general meeting of stockholders.
Netherlands	4	The president and secretary general were appointed by the Crown from two choices submitted by the directors, who in turn were appointed by voting shareholders. The members of the board of directors and board of commissioners were also appointed by shareholders.
Norway	1	The president and vice president were nominated by the king, with the power of dismissal with the supervisory council. The members of the board of directors were elected by the Storting (parliament). The fifteen-member supervisory council and the board of management were also appointed by the Storting.
Poland	1	The president and vice president were appointed by the president of the Republic, on the recommendation of the Council of ministers (cabinet). The general meeting of shareholders elected a two-person council, which in turn submitted nominations for the general manager and board of directors to the minister of finance for approval.
Romania		No data.
Spain	2	The governor was nominated by the government and represented the state. Assistant governors were appointed by royal degree and were proposed by the council, whose members were elected by the shareholders with the approval of the king.
Sweden	2	The president was appointed by the king, and

six directors were appointed by the Riksdag (parliament).

Switzerland   1   The president and vice president, and the five-member Committee of the Bank were nominated by the Federal Council. The forty-member Council of the Bank was nominated in the following way: fifteen by the general meeting, twenty-three by the federal council, and ten (maximum) from the federal/cantonal governments.

United Kingdom   4   The governor, deputy governor, and twenty-four directors were elected by the General Court of stockholders.

United States   2   The governor of the eight-member Federal Reserve Board (which included the Secretary of the Treasury and the comptroller of the currency as ex officio members) was appointed by the President; six of the members were appointed by the President with Senate approval. There was a nine-member board of directors of Federal Reserve Banks, three of whom are chosen by stockholding banks and three designated by the Federal Reserve Board.

Yugoslavia   No data.

CENTRAL BANK SUPERVISION/POLICY CONTROL

Key:

1 = continuous and formal state (executive) supervision/intervention
2 = executive branch has nonvoting policy input
3 = parliamentary supervision
4 = reporting requirement only

Austria   2   The state commissioner might attend all meetings of boards in an advisory capacity, and might protest bank decisions, which were then to be suspended and subjected to arbitration.

Belgium   2   The government commissioner supervised all operations of the bank; he had the right to attend meeting and to be kept informed, but had no formal policy input.

Bulgaria	2	The government commissioner (nominated by the minister of finance) might attend meetings of the administrative council but could not vote.
Canada		No central bank until 1934.
Czechoslovakia	1	The government commissioner could oppose any resolution of the organs of the bank if they conflicted with "laws, statutes, or state interests."
Denmark	4	The bank management was completely separate from the finances of the state. No order of the government was allowed to either directly or indirectly interfere with the bank's management. The Royal Commissioner was a nonvoting chair of the directors' meetings and had access to information on the bank, but was allowed no part in its operations.
France	4	There was no regular system of government input or supervision of the bank, but the minister of finance could ask for information whenever he chose.
Finland	1	The bank carried on its business under the guarantee and supervision of the Diet.
Germany	4	1923–36: The Reichsbank was independent of government control (as a result of foreign reorganization); no formal links between government representative and central bank.
	1	1937–39: The government took control over the bank.
Greece	2	The Ministry of finance might nominate a government commissioner, who had the right to attend all general meetings and meetings of the board of directors and protest their decisions, but not vote.
Hungary	1	The government commissioner had investigatory powers and might attend meetings and protest and suspend decisions, pending arbitration.
Italy	1	The finance minister carried out supervision of note issue and interest rates charged and might annul any decision of the general meeting or of

		the Administrative Council that he believed violated a law.
Japan	1	The comptrollers, acting under the direction of the Ministry of Finance, supervised all matters of the bank, with wide interventionary powers.
Netherlands	2	The commissioner, appointed by the Crown and paid by the state, might attend all meetings, receive information, and have an advisory vote.
Norway	3	The bank had to submit an annual report to the Storting, which was influential in bank administration.
Poland	2	The government delegate might attend meetings and had a right to all information regarding the bank's relations with the state; disputes were subject to arbitration.
Romania		No data.
Spain	1	[No need for government supervision, since bank personnel were appointed by the government.]
Sweden	3	The bank directors were responsible to the Riksdag.
Switzerland	4	There was no explicit government supervision of or liaison with the bank.
United Kingdom	4	An annual report had to be given to Parliament of the amount of exchequer and treasury bills purchased by the bank, or of any sums advanced to the public account.
United States	2	1923–34: The Federal Reserve Board in Washington exerted influence over regional banks. The Secretary of the Treasury and the Comptroller of the Currency were ex officio members of the board. Annual reports had to be made to Congress.
	4	1935–39: Ex officio members (Secretary of the Treasury and Comptroller of the Currency) were removed from the Federal Reserve Board.
Yugoslavia	1	1920–23: Policy was dictated by the Finance Minister.

SELECT BIBLIOGRAPHY

(NOTE: Chapters in edited volumes are not listed separately. See entry under editor's name for citation. In addition, the titles of pertinent newspapers, weekly periodicals, and archives are listed at the end of the bibliography.)

Achen, Christopher H., and Duncan Snidal. "Rational Deterrence Theory and Comparative Case Studies." *World Politics* 41, no. 2 (1989): 143–169.

Aldcroft, Derek H. "Economic Growth in Britain in the Interwar Years: A Reassessment." *Economic History Review* (August 1967): 311–326.

———. *From Versailles to Wall Street, 1919–1929.* London: Allen Lane, 1977.

Alesina, Alberto. "The End of Large Public Debts." In Giorgio Basevi, *High Public Debt: The Italian Experience*, 34–79. Cambridge: Cambridge University Press, 1988.

———. "Macroeconomics and Politics." *NBER Macroeconomics Annual*, 13–51. Cambridge: MIT Press, 1988.

Alesina, Alberto and Allan Drazen. "Why Are Stabilizations Delayed?" Unpublished essay. Harvard and Tel-Aviv Universities, May 1990.

Alesina, Alberto and Lawrence H. Summers. "Central Bank Independence and Macroeconomic Performance: Some Comparative Evidence." Unpublished essay. Harvard University and NBER, 1990.

Alt, James E., and K. Alec Chrystal. *Political Economics.* Berkeley: University of California Press, 1983.

Alt, James E., Randall L. Calvert, and Brian D. Humes. "Reputation and Hegemonic Stability: A Game-Theoretic Analysis." *American Political Science Review* 82 (June 1988): 445–466.

Armella, P. Aspe, R. Dornbusch, and M. Obstfeld, eds. *Financial Policies and the World Capital Market: The Problem of Latin American Countries.* Chicago: University of Chicago Press, 1983.

Arnt, H. W. *The Economic Lessons of the Nineteen Thirties.* London: Frank Cass, 1944.

Aufricht, Hans. *Central Banking Legislation: A Collection of Central Banking, Monetary, and Banking Laws.* Washington, D.C.: International Monetary Fund, 1961.

Axelrod, Robert. *The Evolution of Cooperation.* New York: Basic Books, 1984.

Backus, David, and John Drifill. "Inflation and Reputation." *American Economic Review* 75, no. 3 (1985): 530–538.

Banaian, King, Leroy O. Laney, and Thomas D. Willett. "Central Bank Independence: An International Comparison." *Economic Review*, Federal Reserve Bank of Dallas (March 1983): 1–13.

Bank for International Settlements. *8th Report.* Basel, Switzerland, 1938.

Banks, Arthur S. *Cross-Polity Time-Series Data.* Cambridge: MIT Press, 1971.

Barro, Robert J., and David B. Gordon. "A Positive Theory of Monetary Policy in a Natural Rate Model." *Journal of Political Economy* 91 (1983): 589–610.

————. "Rules, Discretion, and Reputation in a Model of Monetary Policy." *Journal of Monetary Economics* 12 (1983): 101–121.

Basevi, Giorgio. "The Restrictive Effect of the U.S. Tariff and Its Welfare Value." *American Economic Review* 58 (1968): 840–849.

Baudhuin, Fernand. *Dévaluation du Franc Belge*. Brussels: Editions Universelles, 1935.

Baumont, Maurice. *La Faillité de la Paix, 1918–1939*. Paris: Presses Universitaires de France, 1946.

Beck, Nathaniel. "Elections and the Fed: Is There a Political Monetary Cycle?" *American Journal of Political Science* 31 (1987): 194–216.

————. "Parties, Administrations, and American Macroeconomic Outcomes." *American Political Science Review* 76, no. 1 (1982): 83–93.

Beenstock, Michael, and Peter Warburton. "The Market for Labour in Interwar Britain." CPER Discussion Paper No. 105, April 1986.

Benjamin, D., and L. Kochin. "Searching for an Explanation of Unemployment in Interwar Britain." *Journal of Political Economy* 87, no. 3 (1979): 441–478.

Berger, Suzanne, ed. *Organizing Interests in Western Europe and North America*. Cambridge: Cambridge University Press, 1981.

Bhagwati, Jagdish, ed. *Import Competition and Response*. Chicago: University of Chicago Press/NBER, 1982.

Bidaux, F. "La Rôle de l'Etat et de l'Initiative Privée dans la Reconstitution des Régions Devastées." Legal diss., Paris, 1922.

Bienen, Henry S., and Mark Gersovitz. "Economic Stabilization, Conditionality, and Political Stability." *International Organization* 39, no. 4 (1985): 729–754.

Bjerke, Kjeld. *Income and Wealth*, Series 5. Cambridge, Mass., or Cambridge, England: Bowes and Bowes, 1955.

Black, Stanley W. *Politics Versus Markets: International Differences in Macroeconomic Policies*. Washington, D.C.: American Enterprise Institute for Public Policy, 1982.

Blackburn, Keith, and Michael Christensen. "Monetary Policy and Policy Credibility: Theories and Evidence." *Journal of Economic Literature* 27 (1989): 1–45.

Bloomfield, Arthur I. *Monetary Policy Under the International Gold Standard: 1880–1914*. New York: Arno Press, 1978.

Boddy, Rafor, and James Crotty. "Class Conflict and Macro-Policy: The Political Business Cycle." *Review of Radical Political Economics* 7 (1975): 1–19.

Bon, Frédérick. *Les Elections en France: Histoire et Sociologie*. Paris: Editions du Seuil, 1978.

Bordo, Michael D., and Anna J. Schwartz, eds. *A Retrospective on the Classical Gold Standard*. Chicago: University of Chicago Press, 1984.

Bourdrel, Philippe. *Le Mur de l'Argent: Les Gouvernements de Gauche face au Capital*. Paris: Editions Noël, 1985.

Bourgin, G., et al. *Manuel des Parties Politiques en France*. Paris: Editions Rieder, 1928.

Bouvier, Jean. "The French Banks, Inflation and the Economic Crisis, 1919–1939." *Journal of European Economic History* 13 (1984): 38.

Bowles, Samuel, and Herbert Gintiss. *Democracy and Capitalism*. New York: Basic Books, 1986.

Braunthal, Alfred. "The New Economic Policy in Belgium." *International Labour Review* 33, no. 6 (1936): 762–789.

Bredin, Jean-Denis. *Joseph Caillaux*. Paris: Hachette, 1980.

Broadberry, S. N. "Fiscal Policy in Britain During the 1930s," *Economic History Review* 37, no. 1 (1984): 95–102.

Brogan, D. W. *France Under the Republic: The Development of Modern France, 1870–1939*. New York: Harper & Brothers, 1940.

Burton, Herbert. "France and the Depression." *Economic Record* 12, no. 22 (1936): 15–27.

Cahill, J. R. *Report on the Economic and Industrial Conditions in France*. London: His Majesty's Stationery Office, 1925.

Cairncross, Alec, and Barry Eichengreen. *Sterling in Decline: The Devaluations of 1931, 1949, and 1967*. London: Basil Blackwell, 1983.

Capie, Forrest. *Depression and Protectionism: Britain between the Wars*. London: Allen and Unwin, 1983.

Carr, E. H. *Twenty Years' Crisis, 1919–1939*. New York: Harper and Row, 1964.

Cassing, James, Timothy McKeown, and Jack Ochs. "The Political Economy of the Tariff Cycle." *American Political Science Review* 80 (1986): 843–862.

Chapman, Brian. *The Prefects and Provincial France*. London: Allen and Unwin, 1955.

Choudhri, Ehsan U., and Levis A. Kockin. "The Exchange Rate and the International Transmission of Business Cycle Disturbances: Some Evidence from the Great Depression." *Journal of Money, Credit, and Banking* (November 1980), pt. 1: 565–574.

Clarke, S.V.O. *Central Bank Cooperation, 1924–1931*. New York: Federal Reserve Bank of New York, 1967.

———. "The Reconstruction of the International Monetary System: The Attempts of 1922 and 1933." *Princeton Studies in International Finance*, No. 33. Princeton: Princeton University Press, 1973.

Clay, Sir Henry. *Lord Norman*. London: Macmillan, 1957.

Clifford, Germone. *The Independence of the Federal Reserve System*. Philadelphia: University of Pennsylvania Press, 1965.

Cline, William, and Sidney Weintraub, eds. *Economic Stabilization in Developing Countries*. Washington, D.C.: Brookings Institution, 1981.

Collier, David, ed. *The New Authoritarianism in Latin America*. Princeton: Princeton University Press, 1979.

Colton, Joel. *Léon Blum: Humanist in Politics*. Cambridge: MIT Press, 1974.

Columbia University School of Business. *Scandinavian Banking Laws: A Translation of the Act and Regulations Governing the Central Banks*. New York: Columbia University Press, 1926.

Conybeare, John A. C. "Public Goods, Prisoner's Dilemmas, and the International Political Economy." *International Studies Quarterly* 28 (Spring 1984): 5–22.

———. "Tariff Protection in Developed and Developing Countries: A Cross-sectional and Longitudinal Analysis." *International Organization* 37 (1983): 441–463.

———. "Trade Wars: A Comparative Study of Anglo-Hanse, Franco-Italian, and Smoot-Hawley Conflicts." *World Politics* 38, no. 1 (1985): 147–172.

Cook, Chris, and John Paxton. *European Political Facts, 1918–1973*. New York: St. Martin's Press, 1975.

Cooper, Richard N. *The Gold Standard: Historical Facts and Future Prospects*. Brookings Paper on Economic Activity. Washington, D.C.: Brookings Institution, 1982.

Corden, W. M. *The Theory of Protection*. Oxford: Oxford University Press, 1971.

———. *Trade Policy and Welfare*. Oxford: Oxford University Press, 1974.

Coughlin, Cletus, Joseph V. Terza, and Noor Aini Khalifah. "The Determinants of Escape Clause Petitions." *Review of Economics and Statistics* 71 (1989): 341–347.

Cowart, Andrew. "The Economic Policies of European Governments, Part 1: Monetary Policy." *British Journal of Political Science* 8 (1978): 285–311.

Cross, Ira. *Domestic and Foreign Exchange*. London: Macmillan, 1923.

Daalder, Hans, and Peter Mair. *Western European Party Systems*. London: Sage, 1983.

Dam, Kenneth W. *The Rules of the Game: Reform and Evolution in the International Monetary System*. Chicago: University of Chicago Press, 1982.

Danaillow, G. T. *Les Effets de la Guerre en Bulgarie*. Paris: Presses Universitaires de France, 1932.

Davenport-Hines, R.P.T., ed. *Business in the Age of Depression and War*. London: Frank Cass, 1990.

Debeir, Jean-Claude. "Inflation et Stabilisation en France (1919–1928)." *Revue Economique* 31, no. 4 (1980): 622–647.

de Kock, M. H. *Central Banking*. New York: John de Graff, Inc., 1954.

Dornbusch, Rudiger, Stanley Fischer, and John Bossons, eds. *Macroeconomics and Finance: Essays in Honor of Franco Modigliani*. Cambridge: MIT Press, 1987.

Dornbusch, Rudiger, and Mario H. Simonson, eds. *Inflation, Debt, and Indexation*. Cambridge: MIT Press, 1983.

Drummond, Ian. *British Economic Policy and the Empire, 1919–1939*. London: Allen and Unwin, 1972.

———. *Imperial Economic Policy, 1917–1939*. London: Allen and Unwin, 1974.

Duboin, Jacques. *La Stabilisation du Franc*. Paris: Marcel Rivière, 1927.

Dulles, Eleanor Lansing. *The Dollar, the Franc, and Inflation*. New York: Macmillan, 1933.

———. *The French Franc, 1914–1928: The Facts and Their Interpretation*. New York: Macmillan, 1929.

Eichengreen, Barry. *Golden Fetters: The Gold Standard and the Great Depression, 1919–1939*. New York and Oxford: Oxford University Press, 1992.

———. "Sterling and the Tariff, 1929–1932." *Princeton Studies in International Finance*, No. 48. Princeton: Princeton University Press, 1981.

———. "Understanding 1921–1927: Inflation and Economic Growth in the 1920s." HIER, Discussion Paper 1203, January 1986.

Eichengreen, Barry, ed. *The Gold Standard in Theory and History*. New York: Methuen, 1985.

Eichengreen, Barry, and Richard Portes. "Debt and Default in the 1930s: Causes and Consequences." *European Economic Review* 30 (June 1986): 599–640.

Eichengreen, Barry, and Jeffrey Sachs. "Exchange Rates and Economic Recovery in the 1930s." *Journal of Economic History* 95, no. 4 (December 1985): 925–946.

Enzig, Paul. *Behind the Scenes of International Finance*. London: Macmillan, 1931.

———. *The Fight for Financial Supremacy*. London: Macmillan, 1931.

———. *Finance and Politics: Sequel to Behind the Scenes of International Finance*. London: Macmillan, 1932.

————. *Foreign Exchange Crises: An Essay in Economic Pathology.* London: Macmillan, 1970.

————. *France's Crisis.* London: Macmillan, 1934.

Elliot, Arthur D. *The Life of George Joachim Goschen.* London: Longmans, Green, 1911.

Elster, Jon. *Ulysses and the Sirens.* Cambridge: Cambridge University Press, 1979.

Epstein, Gerald. "Federal Reserve Politics and Monetary Instability." In Stone and Harphan, *The Political Economy of Public Policy,* 211–240.

————. "The Political Economy of Central Banking." Unpublished essay. Harvard University, Department of Economics, 1986.

Epstein, Gerald, and Juliet B. Schor. "Macropolicy in the Rise and Fall of the Golden Age." Unpublished essay. Harvard University, Department of Economics, 1987.

Eyck, Erich. *A History of the Weimar Republic.* Vol. 2: *From the Locarno Conference to Hitler's Seizure of Power.* Cambridge: Harvard University Press, 1963.

Federal Reserve Board. *Banking and Monetary Statistics.* Washington, D.C.: National Capitol Press, 1943.

Feinstein, Charles H., ed. *The Managed Economy: Essays in British Economic Policy and Performance Since 1929.* Oxford: Oxford University Press, 1983.

Feis, Herbert. *The Diplomacy of the Dollar: The First Era, 1919–1932.* Baltimore: Johns Hopkins University Press, 1950.

Fitch, Edwin. *Britain's New Tariff.* Illinois: Freeport, 1932.

Flora, Peter. *State, Economy, and Society in Western Europe, 1815–1975.* Frankfurt am Main: Campus Verlag, 1983.

Fraser, Leon. "The International Bank and Its Future." *Foreign Affairs* 14, no. 3 (1936): 453–464.

Frayssinet, Pierre. "La Politique Monétaire de la France (1924–1928)." Ph.D. diss., Department of Political Economy, University of Paris, 1928.

Frenkel, Jacob, ed. *Exchange Rates and International Economics.* Chicago: University of Chicago Press, 1983.

Frey, Bruno S., and Friedrich Schneider. "Central Bank Behavior: A Positive Empirical Analysis." *Journal of Monetary Economics* 7 (1981): 291–315.

————. "An Empirical Study of Politico-Economic Interaction in the United States." *Review of Economics and Statistics* 60, no. 2 (1978): 174–183.

Frey, Bruno S., Werner W. Pommerehne, Friedrich Schneider, and Guy Gilbert. "Consensus and Dissensus Among Economists: An Empirical Study." *American Economic Review* 74 (1985): 986–994.

Frieden, Jeffry A. "Capital Politics: Creditors and the International Political Economy." *Journal of Public Policy* 8, nos. 3/4 (1988): 265–286.

Gallarotti, Giulio. "Toward a Business-Cycle Model of Tariffs." *International Organization* 39 (1985): 155–187.

Gilpin, Robert. *War and Change in World Politics.* Cambridge: Cambridge University Press, 1981.

Glynn, Sean, and John Oxborrow. *Interwar Britain: A Social and Economic History.* London: Allen and Unwin, 1956.

Gold, Joseph. *Conditionality.* Washington, D.C.: IMF, 1979.

Goldthorpe, John H. *Order and Conflict in Contemporary Capitalism.* Oxford: Clarendon Press, 1984.

Gordon, Margaret S. *Barriers to World Trade*. New York: Macmillan, 1941.

Gordon, Robert J. "The Demand for and Supply of Inflation." *Journal of Law and Economics* 18 (1975): 808–836.

Gowa, Joanne. "Bipolarity, Multipolarity, and Free Trade." *American Political Science Review* 83 (1989): 1245–1256.

———. *Closing the Gold Window*. Ithaca: Cornell University Press, 1983.

Grabau, Thomas W. *Industrial Reconstruction in France after World War I*. Ph.D. diss., Indiana University, 1976.

Greene, Nathanael. *From Versailles to Vichy, The Third French Republic, 1919–1940*. New York: Thomas Y. Crowell, 1970.

Gregory, T. E. *The First Year of the Gold Standard*. London: Ernest Benn, 1926.

———. *The Gold Standard and Its Future*. London: Methuen, 1932.

Haggard, Stephan. "The Institutional Foundations of Hegemony: Explaining the Reciprocal Trade Agreements Act of 1934." *International Organization* 42, no. 1 (1988): 91–119.

Haight, Frank A. *A History of French Commercial Policy*. New York: Macmillan, 1941.

Hall, N. F. *The Exchange Equalisation Account*. London: Macmillan, 1935.

Hall, Peter. *Governing the Economy: The Politics of State Intervention in Britain and France*. New York: Oxford University Press, 1986.

Hall, R., ed. *Inflation: Causes and Effects*. Chicago: University of Chicago Press, 1982.

Hamada, Koichi, *The Political Economy of International Monetary Interdependence*. Cambridge: MIT Press, 1985.

Hancock, K. J. "The Reduction of Unemployment as a Problem of Public Policy, 1920–1929." *Economic History Review* 15, no. 2 (1962): 328–343.

Hansen, John Mark. "Taxation and the Political Economy of the Tariff." *International Organization* 44, no. 4 (1990): 527–549.

Harvey, A. S. *The General Tariff of the United Kingdom: Law and Regulation*. London: Sir Isaac Pitman and Sons, 1933.

Hawtrey, R. G. *The Gold Standard in Theory and Practice*. London: Longmans, Green, 1947.

Hibbs, Douglas A. "Political Parties and Macroeconomic Policy." *American Political Science Review* 71, no. 4 (1977): 1467–1487.

Hicks, Ursula K. *The Finance of British Governments, 1920–1936*. London: Oxford University Press, 1938.

Hirsch, Fred, and John H. Goldthorpe, eds. *The Political Economy of Inflation*. Cambridge: Harvard University Press, 1978.

Hirschman, Albert O. *The Passions and the Interests*. Princeton: Princeton University Press, 1977.

Holland, R. F. "The Federation of British Industries and the International Economy, 1929–1939." *Economic History Review*, 2d ser., 34, no. 2 (1981): 287–300.

Homberg, Octave. *La Stabilité Monétaire: Rapports, Travaux, et Comptes Rendus Voeux, et Résolutions de la Deuxième Semaine de la Monnaie*. Paris: Librarie Valois, 1927.

Howson, Susan K. *Domestic Monetary Management in Britain, 1919–38*. Cambridge: Cambridge University Press, 1975.

———. *Sterling's Managed Float: The Operations of the Exchange Equalization Ac-*

count, 1932–39. Princeton Studies in International Finance, No. 46. Princeton: Princeton University Press, 1980.

Huber, Michel. *La Population de la France pendant la Guerre*. Paris: Presses Universitaires de France, 1931.

Hume, David. *Essays: Moral, Political, and Literary*, Vol. 1. London: Longmans, Green, 1898.

Ikenberry, G. John. "The State and Strategies of International Adjustment." *World Politics* 39 (1986): 53–77.

Institut Scientifique de Recherches Economiques et Sociales. *L'Evolution de l'Economie Française, 1910–1937*. Paris: Recueil Sirey, 1937.

Jack, D. T. *The Restoration of European Currencies*. London: P. S. King and Sons, 1927.

Jackson, Robert J., and Doreen Jackson. *Politics in Canada: Culture, Institutions, Behavior, and Public Policy*. Toronto: Prentice-Hall, 1986.

James, Harold. *The German Slump: Politics and Economics 1924–1936*. Oxford: Clarendon Press, 1986.

———. *The Reichsbank and Public Finance in Germany, 1924–1933*. Frankfurt: Knapp, 1985.

Jeanneney, Jean-Joël. *François de Wendel en République: L'Argent et le Pouvoir, 1914–1940*. Paris: Editions du Seuil, 1976.

Jervis, Robert. *Perception and Misperception in International Relations*. Princeton: Princeton University Press, 1976.

Johnson, G. Griffith. *The Treasury and Monetary Policy, 1933–1938*. Cambridge: Harvard University Press, 1939.

Johnson, Harry G. "An Economic Theory of Protectionism, Tariff Bargaining, and the Formation of Customs Unions." *Journal of Political Economy* 73 (1965): 256–283.

———. "Optimum Tariffs and Retaliation." *Review of Economic Studies* 21 (1954): 141–153.

Joll, James. *Europe Since 1870: An International History*. New York: Harper and Row, 1973.

Jones, Kent, "The Political Economy of Voluntary Export Restraint Agreements." *Kyklos* 37 (1984): 82–101.

Kahn, A. E. *Great Britain in the World Economy*. New York: Columbia University Press, 1946.

Katzenstein, Peter J. *Small States in World Markets: Industrial Policy in Europe*. Ithaca: Cornell University Press, 1985.

Kemp, Tom. *The French Economy 1913–1939: The History of a Decline*. New York: St. Martin's Press, 1972.

Keohane, Robert O. *After Hegemony: Cooperation and Discord in the World Political Economy*. Princeton: Princeton University Press, 1984.

Keohane, Robert O., and Joseph S. Nye. *Power and Interdependence: World Politics in Transition*. Boston: Little, Brown, 1977.

Kindleberger, Charles P. *Economic Growth in France and Britain, 1851–1950*. Cambridge: Harvard University Press, 1964.

———. *A Financial History of Western Europe*. London: Allen and Unwin, 1984.

———. *International Economics*. Homewood, Ill.: Richard D. Irwin, 1968.

——. *The World in Depression, 1929–1939*. Berkeley: University of California Press, 1986.

Kirschen, E. S., J. Bernard, H. Besters, F. Blackaby, D. Eckstein, J. Faaland, F. Hartog, L. Morissens, and E. Tosco. *Economic Policy in Our Time. Vol. 1: General Theory*. Amsterdam: North Holland, 1964.

Kisch, C. H., and W. A. Elkin. *Central Banks: A Study of the Constitutions of Banks of Issue, with an Analysis of Representative Charters*. London: Macmillan, 1928.

Krasner, Stephen. "State Power and the Structure of International Trade." *World Politics* 28 (1976): 317–347.

Kuga, Kiyoshi. "Tariff Retaliation and Policy Equilibrium." *Journal of International Economics* 3 (1983): 351–366.

Kydland, Finn, and Edward C. Prescott. "Rules Rather than Discretion: The Inconsistency of Optimal Plans." *Journal of Political Economy* 85 (1977): 473–491.

La Chapelle, Georges. *Les Finances de la IIIème République*. Collection "L'Histoire." Paris: Flammarion, 1937.

Lake, David A. *Power, Protectionism, and Free Trade: International Sources of U.S. Commercial Strategy, 1887–1939*. Ithaca: Cornell University Press, 1988.

Landes, David S. *The Unbound Prometheus: Technical Change and Economic Development in Western Europe from 1750 to the Present*. Cambridge: Cambridge University Press, 1969.

Lange, Peter, and Geoffrey Garrett. "The Politics of Growth: Strategic Interaction and Economic Performance in the Advanced Industrialized Countries." *Journal of Politics* 47, no. 3 (1985): 792–827.

Larmour, Peter J. *The French Radical Party in the 1930s*. Stanford: Stanford University Press, 1964.

League of Nations. *Commercial Policy in the Interwar Years*. Geneva: League of Nations, 1942.

——. *International Currency Experience: Lessons of the Interwar Period*. Geneva: League of Nations, Economic and Financial Committee, 1944.

——. *Memorandum on Commercial Banks, 1913–1929*. Geneva: League of Nations, 1930.

——. *Memorandum on Currency and Central Banks, 1913–1925*. Geneva: League of Nations, 1926.

——. *Monthly Bulletin of Statistics*, various issues.

——. *Quantitative Trade Controls: Their Cause and Nature*. Geneva: League of Nations, Economic, Financial and Transit Department, 1943.

——. *Report on Exchange Controls*. Geneva: League of Nations, Committee on Exchange Controls, 1938.

——. *Tariff Level Indices: A Statistical Inquiry into the Level of Tariffs, in preparation for the World Economic Conference in April-May 1926*. Geneva: League of Nations, Economic and Financial Section, 1927.

——. *World Economic Survey*, various issues. Geneva: Economic Intelligence Unit.

Letiche, J. M. "Differential Rates of Productivity Growth and International Imbalance." *Quarterly Journal of Economics* 69, no. 3 (1955): 371–401.

Leubbert, Gregory M. "Social Foundations of Political Order in Interwar Europe." *World Politics* 39 (1987): 449–478.

Levi, Margaret. *Of Rule and Revenue*. Berkeley: University of California Press, 1988.

Levy, Marc. "Effects and Causes of Central Bank Independence: Do Institutions Matter, and Why?" Unpublished essay. Harvard University, 1988.

Lewis, W. Arthur. *Economic Survey, 1919–1939*. Philadephia: Blakiston Company, 1950.

Liepmann, H. *Tariff Levels and the Economic Unity of Europe: An Examination of Tariff Policy, Export Movements, and the Economic Integration of Europe, 1913–1931*. London: Allen and Unwin, 1938.

Lindberg, Leon, and Charles S. Maier, eds. *The Politics of Inflation and Economic Stagnation: Theoretical Approaches and International Case Studies*. Washington, D.C.: Brookings Institution, 1985.

Lloyd George, David. *We Can Conquer Unemployment*. London: Liberal Party, 1929.

Lohmann, Susanne. "Optimal Commitment in Monetary Policy: Credibility versus Flexibility," *American Economic Review* 82, no. 1 (March 1992): 273.

Maizels, A. *Industrial Growth and World Trade*. Cambridge: Cambridge University Press, 1971.

Maravall, José M. "The Limits of Reformism: Parliamentary Socialism and the Marxist Theory of the State." *British Journal of Sociology* 30 (1979): 262–287.

Marks, Gary. "Neocorporatism and Incomes Policy in Western Europe and North America." *Comparative Politics* 18, no. 3 (1986): 253–277.

Martin, Andrew. "The Politics of Economic Policy in the United States: A Tentative View from a Comparative Historical Perspective." *Sage Professional Papers in Comparative Politics*, No. 01-040. Beverly Hills, Calif.: Sage, 1973.

Marwick, A. *Britain in the Century of Total War: War, Peace, and Social Change, 1890–1967*. London: Penguin, 1968.

———. *The Deluge*. London: Bodley Head, 1965.

Mayer, Wolfgang, and Raymond Riezman. "Endogenous Choice of Trade Policy Instruments," *Journal of International Economics* 23 (1987): 377–381.

McCloskey, Donald N. "Did Victorian Britain Fail?" *Economic History Review* 23, no. 3 (December 1970): 446–459.

McDonald, William. *Reconstruction in France*. New York: Macmillan, 1922.

McHale, Vincent E., and Sharon Skowronski, eds. *Political Parties of Europe; Greenwood Historical Encyclopedia of the World's Political Parties*. Westport, Conn.: Greenwood Press, 1983.

McKeown, Timothy. "Firms and Tariff Regime Change." *World Politics* 36 (1984): 215–233.

———. "Hegemonic Stability Theory and 19th-Century Tariff Levels in Europe." *International Organization* 37 (1983): 73–91.

Meltzer, Allen. "Monetary and Other Explanations for the Start of the Great Depression." *Journal of Monetary Economics* 2 (1976): 455–472.

Mendès-France, Pierre. "Le Redressement Financier Français en 1926 et 1927." Ph.D. diss., University of Paris, 1928.

Meynial, P. "La Balance des Comptes." *Revue d'Economie Politique*. 41, no. 2 (1927): 271–289.

Middlemas, Keith, and John Barnes. *Baldwin: A Biography*. London: Weidenfeld and Nicolson, 1969.

Middleton, Roger. "The Constant Employment Budget Balance and British Budgetary Policy, 1929–1939." *Economic History Review*, 2d ser., 34, no. 2 (1981): 266–286.

Miller, Henry. "The Franc in War and Reconstruction." *Quarterly Journal of Economics* 44, no. 3 (1930): 523–538.

Milner, Helen V. *Resisting Protectionism: Global Industries and the Politics of International Trade*. Princeton: Princeton University Press, 1988.

Mitchell, B. R. *Abstract of British Historical Statistics*. Cambridge: Cambridge University Press, 1962.

——. *European Historical Statistics, 1750–1970*. London: Macmillan, 1975.

——. *European Historical Statistics, 1750–1975*. New York: Facts on File, 1980.

Moreau, Emile. *Souvenirs d'un Gouverneur de la Banque de France*. Paris: Librarie de Médicis, 1954.

Morton, Walter A. *British Finance, 1930–1940*. Madison: University of Wisconsin Press, 1943.

Mouré, Kenneth. *Managing the Franc Poincaré*. Cambridge: Cambridge University Press, 1991.

Myers, Denys P. *Nine Years of the League of Nations, 1920–1928*. Boston: World Peace Foundation, 1929.

Myers, Margaret. *Paris as a Financial Center*. New York: Columbia University Press, 1936.

Mynarski, Feliks. *Gold and Central Banks*. New York: Macmillan, 1929.

National Bank of Czechoslovakia. *Ten Years of the National Bank of Czechoslovakia*. Prague: Orbis, 1937.

Nordhaus, William. "The Political Business Cycle." *Review of Economic Studies* 42 (1975): 169–190.

Nurkse, Ragnar. *The Course and Control of Inflation*. Geneva: League of Nations, 1946.

——. *International Currency Experience*. Geneva: League of Nations, 1944.

Ogburn, William F., and William Jaffé. *The Economic Development of Post-War France: A Survey of Production*. New York: Columbia University Press, 1929.

Oudin, Bernard. *Aristide Briand, Biographie*. Paris: Editions Robert Laffont, 1987.

Oye, Kenneth. "The Sterling-Dollar-Franc Triangle: Monetary Diplomacy, 1929–1937." *World Politics* 38, no. 1 (1985): 173–199.

Ozler, Sule, and Guido Tabellini. "External Debt and Political Instability." NBER Working Paper No. 3772, July 1991.

Paish, F. W. "The British Equalization Fund." *Economica* 2 (1935): 61–74.

Palyi, Melchior. *The Twilight of Gold, 1914–1936*. Chicago: Henry Regnery, 1972.

Parkin, Michael, and Robin Bade. "Central Bank Laws and Monetary Policies: A Preliminary Investigation." Unpublished essay. Research Report No. 7804, Department of Economics, University of Western Ontario, 1978.

Peacock, Alan T., and Jack Wiseman. *The Growth of Expenditures in the United Kingdom*. Princeton: Princeton University Press, 1961.

Peden, G. C. "The 'Treasury View' on Public Works and Employment in the Interwar Period." *Economic History Review*, 2d ser., 38, no. 2 (1984): 167–181.

Philippe, Raymonde. *Le Drame Financier de 1924–1928*. Paris, 1931.

Pollard, Sidney, ed. *The Gold Standard and Employment Policy Between the Wars*. London: Methuen, 1970.

Prate, Alain. *La France et sa Monnaie: Essai sur les Relations entre la Banque de France et les Gouvernements*. Paris: Julliard, 1987.

Putnam, Robert D. "The Logic of Two Level Games." *International Organizations* 42 (Spring 1988): 427–460.

Putnam, Robert D., and Nicholas Bayne. *Hanging Together: The Seven Power Summits.* Cambridge: Harvard University Press, 1984.

Rae, Douglas W. "A Note on the Fractionalization of Some European Party Systems." *Comparative Political Studies* 1 (1968): 413–418.

———. *The Political Consequences of Electoral Laws.* New Haven: Yale University Press, 1971.

Ragin, Charles C. *The Comparative Method: Moving Beyond Qualitative and Quantitative Strategies.* Berkeley: University of California Press, 1987.

Ray, E. J. "The Optimum Commodity Tariff and Tariff Rates in Developed and Less Developed Countries." *Review of Economics and Statistics* 56 (1974): 369–377.

———. "Tariff and Non-Tariff Barriers in the United States and Abroad." *Review of Economics and Statistics* 63 (1981): 161–168.

Redmond, John. "Sterling Overvaluation in 1925: A Multilateral Approach." *Economic History Review*, 2d ser., 37, no. 4 (1984): 520–532.

Remmer, Karen L. "Democracy and Economic Crisis: The Latin American Experience." *World Politics* 42, no. 3 (1990): 315–335.

Roger, Charles. "New Deal for Belgium." *Foreign Affairs* 13 (1935): 625–637.

Rogers, James Harvey. *The Process of Inflation in France, 1914–1927.* New York: Columbia University Press, 1929.

Rogoff, Kenneth. "The Optimal Degree of Commitment to an Intermediate Monetary Target." *Quarterly Journal of Economics* 100 (1985): 1169–1189.

Rogowski, Ronald. *Commerce and Coalitions.* Princeton: Princeton University Press, 1988.

Rooth, T.J.T. "Limits of Leverage: The Anglo-Danish Trade Agreement of 1933." *Economic History Review* 37, no. 2 (1984): 211–228.

Rose, Richard, ed. *Electoral Behavior: A Comparative Handbook.* New York: Free Press, 1974.

Sachs, Jeffrey. *Wages, Profits, and Macroeconomic Adjustment: A Comparative Study.* Brookings Paper on Economic Activity 2, Washington, D.C.: Brookings Institution, 1979. 269–332.

Saint-Etienne, Christian. *The Great Depression, 1929–1938: Lessons for the 1980s.* Stanford: Stanford University Press, 1984.

Sanders, David, and Valentine Herman. "The Stability and Survival of Governments in Western Democracies." *Acta Politica* 12 (1977): 346–377.

Sartori, Giovanni. *Parties and Party Systems: A Framework for Analysis.* Cambridge: Cambridge University Press, 1976.

Sauvy, Alfred. *Histoire Economique de la France Entre les Deux Guerres.* Vols. 2 and 3. Paris: Economica, 1984.

Sayers, R. S. "The Springs of Technological Progress in Britain, 1919–1939." *Economic Journal* 60, no. 238 (1950): 275–291.

Sayers, R. S., ed. *Banking in Western Europe.* Oxford: Clarendon Press, 1962.

Scharpf, Fritz W. "A Game-theoretical Interpretation of Inflation and Unemployment in Western Europe." *Journal of Public Policy* 7, no. 3 (1987): 227–257.

Schmidt, Manfred G. "The Politics of Unemployment and Labor Market Policy." *West European Politics* 7 (1984): 5–24.

Schmukler, Nathan, and Edward Markus, eds. *Inflation Through the Ages: Economic, Social, Psychological and Historical Aspects*. New York: Brooklyn College Press, 1983.

Schuker, Stephen A. *The End of French Predominance in Europe: The Financial Crisis of 1924 and the Adoption of the Dawes Plan*. Chapel Hill: University of North Carolina Press, 1976.

Scitovsky, Tibor. "A Reconsideration of the Theory of Tariffs." *Review of Economic Studies*. Reprinted in American Economic Association, *Readings in the Theory of International Trade*, chap. 16. New York: McGraw-Hill, 1949.

Shepherd, Henry L. *The Monetary Experience of Belgium, 1914–1936*. Princeton: Princeton University Press, 1936.

Sicsic, Pierre. "Was the Franc Poincaré Deliberately Undervalued?" Unpublished essay. Harvard University Department of Economics, November 1989.

Singer, Paul, ed. *Monetary and Central Bank Laws*. Geneva: League of Nations, Economic Intelligence Service, 1932.

Snowden, Philip. *An Autobiography*, Vol. 2. London: Nicholson and Watson, 1934.
———. *The Menace of Protection*. London: Labour Party, 1930.
———. *The Truth About Protection—the Worker Pays*. London: Labour Party, 1930.

Spuler, Berthold. *Regenten und Regierung der Welt: Minister-Ploetz Teil 2*. Würzburg: A. G. Ploetz, 1964.

Stahl, Robert. *L'Organisation du Rélèvement Economique dans le Nord Libéré*. Lille: Thesis, 1920.

Stern, Robert M., ed. *U.S. Trade Policies in a Changing World Economy*. Cambridge: MIT Press, 1987.

Stolper, Wolfgang F., and Paul A. Samuelson. "Protection and Real Wages." *Review of Economic Studies* 9 (1941): 138–151.

Stone, Alan, and Edward J. Harphan, eds. *The Political Economy of Public Policy*. Beverly Hills, Calif.: Sage, 1982.

Stone, N. *Europe Transformed, 1878–1919*. Cambridge: Harvard University Press, 1984.

Svennilson, Ingvor. *Growth and Stagnation in the European Economy*. Geneva: United Nations, 1954.

Sykes, Joseph. "Report of the Colwyn Committee, 1927." In *British Public Expenditure, 1921–1931*. London: P. S. King & Son, 1933.

Sylvestre, Jean. *La Devaluation du Franc Belge*. Paris: Librairie Sociale et Economique, 1939.

Takacs, Wendy E. "Pressures for Protectionism: An Empirical Analysis." *Economic Inquiry* 19 (1981): 87–93.

Taylor, Michael. *Anarchy and Cooperation*. New York: Wiley, 1976.

Taylor, Michael, and Valentine Herman. "Party Systems and Government Stability." *American Political Science Review* 65 (1971): 28–37.

Thomson, David. *Democracy in France: The Third and Fourth Republics*. London: Oxford University Press, 1958.

Tomasson, Richard, ed. *Comparative Social Research*, Vol. 6. Greenwich, Conn.: JAI Press, 1983.

Toniolo, Gianni, ed. *Central Banks' Independence in Historical Perspective*. New York: Walter de Guyter, 1988.

Triffen, Robert. *Gold and the Dollar Crisis*. New Haven: Yale University Press, 1960.

Tsuru, Shigeto, and Kazushi Ohkawa. "Long Term Changes in the National Product of Japan Since 1878." *Income and Wealth*, Series 3, 19–44. London: Bowes and Bowes, 1953.

Tufte, Edward. *Political Control of the Economy*. Princeton: Princeton University Press, 1978.

Turner, Henry Ashby. *Stresemann and the Politics of the Weimar Republic*. Princeton: Princeton University Press, 1963.

Ulrich, Edmond. *Les Principes de la Réorganisation des Banques Centrales après la Guerre*. Paris: Librarie du Recueil Sirey, 1931.

United Nations Secretariat. *International Capital Movements During the Interwar Period*. Lake Success, N.Y.: Department of Economic Affairs, 1949.

United States Department of Commerce/Bureau of the Census. *Statistical Abstract of the United States*. Washington: Government Printing Office, various issues.

Urquhart, M. C., and K. A. Buckley. *Historical Statistics of Canada*. Cambridge: Cambridge University Press, 1965.

Van der Wee, H., and K. Tavernier. *La Banque Nationale de Belgique et L'Histoire Monétaire entre les Deux Guerres Mondiales*. Brussels: Banque Nationale de Belgique, 1975.

Vansittart, Lord Robert. *The Mist Procession: The Autobiography of Lord Vansittart*. London: Hutchison, 1958.

Van Zeeland, Paul. *The Van Zeeland Experiment*. New York: Morteus Press, 1943.

Vinski, Ivo. *Income and Wealth*, Series 9. London: Bowes and Bowes, 1961.

Waight, Leonard. *The History and Mechanism of the Exchange Equalisation Account*. Cambridge: Cambridge University Press, 1939.

Wallerstein, Michael. "Unemployment, Collective Bargaining, and the Demand for Protection." *American Journal of Political Science* 31 (1987): 729–752.

Wasserman, Max J. "The Compression of French Wholesale Prices During Inflation, 1919–1926." *American Economic Review* 26, no. 1 (1936): 62–73.

———. "Inflation and Enterprise in France, 1919–1926." *Journal of Political Economy* 42, no. 2 (1934): 202–236.

Weintraub, Robert. "Congressional Supervision of Monetary Policy." *Journal of Monetary Economics* 4 (1978): 341–362.

Whale, P. B. "The Working of the Prewar Gold Standard." *Economica* 4 (1937): 18–32.

White, Harry. *The French International Accounts, 1880–1913*. Cambridge: Harvard University Press, 1933.

Whiteley, Paul F. "The Political Economy of Economic Growth." *European Journal of Political Research* 11, no. 2 (1983): 197–213.

Winch, Donald. *Economics and Policy: A Historical Study*. New York: Walker, 1972.

Wolfe, Martin. *The French Franc Between the Wars, 1919–1939*. New York: Columbia University Press, 1951.

Woolley, John T. *Monetary Politics: The Federal Reserve and the Politics of Monetary Policy*. Cambridge: Cambridge University Press, 1984.

Yeager, Leland B. *In Search of a Monetary Constitution*. Cambridge: Harvard University Press, 1962.

———. *International Monetary Relations: Theory, History, and Policy*. New York: Harper and Row, 1966.

Zimmermann, Ekkart. "The Puzzle of Government Duration: Evidence from Six European Countries during the Interwar Years." *Comparative Politics* 20, no. 3 (1988): 341–357.

NEWSPAPERS AND WEEKLY PERIODICALS

Bulletin de la Chambre de Commerce de Paris.
Echo de Paris.
The Economist.
La Journée Industrielle.
Lloyd's Bank Review.
Le Matin.
New Statesman and Nation.
New York Times.
Le Populaire.
Le Quotidien.
Le Temps.
Le Temps Financier.

ARCHIVES

Archives Nationales, Paris.
Archives of the Banque de France, Paris.
Archives of the Federal Reserve Bank of New York, New York.
Archives of the Ministère des Finances, Paris.
Lamont Papers, Baker Business Library, Harvard University.
National Archives, Washington, D.C.